A HISTORY
of
SCOTTISH THEATRE

A HISTORY
of
SCOTTISH THEATRE

Edited by

BILL FINDLAY

Contributors

Adrienne Scullion, Barbara Bell,
David Hutchison, Donald Smith

Polygon
Edinburgh

Edinburgh University Press
22 George Square, Edinburgh

Typeset in Sabon
by Pioneer Associates, Perthshire, and
printed and bound in Great Britain by
Bell & Bain Ltd., Glasgow

A CIP record for this book is available
from the British Library

ISBN 0 7486 6220 0 (paperback)

The Publisher acknowledges subsidy from

THE SCOTTISH ARTS COUNCIL

towards the publication of this volume.

Contents

List of Contributors

Barbara Bell is a Lecturer in the Drama Department of Queen Margaret College, Edinburgh. She has worked in arts administration and as an actor-teacher in TIE and in Community Theatre in Britain and the United States. She has published on The Scottish National Drama and stage adaptations of Sir Walter Scott (on which she wrote her doctorate). Her current research interests include issues of national identity in theatre and the role of information technology in Arts Research.

Bill Findlay has co-translated several plays by Quebec dramatist Michel Tremblay: *The Guid Sisters*, *The Real Wurld?*, *Hosanna* (all Tron Theatre); *Forever Yours, Marie-Lou* (LadderMan/Tron); *The House Among the Stars* (Traverse Theatre, and Perth Theatre); and *Albertine in Five Times* (Clyde Unity Theatre). He has adapted Gerhart Hauptmann's *The Weavers* (Dundee Rep Theatre) and Pavel Kohout's *Fire in the Basement* (Communicado Theatre Company). He teaches in the Drama Department of Queen Margaret College, Edinburgh.

David Hutchison is a Senior Lecturer in Communication Studies at Glasgow Caledonian University. His published work has been concerned principally with media policy and Scottish theatre, and includes *The Modern Scottish Theatre* (1977) and *Media Policy* (1998). He was a governor of the Scottish Film Council (1990–5), and a member of the BBC's General Advisory Council (1988–96). He has a particular interest in cultural and media comparisons between Scotland and Canada.

Adrienne Scullion is a Lecturer in the Department of Theatre, Film and Television Studies at the University of Glasgow. Although she has particular interest in Scottish theatre, her research activities cover the broader field of cultural studies: she has published on cinema and theatre history, radio drama, and gender issues in Scottish drama. She edited the Everyman anthology *Female Playwrights of the Nineteenth Century* (1996) and (with the late Alasdair Cameron) *Scottish Popular Theatre and Entertainment: Historical and Critical Approaches to Theatre and Film in Scotland* (1996).

Donald Smith is a graduate of Edinburgh University, where he undertook postgraduate research at the School of Scottish Studies. Since 1983 he has been director of the Netherbow Arts Centre, where he has worked extensively with contemporary Scottish playwrights, and in community theatre, children's theatre, puppetry, and the revival of traditional story-telling. In 1993–4 he documented the National Theatre for Scotland Campaign in *The Scottish Stage* (1994). His other publications include 'Culture and Religion' in *Scotland: A Concise Cultural History* (1992), and *The Edinburgh Old Town Pilgrims' Way* (1995).

Preface

The past quarter-century has seen an extraordinary burgeoning of interest in Scotland's history and culture, as testified by a veritable spate of publications. In the cultural field our neglected or under-appreciated traditions in art, music, language and literature have all benefited from the new mood of recovery and celebration. As regards theatre, since 1970 there has been an unprecedented growth in the writing and performance of indigenous drama, which can be seen as part of this same resurgent national confidence. Study of Scottish drama and theatre history has made advances, too, but rather belatedly, and more incrementally, compared with what has happened in other cultural areas. However, there are now welcome signs of a gathering momentum of interest. Scottish drama is being taught in secondary schools, greatly assisted by the introduction of a Higher Drama examination, and in literature and drama courses in some of our colleges and universities. Research work is expanding both here and internationally, and a publication base is beginning to build (witness the number of recent items listed in the Select Bibliography at the back of this book). This history is both a reflection of this discernible mood and a contribution to its encouragement.

So far as publications are concerned, there are two impediments to advancing study of, and general interest in, Scottish theatre: the want of anthologies of playtexts of historical or canonical importance, and a one-volume history of Scottish theatre from its origins in the Middle Ages to the present. Inevitably, in supplying a one-volume work covering several centuries, compression has been necessary. But the aim has been to highlight key developments in drama and theatre-making down the centuries, and in so doing to draw attention to significant plays, playwrights, playhouses, players and producers. This aim has unified the approach of the five contributors, notwithstanding inevitable differences in personal style. There are also unavoidable differences between the treatment of individual developments in the five period chapters caused by the nature of those developments themselves. For example, while the chapters are otherwise roughly equal in length, Chapter 1 is longer because it covers several centuries of diverse activity; and the mushrooming of theatre activity since 1970 makes detailed discussion of key plays impossible in the post-1950 chapter. A controlling concern throughout has been to make the writing accessible to the serious general reader. With this in mind referencing has been kept to a minimum.

One consequence of the need for compression is that music hall and variety theatre receive relatively limited discussion. However, their importance is signalled, and the Select Bibliography has a section which will direct readers to publications dealing with those popular theatre traditions in more depth. Similarly, and because major developments in modern theatre have tended to centre on Edinburgh and Glasgow, it has not been possible to discuss in more detail the theatre histories of Dundee and Aberdeen, or the major towns; again, the Select Bibliography will direct readers to relevant publications giving fuller information on theatre activity in those places.

Acknowledgements

The Duncan Macrae Memorial Trust generously met the cost of converting into photographic form for reproduction purposes a substantial amount of illustrative material from the Scottish Theatre Archive. I would like to think that Duncan Macrae, who as actor and actor-manager made such a significant contribution to encouraging a distinctive Scottish theatre culture, as acknowledged in Chapters 4 and 5 of this book, would have applauded the trustees' support for a publication promoting greater knowledge of Scotland's theatre tradition.

I must also thank staff of the Scottish Theatre Archive, and Elizabeth Watson in particular, for their patience and attentiveness in assisting me to locate illustrations. The Scottish Theatre Archive is part of the Department of Special Collections in Glasgow University Library, and its rich holdings of archival material and memorabilia make it the principal resource for research into Scottish theatre.

Whilst the Scottish Theatre Archive conveniently supplied the largest number of images of any of my sources, I had to cast my net wide in researching and obtaining copies of other illustrations. I am indebted to a number of institutions and individuals, whom I here thank for their help: British Museum (Department of Prints and Drawings); Ewart Library, Dumfries (Local Studies); Edinburgh Central Library (Edinburgh Room); Edinburgh City Archives (Alison Scott); Edinburgh Festival Theatre (Marion Scott); National Galleries of Scotland Picture Library (Deborah Hunter and Rebecca Thomson); National Library of Scotland (References Section); National Trust for Scotland Photo Library (Isla Robertson); Perth Museum and Art Gallery (Susan Payne); Royal Commission on the Ancient and Historical Monuments of Scotland (National Monuments Record of Scotland); Smith Art Gallery and Museum, Stirling (Michael McGinnis); Sotheby's Department of Printed Books and Manuscripts, London (Jon Climpson); the McCutcheon Stirling Collection; Alex Coupar, Photographer, Dundee; David Liddle, Photographer, Edinburgh;

Brian Lochrin, Photographer, Glasgow; Mark Fisher, editor of *Theatre Scotland*; Citizens' Theatre (Jennie Gardner); TAG (Mary Paulson-Ellis); Borderline Theatre (Eddie Jackson); Pitlochry Theatre (Peter MacIntosh); Tron Theatre (Annie Houston Reddick); Mrs Lydia Skinner; Professor Duncan Macmillan; John McLellan.

I would like to thank Professor Ian Brown of the Drama Department of Queen Margaret College, Edinburgh, for his support in allowing me time to complete the editing of this book.

Dr Jamie Reid-Baxter generously let me have a copy of his acting-text of *Pamphilus* and his unpublished essay on the play. Paul Iles kindly offered bibliographic suggestions.

Finally, my thanks to my co-contributors for their patience in bearing with me through the slower gestation of our book than first anticipated.

Bill Findlay

1 *Beginnings to 1700*

BILL FINDLAY

The origins of Scotland's tradition in drama lie in the Middle Ages, but the massive loss and destruction of burgh, church, guild and court records, including dramatic properties and texts, is a major obstacle to trying to re-create the forms that Scottish medieval drama took. This wreckage was the cumulative result of invasions from England, civil and religious wars, and the iconoclasm of the Reformation. The pre-Reformation records are most affected, but even the post-Reformation ones are incomplete. The surviving evidence was admirably gathered by Anna Jean Mill in her pioneering study *Mediaeval Plays in Scotland* (1927). Her research allows us to see that, notwithstanding the fragmentary state of the records, Scotland had most of the forms of medieval drama found in other western European nations.

A comparison can be made with Scotland's medieval architecture and, as a consequence of those same destructive events causing the dearth of written documents, the shattered state of so many cathedrals and abbeys, where surviving intact examples are rare, and even then are denuded of their internal decorations and fittings. Our perception of those incomplete or ruinous buildings would be radically transformed if we could see them in their original state and adorned with stained-glass windows, sacred paintings and sculptures, carved rood-screens and pews, painted stonework, gold and silver treasures and so on.

Just as we need to make allowance, and attempt to reconstruct the glories of such abbeys and cathedrals imaginatively, we need to approach the fragmentary records of our early dramatic tradition with imaginative sympathy to try to gain a sense of that tradition's full variety and richness. In doing so we should not expect to find that our early drama resembles drama as we now think of it; 'modern' drama begins to emerge in Scotland in the Renaissance period, but throughout the Middle Ages, as in the rest of Europe, the roots of today's theatre are located in various folk, religious and courtly activities of a quasi-dramatic nature.

FOLK DRAMA

The earliest written evidence of activities in which the roots of Scottish theatre can be located is to be found in thirteenth-century Latin records of mandates from the ecclesiastical authorities attempting to ban *ludi* in church precincts. *Ludi*, a Latin term, has a certain ambiguity; it can be translated as 'recreation', 'game', or 'play'. In its Roman original it embraced athletic games such as wrestling, and mimetic 'play' such as mime, dance, pantomime and spoken drama. Whilst the references to *ludi* in Scottish records reflect this ambiguity, the contexts suggest some form of folk pastime of pagan origin, hence church disapproval. On occasion, as in a thirteenth-century statute of the Diocese of Aberdeen, the prohibition is more fully defined as *'turpes et inhonesti ludi'* (shameful and indecent games/plays). What appears to be an example of the latter, and of *ludi* referring to some kind of quasi-dramatic folk ceremony, is recorded in an entry in the *Chronicle of Lanercost* for the year 1282. The offending event occurred at Inverkeithing in Fife in Easter week and, ironically, had a churchman as its instigator:

> The parish priest, John by name, by way of celebrating the profane rites of Priapus, gathered together the little girls from the area around the town, and compelled them to form a circle, and dance round in a ring in honour of Father Bacchus. When he had these females in position, in order to inspire immodesty, he carried a representation of a phallus on a stick in front of the dancers, himself dancing and stamping with the singers, by his miming and lewd language, inciting all those who saw him to lust. Those in the honourable state of matrimony, on account of their dignified station, although unaccustomed to the practice, tempted others to evil out of respect for the principal actor. If any of the bystanders, not participating in the dance, began to speak out amorously on their own account, he became worse, and loudly insulted them.

This is the earliest record of a spring rite in Scotland. Its pagan origin is evident, as is, in its occurrence in Easter week and in the principal part played by the priest, the appropriation of such activities by the Church in order to give them a Christian gloss. We also see in this ceremony those qualities of 'game' and 'play' encapsulated in the Roman term *ludi*, and – in the use here of dance, song, mime and spoken word, all presented before an audience – the evolution of mimetic *ludi* into quasi-drama.

That it is a spring rite recorded at Inverkeithing, with suggestions of a fertility ritual, is significant. Folk drama had its origins in pagan summer and winter festival rites which followed the seasonal and agricultural calendars. Of particular importance was the regeneration of the land in spring and the victory thereby of summer over winter. Folk culture in medieval Scotland had many expressions of this drama of combat between death and resurrection, winter and summer, as seen in animal resurrection cults, ceremonial dances, contests between Summer and Winter Kings and Queens, and various Maying rites. The symbolic representation of death and resurrection characteristic of these folk observances was christianised by adapting it to the story of Christ's Passion and by having the attendant ceremonies sometimes follow the Christian calendar in accordance with the importance of Christmas and Easter. This christianisa-tion was not achieved easily and both the Catholic Church and then the Reformed Church issued edicts against those folk practices which retained traces of paganism. Prosecutions against participants occurred well into the seventeenth century. Where it was deemed acceptable, the Church tacitly sanc-tioned folk festivities, and the municipal authorities gave organisational support, for example in the case of the May games.

References to May festivities celebrating the end of winter and the arrival of summer occur most frequently in the records of the fifteenth and sixteenth centuries. The most popular of these festivities involved the election of a mock king who officiated as lord of the 'May game' or 'May play' (as it is often termed in the records). He had responsibility for organising and leading the event, in which the people themselves performed in costumes and musicians were usually present. This figure had different titles: sometimes he is referred to as 'King of the May', and occasionally 'Queen of the May', but more com-monly as the 'Abbot of Unreason'. Variations on the latter, such as 'Abbot and Prior of Bonacord' (Aberdeen), 'Abbot of Narent' (Edinburgh), and 'Abbot of Unrest' (Inverness), are also found. Although as late as 1600 there is reference to 'ane Abbot play' in Elgin, the presiding figure of the Abbot of Unreason at the May game had by then long been overtaken in popularity by Robin Hood. In 1508, for example, in a city statute organising a Robin Hood event in Aberdeen, able-bodied citizens were commanded to ride 'with Robert huyd and litile Johne quhilk was callit in yeris bipast Abbot and priour of Bonacord' (references to the latter do, however, continue to appear in the Aberdeen records).

The source of the heroic Robin Hood figure in Scottish folk culture is uncertain. He may have derived from mythology, history, or ballad minstrelsy; and there may be a link with the Fool figure who officiated in fertility and sum-mer-heralding rites such as that recorded at Inverkeithing, or with some kind of ritual associated with nature and the forest. Whatever the derivation, by the early fifteenth century his name seems to have been as well known in Scotland as in England, and by the sixteenth century he had become the leading charac-ter in the most popular form of folk play. Just how popular that 'King of the May' folk play was can be judged from the number of places where there are references to Robin Hood or the Abbot of Unreason: Edinburgh, Aberdeen,

Dundee, Perth, Elgin, Inverness, Arbroath, Dumbarton, Haddington, Ayr, Alloway, Peebles, Arbuthnot, Fintray, Lasswade, Cranston and Linton. In addition to burgh support, the May play enjoyed a degree of royal patronage, for there are various entries in the court records indicating payments to the Abbot of Unreason and Robin Hood. On 26 June 1503, for example, King James IV gave four French crowns 'to Robin Hude of Perth'.

The popularity of these May games and the licence they provided for public rowdiness began to alarm civic and church authorities fearful of sedition in the turbulent times of the mid sixteenth-century Reformation (the Roman Catholic Church had earlier begun to voice disapproval of May games for similar reasons). Thus, in 1555, the Reformers, with the support of the civil powers, sought to suppress the traditional May and Yuletide plays by means of an Act of Parliament:

> It is statute and ordainit that in all tymes cumming, na maner of personn be chosin *Robert Hude* nor *Lytill Johne*, *Abbot of Unressoun* [Unreason], *Queenis of Maij* nor utherwyse, nouther in Burgh nor to landwart . . . And gif [if] ony Provest, Baillies, counsall and communitie chesis [chooses] sic ane Personage . . . within Burgh, the chesaris of sik sall tyne [lose] thair fredome for the space of fyve yeires . . . and the acceptar of siclyke office salbe banist furth of the Realme; And gif ony sic persounis sic as *Robert Hude, Lytill Johne, Abbottis of Unressoun, Queenis of Maij*, beis chosin outwith Burgh and uthers landward townis, the chesaris sall pay to our Soverane Lady ten pundis and thair persounis put in waird [prison], thair to remane during the Queenis grace plesoure.

The popularity of such plays, as attested by the perceived need for this legislation, meant that the Act was not wholly successful. In 1561, for example, the Edinburgh bailies banned 'convocatioun and assemblie efter the auld wikit maner of Robene Hude', and they sentenced to death a shoemaker for playing Robin Hood. This occasioned a riot, with the mob smashing the gallows, sealing off the Tolbooth, and forcing the terrified provost and bailies to seek help from an unsympathetic Constable of the Castle. In such ways, and despite official censure and threat, the May games continued to be celebrated. In 1591 the General Assembly of the Kirk was still urging that the Acts of Parliament against 'profaners of the Sabboth day be Robuin Hoodes playis' be vigorously enforced. The Reformers' objective was eventually achieved; the last recorded performance by adults of a Robin Hood play was at Linton in 1610. Elements of the medieval death-and-resurrection drama did however resurface post-1700 in a folk play of Hallowe'en and Hogmanay, 'Galoshins', as Brian Hayward demonstrates in his study *Galoshins: The Scottish Folk Play* (1992). Galoshins plays, for which there are some texts, were performed in local communities well into this century.

An Act of Presbytery of 1589 prohibited 'pasche playis abbot of onresone robene houd & sich uther prophane playis'. There are references like this, in fifteenth- and sixteenth-century records, to summer-heralding plays with a similar variety of names such as King of May plays, May plays, Abbot plays, Robin Hood plays, Pasche or Peace plays, and others. There is, however, an ambiguity in the word 'play', in that it can refer to recreational and festive activity, as well as to a performed drama of some kind. The former meaning seems intended in two mid fifteenth-century poems: the anonymous 'Peblis to the Play', which describes a folk revelry at Peebles, and Alexander Scott's 'Of May', where he describes as a 'game' how 'In May when men geid evrich one/With Robin Hood and Little John,/To bring in boughs and birken bobbins'. The word occurs, too, in a poem attributed to William Dunbar (c.1460–c.1520), 'The Manere of the Crying of Ane Playe' (also titled 'Ane Littill Interlud of the Droichis [Dwarf's] Pairt of the Play'). This poem, which can be read as a monologue, is the one surviving example of a 'cry' (call) to a May play, and it seems to be part of a performed dramatic entertainment, either as a 'bann' to proclaim the start of the play or as an interlude within the play to announce its recommencement. The play to which listeners are being called by a character in the role of 'Welth' (Wealth), who is 'littil as ye may see' – and was perhaps a dwarf as indicated by the alternative title – is a Robin Hood play, as this excerpt shows:

> Quharfor in Scotland come I heire
> With yow to byde and perseveire,
> In Edinburgh quhar is meriast cheire,
> Plesans, disport, and play,   [pleasure]
> Quhilk is the lampe and A *per se* [paragon]
> Of this regioun in all degre,
> Of welefaire and of honeste
> Renoune and riche aray.
> Sen I am Welth cummyn to this wane, [place]
> Ye noble merchandis everilkane
> Addres yow furth with bow and flane [arrow]
> In lusty grene lufraye,   [livery]
> And follow furth on Robyn Hude,
> With hartis coragious and gud,
> And thocht that wretchis wald ga wod, [mad]
> Of worschipe hald the way.

The merchants are to dress in livery and follow Robin Hood, presumably in some kind of processional or pageant 'play'. The narrator 'Welth' says that he also has three companions, 'Weilfare, Wantones, and Play', who 'Sall byde with yow in all affray,/And cair put clene to flicht'. These four allegorical characters would therefore seem to be participants, along with the costumed merchants, in the dramatic entertainment that is the Robin Hood play. There is here a play within a play, as it were, which highlights the ambiguity referred to in usage of the term, in that the 'play' as a drama contains a character, 'Play', who is an allegorical representation of the other sense of the word as game or festivity. Reminiscent of religious drama, the May play may have been a processional event incorporating a performed drama, or a processional riding or pageant leading up to a play at a stationary location. Unfortunately, no text of a May play, if there ever was one, has survived to clarify the matter.

A Plough Play

One text of a medieval folk play in Scotland that has survived is a 'Plough Play' dating from about 1500. Indeed, it is the only surviving text in Britain of a pre-Reformation folk drama. This text has come down to us not as a play but as an anonymous three-part 'Pleugh Song' (also titled 'My Heartly Service'), words of the play having been set to music some time around 1500.[1] The music is in the style of Scots courtly polyphony and was written for a more sophisticated audience than celebrants of the original folk pastime. Also, the text has undergone some modification: when it was first printed in the seventeenth century the older Scots language was anglicised somewhat, and the variation in wording that was introduced has created confusion of meaning on occasion. None the less, it has been confidently claimed that the 'Pleugh Song' essentially preserves the text of a Scottish folk play, and that it is even older than the approximate date of the song's composition in 1500.

As well as May and summer, winter saw folk plays and pastimes, too. Traditionally, plough plays were performed on the first Monday after Epiphany (6 January), when, with the advent of a new year, the new agricultural cycle began. In its association with the old giving way to the new, or death giving way to birth, the surviving Scottish plough play can be categorised as one of the death-and-resurrection folk dramas. In it, ritual death and symbolic resurrection are enacted through the death and replacement of an old and ailing plough-ox:

> He has not a tooth
> And he no longer may be drawn
> I dare say well
> Bot he was never half so thrawn   [stubborn]

> Nor yet so acwart   [awkward]
> Now is he weak and wonder sweer   [wondrous slothful]
> Full sweer is he   [reluctant]
> Out of ane house he may not stire   [stir]
> Suppose ye brod him whill he die   [goad; until]

The old ox belongs to the feudal master – alternatively he could just be the Lord of the revel – who is addressed in the first line of the play: 'My heartly service to you my Lord.' The speaker, the play's only voice (though there is scope for a chorus at points), would appear to be the leader of a group of tenants who both presents and participates in the action. Because the old plough-ox is dying and the ploughing season is nigh, the spokesperson urges his 'Lord', 'better it war that some remeid [remedy] were found in tym . . . to yoke another in his steid [stead]'. He offers his 'fair fresh ox' and 'this pleugh of mine', and requests that 'I contract and hired be' by the Lord. To allow this, the old ox is, evidently, to be killed. To judge by a chorus, 'hey doun a doun a die', which occurs a number of times, the killing is represented in the play.

The speaker then implores the Lord, 'gar call your hyndis' (have your ploughmen called), and reels off all their names. Intriguingly, but not unusually so far as folk drama is concerned, these are a mixture of Christian names (Nicol, Colin, Davie), nicknames (Stra-boots, Ruffie, Ganzel), mythological names (Orpheus, Hector, Arthur), occupational names (Mackay Miller, Sandie Sawer), and names reflecting attributes (False-lips Fergus). He beseeches his master: 'Speir [ask] at them if they will be . . . appleasit for to mell with me'; that is, he wants the 'hyndis' to join with him as a team in drawing the plough. He asks, 'In all Scotland is there sic aught?' 'Aught' can mean either 'eight' or 'draught', and here refers to a ploughing team. If they agree to 'mell' with him, he will come with his ox and his plough equipment, which he itemises in a way which suggests that some kind of ceremonial delivery of the lines was intended:

> Soms of iron stark eneugh   [harness chains; strong]
> The cowter and the pleugh-head   [parts of the plough]
> Sok sheet and mowdie bread
> Rak, rest, and the gluts and the slee band
> The missel and the pleugh-bowl
> The pleugh-staff, the pleugh-shoon
> The mell and the stilt
> And the beam and the heel wedge
> The chock, the yoke, the ring, the sling
> Mine oxen bolls is wreathed and pind

In all probability an actual plough was part of the folk ceremony and the parts of the plough, as indicated above, would have been enumerated accordingly. Also, as was customary in many places, the participants may then have been harnessed to the plough in order to draw it about the village or fields to bestow a bounteous harvest. (This may have derived from an earlier folk custom of transporting a fertility deity around fields on a plough pulled by men.) That the speaker asks the 'hyndis' to make him 'so fast and sicker [fastened and secure] as I wer bound ev'n with ane wicker for to deliver me be the heid' suggests an invitation to harness him.

His ox joins the other oxen, who have evocative names such as 'Trowbelly', 'Chow-bullock', Whyte-horn', 'Humly' and 'Cromack'. The oxen are urged on by name to draw the plough, with exhortations that, if one has a creative stab at adding modern punctuation, seem redolent of authentic farm-speech as the ploughman bullies and cajoles his team, some of whom seem reluctant and wayward:

> The gadwand [prod-stick] is both light and sharp to brod [goad] his belly while [until] he start. Hey! Call about with a shout! Wind [turn] about Brandie! Trow-belly! Trow-belly! Chow-bullock! Chow-bullock! Whyte-horn! Wind Marrow-gaire! I sall brod him while [until] he rair [roars]. The rid stot [red bullock] and the dun, wind about! Hold! Draw him forth, in the Rood's name! [religious oath]

The dynamic quality of such speech suggests performance, with other participants perhaps playing the roles of the oxen. The same, or different, participants may also have taken the roles of the 'hyndis'. Given the nature of some of their names, such as the ones with occupational and mythical associations, the 'hyndis' may have been dressed accordingly as guisers; and so, too, might those playing the individually named oxen.

If we add to these various players the speaker and the 'Lord', we gain a sense of this plough play as a larger performance piece involving many more active participants than might be suggested by its monologue nature and the single controlling voice of the character wishing to hire out his ox. Furthermore, the text, notwithstanding the deficiencies of what has survived, offers obvious possibilities for song and dance, and for mimic action or *tableaux*. Its structure points to dramatic enactment entailing ritual, ceremony and procession. An aspect of these last is the occurrence of religious refrains, such as 'the Trinitie conserve you into Charitie, Amen, Amen, Amen', which can be read as Christianity overlaying paganism. Folk customs such as that reflected in this plough play celebrating regeneration often pre-dated the medieval Church, which, as indicated earlier, in turn accommodated them by adding

Christian elements and adapting them to the church calendar. Epiphany, for example, coincided approximately with the start of the agricultural year, thus regeneration through ploughing could symbolise 'resurrection'.

RELIGIOUS DRAMA

Like their secular counterparts the folk plays, from the Middle Ages through to the Reformation in the sixteenth century, religious plays based on saints' lives and the miracles, or more often the Bible, were an annually recurring event. They served a didactic purpose in dramatising and making familiar to the people, through the immediacy of the vernacular and compelling visual imagery, the stories and moral lessons of the Old and New Testaments. They were also a communal affirmation of faith, for they were staged by and for the community, with the burgh councils combining with the crafts or trade guilds to organise and meet the costs. The plays followed the Holy Days of the church calendar, and were most commonly held outdoors in summer to coincide with the Feast of Corpus Christi, which was tied to the movable feast of Easter and might therefore take place in May or June. There are references in the records to Clerk plays, Candlemas plays, Morality plays and Passion plays, but the most frequent reference is to Corpus Christi plays. The earliest record of a religious drama in Scotland is a Corpus Christi Passion play at Aberdeen in 1440; the first religious play for which we have a title, *Haliblude* (Holy Blood), which was performed in the open air on Windmill Hill in Aberdeen in 1445, was a Corpus Christi play; and the Aberdeen Council records show that Walter Balcancole was paid five shillings in 1449 for copying out a Corpus Christi play text. It is known that there were Corpus Christi plays at Dundee, Perth, Edinburgh, Lanark, Arbroath and elsewhere.

The Corpus Christi plays took the form of a series of pageants dramatising scenes from scriptural history and following a triumphal doctrinal pattern of Fall, Redemption, and Judgement. Each trade guild in a burgh had responsibility for a pageant within a series. For example, the records of the Hammermen of Perth for 1518 show a list of payments to the 'playaris on Corpus Christie Day', with their pageant play featuring Adam and Eve, the Devil and his 'Man', the Devil's Champion, the Angel and 'Marmadin' (Mermaid), and St Eloy (patron saint of the Hammermen). In 1553 it is recorded that George Allan took the part of the Trinity, Robert Colbert was the Serpent, and the parts of Adam and Eve, St Eloy, the Mermaid, and various angels and devils were played by members of the Hammermen. It was important that the pageants should be visually compelling as an assertion of guild pride, as a celebration of the Feast Day, and as an aid to inspiring the people's faith. Sarah Carpenter has observed of the surviving records, fragmentary though they are:

Figure 1.1 The Fetternear Banner, c. 1520, probably made for the Confraternity of the Holy Blood, St Giles Church, Edinburgh. Rare surviving processional banner depicting Christ on the Cross with the Instruments of the Passion. Representations of this scene would have featured in Corpus Christi Passion plays. The banner may have been carried on the processional route of a Passion play. (Trustees of the National Museums of Scotland)

They give us glimpses of the visual style of the plays: the payments in Lanark for 'futyn off the cros' (footing of the cross) in 1503, or the Dundee record of 'a credil & thre barnis (babies) maid of clath' (1520), suggest the emotive realism with which episodes like the crucifixion, or the slaughter of the innocents might be presented; while the 'gold fulye (foil) to Cristis pascione' (Lanark), or 'cristis cott (coat) of lethyr with the hoss (hose) and glufis' (Dundee) shows the ritual splendour with which such naturalism was combined.[2]

The plays could have been performed either on pageant-wagons as 'stations' on a processional route to a church, or as open-air stationary presentations on the same site. The existence of 'playfields' points to the latter being more likely. There were playfields attached to several burghs and it is known that those at Aberdeen, Dundee, Edinburgh and Perth were used for dramatic performances.

A Surviving Passion Play?

It was thought until recently that no text of a medieval religious drama in Scotland had survived. However, Dorothy Riach has argued that a poem, 'The Passioun of Crist', by Walter Kennedy, originally comprised part of a Corpus Christi cycle of plays.[3] Walter Kennedy (c.1460–c.1508) was one of a number of Scottish medieval poets now known collectively as the Makars. Although little known now, he was highly regarded by his contemporaries. He features in 'The Flyting of Dunbar and Kennedie' by William Dunbar, the most significant Makar; and Dunbar names him in his 'Lament for the Makaris', where one of the poets whose passing is lamented is 'Guid Maister Walter Kennedy'. Another Makar, Gavin Douglas, in his poem 'The Palice of Honour', included Kennedy, along with Dunbar, in a list of master poets: 'Of this natioun I knew also anone/Greit Kennedie and Dunbar yit undeid'. Sir David Lindsay, too, praised Walter Kennedy in one of his poems: 'Or quho can now the workis countrafait [counterfeit]/Of Kennedie with termes aureait'.

Aureate diction was a feature of much of the Makars' work, and it is evident in Kennedy's long religious poem 'The Passioun of Crist' (no date), as exemplified by the arresting opening stanza with its declamatory tone:

Haill, cristin knycht, haill, etern confortour, [Christian knight]
Haill, riall king in trone celistiall,   [royal; throne]
Haill, lampe of licht, haill, Iesu saluitour, [Jesus saviour]
In hevin empire prince perpetuall,
Haill, in distres protectour principall,
Haill, God and man, borne of a virgin cleyne,
Haill, boist of balme, spilit within my splene. [small box for ointment,
                                                here balm; heart]

This is the opening to the prologue, which has ten stanzas, and is followed by the biblical story of Christ's Passion in 235 stanzas. The narrative begins with the Creation of Man, followed by his Fall and banishment; allegorical figures then debate Man's case, but God enters and judges the issue by deciding to send His Son to Earth. The story of Jesus's life is then told, culminating in the poem's key concerns: the events of Holy Week, with the Crucifixion and Christ's Passion, followed by the Resurrection, the Ascension and the coming of the Holy Spirit.

The narrative is broken up into sections with Latin and Scots headings such as 'Ferria quarta traditio Domini' and 'At Ew[v]insang'. In a major reassessment of Kennedy's long poem, Dorothy Riach has argued that these sections follow the Festival Days of Holy Week, from Wednesday to Easter Sunday, and the Canonical Hours associated with the structure of church worship. She claims that there are many elements of liturgical drama within the poem which suggest that 'The Passioun of Crist' was originally a Passion play of the Corpus Christi cycle intended for use by a congregation during the Easter season, but to which Kennedy added a prologue to adapt it for a readership. She sees a strong resemblance to extant Mystery play cycles in England, which were centred on the Passion of Christ, and she identifies specific parallels between certain of those plays and parts of the poem. Her close examination of 'The Passioun of Crist' leads her to state: 'Nothing quite like Kennedy's poem is extant in Scots poetry . . . It is both narrative and dramatic, bearing a close relationship with the plays and pageants which were a popular form of instruction in the faith.'

The poem differs from more traditional Corpus Christi-related plays in that it does not have the obvious qualities of a 'script', such as sustained dialogue allocated to characters and stage directions. None the less, it does display features that support the argument for some kind of dramatic performance. Whilst the poem's controlling voice is the narrator, Kennedy inserts direct speech regularly throughout the work. Approximately twenty individual characters are given speech: God, Mary, Christ, Peter, Judas, a Servant, Cayphas, Pilot, a Messenger, Death, Senturio, the Cross, John, Mary Magdalene, Cleophas, Thomas and two thieves. Groups of characters are given choral speech, too, such as Angels, the Jews, the People, Priests of Law, Bystanders, the Disciples and Scribes. Whilst not all of this direct speech takes dialogue form, there are a good number of exchanges between characters. A few of these exchanges are three-way but the majority are between two characters, with Christ being a speaker in most. Notwithstanding this relatively restricted range, Kennedy varies the language and tone of his dialogue, encompassing laments, debates, petitions, exhortations, 'flyting' and so on.

While Kennedy on occasion uses aureate language for stylistic effect and to achieve an elevated tone, for the most part his Scots is straightforward and accessible. Christ in the manger is 'ye bony barne [bairn]'; Mary is 'his moder deir'; the Holy Family live in 'ane sempill hame'; Christ wanders in the desert suffering 'Hunger, thrist, cauld, in wynd & rane'; and when he has been cruelly abused by his captors 'On him to luk yair [your] stomok sair it stoundis'. The use of an accessible and familiar vernacular humanises the drama of the Christian story in a manner reminiscent of the way Corpus Christi plays did so to convey to ordinary people, with emotive realism, both knowledge of the Bible and a graphic sense of their religion's truths. Kennedy's vernacular lends a fluency and immediacy to both the narration and the direct speech, notwith-standing the constraints of his chosen rhyme-royal verse form, as in this extract:

> In ye tolbuth Pilot enterit in,   [prison]
> Callit on Crist, and sperit gif he wes king. [asked if]
> Crist ansuerit, inquirand first at him
> Gif of him self, or vthiris rehersing,   [others]
> He sa inquirit gif he as prince suld ring.   [so; reign]
> Pilot ansuerit: 'I am na Iow to knaw.   [Jew]
> Thy awne pepill hes brocht ye to my law.'   [own]

> Crist said: 'My kinrick into yis warld is nocht, [kingdom; this]
> Bot heir I come to schaw ye verite.   [show]
> As warldly king to regne & I had thocht   [reign]
> My ministeris had maid debait for me,   [argument on behalf]
> Quhilkis fra ye Iowis gret iniquite   [which from the]
> Had me defendit, and keipit fra yair handis:
> Thairfor to regne I come nocht in yir landis.'

> Pilot to ye Iowis geid agane,   [went],
> Sayand: 'Na caus I find to gar him de.'   [cause; die]
> The Iowis cryit, sayand: 'He suld be slane'.

In considering how passages such as this could be performed one has to bear in mind the multi-functional role performed by the narrator. He is both a neutral narrator telling the story and moving it along towards its climax, and an active participant or 'character' in that story-telling. The latter is apparent in his direct speech at those points when he steps outside, as it were, his nar-rator's role and speaks directly to Christ, God, and abstractions such as Man, Pain, Blindness and Death. These speeches are characteristically impassioned and have an emotional force that adds to the impression of a character with a persona, as here where he laments Christ's death:

And fra my hert wald bludy teris spring, [bloody tears]
For thy passioun to murne baith day & nycht, [mourn]
My wofull mynd it wald to confort bring.
Off all solace you had tynt ye sicht.   [lost]
And I salbe besy with all my mycht,   [shall be busy]
And sall nocht ceis to cry quhill I worth hais, [while]
For my kind kingis deid to say: 'Allace.'

There are also occasions when he addresses his listeners/readers directly, reminding them of Christ's sacrifice ('for thy saik wes scornit our saluitour [saviour]'), giving moral commentary, encouraging devoutness and exhorting them with the command 'say' to repeat refrains or prayer-like utterances. The instructor's role he thus adopts extends to explication of words in a way which also indicates that, as a persona, he shares his listeners'/readers' culture: 'Iesu in oure leid [language] is callit saluitor', 'Ane pretius claith [cloth], quhilk [which] we ane syndon call'.

The narrator, then, can be seen as a poet-persona, as both an omniscient voice and an implicated participant. The literary value of this is obvious in the variety it lends to the text, engaging and retaining the interest of readers. But what are the performance implications if we accept that 'The Passioun of Christ' did have its genesis, as Dorothy Riach argues, in a play of the Corpus Christi cycle intended for use by worshippers during Easter Week? At this remove we cannot tell if the poem was adapted from a 'script' or if the poem (minus the prologue provided for a readership) was the 'script'. However, accepting that the latter was the case, then the poem by its nature could not have been an acted playlet of the kind that commonly featured in the Corpus Christi cycle. Rather, the central role of the narrator in the poem suggests that he performed a similar role in performance, which would argue against a more conventional theatrical presentation.

One possibility is that he was a 'Terence-narrator'. This form of presentation stemmed from a medieval misconception of how the comedies of Terence (c.190–159 BC) were performed. It involved a narrator in a booth-like structure speaking the parts of players who mimed their roles in an open area in front of spectators. 'Terence-staging' has been described as an 'elusive but persistent tradition' in European medieval culture,[4] and there is no reason to think that it was not also present in Scotland. If this, or some similar format of presentation, was adopted, Kennedy's narrator could act as a kind of 'cue-master', his narration cueing mimetic action by players to complement events in his story as it unfolds; and perhaps, if he did not himself deliver the direct speech that features so regularly in the poem and is spoken by a wide range of speaking characters, cueing players to deliver the passages of dialogue. In addition to mime and movement, or *tableaux vivants*, Kennedy's poem has scope for inserted music and (religious) song, and it may well have been further enlivened by the splendour of ritual and ceremony associated with church celebrations of Holy Week. The division of the poem into sections may indicate, too, that the poet-persona orchestrated the performance at different locations, either indoors or outdoors, which would have provided further opportunities for enlivening the drama of Christ's Passion.

Because the number of medieval dramatic texts that has survived in Scotland is so meagre, the possibility that Walter Kennedy's 'The Passioun of Christ' preserves just such a text is seductive. However, until further evidence comes to light, a positive identification cannot be claimed and the issue must remain one of tantalising conjecture.

THE REFORMATION AND DRAMA

Like the folk drama, religious drama had its heyday in the fourteenth and fifteenth centuries and declined as the sixteenth century wore on due to opposition from the Reformers. An idea of the popularity enjoyed by communal religious drama before the Reformation can be gauged from the Reformer George Wishart's finger-wagging accusation when preaching to the citizens of Haddington in 1546: 'I have heard of thee, Hadingtoun, that in thee wold have bein at ane vane Clerk play two or three thowsand people.' Contributory to the decline of support for such municipal plays was the burgesses' and guilds' increasing reluctance to contribute effort and money to the performances, and the increasingly rowdy and drunken nature of the attendant revelries (the latter also contributing to the demise of the Robin Hood and May plays). More crucially, in their association with the practices of the Roman Catholic Church – and in the case of the Corpus Christi plays, with the noxious doctrine of transubstantiation in particular – religious plays were vigorously denounced by the Reformers as 'superstitious'. One consequence was that texts, artefacts and records relating to the old religious plays were destroyed (though this was partly due to the more general destruction caused by the Reformation). Old habits died hard, however; in 1577 Lord Rothes and some citizens of Perth were summoned before the Kirk Session and threatened with excommunication for having performed in June of that year an 'idolatrous and superstitious' Corpus Christi play. Baptism was refused to their children unless the players promised 'nevir to mell with sik thingis again'. In Glasgow, a decree of 1599 stipulating citizens' compulsory attendance at a play on Corpus Christi Day suggests a link with the medieval tradition in some form – even though that tradition was by then near to extinction.

The Reformed Church suppressed the feast days associated with Catholicism on which the communal religious dramas traditionally took place; and the keeping of the Sabbath took on a new significance, with consequences for drama. Local Kirk Sessions seem to have been invested with the authority to vet plays and to decide whether permission be granted to allow their performance on a Sunday. In 1574, for example, the Kirk Session of St Andrews granted Patrick Authinleck permission to have performed on a Sunday his *Comedy of the Forlorn Son*, provided that he submitted the text for revision and that the performance did not coincide with the times of preaching. (This was presumably a version, and perhaps a translation, of a play found in a number of Continental countries. In Germany, where it was particularly popular, it was known as *Der verlorne Sohn*.) However, the General Assembly expressed its disapproval of the St Andrews Kirk Session's decision, and this led to the Act of 1574–5 prohibiting all plays on a Sunday:

> Forsamikle as it is considered, that the playing of Clerk playes, comedies or tragedies upon the Canonical parts of the Scripture, induceth and bringeth with it a contempt and profanation of the same . . . It is thoght meit and concludit, That no Clerk playes, comedies or tragedies be made of the Canonicall Scripture, alsweill new as old, neither on the Sabboth day nor worke day, in tyme comeing; the contraveiners heirof (if they be Ministers) to be secludit fra thair functioun, and, if they be vthers, to be punischit be the discipline of the Kirk.

The Act also goes on to say that 'other playes, comedies, tragedies, and others [sic] profane playes *as are not made vpon authentick partes of the Scripture*' (my emphasis) may be allowed, but their texts must be submitted for inspection first and they must not be performed on the Sabbath. An interesting aspect of this Act is the variety of plays named and the inference that can be drawn that these types of plays had been regularly performed. (To judge by the contexts in the records, 'Clerk playes' in Scotland were probably variants of the Corpus Christi play.)

The 1574–5 Act was tested by other cases, and in 1578 the General Assembly was moved to reiterate that the Sabbath had to be strictly observed and that 'mercats, playes, and all other impediments, which may hinder the people to conveen to hear the word, be discharged'. It would seem that local Kirk Sessions were none the less allowed to issue licences for performances, as records reveal was the case in Perth in 1589:

> The ministers and elders give licence to plai the plai, with conditions that no swearing, banning, nor onie scurrility sal be spoken, which would be a scandal to our religion, which we profess, and for an evil example unto others. Alswa that nathing sall be added to what is in the register of the plai itself. If ony one who plais sal do in the contrairie, he sal be *wardit* [imprisoned], and mak his public repentance.

The 'register' was the text submitted for approval. In Stirling, one such submitted text, a Clerk play by a John Brown, was judged to contain 'mekill baning [cursing] & swering sum badrie [bawdry] and filthie baning'. In Dalkeith in 1582, St Andrews in 1595–6, and Elgin in 1600 there are recorded instances of offenders being rebuked for having performed plays without a licence from the Kirk Session.

As discussed above in the section on 'Folk Drama', the Reformers also disapproved of folk plays and pastimes, partly out of alarm at the anarchic behaviour of the participants and the potential for seditious mobbing. The Reformers' antipathy was intensified by their hostility to the wearing of disguises for amusement. This was based on a literal reading of a passage in Deuteronomy forbidding both sexes from assuming disguises because they violated the divine conception of the human form. Folk pastimes involving guising were condemned, as were folk plays with their colourful costumes and props. Although prohibition took several decades to achieve fully, and required further legislative measures, the Reformers' objective was largely secured by the early seventeenth century and the folk drama thereafter declined into comparative insignificance.

The Reformation's adverse infuence on drama, then, is evident in the suppression of feast days and the communal religious dramas that accompanied them, the attempted elimination of folk pastimes and plays, the prohibition of plays drawing on Scripture, the submission of non-Scriptural comedies and tragedies to rigorous censorship, and the rigid adherence to the Deuteronomic injunction regarding disguises. These were policed by the local Kirk Sessions, the Presbyteries and the General Assembly, and were aided by civil legislation, together threatening excommunication and/or imprisonment. Cumulatively these inhibitions constituted a serious impediment to the preservation of existing dramatic forms and the establishment of the roots of a modern drama in the sixteenth century. As will be discussed later, the Royal Court provided a degree of protection for dramatic activity, but that was lost when James VI removed to London in 1603. The Reformers' antipathy to the performance and writing of drama extended into the seventeenth century to stifling effect, and it was not until the mid eighteenth century that moderate forces were mustered and sufficient relaxation was achieved to allow the establishment of theatres and professional acting companies.

REFORMATION PLAYS

Notwithstanding the Reformers' general hostility to drama, in the early days of the struggle for Reformation they encouraged it if it could be used as propaganda against what they saw as the corrupt practices and doctrines of the Roman Catholic Church. It was only once the Reformation had been achieved and was institutionalised, from 1560 onwards, that the people's partiality for entertainment, including dramatic activities, was increasingly condemned as irreligious, and prohibitory edicts were issued accordingly. Even then, if a play served a resolutely moral or sacred purpose it was condoned. Thus, in 1571, John Knox watched with approval a play performed at St Andrews. Written by John Davidson, a regent of the university and a staunch Reformer, the play dramatised the contemporary siege of Edinburgh Castle 'according to Mr Knox's doctrine', and featured the captain and others being 'hangit in effegie'. Drama was also allowed in schools as a vehicle for propaganda and religious instruction. For example, in 1598 a 'comedie' – clearly propagandist and satirical – was performed in Edinburgh High School, with the roles of the Pope, the Cardinal and five friars, being taken by masters and scholars.

The more significant 'Reformation Drama' is found in the first half of the century when Reformation was growing in opposition to the Roman Catholic status quo. John Kyllour, a Dominican friar, wrote a *Historye of Christis Passioun*, which was performed in the Castlehill playfield, Stirling, before King James V, his Court, and the townspeople, on the morning of Good Friday, 1535. Using what was obviously the format of a traditional religious drama, the Passion play, Friar Kyllour, as recorded by John Knox, expressed, in a way that 'the verray sempill people understood', how just as the Priests and Pharisees persuaded the people to refuse Christ, causing Pilot to condemn him, so contemporary Bishops and priests corruptly blinded the people to the real Christ and persuaded 'Princes and Judgeis to persecute sick [such] as professis Jesus Christ his blessed Evangell'. The transparency of Kyllour's attack in his play so angered the Catholic hierarchy that he became a hunted man. He was eventually captured and, by order of Cardinal Beaton, was burned at the stake in Edinburgh in 1539.

It was another reforming Dominican friar who awoke enthusiasm for Reformation in the Dundee merchant James Wedderburn, when, after his education at St Andrews and a spell in France gaining mercantile experience, he became a councillor in 1522. It is recorded that Wedderburn wrote and had performed 'diverse comedeis and tragedeis in the Scotish tongue' which satirised the Roman Catholic clergy. The names of only two of these plays have come down to us through the same contemporary chronicler:

> He composed in forme of tragedie the *Beheading of Johne the Baptist*, which was acted at the West Port of Dundie, wherein he carped roughly the abusses and corruptiouns of the Papists. He compiled the *Historie of Dyonisius the Tyranne* [Tyrant], in forme of a comedie, which was acted in the play-feild of the said burgh, wherein he likewise nipped the Papists.

These are likely to have been performed about 1540. They may have been printed by John Scot in Dundee before his suppression in 1547, but no texts have survived. There is a possibility that some ballads or songs from the plays were included in the *Gude and Godlie Ballates* (1567) – a collection of pro-Reformation verse and songs compiled by Wedderburn's brothers, John and Robert. Wedderburn's dramatic and anti-Papist activities in time led to 'letters of captioun' being issued for his arrest. He fled to France where he spent ten years in exile in Rouen and Dieppe. When he died in Dieppe about 1550, he charged his son: 'We have beene acting our part in the theater: you are to succeed; see you that you act your part faithfullie!' The analogy of life to theatre suggests how strongly James Wedderburn believed in the socially and spiritually transforming power of drama.

In his *Historie of the Kirk of Scotland*, written at the beginning of the sixteenth century, John Row, whose father was the first Reformed minister at Perth, stated that 'There were some theatricall plays, comedies, and other notable histories acted in publict' in the early Reformation period. This suggests that there were more plays than those for which we have names and that much has been lost. The only surviving dramatic texts are George Buchanan's Latin tragedies and, most fortunately, Sir David Lindsay's masterwork, *Ane Satyre of the Thrie Estaitis*. The kind of dangers to which writers of Reformation plays were exposed, such as John Kyllour being burnt alive and James Wedderburn exiled, touched Buchanan and Lindsay, too. Buchanan, after being arrested for heresy in 1539, escaped through a window and fled to France; and Lindsay, as a senior courtier, was protected by the King from the Church's wrath but had his play burned in public. We see in Buchanan's work a parallel with James Wedderburn's in the allegorical use of biblical and historical themes. Also, both wrote plays based on the murder of John the Baptist – a subject used by other Reform-minded dramatists in Europe because it allowed, under the cloak of a biblical story, denunciation of those who would silence a prophet of faith.

George Buchanan's Latin Tragedies

George Buchanan (1506–82) was a humanist scholar and Latinist of European reputation whose writings in Latin and Scots encompassed history, political thought, poetry and drama. Born near Killearn, he studied at the Universities of Paris and St Andrews, and spent some thirty years on the Continent, where he taught in Italy, Bordeaux, Paris and Coimbra in Portugal. His eventful life included fleeing Scotland to escape religious persecution, after writing a satirical poem attacking the Franciscans, and being imprisoned and tried by the Inquisition in Lisbon for his heretical beliefs. He was tutor both to Mary Queen of Scots – later becoming her fiercest critic – and her son James VI. As a Reformer he played a leading role in the Scottish Reformation.

While teaching at Bordeaux (1539–43) Buchanan translated from Greek to Latin Euripides' plays *Medea* and *Alcestis* and wrote two original biblical dramas in Latin, *Jephthes* and *Baptistes*. Three of these works were first published in Paris: *Medea* in 1544, *Jephthes* in 1554, and *Alcestis* in 1556. *Baptistes* had its first publication in London in 1577. As a professor at the Collège de Guyenne in Bordeaux, one of Buchanan's duties was to compose an annual play in Latin for the students to perform, hence these four dramatic works. (One of the student performers of Buchanan's plays was the great French essayist Montaigne.) The Collège de Guyenne was founded to promote the 'new learning' associated with the Renaissance, centring on the study of Ancient Greek and Roman texts, including drama. Drama in the classical languages was thus seen as an educational tool. Buchanan's Latin tragedies should therefore be placed in this context of interest in surviving works by the Ancient Greek and Roman dramatists in turn encouraging the production of translations, adaptations and new plays based on classical principles for performance and study in educational establishments. The translation of plays by the Ancients either from Greek into the more familiar Latin, or from Greek into the vernacular, was seen as leading naturally to imitation of the classics through adaptation or original work, as in Buchanan's case.

The influence of Buchanan's translation work, and of his study of classical tragedy generally, is evident in *Jephthes* and *Baptistes*. Literary historians have identified in them elements of Aristotle, Terence, Horace and, most markedly, Euripides and Seneca. *Jephthes* is modelled on the plot of Euripides' *Iphigenia in Aulis*, and both *Jephthes* and *Baptistes* are so 'Senecanised' in theme, characters, structure and moral didacticism that they have been credited as one of the chief means by which Senecan style became established in Renaissance Europe as the appropriate mode for tragedy. Such classical influences signified a more general shift in European drama away from the medieval tradition of Miracle and Mystery plays and their allegorical characters of virtues towards a Renaissance drama drawing on the structure, language and style of classical drama. Thus, Buchanan's original plays reflect a classics-inspired concern to establish the diction, style and rhetoric appropriate for tragedy and to offer clear moral teaching. As a number of commentators have remarked in relation to Buchanan, such considerations do not necessarily make for good theatre. Elevated expression, lengthy rhetorical speeches and insistent moral didacticism militate against effective performance of his plays. But then, Buchanan's chief influence, Seneca, never intended his plays to be performed; and Buchanan, his literary ambitions for his Latin style apart, was less concerned with his Latin tragedies as performance texts – notwithstanding that they were written for delivery by his scholars – than as educational texts conveying classical ideals and moral instruction.

Both Buchanan's plays are biblical stories dramatising conflicts which turn

SIC BVCHANANVS   ORA SIC VVLTVM TVLIT.
PETE SCRIPTA ET ASTRA.   NOOSSE SI MENTEM CVPIS.

ÆTATIS . 76
AN   1 5 8 1

Figure 1.2 George Buchanan (attrib. Arnold Bronckorst, 1581). (Scottish National Portrait Gallery)

on questions of moral conscience. In *Jephthes*, Jahveh, father of the Jews, sends the Ammonites to fight his own people as a way of punishing them for their disobedience and worship of false gods. Jephthah, leader of the Jews, has led an army to do battle with the Ammonites. His wife, Storge, has a troubled dream where wolves invade the sheep pen but are chased off by a dog which then kills the sheep it is meant to be protecting. Iphis, her daughter, has a premonition that her father will return victorious, which proves to be the case. Jephthah had unsuccessfully attempted to persuade the Ammonites not to raise arms, and in victory he shows again his essential goodness by sparing women, children and old people. God, having punished his sinful people through this conflict with the Ammonites, now expresses his love for Jephthah. In happiness and gratitude Jephthah vows to sacrifice to God the first thing he sees on his return home. To his horror, that proves to be his daughter, Iphis. He confides his predicament to a chorus who determine to warn Iphis and her mother. Jephthah prays for death to avoid sacrificing his daughter. He discusses his moral dilemma with a priest, which allows extended disputation over the competing demands of love and divine will. Jephthah believes that he is acting in good conscience in honouring God's will, but the priest argues that love is the divine will. The priest considers Jephthah obstinate and proud in holding to his vow. Iphis asks her father what wrongs she has committed and asks for pity. He knows that she is sinless but cannot put aside his pride: he still wishes his own death but cannot dishonour his vow to God. Iphis accepts her fate and the chorus praises her.

In *Baptistes*, John the Baptist holds out a religious challenge to a corrupt priesthood and monarchy. The High Priest, Malchus, voices to Gamaliel his criticism of John's hostility to the priests. God, he believes, would not announce a new religion through one so humble in station. Gamaliel is more sympathetic to John's case. Malchus leaves, and Gamaliel expresses his fear that Malchus will poison King Herod's mind against John. In the meantime, Herod is assuring the Queen that John is no threat to their monarchy. The Queen dissents, believing that John can rouse the people against them. She resents Herod's trust in John. When John enters, Herod lists the charges brought against him. John confirms his criticisms but says that he is opposed to violence and has preached only the message of the Prophets; he has criticised the King's adultery because it is a breach of the law. Herod defers judgement on John, but he has inwardly resolved to defend his kingship against him, even if that entails bloodshed.

Malchus pretends friendship to John, who tells him that truth is his only motivation and that God has appointed him the Announcer of that truth. The Jews, he says, have deviated from their traditions and the priests exploit their flock for material gain. Malchus is cynical about John's motives and determines to punish him for his criticisms of the established order. Because he distrusts Herod, Malchus pours his poisonous feelings about John into the Queen's receptive ear. John is warned by the chorus of impending danger and calumny, but he asserts his preparedness to accept death rather than deny his duty towards truth and his greater King in heaven. The Queen, still distrustful of Herod's resolve, ensnares him into acting against John by acceding to her daughter Salome's request that John's head be served up. John duly forfeits his life and the venality of Herod and the priests is thereby further confirmed.

In a preface to *Baptistes* addressed to the young King James VI, Buchanan wrote that the play would show posterity that if the King turned into a tyrant it would be James's fault and not his tutor Buchanan's. The general resemblance of John the Baptist to a Reformer upholding truth against religious and princely oppression was clearly intended. Both *Baptistes* and *Jephthes* deal with moral issues of contemporary moment in Reformation Europe: religious idolatry, tyranny and the duties of monarchs. The critical consensus is that these issues are more successfully dramatised in *Jephthes*, Buchanan's most influential play and his own favourite, which many have found an impressive and moving tragedy. *Baptistes*, which he composed first, is a more static work, deficient in action and characterisation, and with greater emphasis on rhetoric and set-piece debates.

Buchanan's Latin tragedies are part of what is now termed 'academic drama'. Written in Latin, the *lingua franca* of humanist thought and literature, this was an international drama of Europe-wide significance. Because of the language, however, it was a drama intelligible only to an educated élite. Original works were, in the main, written for and performed by young scholars as part of a Latin-medium syllabus embracing rhetoric, public speaking and moral instruction. None the less, *published* drama (and poetry) in Latin – and in vernacular translations from the Latin – was a potent means of propagating humanist and reformist ideals, and was the means by which Buchanan acquired an immense reputation over much of Renaissance Europe before his death and after. *Jephthes*, according to a modern biographer of Buchanan, enjoyed such a vogue throughout Europe that 'its popularity is little short of phenomenal'.[5] In addition to its publication in Latin, *Jephthes* appeared in contemporary vernacular translations in Italy, Holland, Poland, Hungary, France and Germany (there were a number of rival translations in the last two countries). Contemporary translations of *Baptistes* were published in France and Germany (twice in each case), and both plays continued to be published by leading printing houses throughout Europe during the seventeenth and into the eighteenth centuries.

Whilst Buchanan had a general influence throughout Europe as one of the leading humanist dramatists and a seminal exponent of Senecan style, his impact is more measurable in Germany and, most tellingly, in France. In Germany his plays were performed before court society and contributed to the development of Jesuit school drama. In France, where Buchanan spent half his adult life (some twenty-five years), he is considered, as the editors of the most recent (1983) edition of his plays point out:

> As much a man of the French Renaissance as he is of the Scottish Renaissance . . . He was a close friend and professional associate of French humanists and poets during these vital years in the development of French culture; he was shaped by France, and he in his turn helped to shape French scholarship, French poetry and above all French drama.[6]

He has been credited with laying the foundations of French classical drama, where 'academic drama', written in Latin and French, became the national drama. *Baptistes* and *Jephthes* have their place in French theatre history as the first neoclassical dramas to be written in France. Because Jodelle's plays were written in French he has received greater recognition, but his first attempt at neoclassical tragedy, *Cléopâtre captive*, was written a decade after Buchanan's plays. Through their influence on Jodelle and Garnier, their extensive reputation and their availability in print in Latin and French translation, *Baptistes* and *Jephthes* also indirectly influenced the great French classical dramatists of the seventeenth-century golden age in French literature: Corneille, Racine and Molière. Indeed, Corneille justified his use of a biblical subject in one of his classical tragedies in verse with reference to Buchanan's example. It is an indication of Buchanan's reception in France that translations, paraphrases and imitations of his poetry and drama were produced there well into the seventeenth century.

Strands of influence on drama in his native country are detectable in the sixteenth and seventeenth centuries but they are of more limited significance than in France. For three centuries and more after his death, Buchanan was considered one of Scotland's greatest men of letters, but this was mainly based on his poetry and prose. Three translations of his plays into English were published in Scotland in the Victorian period, a Scots translation by the poet Robert Garioch was published in 1959, and an English translation appeared in 1983.

Sir David Lindsay's Ane Satyre of the Thrie Estaitis

Sir David Lindsay (or Lyndsay) (c.1485–1555) wrote what is widely considered the greatest of Scottish plays. Its full title is *Ane Pleasant Satyre of the Thrie Estaitis in Commendatioun of Vertew and Vituperatioun of Vyce*. Now more familiar as *Ane Satyre of the Thrie Estaitis*, the play's theatrical, as against its poetic, importance was neglected from Lindsay's day until modern times when, at the 1948 Edinburgh International Festival, an abridged acting text, prepared by Robert Kemp, was triumphantly staged in the Assembly Hall. The play featured prominently in subsequent Edinburgh Festivals in 1949, 1951, 1959, 1973, 1984, 1985 and 1991. (The acting texts used in these productions, whilst theatrically effective for modern audiences, cut out about half of Lindsay's original text. So far there has been no modern staging of the play in anything sufficiently like its entirety to allow a true sense of its medieval structure.)

Lindsay was the son of a Fife laird. His career was spent at the Court of James V, where he was, variously, usher, herald, Lyon King of Arms and envoy to European courts. He was also a court poet and a deviser and writer of entertainments such as pageants, masques, farces and plays, in which he was known

Figure 1.3 Sir David Lindsay (artist unknown). (The Trustees of the National Library of Scotland)

to perform. Records show that in 1527 he was granted money for a blue and yellow taffeta 'play coat' to participate in a play performed before the King and Queen in Holyrood Abbey. And he is reported to have devised a 'trieumphant frais [farce]' in 1538 for the arrival in St Andrews of the new queen, Mary of Guise, 'quhilk teichit hir to serve hir God, obey hir husband, and keep hir body clene according to Godis will and commandement'. As part of the royal entry devised by Lindsay, at the New Abbey Gate a cloud descended from the heavens and opened to reveal an angel, who offered Queen Mary the keys of the kingdom.

In the prologue to his poem the 'Testament and Complaint of the Papyngo', Lindsay refers to court entertainments, ballets and farces, of which no descriptions or texts have come down to us. But Lindsay's reference confirms James

V's interest in dramatic entertainments and supports the contention that *The Thrie Estaitis* was probably instigated by him. The play was first performed at the Feast of Epiphany, on 6 January 1540, before James V and the Court, 'and the hoole counsaile spirituall and temporall', in the Great Hall at Linlithgow Palace. No text of that performance exists but a summary of it in the diplomatic correspondence of the English ambassador suggests that it was shorter than the later versions, and was therefore more an 'interlude' than a play. We know that it satirised the sensuality and greed of the clergy, and therefore carried a reformist message. During the performance James V and the Player-King sat on thrones at opposite ends of the Great Hall silently listening to the drama. At the end, James summoned the bishops and sternly lectured them on the need to reform the spiritual estate.

There were two subsequent performances of expanded versions: on 7 June 1552 and 12 August 1554. (The 1552 version was further revised and extended for the 1554 performance.) The 1552 performance was an outdoor one in the Playfield at the Castle Hill, Cupar, Fife, again before James V. A short proclamation of 277 lines, announcing the play's performance, has survived.[7] Known as 'The Cupar Proclamation' or 'Banns', it was probably performed by actors in *The Thrie Estaitis*, for which it served as a kind of advertisement, providing information about date and time and urging attendance:

Our purpos is, on the sevint day of June,
Gif weddir serve, and we haif rest and pece, [if weather]
We sall be sene in till our playing place,
In gude array abowt the hour of sevin.
Of thriftiness that day I pray yow ceiss,
Bot ordane us gude drink aganis allevin. [at eleven o'clock, i.e. break time]
Fail nocht to be upon the Castell Hill
Besyd the place quhair we purpoiss to play:
With gude stark wyne your flacconis see ye fill, [strong; flagons]
And hald your self the myrieast that ye may.
Be not displeisit quhatevir we sing or say,
Amang sad mater howbeid we sumtyme relyie. [although; make jokes]
We sall begin at sevin houris of the day,
So ye keip tryist; forswth we sall nocht felyie!   [appointment; fail]

The proclamation ends on a ribald note, advising women that, because of the length of the play, 'faill nocht to teme your bleddir [empty your bladder]' otherwise 'some of you sall mak ane richt wait sark [wet shirt]'. Since the performance was to start at seven o'clock in the morning, with a break at eleven o'clock before presumably continuing for another long stretch, the advice had more than just humorous intent.

'The Cupar Proclamation' is almost a short play in itself, and is significant as the only surviving Scottish example of the medieval genre of farce. It features, in separate cameos, an odd array of stock characters drawn from classical comedy and the *commedia dell'arte*. There is a henpecked husband and his sharp-tongued, quick-fisted wife. They trade insults – 'Besyd yow nane may stand for stink', he says – which ends in her striking him. She won't let him go to see the play in Cupar because she intends going herself, and she orders him: 'speid thee hame speidaly,/. . . and milk the ky [cows]–/And muk the byre or [before] I cum hame!' There is an Auld Man who is cuckolded by his young wife, Bessy, even though 'he lok hir cunt and lay the key under his heid'. She is offered fine clothes and gold by wooers but opts for the Fule because he has a big penis ('the best that evir ye saw'). The Fule succeeds in removing the key from under the Auld Man's sleeping head, and he is none the wiser that he has been cuckolded. And there is Fyndlaw of the Fute Band (Findlay or Finlay of the infantry guard), a warmonger and braggart. The Clerk argues the foolishness of war with him; and the Fule exposes him for a coward by frightening him with a sheep's head on a staff, which he takes for a ghost.

The 1554 performance of *Ane Satyre of the Thrie Estaitis* was another outdoor one, this time in Edinburgh at the newly built Greenside playfield on the lower, northern slopes of Calton Hill (in the vicinity of the present Playhouse Theatre). There are entries in the burgh records relating to the provision of props such as eight 'play hattis' (hats), a crown, mitre, fool's head, sceptre, angel wings, angel headdress, 'chaplet of tryumphe', and gibbet. We know from a contemporary chronicler that the play was presented in front of the Queen Regent, Mary of Guise, second wife of James V and mother of Mary Queen of Scots, and that there was also in attendance 'ane greit part of the Nobilitie, with ane exeding greit nowmer of pepil'. The performance, we are informed, lasted from nine o'clock in the morning till six o'clock in the evening.

Lindsay was described by his fellow poet and dramatist, George Buchanan, as being 'of unsuspected probity and veracity, attached to literature, and invariably opposed to falsehood'. Lindsay's opposition to clerical falsehood as bitingly expressed in *The Thrie Estaitis* so enraged the clergy that they ordered the manuscript to be burned by the public executioner in 1558, three years after his death. Fortunately, the play survived in two texts. One is a manuscript copy by George Bannatyne in *The Bannatyne Manuscript*, compiled in the mid-1560s. This text is much earlier than the first published edition but also much shorter (3377 lines as against 4630). The fullest text we have is the first printed edition, published by Robert Charteris in Edinburgh in 1602, of which only seven copies are extant. (The narrow survival of *The Thrie Estaitis* aside, it is testimony to Lindsay's great popularity *as a poet* in Scotland that between his death in 1555 and the end of the century no fewer than ten editions of his poems were published, and in the seventeenth century there were fifteen editions.)

Ane Satyre of the Thrie Estaitis, then, grew from being an interlude presented in the privacy of the Court to a full-scale drama of several hours' duration presented as a grand communal outdoor event to which all the estates of Scotland were called under the auspices of the widowed Queen Mary of Guise. In expanding it took on a panoramic sweep, embracing Scottish society in its totality with an assurance and an informing vision which no subsequent Scottish play has rivalled. The English critic F. P. Wilson has described it as 'one vast Scottish *comédie humaine*. We have nothing like it in England.'[8] Its monumental dimensions are appropriate to a morality play whose satire carries a polemic calling for *national* reform of the way the three estates conduct their affairs, and which was addressed directly to representatives of those estates, foregathered with the monarch and the people to witness the day-long performance. The reform called for is as much moral as political, with particular emphasis on the need for church reform and for the King to act as moral champion in effecting reformation.

The play is in two parts. The first is an allegorical morality tale concerning the moral illness and cure of the individual, as personified by Rex Humanitas (King Humanity), a young king who aspires to be noble and moral but is easily led astray. The play opens with a herald, Diligence, announcing the coming of Rex Humanitas to make reformation. However, the King proves susceptible to the wayward advice of his courtiers, Wantonnes, Placebo and Sandie Solace: 'Sir, quhill [until] ye get ane prudent Queine,/I think your Majestie serein/Should have ane lustie concubein'. Their supporting argument betrays Lindsay's allegorical intent: 'For all the Prelats of this natioun,/For the maist part,/Thay think na schame to have ane huir [whore],/And sum hes thrie under thair cuir'. They introduce the King to Sensualitie, to whose seductive charms he surrenders. Gude Counsall enters. He has been welcomed in other countries but banished from Scotland. His return home holds out promise of reform, but this hope is extinguished by the entrance of the three Vices: Flatterie, Falset (Falsehood), and Dissait (Deceit). They disguise themselves as clerics, perform a mock baptism, and emerge as Devotioun, Sapience and Discretioun. They inveigle themselves into the King's trust, obtain important positions, and prevent Gude Counsall from advising him. Veritie and Chastitie arrive, representing justice and moral rectitude, but they are consigned to the stocks. The Vices seem to have triumphed but the entrance of Divyne Correctioun, an emissary from God, causes the Vices to flee (taking the King's treasure with them). Sensualitie is despatched to Spiritualitie, and the King, roused from his bed of debauchery and now surrounded by Veritie, Chastitie and Gude Counsall, promises reform. Divyne Correctioun orders the King to call a parliament; and

Figure 1.4 Ane Satyre of the Thrie Estaitis, *Scottish Theatre Company, 1985.*
(Scottish Theatre Archive)

part one ends with the herald, Diligence, summoning the three estates to attend
to make reformation.

Whereas the first part of the play centres on reforming an individual body's moral corruption (the King's), the second broadens out to cover reform of corruption in the body politic. Before the allegorical action recommences there is a realistic interlude involving a Pauper from near Tranent who has been mistreated by avaricious clergy and nobility:

Wee had ane meir that caryit salt and coill,   [mare; coal]
And everie ilk yeir scho brocht us hame ane foill.   [foal]
Wee had thrie ky that was baith fat and fair,   [cattle]
Nane tydier [hyne to] the toun of Air.   [from here]
My father was sa waik of blude and bane
That he deit, quhairfoir my mother maid great maine;   [lament]
Then scho deit, within ane day or two,
And thair began my povertie and wo.
Our gude gray meir was baittand on the feild,   [mare; grazing]
And our lands laird tuik hir for his hyreild.   [mortuary due]
The Vickar tuik the best cow be the heid,
Incontinent, quhen my father was deid;   [straight away]
And quhen the Vickar hard tel how that my mother
Was deid, fra-hand he tuke to him ane uther   [at once].
Then Meg, my wife, did murne both evin and morow,
Till at the last scho deit for verie sorow.
And quhen the Vickar hard tell my wyfe was dead
The thrid cow he cleikit be the heid.   [seized]
Thair umest clayis, that was of rapploch gray,   [homespun clothes]
The Vickar gart his clark bear them away.

He has travelled to Edinburgh to seek justice from the Law Courts but, unsuccessful, is now on his way to St Andrews to seek remedy from the Church. He encounters a fraudulent friar, the Pardoner, who sells pardons and bogus relics. The Pardoner's unconsciously hilarious sales-pitch gives some idea, in its contrast with the Pauper's just-quoted speech, of the range of tones and versification Lindsay uses: 'Bona dies, bona dies!/Devoit peopill, gude day I say yow./Now tarie ane lytill quhyll, I pray yow'. Having arrested their attention, he displays his wares and begins his pitch:

Heir is ane relict lang and braid,
Of Fine Macoull the richt chaft blaid, [Finn mac Coul (legendary
With teith and al togidder;   Gaelic hero);
Of Collings cow heir is ane horne,   cheekbone]
For eating of Makconnals corne
Was slaine into Balquhidder;
Heir is ane coird baith great and lang

Quhilk hangit [Jonnye] Armistrang,
Of gude hemp soft and sound –
Gude halie peopill, I stand for'd,   [vouch for it]
Quha ever beis hangit with this cord
Neids never to be dround!
The culum of Sanct Bryd[i]s kow,   [anus]
The gruntill of Sanct Antonis sow,   [snout]
Quhilk buir his haly bell –   [bore]
Quha ever he be heiris this bell clinck,
Gif me ane ducat for till drink,
He sall never gang to Hell,
Without he be of Baliell borne.   [Belial]

A Sowtar (cobbler) and his wife ask the Pardoner to divorce them, which he illegally does by means of a bawdy ceremony in which they have to kiss each other's 'arses', the Sowtar appealing, 'I pray yow, Sir, forbid hir for to fart!' The Pardoner cheats the Pauper out of his last groat, and as they fall to fighting, Diligence enters and chases them away.

Diligence now announces the commencement of part two of the play and the arrival of 'The Thrie Estaitis of this natioun', the realm of Scotland. The first estate, Spiritualitie, is the clergy; the second, Temporalitie, is the secular lords; and the third, the Burgessis, comprises the merchants. In dramatic style, and symbolising their moral turpitude, the three estates enter backwards, led by their vices. Once all are seated, Rex Humanitas declares his intention to reform abuses and punish wrongdoers with the help of Divyne Correctioun. He reminds the estates that he is head of the body politic: 'ye are my members, suppois I be your head'. All those who have suffered abuses are summoned to appear and voice their complaints. Johne the Common-weill – a key character, symbolic of the people's welfare – steps forward and denounces the Vices and the three estates. Flatterie, Dissait and Falset are put in the stocks, and Coventice (Covetousness) and Sensualitie are chased away. The lay estates – the merchants and nobles – express their willingness to reform, and call for the assistance of Gude Counsall. The clergy play for time but are castigated by Johne the Common-weill for their greed, lechery and incompetence as preachers, and are publicly humiliated. Diligence is instructed to seek out honest preachers, and he returns with three whose example is an indictment of Spiritualitie's corruption. The Vices are stripped of their disguises and the wayward clergy of their dignities. By contrast, gorgeous garments are bestowed on Johne the Common-weill, who takes his seat at the heart of Parliament. Diligence proclaims fifteen Acts of Parliament for reform of the nation, and the three Vices are sentenced to the gallows (only Falset and Dissait are executed, because Flatterie is allowed to escape). The play ends with a short interlude, essentially comprising a sermon on folly serving to show that Rex Humanitas is now capable of ensuring probity in the body politic and good government in his realm.

The epic scale of *Ane Satyre of the Thrie Estaitis*, and the play's extraordinary outspokenness in calling directly to a monarch and a nation's estates for moral and political reform, makes it a work of European significance. Its panoramic sweep embraces a spectrum of society from disenfranchised pauper to all-powerful king, mirrored in varieties of living Scots speech, from the coarsely colloquial to the learned and courtly, and reflecting the then status of the language as a *national*, all-purpose medium. Satirical comedy and farce co-exist with didacticism and high moral seriousness, varieties of metre are skilfully deployed to fit characters and situations, and allegorical abstractions are given a rootedness in real, shared experience. The dramatic qualities of Lindsay's verse-dialogue, and his evident awareness of dramatic structure and stagecraft, testify to both his skills as a poet and his long experience of composing and realising dramatic entertainments for the Court. Lindsay's artistry and almost encyclopaedic knowledge of his country and compatriots combine to provide vivid insights into a nation on the brink of momentous change. *Ane Satyre of the Thrie Estaitis* contributed to and heralded the arrival in Scotland of the Reformation, whose chief poet and dramatist Lindsay was.

COURT DRAMA

The earliest recorded example of a rudimentary court masque in Britain took place in 1285 as part of the marriage banquet of King Alexander III in Jedburgh Abbey. Dancers and musicians fell hushed as the figure of Death – 'ane ymage of ane dede man, nakitt of flesche & lyre [skin], with bair banys [bones]' – interrupted the celebrations as a potent reminder of human mortality. Progressively, from this period down to the departure of James VI to London in 1603 – and especially during the fifteenth and sixteenth centuries (court revels in Scotland being well documented from 1446 onwards) – dramatic and quasi-dramatic activities such as masques, mummings, pageants, tournaments, spectacles, royal entries, farces and plays were integral to court life. They were part of a larger court culture in which music, song, poetry and dance featured large, as evidenced in William Dunbar's poem 'Remonstrance to the King', in which he describes court life in the time of James IV (1488–1513), with its 'Musicianis, menstralis and mirrie singeris,/Chevalouris, cawandaris, and flingaris [dancers]'. Minstrels were employed at court from the time of Robert the Bruce, as were fools and tumblers. By the early sixteenth century, reflecting the cosmopolitan nature of the Courts of James IV and James V, bands of French and Italian minstrels were retained and Scottish minstrels were given royal grants to allow them to perfect their art at minstrel schools on the

Figure 1.5 Fool or jester in the costume of his profession. Note the many bells and the hood with asses' ears. One of the Stirling Heads, a series of medallions carved c. 1540 for the King's Presence Chamber, Stirling Castle. (Crown Copyright: Royal Commission on the Ancient and Historical Monuments of Scotland)

Continent. Semi-professional players, guisers, jesters, jugglers and tale-tellers were also employed as required. Nominated officers of the Court, such as Sir David Lindsay, were charged with devising entertainments, with texts provided when necessary by court poets.

Monarch and courtiers were themselves sometimes participants in those semi-dramatic and song–dance entertainments, playing instruments and 'disguising' in costumes or 'play coats'. For example, two 'mummyng gouns' were made for King James IV in 1506–7, red and yellow taffeta was ordered for James V's 'play coit' in 1533–4, and 'certane play gounis to the Kingis grace to pas in maskrie' were supplied in 1535.

The Court also provided a degree of patronage for folk and religious drama through financial donations and through royal attendance. Thus, figures in the folk drama such as the King of Bean, Abbot of Unreason, Queen of the May and Robin Hood appeared at court on the special days associated with them; and 'moralities' and Corpus Christi plays were enjoyed, as in 1504 when John Doig was paid for laying down grass 'on Corpus Christi Day, at the play, to the Kingis and Quenis chamires [chambers]'.

Some of the court entertainments were spectacular. By the sixteenth century, tournaments were more than just jousts, entailing the adoption of roles, in costume, and the enactment of a chivalric adventure, sometimes drawn from romantic literature. Such semi-dramatic tournaments were common throughout western Europe. The most notable held in Scotland were the two tournaments of 'The Justing of the Wild Knycht for the Blak Lady', which were held in Edinburgh in June 1507 and May 1508, and in which James IV participated. These were international events, to which combatants were invited from Europe through illuminated proclamations sent to France. The 1507 tournament was so successful that it was repeated in even more elaborate form in 1508, to the enhanced international prestige of James IV's Court, as Sir David Lindsay claimed in his poem 'The Testament of the Papyngo':

> And of his court, throuch Europe sprang the fame
> Off lustie Lordis and lufesum Ladyis ying,
> Tryumphand tornayis, justing and knychtly game,   [tournaments]
> With all pastyme accordyng for one kyng.

The 'Blak Lady', in whose honour the 1507 and 1508 tournaments were held, was one of a number of blackamoors at James's Court, and may have been the one in whose honour the court poet William Dunbar wrote his poem 'Of ane Blak Moir'. The jousting was held in the allegorical Field of Remembrance, situated between the Castle and the Secret Pavilion. In the Garden of Patience in this Field was the Tree of Esperance (Hope) bearing carvings of the leaves of Pleasance, the flowers of Noblesse and the fruits of Honour. Before jousting, combatants were to proceed to the Tree and touch the White Shield in the keeping of the Black Lady, who had been borne in a triumphal chair from the Castle to the tournament ground by fourteen costumed attendants. The tournament featured 'wild men' dressed in harts' horns and goatskins, 'wild beasts' with reins and saddles, and winged monsters made from canvas. The 1508 tournament culminated in a three-day festival at Holyrood House, with a grand banquet enlivened at intervals by entertainments: 'Betuix everie service thair was ane phairs [farce] or ane play', some spoken but some contrived by 'craft of Igramancie quhilk causit men to sie thingis aper [appear] quhilk was nocht'. One use of the word 'phairs' at this time meant a spectacular effect achieved by mechanical means. On the last day of the banquet there was a climactic spectacular 'phairs' involving Andrew Forman, the Bishop of Moray, 'quha was ane Igromancier'. He appeared as a sorcerer and spirited away the Black Lady in a cloud that descended from the ceiling of the hall. An insight into the ingenious mechancial device that must have been employed can be gained from the record of a payment 'for bukkilling and grathing [equipping] of Martin and the blak lady agane the bancat'.

The machinery deployed at state banquets might also feature 'pageant cars' used to dramatic effect. The baptismal feast of Prince Henry at Stirling in 1594 was punctuated by the entry of a huge triumphal chariot drawn by, remarkably, a single blackamoor (the original intention to have a real lion draw in the chariot had been abandoned as too dangerous). Six costumed ladies performed a 'silent comedie', then served dessert from a banqueting table borne in the chariot. There then entered the hall by invisible means a ship 'eighteen feet long, eight feet broad, and forty feet high', on a sea twenty-four feet in length and 'lively counterfeit with all colours'. Discharging her guns as she went, the ship carried the figures of Neptune, Thetis, Triton and 'all the marine people', who recited Latin verse to the accompaniment of fourteen musicians and Arion with his harp.

Royal entries to burghs might see machinery used, too. As mentioned earlier, Sir David Lindsay, who was skilled in such events, organised one in welcome for King James V's second French bride, Mary of Guise, on her entry to St Andrews in 1538. Above a triumphal arch a cloud descended from the sky and opened in two halves, from which 'apperit ane fair lady most lyke ane angell havand the keyis of haill Scotland in hir handis', which she presented to the Queen. Similar royal entries, where a cloud or globe descended revealing an angel bearing keys, were enacted elsewhere. Entries might also feature pageantry of a religious, national, or classical nature. William Dunbar describes in his poem 'Blyth Aberdein' the entry to that city of Queen Margaret in 1511. As she proceeded through streets hung with tapestries the Queen was entertained with a succession of pageants depicting biblical scenes (probably derived from the communal religious drama) and two affirming the legitimacy of the Stuart monarchy. One of the latter featured a representation of Robert the Bruce as 'nobill, dreidfull, michtie campioun [champion]'. Similar allegorical pageants for royal entries were sometimes performed on decorated scaffolding of one or more tiers. In his 'Deploratioun of the Deith of Quene Magdalene' (1537), Sir David Lindsay refers to 'Disgaysit folkis, lyke creaturis divyne/On ilk scaffold to play ane syndrie storie'. To what extent such 'syndrie storie' resembled drama as against *tableaux vivants* is difficult to determine. However, it is interesting to note that, although not a royal entry as such, on the occasion of Mary Stuart's marriage to the Dauphin of France in 1558, a celebratory 'Triumphe and Play' was performed in Edinburgh which reproduced some of the conventional features of an entry alongside dramatic entertainment.

Scaffolding was erected at different locations, to which the players were brought by horse-drawn cart, and the stages on the scaffolding were laid with turf to deaden the noise of the players' feet. Anna Jean Mill believes that the 'play' that was part of the celebrations, and which was probably written by either William Lauder or William Adamson, was performed on the scaffolding at the Tron. She says it looks as if the scaffolding erected there was 'reserved for a genuine play . . . [for] the stage was carefully covered with clay and woodbines, into which yellow flowers were stuck erect, and the *pièce de résistance* was a tree decorated with two dozen gilded tennis balls and a hundred cherries'.[9] The colourful celebrations also featured minstrels, dancers, banners, gun salutes and fireworks.

Whereas the pageantry associated with royal entries and state banquets served particular purposes, the Court also enacted quasi-dramatic entertainments for purely social pleasure, as with amateur disguisings (mumming) and masques. Evidence from 1460 shows that festive seasons were celebrated with 'disguisings'. Their nature is not clear, but the payment to a painter at Christmas 1465 suggests that some kind of 'scenery' might have featured. Masques, in which courtiers danced, sang and acted, seem to have been particularly common during Mary Queen of Scots' reign, perhaps reflecting her formative years at the French Court. John Knox railed against such 'vanitie', alleging that following her return to Scotland 'thair began the masking, which from year to year hath continewed since'. It is known that George Buchanan wrote Latin texts for Mary's masques; that the court poet Alexander Montgomerie provided poems in Scots ('The Navigatioun' and 'A Cartell of the Thre Ventrous Knichts') to be spoken at masque-like entertainments at the Court of Mary's son, James VI, in 1579; and that James VI himself composed a masque for the celebrations at a wedding in 1588.

While there are elements of drama in all these court-related activities, the question arises of to what extent the Court nurtured what we would now regard as more conventional drama. Unfortunately, the surviving evidence is tantalisingly fragmentary. Although Lindsay's *Ane Satyre of the Thrie Estaitis* was earlier discussed as an example of Reformation drama, it can also be considered a court drama. Lindsay was a senior courtier, his play was written with the approval of the King and was first performed before King and Court at Linlithgow Palace. Lindsay's is such an accomplished work that it is difficult to believe that he had not learned from other performed drama. As an envoy to a number of European courts he may have seen plays performed there. More crucially, he may have learned from Scottish exemplars now lost, such as those by Sir James Inglis, whom he mentions with admiration in 'The Testament of Papyngo' (1530), which includes a list of poets reflecting the rich court culture of James V:

> And, in the courte, bene present, in thir dayis,   [are]
> That ballatis, breuis lustellie and layis,   [these]
> Quhilks tyll our Prince daylie thay do present.
> Quho can say more than schir James Inglis says,
> In ballatts, farses, and in plesand playis?

(The reference to farces in this context is probably to short comedies rather than spectacular allusions.) Sir James Inglis, as Royal Chaplain, Chancellor of the Chapel Royal and Secretary to the Queen, was well placed to influence Lindsay. Lindsay names other writers in his list whose work has not survived and who may also have written dramas. Another court poet, but of the previous generation to Lindsay, William Dunbar, has a poem 'Lament for the Makaris', in which he similarly lists authors whose work is lost but who may have written dramatic texts. Two of them, 'Maister John Clerke and James Afflek', would certainly seem to have, since Dunbar says that they wrote tragedies. Dunbar also mentions a writer called 'Patrik Johnestoun'. Johnestoun is named in court records as having received payments for providing, in 1475, 1476 and 1477, what would appear to have been dramatic texts. This sits with other evidence that he was a play-actor and producer of entertainments who performed at court with the 'playaris of Lythgow' (Linlithgow) in 1488 and 1489 – a payment of 1488 being made 'to Patrick Johnson and his fellows that playt a play to the King in Lithgow'. A fifteenth-century poetic fragment attributed to William Dunbar, 'The Manere of the Crying of Ane Playe' (or 'The Interlude of the Droichis [Dwarf's] Part of the Play'), also points to the existence of a specimen of more formal drama written at court. Other fragmentary evidence records that William Lauder wrote a play, performed in 1549 at the marriage of Lady Barbara Hamilton, and perhaps the one performed to mark the marriage, in 1558, of Mary Stuart and the Dauphin; and that Robert Sempill wrote a play performed in Edinburgh in 1568 before the Regent Moray and the nobility. Alas, of these recorded and potential court plays performed, only the texts for Lindsay's *The Thrie Estaitis* and the anonymous *Philotus* (see below) have survived.

JAMES VI AND THE UNION OF THE CROWNS

King James VI (1566–1625) is of particular significance in the story of Scottish theatre for two reasons: his resistance to the Reformers' antipathy to drama; and the loss of that resistance, with the concomitant loss of royal patronage of drama, with his decision to relocate his Court in London on the Union of the Crowns in 1603 when he became James VI and I. While still resident in Scotland, James wrote and published poetry, formed a 'Castalian Band' of

Figure 1.6 Animated young man in fanciful costume in what may be a performance pose. One of the Stirling Heads, carved c. 1540, King's Presence Chamber, Stirling Castle. (Crown Copyright: Royal Commission on the Ancient and Historical Monuments of Scotland)

court poets whose work he guided, and encouraged the kind of dramatic entertainments at Court that his mother, Mary Queen of Scots, had nurtured in the face of Reformers' disapproval. He had become king as an infant in 1568 and was in tutelage until 1579 when he was 13 years old, so it is in the period from the last decade of that century until his departure from Scotland in 1603 that we find his influence on dramatic activities exerted.

James granted licences to visiting companies of English players in 1593–4, 1599 and 1601. All that is known about the 1593–4 visit is that payment was made 'to certane Inglis commedianis' for performing at Holyrood Palace. Much more is known about the 1599 visit. The players were led by Laurence Fletcher and Martin Slater. After playing before the King at Holyrood they were given a licence by him to perform in public and a warrant for the Edinburgh bailies to provide a 'pastyme hous' for that purpose. One was obtained in Blackfriars' Wynd. It can be considered the first public playhouse in Scotland. The King met the expense of fitting out the house; and the players sent trumpets

Figure 1.7 Painted ceiling, Crathes Castle, 1590s. Inscribed with Scots poetry and depicting women playing musical instruments. In the 16th century, poetry and music, song and dance, featured prominently in Scotland's court culture and in quasi-dramatic court entertainments. (National Trust for Scotland)

and drums through the town advertising their performances at the new play-house. However, the Kirk Sessions passed an Act that 'none resort to these profane comedies, for eschewing offence of God'. The King faced down the clergy and angrily demanded that they account for their actions. They sought to defend themselves by appeal to an Act of Parliament prohibiting stage plays and 'slanderous and undecent comedies', and by slyly adding: 'We heard that the Commedianis in their plays checked your royall person with secreit and indirect taints and checkes; and there is not a man of honour in England would give such fellowes so much as their countenance.' James would have none of it and the ministers were humiliatingly forced to rescind their Act and to issue a proclamation in favour of the 'Inglische Commedianis'. Permission was given to the inhabitants of the city 'to friely at thair awne plesour repair to the saidis commedeis and playis without ony pane, skaith, censureing, reproche or sclan-der to be incurrit'.

The King also used his authority to stay kirk opposition when in 1601, and again with Laurence Fletcher as manager, the company of players performed in Edinburgh, probably at James's invitation. It has been suggested that William Shakespeare was a member of Fletcher's company then, but the evidence is tenuous. After a residency performing in Edinburgh, the company was directed by the King to travel to Aberdeen to amuse the citizens with 'plays, comedies, and stage plays'. As the 'King's Servants', he furnished them with a letter of recommendation addressed to the magistrates. They were fêted by the City, entertained to supper by the council and remunerated with thirty-two merks for their services. Laurence Fletcher was admitted burgess of guild of the burgh and he and each of the players was given the freedom of the city. The company also performed in Dundee and was similarly well received.

Whilst royal protection and patronage of theatre in Scotland was lost with the removal of James VI to London in 1603, by the time James was old enough to have an impact on the culture of the Court and of his nation, the forms of medieval folk and religious drama in Scotland were already in terminal decline. Moreover, the Court he inherited had been adversely affected by the instability of his long minority and the civil and religious strife that marked it, as Scotland changed from a medieval Catholic country to an early-modern Protestant one. The previous two infant minorities in the same century, with their precarious regencies, the Earl of Hertford's invasion in 1544, the Reformation upheavals of 1559–60 and the civil war that followed Mary's abdication in 1567, also con-tributed to a dislocation of court culture throughout much of the century. These events also meant that there was no settled courtly or civic means of fostering the emergence of theatre companies.

England experienced not dissimilar difficulties during this period but forces were operating to replace the declining medieval drama with new forms, and the patronage of Queen Elizabeth and the nobility helped to protect theatre companies from the Puritan displeasure of the London civic authorities. James VI was to continue Elizabeth's royal patronage; only a few days after ascending his throne in London, he granted the first dramatic licence in England to the same Laurence Fletcher whose company had performed in Scotland, and to William Shakespeare and others. Had he remained in Edinburgh, and continued his defence of theatre against kirk censure, James VI might have similarly contributed to creating a hospitable environment in which new Scottish drama and native theatre companies could have emerged.

Two playtexts from the late period of James's reign in Scotland illustrate what the development of a native modern drama might have gained had he remained; a third exemplifies a consequence of his departure south. *Philotus* seems to have been written by a court writer in the 1580s or 1590s and to have been performed at court. Its theme indicates court toleration of subject matter that would have appalled the clergy of the Reformed Kirk, and its language confirms the potentialities of Scots as an effective medium for an emergent post-Reformation drama (and suggests that the play must have been performed by Scottish players rather than a visiting English company). *Pamphilus* is a play translation probably commissioned by a senior member of James VI's circle about 1590. Although apparently intended as a play to be read, it displays the dramatic strengths of Scots. The four-part *Monarchicke Tragedies* (the first was published in Edinburgh in 1603, the others subsequently in London) symbolises the cultural disruption caused by James VI's departure. The author, a member of the Court who moved to London with the King, has his eye on a London readership (the plays were 'closet' ones to be read) and the language now is a rhetorical, lifeless English, to the detriment of his artistry and any sense of cultural rootedness.

Philotus

Philotus and Lindsay's *Ane Satyre of the Thrie Estaitis* are the only surviving specimens of Scottish court drama written for performance. An anonymous work, *Philotus* is a verse-comedy in Scots, composed in the 1580s or 1590s. No manuscript has survived but the text was published by Robert Charteris in Edinburgh in 1603 with the title *Ane verie excellent and delectabill Treatise intitulit PHILOTVS*. That it seems to have enjoyed some popularity is suggested by the publication of a second edition in 1612, again in Edinburgh, by Andro Hart, who had taken over Robert Charteris's business. This second edition saw the replacement in the title of 'Treatise' with 'Comedie' and revisions to the text in the direction of anglicising the spelling (this being a feature of Andro Hart's printing policy and a symptom of the consequences for Scots' literary status of the Court's move to London).

Philotus was published as an anonymous work, but literary historians have since proposed three possible authors, all of whom were poets: Robert

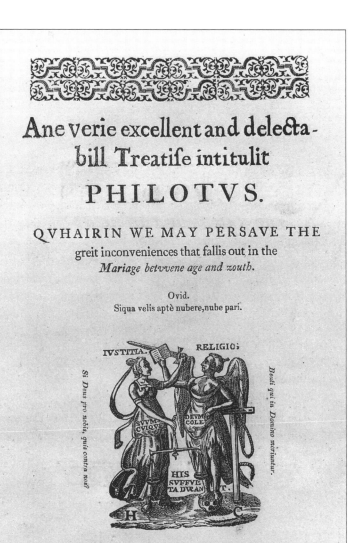

Figure 1.8 *Title-page of an anonymous play,* Philotus, *published in Edinburgh in 1603.* (Scottish Theatre Archive)

Sempill (or Semple), Alexander Montgomerie and King James VI. One reason why each of these has variously been suggested is that each wrote dramatic entertainments for the Court: Sempill entertained Regent Morton with a play in 1567 and King James with a 'pastyme' at Glasgow in 1581; Montgomerie wrote verse to be spoken as part of a court spectacle in Edinburgh in 1579; and

James VI wrote a masque that was performed as part of the festivities at the Earl of Huntly's wedding at Holyrood in 1586. Authorship of *Philotus* remains inconclusive, but the consensus is that the author must have been someone closely connected to the Royal Court.

No record of a contemporary performance of *Philotus* seems to have survived, but it has been convincingly argued that the play was written specifically for court performance before James VI. In Reformation Scotland only the Court could have proven hospitable to public performance of a play about an 80-year-old man seeking sexual pleasure through marrying a girl of 14; and only the Court could have had the liberality to accept the play's explicit and sometimes ribald language. As regards the latter, for example, one character says of the octogenarian lecher:

> I lauch to sie ane auld Carl gucke:
> Wow wow sa faine as he wald fuck,
> Fra he fall till his fleitching.
> [I laugh to see an old codger behave foolishly:
> Wow! Wow! so eager to fuck
> From as soon as he starts his flattering.]

The text contains courtly allusions, such as to two court Fools, and at points an assumed audience is addressed. These two elements come together in an epilogue spoken by 'The Messinger', who appears to have been the author. His epilogue addressed to the audience begins, 'Gude sirs, now have ye hard and sene this ferse [farce]/Unworthie of your audience I grant/[but] . . . I hope sall of your courtesies excuse mee'. He refers to 'The Courteours that Princes Hallis do hant [frequent]', and concludes: 'Last sirs, now let us pray with ane accord,/For to preserve the persoun of our King'. Philotus, then, would seem to have been performed before the Court and probably in the presence of King James VI.

There is further evidence from the text that the play was a performance piece. The published versions of 1603 and 1612 give only a limited sense of the stagecraft implicit in the work. A list of *dramatis personae* is provided and characters' names are placed beside their speeches throughout the text but there is no division of the play into acts and scenes, and no indication of exits and entrances. Although these deficiencies create the appearance of abrupt shifts in the action, any puzzlement they create is soon resolved. The twists and turns of the plot are straightforward to follow and, if one imagines the text performed, it is easy enough to insert the omitted exits, entrances and scene changes. Admittedly, scenes are sometimes very brief, but this poses little problem if the 'acts' and 'scenes' are viewed more as 'episodes', allowing a fluidity of action unencumbered by set changes and the like, and if it is borne in mind that *Philotus* is a short work likely to have been presented at a single unbroken sitting. (Modern productions, it should be said, have confirmed the play's stageability.) The 1612 edition prefaces the play with a résumé of the plot which still serves as an effective summary today. Headed 'The Argument' in the published text, this résumé is also of intrinsic interest, for it may have been intended for reading out at the beginning of a performance of the play:

> PHILOTUS, an olde rich man, is enamoured with the love of *Emilia*, daughter to *Alberto*, who being refused, imployeth a *Macrell* or pandrous [a bawd] to allure her thereto, but all in vain: afterward he dealeth with her father *Alberto*, who being blinded with the man's wealth, useth first faire words, and thereafter threatnings to perswade her thereto: the mayde still refuseth. In the meane time *Flavius*, a young man, enters in conference with the mayde, and obtaineth her consent, who being disguised, conveyeth her selfe away privilie with the said *Flavius*. Her father and *Philotus* searches [sic] for her in the house. *Philerno* the maydes brother laitlie arryved out of other countries, (being verie lyke her) is mistaken by her father and *Philotus* to be *Emilia*, who takes the person of his sister upon him: and after diverse threatnings of his father, consenteth to marrie *Philotus*: and so *Philotus* commiteth *Philerno* to the custodie of his daughter *Brisilla*, untill the mariage should be accomplished. *Philerno* faines himselfe to *Brisilla*, to be transformed in a man, and so maketh himselfe familiar with her. Thereafter, *Philerno* is maried to *Philotus*, who fearing to be discovered, maketh a brawling that same night with *Philotus*, and abuseth him vylie, and to colour the mater the better, agreeth with a whore to go to bed with *Philotus*. *Flavius* seeing the supposed *Emilia* to be maried to *Philotus*, imagines the right *Emilia* to be a devill, and, after many conjurations, expelleth her his house, she returneth to her father *Alberto* acknowledging her misbehaviour, and lamenting her case. *Flavius* being sent for, perceiving how he had mistaken *Emilia*, revealeth the whole trueth, and so taketh her home agane to [be] his wife, and *Philerno* [marries] *Brisilla*. In the end *Philotus* bewaileth his follie, for pursuing so unequall a match, warning all men to beware, by his example.

The source of this plot is a tale, *Of Phylotus and Emilia*, by the English writer Barnabe Rich from his series *Riche, his Farewel to Militarie Profession* published in 1581. (Shakespeare drew on the same work, though more loosely, for *Twelfth Night*.) More indirect influences were classical authors, such as Terence and Plautus, and sixteenth-century Italianate comedies (stock characters from which feature in *Philotus*).

Philotus is a kind of comedy of errors involving disguises and mistaken identity as crabbed age, 'led with lewd licentious lust,/And beastlie appetyte', attempts to ensnare youth into marriage but gets its comeuppance. A flavour of the comedy can be gained from this passage where Philerno, dressed as his sister Emily and having thus hoodwinked his father Alberto and Emily's would-be suitor, the 80-year-old Philotus, is accepting his father's wish that he marry the despicable 'auld Carle'. Philerno doubtless speaks in an adopted 'girly' voice, and Philotus fights to suppress his licentious glee while exuding sham solicitousness:

> *Philerno*. Father, I hartlie am content,
> And heirto gives my full consent,
> For it richt sair wald mee repent,
> Gif I sould you gainstand.   [if; oppose]
> *Philotus*. Heir is my hand my darling dow, [dove]
> To be ane faithfull spous to yow,
> Now be my saull Gossop I trow,   [familiar form of address]
> This is ane happie meiting:
> This mater Gosse, is sa weill drest, [resolved]
> That all things are cumde for the best,
> Bot let us set amang the rest,
> Ane day for all compleiting.
> *Alberto*. Ane Moneth and na langer day,   [month]
> For it requyres na grit delay,
> Tak thair your wyfe with yow away,
> And use hir as ye will:
> *Philotus*. Forsuith ye sall ga with me hame,
> Quhair I sall keip you saif fra schame,
> Unto the day, or than mee blame,
> That scho sall have nane ill.

If a stage direction were to be inserted here, it would be: 'All exit. Enter Pleasant.' For suddenly now appears Plesant (Pleasant), a character who is the reverse of his name. He is invisible to the others and, in effect, stands outside the play, randomly interjecting and offering earthy commentary on the action (in a way which also suggests that the author wrote for an audience). Here he colludes with us, the audience, and scathingly mocks Philotus and Alberto:

> *Plesant*. Quha ever saw in all thair lyfe,
> Twa cappit Carles mak sik ane stryfe, [crabbed churls]
> To tak a young man for his wyfe,
> Yon cadgell wald be glaid: [wanton fellow]

The feind resave the feckles frunt,   [receive; helpless; face]
Put doun thy hand and graip hir cunt,   [grope]
The Carle kennis not, he is sa blunt.   [stupid]
Gif scho be man or maid.

Auld guckis the mundie, sho is a gillie,   [lad]
Scho is a Colt-foill, not a fillie,   [colt-foal]
Scho wants a dow, bot hes a pillie,   [penis]
That will play the ane passe:
Put doun thy hand vane Carle and graip, [grope]
As thay had wont to cheis the Paip,   [choose the Pope]
For thow hes gotten ane jolie jaip,
In lykenes of ane Lasse.

The savageness of this humour belies the author's description of his work as a 'ferse' (farce), as does the nastiness underlying the shenanigans of Philotus and Alberto – fathers who are prepared to force their respective daughters to marry and thereby be molested by repulsive old men. One of those daughters, Emily, voices her dread of how it would be to have as her husband the octogenarian Philotus:

His eine half sunkin in his heid,   [eyes]
His Lyre far caulder than the leid,   [skin; lead]
His frostie flesch as he war deid,
Will for na happing heit,   [covering]
Unhealthsum hosting ever mair,   [coughing]
His filthsum flewme is nathing fair,   [phlegm]
Ay rumisching with rift and rair,   [making noise; belch; roar]
Now, wow gif that be sweit.

There is a realism here, characteristic of the Scottish literary tradition, which acts as a restraint on the humour and makes *Philotus* more black comedy than farce. In keeping with the conventions of the time, at the end of the play the four youngsters find true love and Philotus recants and realises the folly of his behaviour. On one hand, this unlikely scenario runs counter to the play's realism; on the other, the moral didacticism explicit in the conclusion, which was an inevitable aspect of a dramatic work at this time, is more forceful because it is grounded in preceding events that are as much sordidly realistic as comic.

In contrast with Lindsay's *Ane Satyre of the Thrie Estaitis*, where it is insistent and extended, the moral teaching is relatively brief in *Philotus* and is principally confined to the final speeches. There are other points of contrast with Lindsay's work: *Philotus* is much shorter; it centres on what is essentially a 'domestic' situation (inspiring one writer to describe it as a 'bourgeois comedy'); it shows a clear sense of structure and plot; and its characters are identifiably human in their motivation and interaction, rather than allegorical as in Lindsay. In sum, notwithstanding the use of stock characters drawn from Italian comedy and some concomitant stock improbabilities in the plot, *Philotus* has a more modern cast than Lindsay's markedly medieval masterpiece, signifying changes in literary taste that had developed as the sixteenth century drew to a close. Unfortunately, the playwriting promise displayed by the anonymous author of *Philotus* had no opportunity to develop further. In 1603, the year that the work was first published, the Union of the Crowns was ratified and the Scottish Court decamped to London, taking with it the patronage and audience that any such playwright would require.

Pamphilus

Pamphilus speakand of Lufe is a verse translation into Scots by the Edinburgh poet John Burel (fl.1590–1601) of a Latin *comoedia*, *Pamphilus de Amore*, written around the year 1100 by an anonymous author somewhere between northern Italy and the Loire Valley in France. Aside from that translation and some published poetry, little is known about John Burel. He has traditionally been identified with the goldsmith and royal mint printer of that name, but there was also a contemporary merchant in Edinburgh called John Burel. A tantalising clue to a court connection lies in his dedication of *Pamphilus speakand of Lufe* to Ludovic Stuart, second Duke of Lennox and one of James VI's intimates. In translating the Latin work, Burel chose a text that had been popular throughout Europe in the four centuries since its composition and had become a standard school text. It had been translated into several languages and inspired adaptations and original work. Its direct and indirect influence can be seen in such important works as the *Roman de la Rose*, Fernando de Rojas's *Celestina*, and Shakespeare's *Romeo and Juliet*.

   Until very recently Burel's *Pamphilus* was an almost entirely unknown work, only surviving in a single copy published around 1590/1. Its recovery is largely due to Jamie Reid-Baxter, who has championed its importance as a dramatic text. Although Burel may have intended *Pamphilus* as a closet drama, for it seems never to have been performed in his day, Reid-Baxter's belief is that the speakability of the verse, and Burel's division of his text with brief 'stage directions', invites performance. He demonstrated this when he presented *Pamphilus* as a ninety-minute, five-act drama, supplemented with music and mime, in a semi-professional performance at St Hilda's College, Oxford, in 1996 as part of an international conference on Scottish Medieval and Renaissance

Literature and Language. The enthusiastic response to that performance confirmed the stageability of *Pamphilus* and led Reid-Baxter to conclude: 'From the point of view of Scottish theatre, Burel's translation is a major acquisition . . . We are hardly so rich in Middle Scots texts susceptible of effective performance that we can afford to ignore [it].'[10]

In Burel's translation (in Reid-Baxter's unpublished performance edition), Act I sees the lovestruck Pamphilus unable to approach the girl he loves, Galathea, so he prays to Venus for help. Venus appears and counsels him at length, but his lovesickness still torments him. To his consternation, Galathea then happens to come by and he has to face her and admit his love. She is concerned to protect her honour but eventually agrees to tryst with him on condition that 'Tae kis and clap [stroke] I will permit and spair,/Providing that ye do nae mair nor this'. Pamphilus is ecstatic but has nagging doubts about his good fortune. In Act II, he seeks the help of an old woman, Anus. She will help him if properly rewarded, and he promises that 'baith my hous an aa things sall be thine'. She guilefully sings Pamphilus's praises to Galathea. Galathea again expresses her concerns about losing her honour ('the comoun sclander, quhilk I feir'), but overcomes her reservations and asks Anus to speak to Pamphilus on her behalf.

Act III sees the duplicitous Anus tell Pamphilus that Galathea's parents are secretly marrying her to someone else. Pamphilus is beside himself with a despair which is not a little self-regarding, and which Anus rudely deflates: 'Daft Pamphile, quhat madnes muves thy heid?' Craftily, she questions both his good faith and his intention to reward her. Reassured by Pamphilus, she promises to bring he and Galathea together. In Act IV, Anus accuses Galathea of making Pamphilus ill through her coolness to him. In fact, Galathea is in turmoil, torn between safeguarding her honour and abandoning herself to love of Pamphilus. She admits to Anus, 'That quhilk ye seik, I wisch wi full intent,/ For in the warld nocht deirer is to me'. However, she cannot tryst with Pamphilus because 'aa our faimily at hame,/Baith nicht and day attendance on me taks'. Anus stills her fears and leads her 'hame to my hous, with me for to remaine'. There she urges her to embrace love: 'Intae thy youth, tak up ane wantoun tred,/And all thy fleschly pleasours see thou feid'. Pamphilus makes a 'surprise' visit and Anus makes an excuse to leave:

> My nichbour me incalls, as ye may heir;   [neighbour]
> I will hir speik, and syne return richt snell, [then; quickly]
> For grittumlie forsuith I dreid and feir   [greatly]
> That tae my hous sche sall cum in hir sell.
> [*Calling out to the feigned neighbour wife.*]
> I dae draw neir - quhat gars you cry sae fell? [causes; call so urgently]

Pamphilus cannot contain his lust. Galathea rebuffs his advances and curses 'the wikit auld wife', Anus, for her deceitfulness. Eventually she gives in to Pamphilus, but she warns that their love will then 'broken be betwixt us twa for ay [always]'.

In Act V, Pamphilus alternates between apology for this 'maist filthy and profane' deed and accusation that Galathea had inflamed his desire for her. Anus returns and Galathea rages at her for the art and part she played in assisting Pamphilus to deflower her, to which Anus feigns hurt innocence. Galathea is distraught:

> Quhat sall I dae, tae quhat pairt sall I ply?
> I wander maun throu aa the warld astray!   [must wander]
> My parents justly may me nou deny,
> And at thair door debar me oot for ay!   [always]
> Wi wavering een I luik tae every way,   [eyes]
> Quhyles heir, quhyles thair, in every airth athort; [from one direction to
> I see nae comfort quhairupoun tae stay,   another]
> Maist caitif woman, void of aa support!   [despicable]

Anus points out that it is Galathea's immoderate love which has entrapped her, and counsels her to learn wisdom and 'guid discretioun'. After all, Anus says, the means that she provided has obtained the end that both lovers wished her to achieve for them. She wishes them well in married life. Her, and the play's, final ironic words to them are, 'of me hae gud [good] remembrance ay'.

In his preface to the work, John Burel offers an explanation of his approach to translating his Latin original. He has eschewed 'rethorik', 'prolixnes', and 'polist [polished] terms', preferring 'simpill wourds' to 'imitat my author lyne be lyne'; he has 'amplifiet the mater plane' and 'subcinctlie [succintly] as I culd or micht,/The sentence I haif prosecute aricht'. His concern to make his text as accessible as possible to avoid the reader 'reciting one thing ouer agane' is evident even to modern eyes from the short quotations in the plot summary just given. His language is direct and lends a beguiling fluency to his charac-ters' speech. Even though he writes within the constraints imposed by 'ballad royal' verse form, his rhymes are deftly handled and have a natural ease that serves to drive on the dialogue rather than hinder it. This can be seen in a passage of dialogue where Pamphilus is pressing Anus to find out if Galathea loves him:

> *Pamphilus*: Can ye no ken, nor nae cognoscens haife,
> Quhither that sche dois lufe me ill or weill?
> Lufe scarse can hide or quietly behave
> The inwert hart, the quhilk it suld conseill.

Anus: Quhen untae hir o you report I mak,
Hir mynd an will I find tae be discreit.
Untae my talk sche dois attendence tak
In modrat maner, quhilk apeirs maist sweit.
Wi tender words sche dois me ay intreit,
And me imbraces roond aboot the neck,
Requeisting me for tae tell and repeit
Those words, the quhilk ye till hir did dereck. [direct]
Quhan that occasioun can it sell present
Tae nominate your name in ony sort,
Sche stands intae ane gret astonisment
Quhan o the samyn sche dois heir report.   [same]
An quhan o you we chance tae speak or sport,
Quhyles sche growes reid, quhilis pail, as sche wer seik;
Quhan I keip silence, sche will me exort
And me command that I againe suld speik.

Pamphilus speakand of Lufe is written throughout as speech, but features dialogues and monologues of a length which makes for relatively static action and generally militates against conventional dramatic performance. Whilst this would seem to confirm that it *was* conceived as a closet drama to be read, there is none the less, as Jamie Reid Baxter argues, such a drama-like quality to the language that the work demands to be spoken for full effect and is thereby, in his words, 'susceptible of effective performance' today. There is modern appeal, too, in the witty and pervasively ironic way in which Burel unfolds this story of adolescent infatuation and sexual obsession, climaxing in an ambiguous and thought-provoking ending. Are the lovers victims or winners? That this is in effect a troubling ending is testimony to how well Burel realises his characters as recognisable individuals with whom a modern reader can still empathise.

The Monarchicke Tragedies

Sir William Alexander, Earl of Stirling and Viscount Canada (1577?–1640) was born in Menstrie. He built, in nearby Stirling, Argyll's Ludging, which is, today, the finest surviving example of a seventeenth-century Scottish town house (now in the care of Historic Scotland and open to the public). As a schoolboy his teacher was George Buchanan's nephew, Thomas. Alexander himself became tutor to Prince Henry, partly through the favourable impression that one of his verse-tragedies made on King James VI. With the Union of the Crowns in 1603 he moved with the Scottish Court to London, enjoying the patronage of James VI and Charles I, acquiring titles, and rising to become Secretary of State for Scotland. His role in attempting to force Episcopacy upon the Church of Scotland, and in passing the Vagrancy Act severely inhibiting the admission of Scots to England, made him venomously detested in his native land. In 1621 James VI granted him Nova Scotia and large tracts of Canada, which, from the distance of London, he sought to have colonised. The venture ended in financial disaster and he died a bankrupt in London, bereft of the social and political power he had once yielded. A contemporary verse-epitaph conveys the depth of dislike of him in Scotland: 'A vain, ambitious flattering

Figure 1.9 Sir William Alexander, Earl of Stirling (artist unknown). (Scottish National Portrait Gallery)

thing,/Late secretary for a king;/Some tragedies in verse he pen'd,/At last he made a tragic end.'

As well as a substantial body of poetry, Alexander composed four tragedies in verse, which show the influence of George Buchanan and French classical tragedy. These were published in London in 1607 under the collective title *The Monarchicke Tragedies*. The individual works were *Darius* (first published in Edinburgh in 1603), *Croesus* (first published in London in 1604), *The Alexandrean Tragedy* and *Julius Caesar* (both published in the 1607 omnibus edition for the first time). After first publication, subsequent editions were revised by him, including reworking of plot and greater anglicisation in language. The latter is most obvious in his first tragedy, *Darius*, which was composed and published before he removed to London, and was written in a mixture of English and Scots. In that first 1603 Edinburgh edition, he provided a preface to the reader in which he said that the language of his verse-tragedy was

> mixt of the English and Scottish Dialects; which perhaps may be un-
> pleasant and irksome to some readers of both nations. But I hope the
> gentle and Judicious Englishe reader will beare with me, if I retaine
> some badge of mine owne countrie, by using sometimes words that are
> peculiar thereunto, especiallie when I finde them propre, and significant.
> And as for my owne country-men, they may not justly finde fault with
> me, if for the more parte I use the English phrase, as worthie to be pre-
> ferred before our owne for the elegance and perfection thereof. Yea I am
> perswaded that both countrie-men will take in good part the mixture
> of their Dialects, the rather for that the bountiful providence of God
> doth invite them both to a straiter union and conjunction as well in
> language, as in other respects.

This preference for English over Scots, and his association of English with 'elegance and perfection', led to the progressive eradication of Scots from Alexander's work in a way which mirrors his ambitious eye for the main chance once in London and his political hostility towards Scotland. It is also symptomatic, as was indicated earlier, of a wider problem that would afflict Scottish literature and drama as the seventeenth century progressed; namely, the removal of the Scottish Court to London entailed the loss of court culture, court writers, royal patronage and status for the Scots language, and bred a new tendency in Scots of Alexander's class to defer to London in matters of taste.

The willed nature of his politically influenced language choices had delete-rious consequences for Alexander's verse. His tragedies are preoccupied with language at the expense of action. He vainly tries for a noble and sonorous rhetoric, as in this speech from *Darius* where Darius, King of Persia, laments his overthrow through treachery (the victor he refers to is Alexander the Great):

> O pow'r supreame! that of great states disposest,
> And ratifi'st thy will with fearfull thunder,
> Who as thou pleasest, placest, and deposest
> Vncertaine worldlings, now above, now under:
> I pray thy Deitie in my soules distresse,
> If that th' inhabitants of heaven can heare
> The plaints of them who this low point possesse,
> Or that th'immortals can give mortals eare,
> This favour last I onely doe require,
> Establish first the Scepter in my hand;
> But if through my desert, or thy desire,
> The race of *Cyrus* must no more command,
> Since angry heaven so high a hate contracts,
> That I must needs my Diadem foregoe,
> Let him succeed, who proves in all his acts,
> So milde a Victor, and so just a foe.

There are occasional redeeming passages in Alexander's work, but these are drowned in a sea of prolix rhetoric and leaden rhymes, with alliteration, antithesis and mannered conceits holding sway, and the author's meditations rarely rising above the platitudinous.

The Monarchicke Tragedies deal with the successive fall of four ancient monarchies. *Darius*, set in Babylon, portrays the downfall of Darius, King of Persia. Alexander the Great defeats Darius in battle and captures his mother, wife and children. Alexander treats them honourably but Darius's wife dies in captivity. Darius plans a desperate assault on Alexander's army but falls victim to a plot by two traitors in his own army. On learning of Darius's death, the ever-honourable Alexander promises a royal funeral and threatens vengeance on the traitors.

In *Croesus*, the eponymous hero, King of Lydia, has invited to his court the Athenian phioloopher, Solon. To Croesus's displeasure, Solon mocks his pride in his wealth and dissents from the courtiers' flattery of the King. Croesus has a dream that his son, Atis, is killed by a dart. To prevent his dream becoming reality he forbids the use of darts in his kingdom. But, notwithstanding his fears, he accedes to his son's pleas that he be allowed to help kill a wild boar that has been terrorising peasants in the countryside. Inevitably, Croesus's dream is realised, and, to assuage his grief over his son's death, he embarks on a war against Cyrus, King of Persia. He is defeated, captured, and consigned to the stake for burning. As the fire licks at him he remembers the philosopher Solon's moralising on vanity and materialism and cries out Solon's name so loudly that Cyrus halts the execution. Learning the reason for the cry, he sets Croesus free, now a desolate father and a fallen king.

The futility of worldly ambition again provides the central theme in *The Alexandrean Tragedy*, which opens with the ghost of the recently murdered Alexander the Great disowning ambition and lamenting the conflict that exists between his surviving generals over how best to govern his disintegrating empire. The generals' squabbling leads to internecine plotting and murder. Alexander's mother and wife resolve to intercede and save the empire. Olympias, the mother, goes to war against Cassander, a general, but is defeated and condemned to death, which provides an opportunity for more meditation on the futility of monarchic ambition. Cassander proves the most ruthless of the generals, and his worldly ambition triumphs in a trail of bloodshed.

The final tragedy in the series, *Julius Caesar*, covers most of the familiar story of Caesar's murder. Brutus and Cassius plot the assassination of the new emperor. On his way to the Forum, where he will be assassinated, Caesar is held back by Calphurnia's dream, yet continues to his fatal destination.

The likely origin of Alexander's emphasis on royal characters, and his choice of *The Monarchicke Tragedies* as the collective title for his four verse-dramas, is Senecan tragedy, including French neoclassical drama (particularly the plays of Robert Garnier). Monarchs, kings and princes conventionally featured in Seneca's tragedies; similarly, the traditional theme of sixteenth-century French classical tragedy, which was heavily influenced by Seneca (in large measure through George Buchanan's Latin plays), was monarchy. This made such tragedies well suited for instructive reading by kings and princes. Thus, George Buchanan, in 1576, dedicated his *Baptistes* to his pupil, the young James VI, cautioning him on the duties of a monarch. *The Monarchicke Tragedies* were also dedicated to James VI, having been written partly as instruction for his son, Prince Henry.

If we accept that Alexander's poetic tragedies were intended as closet dramas to be read rather than performed, we can better excuse their unactability. In this they follow the example of Seneca's plays, which were originally intended to be studied, not staged. In Seneca's work, the rudiments of action and dialogue are disregarded in favour of emphasis on endless meditative monologues, written in an elevated rhetorical style, inviting at best a declamatory delivery. In fairness, Alexander has been described by the editors of his collected works as 'the most considerable and the most representative of British authors of "classical tragedy"'.[11] This is in the context of a small group of English writers contemporaneous with him who, between 1590 and 1607, followed rigidly classical French Senecan models. However, since that group is now but a footnote in English theatre history, the judgement on Alexander is faint praise.

MISCELLANEOUS DRAMATIC ACTIVITY: 1603–1700

In common with the sixteenth, the seventeenth century was afflicted by religious, political and constitutional upheavals. Civil and religious wars, including the struggles of the Covenanters, Cromwell's subjugation of Scotland, the 'Killing Times' under Charles II and the 'Glorious Revolution' of 1688, all contributed to an unstable and divided society for much of the century. Dramatic activity was one of many cultural casualties. A compounding factor was the absence of a resident monarchy. Aside from royal visits in 1617 and 1633, and a short period of residence by James, Duke of York (later James VII and II), in 1679–82, Scotland lacked the focus of a Royal Court. Not only was sustained patronage of playwriting and play-going thereby removed, but so too was a potentially powerful counterweight to the authoritarian tendencies of the Kirk in attempting to suppress, with the help of civic legislation, popular enjoyment of drama and other entertainments. The absence of a monarchy left a vacuum that was filled by the Kirk, to the detriment of those cultural activities, including drama, that had developed with the assistance of Scotland's Royal Court over the previous two centuries. The Kirk had developed a distinctive form of Calvinism hostile to imaginative art, whether literary, visual or dramatic, unless it served a religious purpose consonant with Presbyterianism. The consequences of this antipathy, and the absence of opposing Stuart influence, can be seen in the fact that after James VI's departure in 1603 no stage play was written in Scotland until 1663. Even then, only three plays were written between 1663 and 1700, two staged and one unstaged. That the three authors were Episcopalians and royalists, and therefore scornful of kirk diktat, is not without significance; nor is the fact that the two performed plays enjoyed court patronage.

Before discussing those three post-1660 plays, it should be acknowledged that there is fragmentary evidence of the existence of miscellaneous forms of dramatic and semi-dramatic activity other than formal stage plays in the seventeenth century.

Royal Pageantry

From the time of his departure to London in 1603 until his death in 1625 James VI and I visited his native kingdom only once, in 1617. There was much pomp and circumstance, and flowery orations of greeting, sufficient to fill over three hundred pages of a folio volume, but there seems to have been no pageantry or quasi-drama of the kind traditionally associated with royal entries. Thereafter the Stuarts visited Scotland infrequently.

James's son, Charles I, who had been born in Dunfermline Palace in 1600, returned to Scotland for his coronation in 1633. Charles was an enthusiastic patron of the visual arts and a spectacular royal pageant was devised for his entry to his family's ancient capital, Edinburgh. A series of allegorical *tableaux* and pageants were contrived by the Aberdonian portrait painter George Jamesone and the poet Sir William Drummond of Hawthornden in emulation of the elaborate court masques organised in London by Inigo Jones and the poet and playwright Ben Jonson. (Ben Johnson was a friend of Drummond, having been a guest in his house at Hawthornden outside Edinburgh for part of his six-month sojourn in Scotland in 1618–19.) Jamesone attended to the visual aspects and Drummond provided the speeches, in poetry and prose, to be delivered by mythical characters and personifications welcoming Charles to Edinburgh with customary flattery. Drummond's texts survive under the title *The Entertainment of the High and Mighty Monarch Charles, King of Great Britain, France, and Ireland, into his ancient and royal city of Edinburgh*.

Detailed descriptions of the event exist, confirming that it was the most elaborate public spectacle staged in Scotland in the seventeenth century. At the West Port there was a great arch representing a city on a rock, and under the arch was a theatre shaped like a mountain on which appeared the Genius of the City in the form of a nymph costumed in a 'greene velvet mantle, her sleeves and under roabe of blue tissue, with blue buskins on her feete; about her necke shee wore a chaine of diamonds; the dressing of her head represented a castle of turrets, her locks dangled about her shoulders'. After she addressed the King, the Magistrates presented him with the keys of the city 'in a silver basin, into which there were showered a thousand gold coins'. The procession moved on to the West Bow, where there was another arch and theatre repre-senting the Grampian Mountains 'with their wild scenery and animals, and Romans fighting with Picts'. Here another nymph, representing Caledonia, accompanied by an Indian-looking maid representing Nova Scotia, again delivered a speech to the King. The royal entourage continued, to musical accompaniment, through streets hung with flags and decorated by the city's artists and craftsmen. In the High Street there was an even more lavish arch and theatre, on which George Jamesone had lavished most of his efforts:

> When the curtain of the theatre before the arch was drawn, Mercury was seen, with his feathered hat, his caduceus, and a hundred and seven Kings, the Scottish progenitors of Charles, from Fergus the First down-wards . . . King Fergus was overjoyed at seeing his 108th descendant, and expressed his feelings in a Latin speech. Next there came in sight figures of Bacchus, Silenus, Sylvanus, Pomona, Venus, and Ceres; and still further down the street there was Mount Parnassus, with Apollo and the Muses on it . . . [including] portraits of the chief literary celebrities of Scotland, from Sedulius and Joannes Scotus down to Sir David Lindsay and George Buchanan.[12]

At the Netherbow there was yet a further arch and stage 'representing Heaven itself, with stars of all magnitudes, the Earth beneath and the Titans prostrate on it, the Fates, and the Seven Planets, each sitting on a throne, and Endymion among them'. A Horoscopal pageant was performed by the Seven Planets, introduced and concluded by a prologue and epilogue from Endymion. As Terence Tobin has observed, the whole extravaganza 'indicates a theatrical sophistication', for 'the coordination of set, costume, and speech, for a single effect, indicates that Drummond of Hawthornden and the others responsible for the display were not unaware of theatrical technique'.[13]

Charles also visited Perth, where, as part of the town's welcome to him, he viewed, from the Earl of Kinnoul's garden, an entertainment on a stage in the River Tay. The main event was a sword-dance performed by costumed members of the burgh's Incorporation of Skinners and Glovers. The performance was recorded in the Guild's minutes:

> His Majesty's chair being set upon the wall next the Water of Tay where-upon was a floating stage of timber clad about with birks [birches], upon the which for his Majesty's welcome and entry thirteen of our brethren of this our calling of Glovers with green caps, silver strings, red ribbons, white shoes and bells about their legs, shearing [sharp] rapiers in their hands and all other abulzement [equipment], danced our sword dance with many difficult knots [sword formations] and allapallajesse [nimble feats], five being under and five above upon their shoulders, three of them dancing through their feet and about them, drinking wine and breaking glasses. Which (God be praised) was acted and done without hurt or skaith [injury] to any.[14]

A costume reputedly worn by one of the performers has survived and is in the care of Perth Museum and Art Gallery. Adorned with numerous bells, the garment is of special significance, as no comparable costume for sword or morris dancing has survived in Europe. (An interesting link with later developments in Scottish theatre and the establishment of a National Drama, as discussed in Chapter 3, is that the surviving costume was worn by an actor in a dramatisation of Sir Walter Scott's *The Fair Maid of Perth*, performed at the Theatre Royal, Perth, in 1828.)

School Drama

A playbill survives for a school drama in Latin performed in public by students of Kelso Grammar School in 1681. It is the earliest known amateur playbill in Britain, and it announces two performances of Terence's play *Eunuchus*. The students had first performed the play at the end of their school term in Kelso,

Figure 1.10 Surviving sword-dance dress worn in 1633 as part of an entertainment staged in Perth for Charles I. (1840s watercolour courtesy of Perth Museum & Art Gallery, Perth & Kinross Council)

and the playbill is for two further performances at a public theatre in Edinburgh (some of the Kelso students having then entered Edinburgh University). The playbill is written in Latin, and includes Latinised versions of the Borders scholars' names, such as *Gulielmus Knoxius, Robertus Maxwellius, Georgius Humius, Walterus Riddelus* and *Joannes Spotswodius*!

Plays had sometimes been performed by students in schools in the late sixteenth century as a means of religious instruction and of propagating Protestant doctrine. In the seventeenth century the use of school plays for similar didactic purposes, and as a vehicle for students to practise Latin, English and public speaking continued. Normally such plays were performed during the annual visits of church and civic dignitaries at the end of the academic year when students were examined (as in the Kelso example). The most commonly performed drama was *Bellum Grammaticale*, written in the time of James VI by Alexander Home, a schoolmaster in Dunbar. Henry Grey Graham, in his *The Social Life of Scotland in the Eighteenth Century*, describes *Bellum*

Grammaticale as 'a serio-comic piece of portentous dullness, in which the various parts of speech are personified, and appear to argue forth their respective claims to precedence over the rest'. This 'pedagogic moral play', he says, rather than encourage youthful interest in drama, was 'admirably fitted to extinguish

Figure 1.11 Latin playbill for student performance of Terence's Eunuchus *in Edinburgh in 1681. The earliest known amateur playbill in Britain.* (Scottish Theatre Archive)

utterly all fondness for the stage in juvenile breasts throughout their natural life'.[15] As Graham testifies, *Bellum Grammaticale* was still the favourite work for school performance well into the eighteenth century.

Folk Drama

Kirk hostility to folk pastimes continued into the seventeenth century, even though such pastimes had declined markedly. In 1608 the Presbytery of Glasgow directed the minister of Rutherglen to summon for public repentance those people 'quha in ye tyme called Yule days used Gysrie [disguising] superstitiouslie and troublit yr nichtboars [neighbours] in ye nicht tyme to ye great offence of God and his Kirk'; and in 1610 participants in a Robin Hood play in Linton were censured. In mid century (1663), the Kirk Session of Rothiemay banned participation in seasonal festivals, with their singing, guising and masking. Some folk drama did nevertheless continue. The Lammas play in Midlothian, for example, where, in Alasdair Cameron's words, 'rival villages tried to storm towers built of turf and decorated with ribbons'.[16] There were, too, the 'Clark-plays' referred to in Robert Sempill's poem 'The Life and Death of Habbie Simson the Piper of Kilbarchan', written about 1640 and citing a number of communal traditions. The lamented Habbie played 'At every play, race, feast and fair', including the seasonal festivals of Beltane (May) and Saint Barchan (December). Sempill's poem has been interpreted as championing those old folk traditions, including open-air plays, that the Kirk was attempting to stifle as profane. The Falkirk Kirk Session in 1701 warned a group of young men for going 'about in disguise acting things unseemly' at Hogmanay. This suggests a visiting custom, dramatic in nature, that was a recurrent annual event and therefore had been practised in the previous century. But, overall, suppression of folk customs by the Kirk did have a destructive impact and the seventeenth century proved one of decline and transition for folk drama. Certain lines of continuity can be found in the eighteenth century but by then feeding into the Galoshins folk play that emerged after 1700.

Popular Entertainments

For a number of centuries wandering minstrels and strolling players were common in Scotland. Some were licensed and attached to the burghs or the Court. As early as 1278 there is a record of payment to 'minstrels of the King of Scotland' (as well as to his harper and trumpeters). Others lived an itinerant existence on the margins of society and sometimes ran foul of authority. An Act of Parliament of 1449 against beggars included destitute minstrels, who were to be punished by having their ears nailed to a tree, followed by banishment. The tradition of itinerant entertainers, such as strolling players and musicians, continued into the seventeenth century, but with the addition of what seem to have been new kinds of street entertainment. Some involved performing animals such as dancing horses, or exotic animals like the camel and baboon exhibited in Edinburgh in 1658. These were viewed for payment, as were exotic people like the three Turks toured by a Dutchman in 1691, and human freaks such as 'ane Italian man monster' who toured Scotland in 1642, and who had a Siamese double 'growing fra the breist upward'. In Aberdeen, the Italian 'had his portraiture with the monster drawin, and hung out at his lodging, to the view of the people', and he sent round the town 'ane trumpettour who soundit at such tyme as the people sould cum and sie this monster'.

Acrobatic acts were particularly common, and were often included as part of a larger street entertainment performed on a temporary stage and devised by quack doctors as a means of drumming up business for their medicines. These acrobats, or 'tumblers' as they were popularly called, performed juggling and vaulting feats, and 'rope-dancing' (the performance of tricks on a tightrope). Most of the 'doctors' were from the Continent. German, Dutch and Italian ones are recorded, with names like Joannes Michaell Philo (1672), Cornelius a Tilbourne (1684), Mathias Sasse (1691), John Arnold Carner (1692), and Joanna Baptista Quarentina (1660s and 1670s); the last, unusually, a woman.

Figure 1.12 Gyserts *(guisers), an original sketch of a Galoshins folk play in Stirling drawn by James Chrystal about 1830. The Galoshins play emerged after 1700 but has lines of continuity with earlier folk drama.* (The McCutcheon Stirling Collection)

They toured widely to, among other places, Edinburgh, Glasgow, Dundee, Aberdeen, Perth, Cupar, St Andrews and Stirling. The mountebank about whom most is known is a German, Doctor John Pontus, who brought his troupe to Scotland in 1633, 1643, 1662 and 1663. A contemporary diarist, John Nicoll, has left a description of the 1662 event in Edinburgh when Pontus's tumblers performed for

> two houris togidder without intermissione, volting, leaping, and dancing up and doun without help of handis, except ane poyll [pole] of timber, great and long to gyde his body in the dance. Lykewyse, thair wes ane great tow [rope] affixit fra the south syde of the Hie streit of Edinburgh to the north syde of the streit, quhairon [one of them] discendit upone his breast, his handis lows [loose], and streatched out lyke to the winges of a foull [fowl], to the admiration of many.

Of particular interest is that, in addition to tumblers and fools, the stage-shows employed by the mountebanks included drama of some kind. When Pontus was in Aberdeen in 1643 an observer (John Spalding) noted that his show featured '*sum stage playis*, quhilk drew the people'. Afterwards, from the stage, Pontus 'sold certain balmes, oyllis, and uther phisicall oyntmentis, quhairof he maid gryte gane', and 'thairafter he went north to uther burrowis [burghs] and did the like'. John Nicoll records of the 'sindrie strangeris' from the Continent who 'gave out thameselffis to be physicianes', that they '*actit commedeis*, [and] erectit stages at the Mercat Croce of Edinburgh, and uther pairtes of the citie, haveand his Majesteis warrand to that effect'. In 1662 Pontus and his troupe were granted permission by Edinburgh Town Council 'to build a stage doun about Blackfreir Wynd head, for publict view, they *acting* no obscene thing to give offence'. In 1677 the same Town Council gave permission to John Mash to erect a stage within the tennis court opposite the Tron 'for *acting his playes* and [rope-dancing] showes'. Whilst such references (the emphases are mine) make clear that dramatic entertainments were part of the general stage-show of street entertainers, it is difficult to determine if these took the form of silent pantomimes or were dramas with words.

FORMAL DRAMA: 1660–1700

From 1603 to 1660 there is scarcely a trace of any performance of formal dramas in English or Scots. For those we have to look to the period when, in the wake of the Restoration of Charles II in 1660, aristocratic patronage of dramatic and other entertainments was able to withstand kirk displeasure, though the Kirk's hostility to theatre was reasserted, with the aid of civil discipline, from the mid 1680s.

Marciano: 1663

Marciano; or, The Discovery was performed and published in Edinburgh in 1663; it was the first post-Restoration drama written in Scotland. The title-page describes it as 'a Tragi-comedy, Acted with great applause, before His Majesties high Commissioner, and others of the Nobility, at the Abby of Holyrudhouse, on St Johns night: By a company of Gentlemen'. The latter were amateurs and may have included the play's author, an Edinburgh advocate, William Clark or Clerke (fl.1663–99?). The Commissioner before whom *Marciano* was acted was the Earl of Rothes, who had come 'down fra court with sindrie of the nobilitie that haid bene in England a long tyme befoir . . . to Halyrud hous'. That this courtly visit from London by Scottish aristocrats should encourage the writing and performance of a play reveals again the adverse consequences for Scottish drama of the loss of a resident court in Edinburgh. It also demonstrates how court and aristocratic patronage could protect a would-be dramatist from church censure and, importantly, provide a stage for his work. The Tennis Court Theatre in the grounds of Holyrood House was the only permanent theatre in post-Restoration Edinburgh, and it was able to withstand church-inspired hostility towards plays because its patrons were exclusively the nobility.

The hold which church censure had on dramatic activity is evident from the combative preface that William Clark felt he had to supply to his published play, and where he says:

> Although . . . it is not ordinar to apologize for Playes in general, at the publishing of any particular one; Yet, because this now appears as a City-swaggarer in a Country-church, where seldom such have been extant; and that the peevish prejudice of some persons, who know nothing beyond the principles of base, greazy, arrogant, illiterate Pedants, who, like the grasshoppers of Egypt, swarm in every corner of this Nation, and plague all the youth accordingly, is such, that they cannot have patience to hear of a Comedy, because they never see one acted.

(One such pedant, and tutor to a youth, features in *Marciano* and condemns plays as 'profane . . . abominable, yea, abominably abominable'.) Clark goes on in his preface to argue for the dignity and moral value of plays, and for the benefits of poise and oratory that can accrue to the young nobility through acting in them. He cites how great monarchs of the past, from classical times on, encouraged both dramatists and theatres and, this a jibe at the Church, how 'plays of all sorts' flourished throughout the Christian world from the time of Jesus without reproof. He also sees the suppression of the 'innocent and usefull recreation' of plays as having contemporary political significance:

MARCIANO;

OR,

THE DISCOVERY.

A

TRAGI-COMEDY,

Acted with great applause , before His
Majesties high Commissioner, and others
of the Nobility, at the Abby of *Holyrudhouse*, on St. *Johns* night :

By a company of Gentlemen.

Segnius irritant animum demissa per aurem,
Quam quæ sunt oculis subjecta fidelibus———
Hor. *de art. Poet.*

Edinburgh , Printed in the year , 1663.

Figure 1.13 Title-page of Marciano *by William Clark, the first post-Restoration play written in Scotland. Published and performed in Edinburgh in 1663.* (Scottish Theatre Archive)

For no sooner had those hell-hounds, assassinats of our liberties, snatch'd the very reins of Government into their hands, but as soon they thought it expedient to vote down all Scenick Playes so that they should suffer in that same sentence with Monarchy; upon whom they [i.e.

plays] have such a dependance, that at the thrice auspicious restaura-
tion of our Royal Soveraign, they were not only by him re-established,
but also more gloriously adorned with priviledges, than formerly.

Whilst due allowance must be made for the Royalist and anti-Presbyterian
sympathies informing this tirade, it does confirm again the real impact of those
forces conspiring to inhibit the development of playwriting and play-going in
Scotland.

Clark's preface reveals that, in writing *Marciano*, he had the assistance of
'a certain ingenuous Gentleman' in placing a comic interlude within his
tragedy to satisfy those who 'expected nothing from the Stage but mirth'.
Disarmingly, he admits that it was 'a difficult task to have arrived at a happy
Catastrophe, seeing how hard it is to carry on two different plots in one single
Play'. The tragic main plot and comic sub-plot alternate in different scenes,
with separate sets of characters; the two are only brought together in the final
scene, and then unconvincingly. The division is further marked by the tragedy
being in blank verse and the comedy in prose. In effect, the two plots are separate plays which should have stood alone. The awkward yoking of them
together is reflected in Clark's use of two titles, for *Marciano* refers to the
tragedy and *The Discovery* to the comedy. Both plots are set in Florence at the
same time, and it could be argued in the play's favour that one deals with
public affairs and the other with private ones, thus showing how ordinary life
carries on even in times of violent unrest, but such a linkage would be decidedly
tenuous.

The tragic plot centres on a rebellion, headed by Barbaro, which has forced
Cleon, Duke of Florence, to flee from his city. The Duke instructs his general,
Marciano, to rally what forces he can find. Marciano's forces are routed and
he is captured by Barbaro's captain-of-guard, Borasco, and condemned to die.
Arabella, Marciano's beloved, who has been searching for him, is separately
taken prisoner by Borasco. Borasco is smitten by her and instructs that she be
treated well and allowed to visit Marciano in his prison. This allows her to participate in a plan to help Marciano to escape. At first Marciano is reluctant
because he fears that she will be executed for helping him but eventually he
agrees and escapes. Arabella is condemned to execution for her part in the
escape plot. Borasco is prepared to plead with the Senate to pardon her but
would expect sexual favours in return. Arabella refuses. Events overtake matters
with the death of Barbaro, the fall of the rebellion, and the restoration of
Cleon. The Duke is enthroned and the reunited Arabella and Marciano are
wed.

A play dealing with the overthrow and restoration of a high-born ruler was
clearly meant to have contemporary relevance to the recent Restoration of the
British monarchy. That relevance is made quite pointedly within the play at

regular intervals, and one can well imagine Clark's audience of aristocratic visitors from the Court in London nodding vigorously in assent at such lines as 'When men begin to quarrel with their Prince,/No wonder if they crush their fellow subjects'. Unfortunately, the play itself is dire. It insistently strives for a high rhetoric, requiring characters to strike heroic poses. The combined effect is wearingly monotonous. The characters are merely ciphers for rhetorical vapouring, which probably reflects Clark's view, as expressed in his preface, that drama can have value as a kind of exercise performed by young noblemen to improve their powers of oratory.

Whilst the tragic plot thus resembles a closet drama more than a work for performance, the comic plot is eminently stageable and could still be performed effectively as a stand-alone piece. There are seven characters: Cassio and Leonardo (friends and 'noble Gentlemen of quality'); Chrysolina and Marionetta (sisters and 'Ladies of honour'); Pantaloni and Becabunga ('two rich gulls, in favour with the [aforementioned] Ladies'); and Manduco ('an arrogant Pedant' who is tutor to Becabunga). The two ladies are courted by Cassio and Leonardo but they rebuff them because they are more interested in Pantaloni and Becabunga as suitors. Pantaloni and Becabunga in turn court the two ladies, but Pantaloni only does so at his mother's insistence, and Becabunga, who is something of a naïf, does so under thrall to his domineering tutor, Manduco, who instructs him in courtship. Cassio and Leonardo devise a ruse to make Pantaloni and Becabunga look despicable in the ladies' eyes. Cassio gulls Pantaloni into believing that Becabunga is plotting that he will have Marionetta and Leonardo will have Chrysolina (Pantaloni's intended). Cassio urges Pantaloni to challenge Becabunga to a duel. Leonardo advises the reluctant Becabunga to accept the challenge. Come the day of the duel, Becabunga and Pantaloni squirm out of fighting by renouncing interest in their respective ladies. Leonardo and Cassio pretend disgust at this cowardly and unchivalrous behaviour and have them sign a document testifying that Leonardo and Cassio at least were prepared to duel; in fact, they have signed a document renouncing their love for the sisters. When the sisters read this, they tell Pantaloni and Becabunga that they are finished with them. After their pleading falls on deaf ears, Pantaloni and Becabunga become abusive, which reveals, hence the play's sub-title, 'The Discovery', that they never loved the ladies anyway. The way is clear for Cassio and Leonardo to woo Marionetta and Chrysolina, who now see the gentlemen in a more favourable light.

The to-ing and fro-ing of the interrelationships that make up the action is deftly handled, the characterisation is assured and individualised, and the dialogue and situations are successfully funny. The tutor Manduco is a wonderful comic creation whose pedantic speech is larded with polysyllables, circumlocutions and Latin words and tags, to riotous effect. Here he calls on the sisters

with a letter of courtship from his pupil, Becabunga, whom he assures 'flagi-
tates to see you'. He offers some information about Becabunga:

> I shall, *paucissimis*, insinuate to you the method of his education. –
> *Primo*, then, when he came under my gubernation, which was about
> the year of his age, *Anno Domini*, (let me see) *millesimo, sexcentesimo,
> quadragesimo sext*, it being then Leap-year; he was, *inquam*, a very per-
> verse youth, vitiat in his behaviour, knowing nothing but what he had
> learned amongst the *ancilla's* (what d'you call 'em) Chambermaids . . .
> But, so soon as I took him in hand, I did so belabour his *nates* with my
> *ferula*, that *profecto* I have whipped him, whip'd him thus – for half an
> hour together, until his abundant lachrymation had mov'd compassion:
> but, I knew that was the only way to disciplinate him.

He goes on to itemise the instructions that he gave Becabunga, which included
being 'terse in his habit, with hair in the same longitude as you see mine',
and 'how to keep a clean mundified nose, not with his sleeve, but with his
fudarium, or handkercher'. He enumerates these instructions in Latin – *Primo*,
Secundo, *Tertio* and *Quarto* – and arrives at the all important warning,
Quinto: '*maximè à crepitando & eructando*; that is, from emitting ventosities
or flatuosities from his concavities'.

The witty utterances of Cassio and Leonardo are another source of
humour. Here they bemoan their lack of success in courting the sisters
Chrysolina and Marionetta:

> *Cass.* . . . How does thy Mistress, the Lady you know of,—ha?
> *Leon.* – Why, faith as unreasonable as ever.
> *Cass.* How! Unreasonable . . .
> *Leon.* Yes – unreasonable, she will admit of no tearms whatsoever, so
> that I fear I shall be forc'd to storm her: 'slid, I can have scarce liberty
> to survey her very parapet and out-works for fear of a thing . . . suspi-
> cion, I think she calls it; and for thee, I beleeve thou art in no better
> condition, for her Sister, thy Mistress (otherwayes in my opinion plyable)
> is rul'd by her, and both by an old urinal-peeping, onyon-breath'd hag,
> whom they call the Countesse of *Saromanca* forsooth, so that now she
> is impregnable.
> *Cass.* A devil she is, 'slid, I think it is become an epidemical disease
> amongst that sexe, they intend, I think, to imitate the times and erect a
> new Commonwealth of themselves, excluding all masculine society,
> and to be called *the new assembly of zeal-copyholders*.
> *Leon.* Yes, yes, for now they hold it a cryme to court.

Cass. Since Monarchy fell, that trade is totally decayed, thou must now either Marry at first sight or else march off; as if who should throw the Dye for a maydenhead, Boy.
Leon. Goodness, I think, by and by, we shall be constrained to make love to one another, and so thou shalt be my Mistress, Cassio; for our modern Criticks will not allow us women's flesh, even upon holy-dayes.

Marciano; or, The Discovery shares with *Philotus* an Italian setting and some Italian influence, but the modern spirit that was noted in *Philotus* is taken further. The awareness of stagecraft implicit in *Philotus* is made explicit in *Marciano*, and for the first time we have a Scottish play which looks modern in layout on the page *as a performance text*, with clear divisions into acts and scenes, and detailed and comprehensive stage directions throughout. Also, the traditional Scottish preference, still evident in *Philotus*, for dialogue in rhyming verse, even after the successful introduction of blank verse to the Elizabethan stage in England, is relinquished in *Marciano* in favour of blank verse and prose. Another contrast with the Scots-medium *Philotus* – reflecting changes brought about by the Union of the Crowns as referred to before – is that *Marciano* is written in English with only a few covert Scotticisms. (Sir William Alexander's closet dramas were, as we saw, originally written in Scots but he progressively anglicised them in revision once the Court moved to London.) The modern sensibility informing *Marciano* is most evident in the comic plot, and it is therefore to be regretted that the author did not go on to write full-length comic dramas.

Tarugo's Wiles: 1668

The next Scottish play after *Marciano* was *Tarugo's Wiles: or, The Coffee-House* by Thomas Sydserf (fl.1667–1689?), whose name is also written as Sydeserf or St Serfe. He has the double distinction of founding, in 1661, Scotland's first newspaper, the *Caledonian Mercury*, and being the first Scot to have a play premiered in London. *Tarugo's Wiles* opened there on 5 October 1667, with a subsequent production in Edinburgh at the Tennis Court Theatre in 1668. It was published in London in 1668, and the title page, which gives the author's name in the form Thomas St Serfe, describes the play as 'A Comedy as it was acted at his Highness's, the Duke of York's Theatre'. The dedication of the play to the Earl of Huntly shows the author lamenting 'our late Fanatick Commotions' and extolling, like William Clark in the preface to *Marciano*, the monarchist cause. (Sydserf, a son of the Bishop of Galloway, fought in the civil war on the Royalist side under Montrose.) He says, this 'Comical Tale, which I dedicate to your recreation, like most other Playes, has its useful moralities'. The published play also contains a prologue which was delivered at the beginning of the London performance. In it, Sydserf uses exchanges between characters about 'the Author of this new Play' to forestall criticism of the kind of work he has written. In answer to whether the play is in 'Blank verse, Rhyme, or Prose', it will be in prose because the author is a 'stranger to our Language, Learning and Ryme [sic]'. There is, however, no indication that this is so as regards language, for the play is written throughout in English. The Earl of Dorset wrote in a poem in praise of *Tarugo's Wiles*, 'To my friend Master Thos. St. Serfe', that the play could 'teach ev'n English men the English tongue'.

Two influences on the composition of *Tarugo's Wiles* have been identified: the early plays of Molière, with the themes in *L'École des maris* being especially reminiscent of Sydserf's; and, more directly, Spanish romance, particularly *No puede serl* by Augustin Moreto y Cabaña. (Not knowing about Sydserf's play, the English dramatist John Crowne based his 1685 work, *Sir Courtly Nice*, on the same source.) Betraying its Spanish models, *Tarugo's Wiles* is set in Spain. But Sydserf breaks the structural mould of his Spanish sources by placing his third act in a coffee-house – a coffee-house which is patently more London than Spain, notwithstanding the limp effort to give it Spanish 'colour'. Also, references are made to England throughout the play, usually contrasting customs there with Spanish ones. Sydserf achieves this mainly through the unconvincing device of the eponymous Tarugo having lived for some time in England, from where he has recently returned. Some of Tarugo's wiles are attributed to English influence and are obviously intended as a source of humour for a London audience. When, for example, Tarugo is accused of playing 'tricks to avoid [paying] a just debt', he laments, 'farewell sweet England, where what you term tricks are accounted acts of thrift'. Unfortunately, in most cases such references are – like the 'London' coffee-house scene – gratuitous and serve as distractions to smooth progress of the plot.

Tarugo is cousin to Don Horatio, a knight. Horatio has fallen out with his friend, another knight, Don Patricio, over Patricio's unreasonable argument that 'the best way to secure a woman's honesty is close imprisonment, and that freedom furnish'd 'em opportunity to looseness'. Patricio has acted on his belief by confining his sister, Liviana, to their house and denying her visitors. Sophronio is Don Patricio's betrothed but she is alarmed by his tyrannical treatment of Liviana and is disinclined to marry him unless he can be brought to see the error of his ways. Horatio's concern for Liviana's virtual imprisonment stirs love in her for him, which he reciprocates (ironically, Patricio's confinement of her has thereby served to encourage what he wished to prevent). But Patricio has chosen a husband for Liviana, Don Roderigo, and is arranging the marriage against her will.

Tarugo hatches a plot to help Liviana and Horatio. He pretends to be Don Chrisanto, 'a Cavalier of Peru', and a kinsman to Patricio's friend in the West Indies, Marquiss Villana, from whom he brings gifts for Patricio. Consequently, he is invited to lodge in Patricio's house. To overcome Patricio's concern for Liviana's chastity, Don Chrisanto/Tarugo makes out that he suffers from an affliction whereby the sight of a woman of youth and beauty sends him into a potentially fatal fit. Out of consideration for his guest, Patricio removes Liviana and her maid to a remote part of the house. Tarugo then smuggles Horatio into the house to see Liviana; and he conspires to let Patricio overhear Horatio lamenting the breach that has arisen between them and how much he still respects Patricio. To Patricio's gratitude, Tarugo undertakes to act as a go-between to effect a reconciliation. However, Patricio remains adamant that Liviana will obey his will and marry Roderigo that night.

Patricio is en route with Roderigo to the wedding ceremony, but Sophronio uses a ruse to divert them to her house. Meanwhile, Tarugo helps Liviana to escape from her confinement and to make her way to Sophronio's house where Horatio is awaiting her. Sophronio confronts Patricio with 'my new marry'd couple', Horatio and Liviana, and Liviana tells the dumbfounded Patricio that Horatio's courage 'has rescu'd me from your unjust slavery'. To add to Patricio's astonishment, Don Chrisanto reveals himself to be Tarugo. Patricio acknowledges his error in thinking that a woman's will can be fettered. With this admission, Sophronio is now happy for her marriage to Patricio to proceed.

The final line in the play is, 'In this there's nothing new, only you see a fresh experience of the impossibility of restraining a Woman's Will.' This reference to lack of originality can stand as an apt assessment of *Tarugo's Wiles*, which, according to a contemporary commentator, 'expir'd the third day' of its run in London. That the plot is awkward and contrived, with an entirely irrelevant central act (Act III in the coffee-house) and a cursory and wholly unconvincing final resolution in the last act, would matter less if the humour in this supposed 'comedy' was lively. Unfortunately, it is mostly forced and lame, as here where Tarugo has been interrupted in his attempted seduction of Sophronio's maid, Stanlia:

> *Stan.* O Madam! your call came in good time. Certainly this man has been bred Commander in a Scotch Privateer.
> *Sophr.* Why so, Stanlia?
> *Stan.* Because I suppose he fancied me a Dutch bottom, who for not striking at first, he was ready with his Grapler to have laid me aboard; and I verily think had made me prize, if the Authority of your call had not so seasonably come to my relief.
> *Sophr.* What a mad way of expression this same Wench uses. But don't you know the English humour, with which he hath been so lately accustom'd, is not really so dangerous as it seems.
> *Stan.* I am sure 'tis altogether Anti-platonick . . .

This would-be humorous exchange also shows how Sydserf's incorporation of regular references to England works against the grain of the play's Spanish setting and can sometimes prove – as with the reference to a 'Commander in a Scotch Privateer' – disorientating. A key problem, too, is that the 'excuse' for the English references, the character Tarugo, whose 'education abroad has wonderfully improv'd him in dextrous stratagems', is a deficient creation who does not achieve the level of wit or comic business that would have been necessary to rescue the play. Where the play does retain a degree of interest is in the theme of male domination of women – or, 'the impossibility of restraining a Woman's Will', to quote the final line – and in the spirited way in which Liviana and Sophronio express their resistance to Patricio:

> *Liv*. Brother, let me tell you, your groundless jealousie was temptation enough for me to have gone astray, if my own honour had not govern'd me better. If I have done amiss, you are to blame as well to conceal it as not to punish it: and take notice, your austerity has awak'd desires in me that might have slept. If I chance to miscarry, I must attribute all to your idle humour. I'm confident this sottish distrust in men, thinking to overcome our Wills with violence, has been, and is still the onely great cause that creates vicious Women.

Although he only wrote one play, Sydserf contributed in other ways to the development of Scottish theatre. He was the manager, from 1667, of the same Tennis Court Theatre where *Marciano* had been performed in 1663, and he managed an acting company based in Edinburgh's Canongate (and therefore in the vicinity of the Tennis Court Theatre). We know about this company from a legal action that Sydserf raised against one Mungo Murray in June 1689. Murray had interrupted Sydserf's company during rehearsals, using personal violence, and the legal records make reference to Sydserf's 'hous in the Canongate, quher he keeps his theater for acteing his playes'. It seems a fair assumption that, in the years between 1663 and this 1689 reference, Sydserf continued to manage for some or all of the time a company presenting plays.

Sir John Foulis: 1669–72

Sir John Foulis of Ravelston is likely to have seen performances by Sydserf's company. He attended the theatre in Edinburgh regularly between 1669 and 1672, as documented in his Account Books. The following sample entries give a flavour of his theatre-going:

1671, *Dec.* 1. A Dinner at Leith to Sir James, Lady Grissell, Cristian, Antie, &c., and for the play, £11, 4s.

1672, *Jan.* 26. When we went over to Bruntiland, for coatches, fraught, dinner, and the play, £20, 5s.

1672, *Feb.* 27. Spent at Newhaven, and Leith, and at the play, with young and old Ratho, Sir James Hay, Marg. spouse, Lady Ratho, my wife, &c., £6.

1672, *March* 9. Payed for myselfe, my wife, and Cristian, to see Macbeth acted, and for sweetmeats to Lady Colingtoune, Lady Margaret M'Kenzie, and others, £6, 2s.

1672, *June* 21. To see the comedie when the Commissioner [John, Duke of Lauderdale] was ther, and for oranges for gentlewomen, £2, 8s.

1672, *June* 25. To let the Lady Pittaro and Sir James Sinclair's Lady see the Comedie, and for oranges and cherries to them, £5, 12s. 9d.

1672, *Nov.* 28. To my wife and Cristian to see the comedie acted, £2, 18.

1672, *Dec.* 21. To see Sir Solomon acted, £1, 9s.

Foulis's Account Books provide an invaluable insight into Restoration theatre in Edinburgh. In addition to incidental information about 'orange-sellers' plying their wares to theatre-goers, we glean that play-going was expensive and therefore socially selective, as also evidenced by aristocratic patronage. Unfortunately, Foulis usually describes what he saw as a 'play' or 'Comedie' and only occasionally provides a title. None the less, we learn that the repertoire of the Tennis Court Theatre followed the London repertoire, and that no new Scottish plays featured after *Marciano* and *Tarugo's Wiles*.

We know the titles of three plays staged by visiting English companies in Edinburgh during the same period covered by Foulis. In 1669 the Town Council granted a licence to 'inglishmen' Robert Clerk and Stephen Grege, 'to act thes motions or plays within the citie or suburbs, called *pollishingello*, or the *beateing of the sea*, or such uther rather motions grin they ar expert, or can exercise'. In the next year, 1670, the Council gave James Underwood permission to stage the 'motion or play called the *Judgment of Soloman* and other playes'. 'Motions' were plays involving puppets – and were presumably what Sir John Foulis refers to when he notes that he occasionally went to see a 'puppie [puppet] show'. It is also recorded that in 1682 the Town Council gave a merchant in Edinburgh, William Heartly, permission 'to erect and caus build ane timber house of fourty foot of length, and twenty foot of breadth, upon the high street, below the Blackfrier Wynd head for showing a motion called *The Indian*, or the *German Wooks*'.

Duke of York at Holyrood: 1679–82

The Duke of York, the younger brother of Charles II who was to become James VII, was resident in Edinburgh at Holyrood Palace with his wife Mary of Modena from 1679 to 1682. He encouraged court masques and seasons of plays at the Tennis Court Theatre, having brought with him from London a company of actors, as alluded to by the poet and playwright John Dryden in one of his prologues. Dryden laments the politically inspired troubles then afflicting the London stage and mock-ruefully ponders the loss of the company that has gone to Edinburgh:

> Discords and plots, which have undone our age,
> With the same ruin have o'erwhelmed the stage.
> Our house has suffer'd in the common woe,
> We have been troubled with Scotch rebels too.
> Our brethren are from Thames to Tweed departed,
> And of our Sisters, all the kinder-hearted,
> To Edinburgh gone or coach'd or carted.
> With bonny bluecap there they act all night
> For Scotch half-crown, in English three-pence hight.
> One nymph, to whom fat Sir John Falstaff's lean,
> There with her single person fills the scene.
> Another, with long use and age decay'd,
> Div'd here old woman, and rose there a maid.
> Our trusty door-keepers of former time
> There strut and swagger in heroic rhime.

How justified was Dryden's satirical dismissal of the company that the Duke of York brought north is difficult to know. That he may be an unreliable source is suggested by the fact that at least two actors from the Duke of York Theatre in London, Mr Clark and Mr Goodman, are known to have come to Edinburgh. Both had appeared in London in Nathaniel Lee's play *Mythridates, King of Pontus*, which received its premiere in London in 1678.

Princess Anne, the future Queen, joined the Court at Holyrood in 1681, where she acted in a performance of that same play for the pleasure of her family, as recorded by Lord Fountainhall:

Novembris 15, 1681, being [the Queen's birthday] it was keeped by our Court at Halyruid house with great solemnitie, such as bonfyres, shooting of canons, and the acting of a comedy [sic; it was a tragedy] called *Mithridates, King of Pontus* before ther Royal Hyneses, &c., wheirin Lady Anne, the Duke's daughter, and the ladies of honour ware the onlie actors.[17]

The Duke of York's presence in Edinburgh also attracted a company of Irish players, numbering thirty, who sailed to Scotland to perform for him, bringing with them their costumes.

With the Duke of York's departure it seems that Presbyterian hostility to drama reasserted its authority. In October 1682 Edinburgh Town Council ordered that a wooden theatre then being built should be demolished, and ordained 'that from hencefurth noe stadge or playhouse be erected or built upon any part of the high street of this city'. Thomas Sydserf, as we saw, still had a company of players in 1689, but perhaps his location in the Canongate exempted him from the Town Council's ordinance. Significantly, it was noted that in the 1690s, the citizens of Edinburgh, by coach and on foot, sought diversions in Leith, themselves 'having no Play-house, Musick-meetings, or Spring-Garden to tempt them to those superfluous Expences'.

The Assembly: 1692

Archibald Pitcairne (or Pitcairn) (1652–1713) was the author of the satirical play *The Assembly*, written in 1692, and described as 'a venomous caricature of Presbyterianism'. Son of a merchant in Edinburgh, he studied in Leyden and Paris, qualified as a doctor in Rheims, became the most distinguished medical man of his day and was a founder of the College of Physicians in Edinburgh. In addition to *The Assembly* he wrote a lesser play satirising the Presbyterian Church, *Tollerators and Contollerators; a Comedy Acted in My Lord Advocats Lodgeing, June 10, 1703* (probably written in 1703, but not published until 1830); a long poem, 'Babell', satirising the General Assembly of the Church of Scotland; and some Latin verse. When Pitcairne died in 1713, the poet, playwright and theatre-company manager, Allan Ramsay (see Chapter 2), wrote an appreciative verse-epitaph, 'A Poem to the Memory of the Famous Archibald Pitcairn, MD'.

As a staunch Jacobite, publicly avowed atheist and fierce critic of religious bigotry, Pitcairne was no stranger to controversy. It is a mark of his outspokenness that *The Assembly* was not staged in his lifetime, and that, although copies circulated in manuscript, the play was not published until 1722, some thirty years after its composition and well after Pitcairne's death. In contrast with the foreign settings of earlier Restoration plays by Scots, *The Assembly* deals with contemporary Scottish events and characters. The title refers to the General Assembly of the Church of Scotland, and to the Assemblies of 1690 and 1692 in particular. Pitcairne drew on those Assemblies in composing his satire of Presbyterian cant and in lampooning thinly disguised real churchmen. To compound the play's gross offence (had the Presbyterian leaders seen it), the subject matter is often lewd and the language scurrilous. It is therefore easy to understand why *The Assembly* could not have been published in Pitcairne's day.

A preface provided to the 1752 edition makes clear that the play drew on real events, and it identifies by name the people on whom characters were based. It also addresses a number of 'objections that may be made against the manner of writing' the play (perhaps reflecting criticism voiced after publication of the first edition in 1722). The first such objection answered is:

> The critics perhaps will say, that our play is made up of two plots, the one of love, the other about the General Assembly. Suppose this were true, we might defend ourselves by examples of some of the ancients and moderns too, of no small note, who have done this. But we are not obliged to seek shelter under authority, for reason will sufficiently defend us. Our entire and uniform plot is to represent the villainy and folly of the Presbyterians in their public meetings, and the private transactions of their lives; and, how we have succeeded in both, we leave it to the judgement of the ingenuous reader.

As noted earlier, *Marciano* is another play with two separate but supposedly linked plots, respectively treating of the public and private consequences of political circumstances. The disjunction between the two plots is less marked in *The Assembly* than in *Marciano*, but it is unsatisfactory none the less. When the preface says that 'our entire and uniform plot is to represent the villainy and folly of the Presbyterians', this is so if 'plot' is understood as a stratagem to attack the Presbyterians, but it is not so if 'plot' is taken in the literary sense; that is, the anti-Presbyterianism evident in both plots is 'entire and uniform', but artistically those plots do not cohere into a satisfactory whole.

The love plot centres on relationships involving the daughter and nieces of a Presbyterian bigot known only as the Old Lady. Her daughter, Rachael, spouts the same pious cant and gives the nieces dire warnings against 'the scandalous custom of speaking with men'. Hypocritically, however, Rachael has been having carnal relations with her Presbyterian chaplain and dominie, Mr Wordie, and is six months pregnant. Indeed, when we first meet them, Wordie is tutoring Rachael in the Scriptures, yet, under the stern gaze of her mother, they indulge in sexual innuendo. The Old Lady invites 'Mas James' (Master James) to sit down:

> *Rach*. No mother, he exerciseth best standing, 'tis more convenient, I think.
> *Old L*. But 'tis more convenient for Mas James.
> *Wor*. No madam, I give o'er in time.
> *Old L*. I know such is the frailty of her nature, she will weary first.
> *Rach*. Indeed, no mother, Mas James can tell I love it very well . . . But much exercising makes him dry, mother, and he's forc'd to give over, God knows, sooner than I wish many a time.
> *Old L*. Teach her, Mas James, to drink in the sincere milk of the word, that she may grow thereby.

Wor. In troth, she's a very pliable scholar.
Rach. The truth is, mother, I know myself growing by it these six
months bypast extremely.

When her mother learns the truth at the end of the play, her concern to avoid
scandal outweighs her vaunted religious scruples and she accedes with alacrity
to the offer by a Presbyterian minister to give out the lie that he had married
them eight months previously.

The nieces, Violetta and Laura, attract the attention of two gentlemen, Will
and Frank. The latter are of the party which is anti-Presbyterian, Tory, and
pro-King James, as against the opposing party which is Presbyterian, Whig,
and pro-King William. The divisively bipartisan nature of political and religious
affiliations in Scotland at that time provides the background to both plots.
Edinburgh, where the play is set, is riven with this division, as Will explains to
Frank who has newly returned from the Continent and enquires about 'the
state of the nation':

> Gad, 'tis a most monstrous body politic, I have neither time nor
> rhetoric to describe it to you; you may have an abridgement of it, by
> conversing with the people in town: a man who had walked betwixt
> the Strait-bow and the Cross, wou'd imagine, by their converse, he had
> marched out of King William's territories into King James's. They have
> both their kingdoms in this town . . .

The depth of hostility between the camps can be gauged from the intemperate
language by which a Whig character, Visioner, refers to the Prince of Wales as
'a shitten bastard, a mere impostor'.

Will and Frank abhor what Will describes as 'the religious nonsensical cant
of the right reverend godly blockheads of the fanatic order'. Their rakish
dislike of Presbyterian censure of amusement and wooing appeals to the rebel-
lious-minded sisters, who are heartily sick of their aunt's 'impertinent religious
nonsensical clatter'. Will and Violetta are the more spirited of the couples, as
seen when they first meet in church at the public arraignment of a woman for
committing 'the filthy sin of fornication'. They flirt by means of chosen biblical
passages, with Violetta pointing this one out for Will to read: 'O that thou wert
as my brother, who sucked the breasts of my mother!' However, she won't
countenance consummation unless they are married, so Will agrees to marry
her. Meanwhile, Frank has fallen in love with Laura and wants to marry her.
As a trial of their love, and as a means of allowing them all to meet again, Will
and Frank are persuaded by Violetta and Laura to don the disguise of
Presbyterian ministers and come to their aunt's. They will tell their aunt that

they have invited two ministers, just arrived from Holland, to come and dine.

Will and Frank attempt to act out their parts with the Old Lady. Will exchanges Presbyterian-speak with her, to humorous effect:

> *Will.* O but 'tis a sad world this, . . . an abominable, curst, unjust, malicious, ill-natur'd world.
>
> *Old L.* A prying, censorious, soul-seducing, gospel renouncing world! A malignant, backsliding, covenant breaking, minister mocking, a filthy, idolatrous, Sabbath breaking, parent dishonouring world! A murdering, whoring, lying, coveting world; 'tis, in a word, an uncharitably worldly world.
>
> [*Maid enters.*]
>
> *Maid.* There's a poor man, Madam, says he lost his means by the west country rabble.
>
> *Old L.* Come you to tell me that, you baggage! Beat him down stairs.

To Frank's consternation, the Old Lady asks him to offer commentary on a passage from the Bible. In the bluster to avoid doing so a saint's name is mentioned, which idolatry conveniently causes her to faint. The entry of two clergymen creates a diversion which allows the four lovers to escape next door to an Episcopal curate who marries them. Meanwhile, Rachael and Wordie have arrived and the Old Lady has learned about the pregnancy and agreed to the cover-up. Will and Violetta, and Frank and Laura return and inform the Old Lady that they are married. With typical hypocrisy, she can accommodate her pregnant daughter cheating her but not her (virgin) nieces, and she tells them she never wants to see them again. In a parting shot, Violetta and Laura remind Rachael of her diatribes to them against the 'wicked customs' of consorting with men, and reveal to her that they knew all along about her fornication with Wordie.

The other plot, about the General Assembly, is less satisfactory as drama, for it has no story or action to it. It is static, comprising deliberations in the Assembly involving a narrow group of characters. There is some differentiation between the characters in terms of personality and style of speech. One, for example, speaks a north-east Scots, as in his indignant response to 'the very thunder-bolt of excommunication' having been taken from the Kirk by Act of Parliament: 'Fat ha' they deen? If that be true, we are but a beik of bees without stangs.' But the author's preoccupation with making the Assembly members mere butts for his political and religious satire prevents the characterisation from rising above the level of caricature. His partisanship is so unrelieved, and often so blunt, that the cumulative effect is to dull the satire. That said, there are many amusing moments, such as this discussion about deposing Episcopal curates who are not prepared to comply with Presbyterian practice, where the Assembly men are typically shown to indulge in absurd procedural and seman- tic wrangles which betray their petty-mindedness, incompetence and stupidity:

> *Cov.* To what our brother has said, I have two queries, two difficulties, one fear, and a proposal; or rather two proposals, two queries, one dif- ficulty, and a fear. My proposals are, that there be an act prohibiting all answering of libels, either by word or writ, and that the curates be libelled on faults to be done as done. My first question is, Whether we should plant their kirks ere we depose them, or depose them ere we plant their kirks? My second question is, How is it possible to reach those curates that are neither on this nor on the other side of Tay?
> *R. Eld.* Let 'em come in by a class of their own, which, with the other two – let me see – two and one, make just three.
> *Cov.* Well, my difficulty is, Whether this libel should be written or printed; and my fear is, that the curates call this indirect dealing, and judging in our own cause.
> *Turb.* What, will not Christ be judge in his own cause at the last day? Did Joshua, when he extirpated the idolaters, cite every man to per- sonal compearance, and give him a copy of his libel aforehand? Did Christ, when he whipt the buyers and sellers out of the temple, take every particular huckster-wife by the lug? I trow no. –
> *All.* All strong sense!

The only points of overlap between the two plots is that they share the same contemporary background of religious and political division, the same satirising of Presbyterian bigotry and hypocrisy, and that one or two Assembly men make appearances in the love plot; otherwise, they are in effect separate plots. This, and the static nature of the General Assembly plot, which is more satire-dialogue than drama, makes *The Assembly* problematic as a stageable play. There is the added difficulty presented by some gratuitous scenes inserted merely to serve a polemical rather than a dramatic purpose, such as when Will and Frank anatomise at length passing Presbyterian politicians and judges, or when two minor characters absurdly dispute the merits of 'Presbyterian Latin' over 'Romish Latin'! Pitcairne seems to have been aware of *The Assembly*'s shortcomings, for the epilogue states: 'Our play is done, that circumstance, the plot,/Our authors have of mere design forgot'.

In a way, Pitcairne's failure can be interpreted as a larger consequence of living in times inimical to encouragement of drama. As the prologue to *The Assembly* says:

'Tis a long while since any play hath been,
Except rope-dancing, in our nation seen;
But now, in this our all-reforming age,
We've got a play – The pulpit's turn'd a stage!

The lack of a recent tradition of staged drama, kirk censure of theatres and plays, and the conception of *The Assembly* as a 'pulpit' for political diatribe in the form of satire, were to handicap Pitcairne as a would-be dramatist (entertaining satirist though he is). His prologue was written in the last decade of the seventeenth century, and, if one surveys the period from medieval times till 1700, his dispiriting comments on the state of theatre in Scotland on the eve of the eighteenth century raise a more general question: with the loss by then of the medieval tradition in folk and religious drama, with no resident court culture, no professional theatre, and next to no playwrights, could Scottish theatre in the next century deliver more than 'rope-dancing'?

2 *The Eighteenth Century*
ADRIENNE SCULLION

The eighteenth century begins with erratic and irregular theatrical entertainments at the Tennis Court Theatre, Holyrood, and a handful of plays by Scots being played in London. In the following decades Scottish theatre came of age. The eighteenth century saw the establishment of a permanent playhouse and a resident company in Edinburgh, then a hard-fought battle for a Patent house in the capital and the subsequent development of a vital minor house tradition. In these years actors and managers found employment and celebrity, fortune and notoriety on the Scottish stage. Despite religious opposition, a theatre culture was established and a wildly enthusiastic, increasingly knowledgeable and eminently partisan audience quickly developed. By the mid-century there were regular clashes between supporters of the theatre and religiously motivated opponents. Although it would be an exaggeration to suggest that blood was spilt in these arguments, much spleen was vented and much ink poured forth in elaborate and protracted pamphlet wars. Occasionally these paper wars became violent: at least one playhouse was destroyed by religious zealots. None the less, by 1800 there were nine permanent playhouses in Scotland. In addition to these institutional developments, some of the most significant plays in the history of Scottish theatre were written and produced.

This chapter will describe and account for some of the features of eighteenth-century Scottish theatre. Inevitably the focus will be on events in Edinburgh, but developments across the whole country will be considered. The lives and careers of the most influential figures in the history of the Scottish stage will be highlighted and some of the plays which responded to and shaped theatre practice will be examined.

SCOTTISH PLAYWRIGHTS IN LONDON

At the start of the eighteenth century there was little suggestion that the Scottish theatre would soon spring into new and popular life. Religious opposition restricted theatre and other public entertainments to a remarkable degree and individuals ambitious of a career in drama had to travel south, perhaps picking up work with the provincial companies scattered across England or travelling on to London where a rich professional theatre culture had flourished since the Restoration in 1660. Several Scots chose this option and the beginning of the century saw a number of plays by Scots being produced on the London stage. Most significant were those by David Crawford (printed as Craufurd) and Newburgh Hamilton who wrote witty social satires designed for the highly organised, professional companies of the Drury Lane and Lincoln's Inn Fields theatres with their strict hierarchy of players, tight production schedules and knowledgeable, and occasionally fickle, audiences.

David Crawford (1665–1726) wrote typical Restoration comedies featuring true and false lovers, fops, coquettes, courtesans, cuckolds, sophisticates, innocents, deceit, infatuation, disguise, intrigue and a dubiously moral conclusion. His first play, *Courtship A-la-mode*, was premiered at the Theatre Royal in Drury Lane on 9 July 1700, his second, *Love at First Sight*, first played at Lincoln's Inn Fields on 25 March 1704. The printed edition (1700) of *Courtship A-la-mode* includes a preface, in which Crawford describes the trials he encountered when he first offered his play to Thomas Betterton and his Duke's company at Lincoln's Inn Fields:

> It was enter'd in the other House, where Mr Betterton did me all the Justice I cou'd indeed reasonably hope for. But that Example he gave, was not it seems to be follow'd by the whole Company, since 'tis known that Mr Bowman . . . kept the first Character of my Play six weeks, and then cou'd hardly read six lines on't . . . Some who valued their reputations more, were indeed rarely or never absent. To these I give my thanks; but finding that six or seven people cou'd not perform what was design'd for fifteen, I was oblig'd to remove it after so many sham Rehearsals.

Frustrated at the slipshod standards of Betterton's players, Crawford had an altogether happier experience when he offered his play to Christopher Rich and his King's company at Drury Lane. It was accepted immediately and produced less than three weeks after it had been submitted. Rich clearly responded to the play's traditional tale of true love confronted by the conventional opposition of an ambitious and mean *paterfamilias*, and to its good-humoured salaciousness. Scheming servants, foolish youths, virtuous young ladies and frustrated lovers also played their part.

Sir John Winmore, jaded in his devotion to his long-time lover, the courtesan Lucy, sets his cap at Timandra, the niece of Alderman Chollerick. Winmore determines to put aside his rakish past and reform. When he confides these intentions to his servant, the prurient Scowrer, he is cynically scolded:

> Have you consider'd the state of Matrimony, the Plague of that dull insipid Partner of your bed, distinguish'd by the name of Wife; from that charming easie loving kind thing, call'd a *Mistress*?

Winmore's friend, Captain Bellair, newly returned from the country, is also in love. He is determined to win the hand of Flora, whose father, Sir Anthony Addle, keeps her from society. Winmore convinces Bellair to engage the matchmaker Decoy to help him in his suit. Decoy (who is also Chollerick's housekeeper) is despatched with a love letter for Flora. Timandra's brother Ned is in love with Flora's sister Melintha (Sir Anthony's eldest daughter), despite the fact that Chollerick plans to marry her. The fop Freelove arrives lamenting the fact that his several lovers have all jilted him.

The second scene mirrors the first as Crawford introduces Flora and Melintha. Like the male characters, they talk animatedly about their lovers. Flora affects a facade of coolness, but it is clear that she is not indifferent to Bellair's affections. Sir Anthony insists upon his plans to wed Melintha to his friend Chollerick and keep Flora unwed as his housekeeper. Flora finds the match preposterous but Melintha is sanguine, despite the fact that she holds some affection for Ned. The matrimonial plans hatched by Sir Anthony and Chollerick are even more ambitious, extending to Sir Anthony's son Dick, who is to marry Timandra. Freelove then engages Decoy to find him a new lover. She sets upon an ambitious plan to join the true lovers and gull their guardians while matching Freelove with the abandoned courtesan Lucy. Lucy and her maid Betty lament Winmore's disaffection but are encouraged by a note from Decoy promising a rich new lover in the form of Freelove.

Winmore is determined to abandon his dissolute past to marry Timandra. Freelove, too, besotted with his new love 'Lucinda', declares that he will change his ways. So as to make a good impression when he courts Lucinda, Freelove engages Bellair's servant, Willie Beetlehead. In his preface Crawford describes Willie as 'a down-right ignorant Clown', though in the play Winmore is rather more generous, describing him as 'a troublesome, unmannerly Rogue, and sometimes possest with the Spirit of Contradiction, but of undoubted honesty'.

Beetlehead is, perhaps, an early version of the stage Scotsman. His first question on hearing that he is to serve Freelove concerns money: 'Aun whau wull pay me for my pains . . . ?' Thus supported, Freelove goes forth to woo Lucy. Willie immediately proves his shrewdness, counselling his new master against Decoy, who has arranged an interview with Lucy, but will charge the suitor £1000 if a marriage follows. Willie is himself soon besotted of Lucy's maid, Betty, thus completing the elaborate set of Crawford's lovers:

> *Willie*. Hear ye me, *Jo*: how waud ye like me for yer good man? I hea a brau Estate in *Scotland*.
> *Betty*. Like you?
> *Willie*. Ay, that is, lye wi me au yer days; warm me bed in au caul Winter-neight, aun let me get bairns upon ye.
> *Betty*. Is that your way of Courtship in *Scotland*?
> *Willie*. Ay, aun this way tea be me Saul – [*Kisses her rudely*]

Timandra, Flora and Melintha are then wooed by Winmore, Bellair and Ned, but Dick spies on the tryst and exposes the lovers to Sir Anthony. The girls and their beaux turn to Decoy for help, each one paying the matchmaker's fee, and she hatches a daring last-minute plan. Thinking themselves triumphant, Sir Anthony and Chollerick arrange the wedding of Dick and Timandra. The minister and the lawyers they engage for the ceremony are, of course, the closely disguised Ned, Winmore and Bellair. The lovers trick Sir Anthony and Chollerick into believing that Dick is to be arrested for a debt. When the two dupes leave to pay his bail the lovers effect a hasty exit and, with miraculous speed, are each married. They return seeking the blessing of Sir Anthony, who admits his errors and, seeing some advantage in the matches his daughters have struck, blesses their unions. Freelove arrives with Lucy, whom Sir John promptly exposes as a courtesan. Decoy holds bonds which, she insists, mean that the couple are legally married. Winmore buys the bonds from Decoy and Freelove is released from the contract. As the play closes Willie and Betty arrive, they too being newly married. Although Chollerick cannot be mollified, Sir Anthony is sanguine: '. . . who knows', he confides in the jilted Chollerick, 'I may live to get another Daughter for ye?'

Crawford's play is capable and entertaining, assured in word and comic in stage-business. It is typical of contemporary comedies that his servants are both witty and wise, and he certainly gives them some of his liveliest dialogue. Willie's language is particularly interesting, being energised by an idiomatic and phonetically rendered Scots that is no mere facade. His linguistic identity is fully integrated into his dramaturgical role and does not reduce him to mere ethnic stereotype, for his role as 'Scot' is pregnant with a more general significance:

> *Freelove*. And so she bid me stay in the Room till she came – Was it not so?
> *Willie*. What a deel Sir aur ye deef, shoe baud ye tarry here aun no gang awau till she caum been.

Freelove. Ben – but 'tis no matter; *Willie*, you must forget *Scotland*, and
conform yourself to the Customs of *England*; learn our Accent.
Willie. Nau sir, sheam fae me thaen, Customs o *Englaun* quo? Nau,
nau, I'se do aus our Maest *Johaon* does pray for yer reformaution in
good-bred *Scots*. Aus for yer accent Sir, I speak as Father *Audaum*
spauke before me.
Freelove. Then *Adam* spoke *Scotch*?
Willie. Goad aun that he did, Sir.

Crawford's second play, *Love at First Sight*, celebrates, as was conventional,
virtue and true love winning over vice and fashionable posturings. It features
a love entanglement similar to that in *Courtship A-la-mode*. It was, if anything,
less successful than Crawford's first play, being performed only once by
Betterton's company.

With these two plays Crawford retired from the theatre but not from
public life; in 1705 he became Historiographer Royal for Scotland. His other
notable publications include three epistolary novels, published together as *The
Unfortunate Duchess* (1700), and a history, *Memoirs of the Affairs of Scotland*
(1706).

Newburgh Hamilton (fl.1715–1760) also wrote two comedies for the
London stage, *The Petticoat-Plotter* and *The Doating Lover; or, The Libertine
Tam'd*, as well as the lyrics of Handel's oratorio *Samson*, based on Milton's
Samson Agonistes. *The Petticoat-Plotter* was first presented at Drury Lane, on
5 June 1712, as an afterpiece to *Macbeth*. It is a pacy and, despite its utter
predictability, an appealing and witty comedy. Isabell loves Truelove but the
match is opposed by her father, Thrifty, who wants her to make a more advan-
tageous match with the aged, but rich, Sir Simon Scrapeall. To foil this plan
Truelove's servant, Plotwell, becomes the Petticoat-Plotter. Disguised as a
Spanish lady, Plotwell enters Thrifty's house where he is assumed to be
Theodosia, Thrifty's late brother's lover. Truelove, too, adopts a new identity,
that of Ananias Scribe, to gain entry to the house and so make off with Isabell,
only to be exposed when the real Scribe arrives. Truelove and Isabell are only
joined when he, and a parson, have themselves delivered into Thrifty's house
inside two trunks. Truelove throws Sir Simon and Nincompoop, a slow-witted
servant, into the street and wins Isabell.

It has been suggested that some of the play's comic business (disguise, con-
cealment and subterfuge) was used by Susanna Centlivre in her 1718 play, *A
Bold Stroke for a Wife*, while William J. Burling, in *A Checklist of Plays and
Entertainments on the London Stage, 1700–1737*, goes so far as to suggest
that Centlivre's work is actually based on Hamilton's. Beyond these comments
the play has received little attention, contextualisation or criticism.

The same might be said of Hamilton's second play, *The Doating Lover; or,*

The Libertine Tam'd, which was premiered at Lincoln's Inn Fields on 23 June 1715. A comedy with a much more sophisticated, not to say more modern, structure than *The Petticoat-Plotter*, *The Doating Lover* shows a real command of the plot conceits, comic techniques and character motifs of the early eighteenth-century stage. The rake, the virtuous and witty young lady, the vain fop, the choleric father and several comic servants feature in a plot of conventional intrigues involving the deception and humiliation of those who oppose true lovers. The main plot, charting the love affair between Lord Gaylove and Cosmelia, is an engaging and vitriolic battle of the sexes. An equally appealing sub-plot, recounting the love of the servants Prate and Decoy, features comic banter as witty and vibrant as their masters'. As expected in comedies of the period, each sex passes mordant comment on the other and age is no guarantee of respect or honour. Hamilton also provides a merry, wildly excessive and ultimately repentant fop, Sir Butterfly, who is infatuated with the heroine Cosmelia but is no match for her superior wit. Butterfly's passion for Cosmelia precipitates his humiliation when, set to seduce her, he is tied helplessly to a chair while she wickedly taunts him as 'a poor Pretender to Foppery and Debauchery, and but a burlesque Image of either Beau or Rake'.

The plot twists of Hamilton's comedies show that he had a keen eye for contemporary theatricalities. Cosmelia, for example, effects the repentance of Gaylove with an elaborate masque in which he comes upon a splendid funeral procession. Enquiring of the mourners he discovers that the casket is for himself. Cosmelia declares to Gaylove that the coffin is there because 'You are dead to Virtue, without which, Life is but Death's Twin-Sister.' The play contains the expected heady mix of high comedy, pious virtue, bald immorality and complicated plottings, neatly encapsulated by Decoy's assertion that 'Stratagems gain Gold and Friends'.

The cross-dressing used effectively in *The Petticoat-Plotter* is heightened in *The Doating Lover* in an elaborate masquerade of gender roles, with Lady Youthful, Decoy and Prate all involved in politic transvestism. This reaches dizzying heights when a cross-dressed Sir Butterfly weds Lady Youthful in strident opposition to the wishes of Cholerick. The play ends with Lady Youthful promising to turn the unreformed Sir Butterfly into a cuckold – the only suitable punishment for such a fop in Restoration comedy.

One of the most successful of the turn-of-the-century London playwrights, Catherine Trotter (1679–1749), later Mrs Cockburn, was born in London of a Scottish family and, after her playwriting career ended, lived in Aberdeen. She enjoyed some success as a literary figure during the reign of George I and was prominent as a writer on ethics.

Trotter's first significant play was a version of *Agnes de Castro*, an adaptation of Aphra Behn's own adaptation of a French novel founded on an event from Portuguese history. It was probably played in late December 1695, when

Trotter was just 17 years old, and was published in 1696. Her second play, *Fatal Friendship*, a verse-tragedy, produced with moderate success at Lincoln's Inn Fields in 1698, is significant because it was anthologised in a two-volume edition of her works by her first biographer, Thomas Birch. Of her subsequent plays, *Love at a Loss; or, Most Votes Carry It* was a comedy produced at Drury Lane in 1700, at Covent Garden in 1701, and later revised (but not produced) as *The Honourable Deceivers or All Right at the Last*. *The Unhappy Penitent*, a verse-tragedy, played at Drury Lane in 1701; and *The Revolution in Sweden*, also a verse-tragedy, was premiered at the Haymarket in 1706.

Trotter's success was such that by 1696 she was already well enough known to be satirised in *The Female Wits* alongside Mary Pix and Delarivière Manley. Her best play, *Fatal Friendship*, should be considered in any analysis of Restoration plays by women, if only because it was produced by Betterton's company with the leads played by his co-managers and starring ladies, Ann Bracegirdle and Elizabeth Barry. Nevertheless, it is probably Trotter's prose writing, in particular *A Defense of the Essay of Humane Understanding*, a response to Locke's theories and other works on moral philosophy, which will secure her lasting reputation. An epistolary novel, *Olinda's Adventures; or, the Amours of a Young Lady* appeared in 1718.

The London theatre world of these Restoration Scottish dramatists was far removed from the politics and morality which so restricted the drama in Scotland. While the brief dramatical careers of Crawford, Hamilton and Trotter are easily swept away in the procession of the more splendid comedies of William Wycherley, Aphra Behn, George Farquhar, Mary Pix and Susanna Centlivre, it is important to recognise that, in 1700 just as much as today, London was an important market for the work of Scottish writers.

'ILLEGITIMATE' THEATRE IN THE FIRST HALF
OF THE CENTURY

The domestic Scottish theatre was a more haphazard, not to say illicit, affair. The Church influenced the development of the Scottish stage more than any other single factor, as Terence Tobin has argued in *Plays by Scots 1660–1800*:

> Of the various elements which explain the poverty of the Scottish stage, religious censure is paramount. While it may seem simplistic to attribute clerical condemnation as the major reason for the precarious position of the drama, the controversy which John Home's *Douglas* provoked in the mid-eighteenth century illustrates the prime importance of religious censorship. And it was not until the late eighteenth century, when the Enlightenment had become sufficiently widespread

to shake theocratic power, that the Kirk ceased to be the 'devil's advocate' of the theatre.[1]

The Church's hostility towards the theatre can be accounted for on a number
of levels. As noted in Chapter 1, from the earliest times drama had been related
to religious observances but these connections were now inconceivable within
a Reformed and Calvinist society. For much of the period secular and religious
politics are either indistinguishable or intractably intertwined and, while both
were legitimate topics of verse, prose and closet drama, it verged on the sacrile-
gious for such topics to reach the stage. The theatre was to be neither encouraged
nor condoned, however indirectly. If real political power was increasingly to
be found in London, the Reformed Church in Scotland was determined to keep
a tight grip on local government and was perennially preoccupied with the
monitoring of licensing arrangements and the censoring of public displays and
entertainments. Robb Lawson expands on this point in *The Story of the Scots
Stage*, arguing that:

> In the face of the ecclesiastical and legislative opposition that existed no
> company of players would risk the financial uncertainty of a visit to
> the Scottish domains. The people, too, fell into a state of indifference in
> regard to the drama. The fear of incurring the displeasure of the Kirk,
> and the inconvenience connected with any breach of civil discipline,
> deterred them from seeking out those pleasures for which they had
> previously striven so zealously.[2]

Strolling companies did occasionally venture into the Scottish capital,
although evidence is sketchy to say the least. It is certain, however, that a company of almost completely anonymous strolling players began a residency in
Edinburgh in 1715. Opposition from the religious authorities was fierce but
the actors seem to have been resident on two separate occasions in the course
of the year, performing, first at Holyrood and later at the Old Magazine House
at the foot of the Canongate, a standard repertory which included *The Beaux
Stratagem, Macbeth, The Inconstant; or, the Way to Win Him, Love for Love*
and *The Spanish Friar*. One of the Presbytery's statements in opposition to
these players indicates the tone they would continually adopt in confronting
theatricalities:

> The presbytery taking to their consideration that the stage hath been
> condemned by diverse ecclesiastical Councels and many eminent
> divines, as a nursery of Impiety and vanity, and considering how much
> it hath been found to corrupt peoples morals; and being informed that

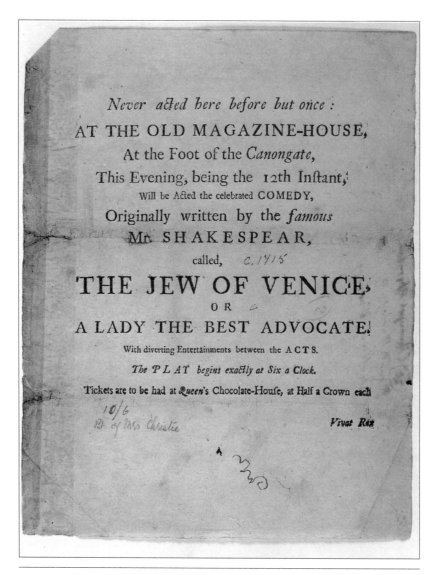

Figure 2.1 Edinburgh playbill c. 1715 for what seems to have been a version of Shakespeare's The Merchant of Venice. *(Edinburgh City Library)*

some comedians have lately come to the bounds of this presbytery, and do act within the precincts of the Abbey to the great offence of many, by trespassing upon morality and those rules of modesty and chastity, which our Holy Religion obligeth all its professours to a strict observance of, therefor the presbytery Recommends to all their members to use all proper and prudent methods to discourage the same. (*Edinburgh Presbytery Records*, 23 March 1715)

The final reference to these pioneering players is an announcement, in the *Scots*

Courant of 16 December 1715, that the company, strengthened by 'some new actors just arrived from England', would give *The Unhappy Favourite; or, The Earl of Essex.*

Although an Irish company had toured to Scotland as early as 1681, at this time most such touring companies were English. The plays they performed were English repertoire pieces which rarely, if ever, contained a Scottish character, except as a rustic figure of fun, in the style of Crawford's Willie Beetlehead or, equally inappropriately, Macbeth.

In the winter of 1726–7 the roguish English actor Anthony Aston (fl.1712–31), a friend of poet and playwright Allan Ramsay, was performing in Skinner's Hall, just off the High Street in Edinburgh. Aston was a remarkable figure, generally credited with being the first professional actor to appear on stage in the American colonies, performing there as early as 1703. He may have been producing drama in Edinburgh from the winter of 1724–5 and certainly he managed a company in Edinburgh consistently from 1726 until he was forced by magistrates and creditors to quit the city.

Initially at least, Aston and his actors were welcomed and supported by the civil authorities and by local society. Allan Ramsay penned a special prologue for Aston to give on the first night of that season:

> Tis I, dear Caledonians, blythsome Tony,
> That oft, last winter, pleas'd the brave and bonny,
> With medley, merry song, and comic scene:
> Your kindness then has brought me here again
> After a circuit round the queen of Isles,
> To gain your friendship and approving smiles.
> Experience bids me hope: – Th[o]' south the Tweed,
> The dastards said, 'He never will succeed![3]

Aston's fortunes changed in the autumn of 1727 when power on the local council shifted and a new provost was elected. Magistrates fined Aston and even locked him out of his hall, claiming that it was unsafe for public meetings. A legal battle commenced when Aston appealed to the Court of Session. He won, but the council entered another writ claiming that, if Aston were permitted to play, an unhealthy and immoral precedent would be set. The Edinburgh Presbytery issued a lengthy *Admonition and Exhortation . . . concerning Stage Plays* to be read from the pulpit of all the churches of the Presbytery:

> The Presbytery taking to their Consideration, That there is lately come into this City a Company of Stage players who are Acting plays within the precincts of it, and have begun, with acting one, which is filled with horrid Swearing, Obscenity, and Expressions of a double Meaning,

tending directly to Corrupt the minds of the Spectators, and to the practice of the Grossest Immoralities . . . The presbytery Judge it their duty,
out of Concern for the Glory of God, the Interest of Religion, and the
good of our Souls, committed to their Charge, plainly to declare their
Sentiments, and to warn all within their Bounds of the danger they incur,
by encouraging or frequenting these plays. (*Edinburgh Presbytery
Records*, 29–30 November 1727)

Aston vehemently denied implications of immorality, reminding the Court that
he had played for George I and his London Court, but the combined opposition of the Presbytery, the bailies and the provost was too great for him.
Although he won an appeal to the Court of Session, the council itself appealed
the decision arguing that such a judgement would create

> a precedent and would open doors, not only for multitudes of players,
> comedians; but at the same time for Merry Andrews, Rope Dancers,
> Tumblers, Leaders of Bears, Munkies and other Shows.

Aston had finally to admit defeat when, on 1 December 1727, Lady Morrison,
who lived below the Skinner's Hall, lodged a complaint that the audience were
in danger of coming through her ceiling. When tradesmen checked the building it did prove to be unsafe.

There were also public demonstrations. On 14 December 1727 the *Caledonian Mercury* recorded that:

> Yesternight an idle giddy mob got up a little below the Guard-house,
> who without the least Shadow of Provocation, insulted several Persons
> of Quality and Distinction, etc, as they were passing the Streets, to see
> the play call'd the *Earl of Essex* acted by Anthony Aston's company of
> comedians.

In the course of this skirmish a flurry of statements was issued both by Aston's
supporters and by his opponents. They give an interesting indication of attitudes to the theatre in the early decades of the eighteenth century. The drama
was described variously as irreligious, immoral and wickedly seductive, or as
improving, and harmlessly diverting. The hard-campaigning opposition was
most sustained and effective. Edinburgh proved itself a determined opponent
to theatre and its personnel. Aston and his company quit the city sometime
after 15 April 1728, leaving unpaid bills.

Within six months of Aston's departure, however, a new company of players
was attempting to woo the capital. If anything they proved less successful than
Aston, lasting only six months. The *Edinburgh Evening Courant* claims that

on 12 March 1729: 'The Scots Company of Comedians, as they call'd themselves, have, all of a Sudden, elopt, without counting with their Creditors.'

In the face both of trenchant opposition from pamphleteers, council and Presbytery, and of evidence, in the failure of yet another company, of uncertain public support, one voice of reasoned determination came to prominence. Allan Ramsay not only wrote the most significant pastoral of the eighteenth century and a strongly worded pamphlet (*Some Hints in Defence of Dramatic Entertainments* (1727 or 1728)) supporting the drama in general and Aston in particular, but achieved the apparently impossible, a regular theatre in Edinburgh.

Ramsay was born on 15 October 1686 at Leadhills, Lanarkshire. Around 1701 he settled in Edinburgh and was apprenticed to a wigmaker. Completing his training he opened his own wigmaker's shop and in 1712 was married. His first piece of theatrical writing, *The Nuptials: a masque on the marriage of his Grace James Duke of Hamilton and Lady Anne Cochrane*, appeared in 1723. Around 1725 Ramsay established Scotland's first circulating library, which he operated from his shop. In 1728 Edinburgh magistrates attempted to close Ramsay's library, which they deemed was contributing to immorality and obscenity among the town's youths.

Although a version of Ramsay's pastoral *The Gentle Shepherd* was first published in 1725, it was not until 22 January 1729 that, revised into a ballad opera, it was performed by pupils of Haddington Grammar School at Taylor's Hall in Edinburgh's Cowgate. Based on two of Ramsay's earlier pastoral poems, 'Patie and Roger' (1720) and 'Jenny and Maggy' (1723), and a song, 'By the delicious warmness of the mouth' (1721), which is incorporated into the entertainment, the play reworks a conventional plot. A lowly shepherd, unaware of his noble birth, falls in love with an equally lowly shepherdess who, eventually, is also revealed to be a gentlewoman. Patie, the gentle shepherd of the title, loves Peggy. Roger, another, richer shepherd, loves Jenny. Simon and Glaud are two local tenants of Sir William Worthy, the long-absent laird. Mause is an old woman, allegedly a witch but merely educated and independent. Elspa is Symon's wife and Madge is Glaud's sister. Bauldy, a hind (farm worker), takes the place of the traditional satyr of classical pastorals.

The play opens with Patie and Peggy about to announce their love. However, Sir William arrives, reveals himself as Patie's father and, opposing his son's match with a peasant girl, insists that he undertake a long journey away from such rustic temptations. The necessary happy ending is achieved when Mause reveals that she knows Peggy to be the daughter of Sir William's sister. Satisfied that Peggy is his son's equal, Sir William gives the lovers his blessing.

While the pastoral is an essentially artificial form, *The Gentle Shepherd* has an unexpected naturalness. Its vibrant, idiomatic diction breathes new life into the constrained neoclassical conventions and the unaffected emotional realism of Ramsay's secondary characters is particularly effective. Thematically it ranges widely, touching on contemporary politics, the aftermath of war, social hierarchies and class, the power of the laird and of the Church, the role of women, and even the presence and fear of the supernatural.

Figure 2.2 Allan Ramsay (1686–1758) poet, playwright and theatre company manager (by his son Allan Ramsay, 1729). (Scottish National Portrait Gallery)

The Gentle Shepherd became the most popular pastoral in eighteenth-century British theatre and its success inspired a host of imitators throughout the century. Among the earliest is Theophilius Cibber's ballad opera *Patie and Peggy; or, the Fair Fondling*, which was played at Drury Lane on 20 April 1730. Others include versions by Cornelius Vanderstop (1777), Thomas Linley (1781), Richard Tickell (1781), Charles Bonner (1783), W. Ward (1785), Andrew Shirrefs (1787), Margaret Turner (1790) and Archibald MacLaren (1811).

Between 1730 and 1736, Ramsay supported a company of actors called the Edinburgh Players. Although based in the capital, this troupe seems also to have toured to Dundee, Montrose, Aberdeen, Newcastle and Scarborough. Ramsay also organised visits of London theatre companies to Edinburgh. But his principal goal was to win for Edinburgh a permanent, legitimate theatre, free from the overt or even covert influence of church and state. Following the demise of the Edinburgh Players, in the summer of 1736 he acquired the Carruber's Close theatre as a more permanent home for a new company. Established around 1715 as a venue for musicians, acrobats, clowns and other strolling performers, it was associated mostly with Signora Violante, an Italian performer and singer. Ramsay's new company, which included some actors from the Edinburgh Players, opened there on 8 November 1736 with productions of *The Recruiting Officer* and *The Virgin Unmask'd*.

Carruber's Close is generally considered to be the first regular theatrical establishment (a venue with its own company committed to producing regular seasons of plays) in Scotland. The prologue spoken by the actor Mr Bridges at the theatre's first night insisted on the venerable social, cultural and, indeed, moral role of the theatre, and took a swipe at its opponents:

> Long has it been the business of the stage
> To mend our manners, and reform the age.
> This task the muse by nature was assign'd,
> Ere Christian light shone in upon the mind;
> Ev'n since these glorious truths to men appear'd,
> Her moral precepts still have been rever'd,
> And when the sacred monitors have fail'd,
> Just satyre from the stage has oft prevailed.
> Tho' some sour criticks full of phlegm and spleen
> Condemn her use as hellish and obscene;
> And from their gloomy thoughts and want of sense,
> Think what diverts the mind gives Heav'n offence.[4]

Despite the venture's promise Ramsay's theatre was closed by the 1737 Licensing Act, passed in the aftermath of *Tom Thumb*, Fielding's bitter satire against the Walpole government. The Act forced the closure of all but the two London houses and theatres in places where the sovereign might temporarily reside. Based on the 1713 'Act for Reducing the Laws relating to Rogues, Vagabonds, Sturdy Beggars, and Vagrants', the new measure clarified the legal definition of 'rogue and vagabond', but went even further in restricting theatrical activities, insisting that any theatre presenting spoken drama had first to be granted a Royal Patent, itself requiring an Act of Parliament. Not only were venues to be licensed but so too were new plays, prologues and epilogues. All texts were to be submitted to the office of the Lord Chamberlain no less than fourteen days in advance of scheduled performance. Offences against any part of the Act incurred a fine of £50. In Scotland the Act was immediately enforced with the authority of the Court of Session. Ramsay took to versification:

> Shall London have its houses twa
> And we be doomed to none ava'?
> Is our metropolis, ance the place
> Where langsyne dwelt the royal race
> Of Fergus, this gate dwindled down
> To a level with ilk clachan town,
> While thus she suffers the subversion
> Of her maist rational diversion?[5]

Ramsay tried to reopen his theatre in August 1738 and again in 1739. Both attempts failed; the latter effort overshadowed by events of January and February 1739 when a touring company of actors attempting to play in Edinburgh in defiance of the Licensing Act was called before the town council and fined £50 each. These players vanished before paying the fine.

Theatre and the drama continued to occupy the minds of Edinburgh society. On 4 April 1739 Lord Glenorchy introduced a bill into Parliament in favour of a licensed Patent theatre for Edinburgh but it was opposed by Edinburgh's magistrates, clergy and University. The Town Council minutes record the bailies' objections to a Patent house:

[The Town Council objected to the] many Inconvencys and mischiefs will arise to This City by Establishing of a play House therein and particularly that the same will occasion expenses such as the Small Extent of the Wealth and Trade of this City cannot well affoord [sic] to bear and that the Manners of the Youth will be in great danger of being corrupted of whom there are great numbers Residing within this City, as being the Seat of the University, and a Place Chiefly frequented for all parts of the Education of Children of Both Sexes, besides the Considerable number of Apprendices in it.

Such local opposition ensured that Glenorchy's bill would fail. However, on 18 December 1739 a group of actors initiated a ruse that was to prove an effective and quite legal subterfuge for theatre in Edinburgh and elsewhere. On that night *The Provok'd Husband* was played free as an afterpiece to a concert. Despite the success of this minor deceit, the shock waves from the Licensing Act and the prosecution of the actors in 1739 endured and it was not until December 1741 that dramatic production returned to Edinburgh on anything resembling a permanent footing, when Thomas Este began a series of concerts and plays at Taylor's Hall, a popular venue for strolling companies. Este was a prolific and effective manager, who won the patronage of the Duke of Hamilton. His company was well respected and drew comparisons with the performers of the London houses.

One of the most influential figures in the development of a professional theatre in Scotland in the eighteenth century was a member of the company established by Este, the actress Sarah Ward. Although little is known about her early life she was probably born in 1727, the daughter of York-based actor Thomas Achurch. She began her theatrical career in the early 1740s at York and married fellow actor and minor playwright Henry Ward (fl. 1734–58) when she was barely 17 years old. Henry Ward was a member of the York company from 1742 to 1744 and is billed, sometimes in his own plays, with Mrs Ward from 1744. Although she certainly had children with Henry Ward (one of her sons, named for her father, Thomas Achurch Ward, married the actress Sarah Hoare) and, even in later life, occasionally appeared on the same bill as him, their match was unconventional in that it did not restrict her from an independent career, or from a tempestuous liaison with the actor West Digges (1720?–86).

Around 1745, Sarah Ward moved to Edinburgh, joining the Taylor's Hall company, which had been led by Este. Following internal disputes the company split into two groups, one led by Ward, the other, by the actor Salmon. Ward's group planned to open a new theatre in the Canongate. With money raised from public subscription and credit from Edinburgh tradesmen and craftsmen they began building their new playhouse. The theatre was being erected without legal sanction and in bold defiance of the Licensing Act; nevertheless, the Covent Garden actor Lacy Ryan laid the foundation stone in August 1746. With only a temporary base available in Edinburgh while the new theatre was being built, Ward led her company to Aberdeen, intending to perform a season there. However, the Aberdeen magistrates, inflamed by the local clergy, forbade them from performing in the city and the company was forced to return to the capital.

On 16 November 1747 the new Canongate Concert Hall opened, with a performance of *Hamlet* under the, by now usual, cover of a musical concert (the theatre was called a 'Concert Hall' as part of the same ruse). The theatre

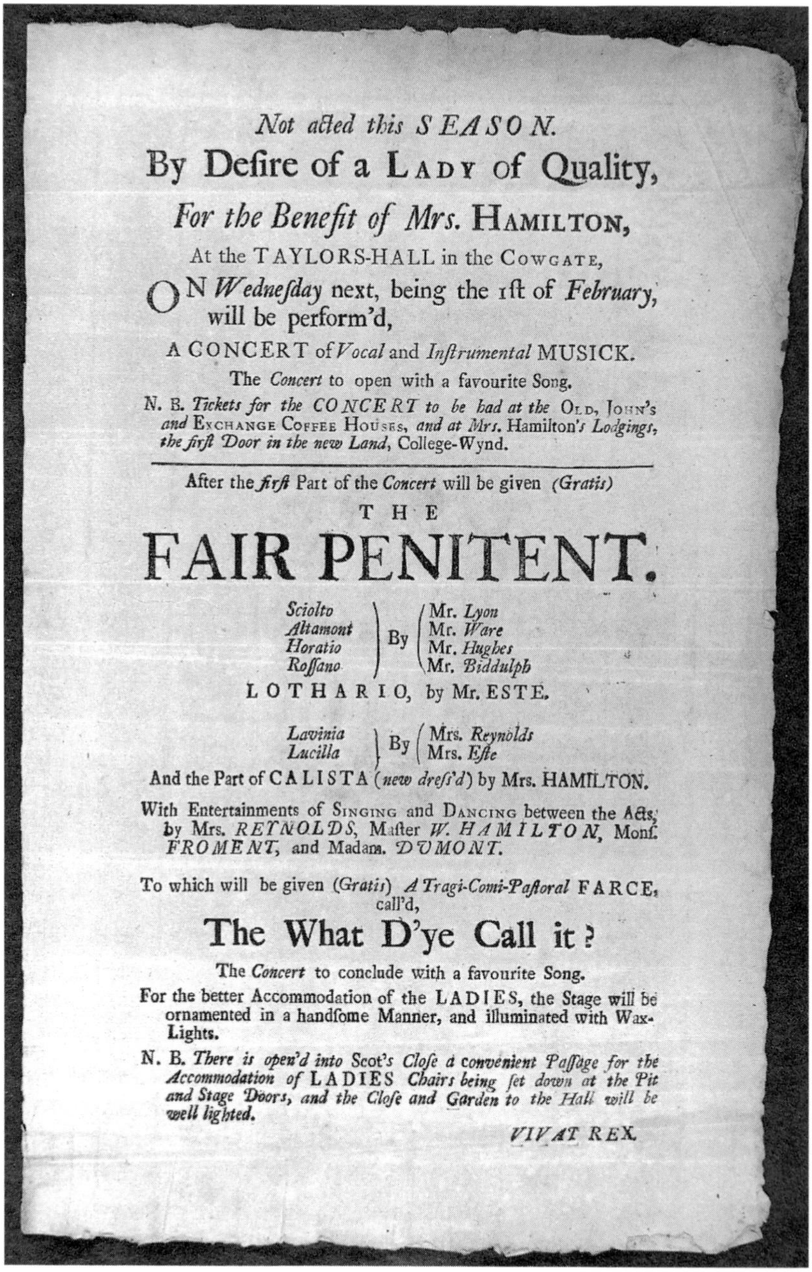

Not acted this SEASON.

By Desire of a LADY of Quality,

For the Benefit of Mrs. HAMILTON,

At the TAYLORS-HALL in the COWGATE,

ON *Wednesday* next, being the 1st of *February,* will be perform'd,

A CONCERT of *Vocal* and *Instrumental* MUSICK.

The *Concert* to open with a favourite Song.

N. B. *Tickets for the* CONCERT *to be had at the* OLD, JOHN's *and* EXCHANGE COFFEE HOUSES, *and at* Mrs. Hamilton's *Lodgings, the first Door in the new Land,* College-Wynd.

After the *first* Part of the *Concert* will be given *(Gratis)*

THE

FAIR PENITENT.

Sciolto		Mr. *Lyon*
Altamont	By	Mr. *Ware*
Horatio		Mr. *Hughes*
Rossano		Mr. *Biddulph*

LOTHARIO, by Mr. ESTE.

| Lavinia | By | Mrs. *Reynolds* |
| Lucilla | | Mrs. *Este* |

And the Part of CALISTA *(new dress'd)* by Mrs. HAMILTON.

With Entertainments of SINGING and DANCING between the Acts, by Mrs. *REYNOLDS,* Master *W. HAMILTON,* Monf. *FROMENT,* and Madam. *DUMONT.*

To which will be given *(Gratis)* *A Tragi-Comi-Pastoral* FARCE, call'd,

The What D'ye Call it ?

The *Concert* to conclude with a favourite Song.

For the better Accommodation of the LADIES, the Stage will be ornamented in a handsome Manner, and illuminated with Wax-Lights.

N. B. *There is open'd into* Scot's *Close a convenient Passage for the Accommodation of* LADIES *Chairs being set down at the Pit and Stage Doors, and the Close and Garden to the Hall will be well lighted.*

VIVAT REX.

Figure 2.3 Playbill for Taylor's Hall in the Cowgate, Edinburgh, showing the ruse of advertising a concert (on 1 February 1744) after which two dramas will be performed 'gratis': The Fair Penitent (by Nicholas Rowe) and The What D'ye Call It? (a 'tragi-comic-pastoral farce' by John Gay). 'For the better Accommodation of the LADIES , the Stage will be ornamented in a handsome Manner, and illuminated with Wax-Lights.' (Edinburgh City Archives)

was situated in an area behind St John's Cross that later became known as Playhouse Close. It was the first building in Scotland constructed solely for theatrical purposes and quickly established itself as the theatrical centre of Edinburgh with a company initially led by Lacy Ryan, Sarah Ward and West Digges. Its success was such that the following year Salmon and his company gave up Taylor's Hall and were reconciled with their former colleagues.

A brief detour here to look at a few years in Sarah Ward's acting career will give some idea of the travels undertaken by many eighteenth-century actors and theatre managers, and give an indication of how Scottish theatre was increasingly part of a larger circuit.

In 1748 Ward began her London career when she joined John Rich's company at Covent Garden. She made her debut as Cordelia and continued in equally prominent roles, quite overshadowing the career of her husband. Mrs Cibber falling ill, David Garrick was keen to secure the services of the young actress, who made her Drury Lane debut in October 1749, playing Cordelia to his Lear. She spent at least the summer season of 1750 with Linnett's company at Bath and Bristol, returning to Drury Lane in the autumn. For the summer season of 1751 she returned to Scotland and made another attempt to tour a company to Aberdeen. Again the local magistrates and clergy refused to license such activities. The company attempted to thwart the authorities by erecting a fit-up theatre outside the city's boundaries, somewhere in the Spittal, but the populace failed to attend the performances in sufficient numbers and the tour collapsed. After another season at Drury Lane (1751–2) Ward returned to Edinburgh with John Lee, another former Drury Lane actor, who, quarrelling with Garrick, had quit the London house to assume management of the Edinburgh theatre. Lee's company, including Digges, Love, Stampier and Ward, attempted another tour, this time to Glasgow, where it met with familiar opposition. A booth theatre was erected against the wall of the Bishop's Palace but religious zealots protested against the players and it was hastily dismantled. It appears that it was during this season that Ward and Digges began their affair, for after Glasgow they progressed together to Liverpool to embark for Cork, where Ward passed the summer season. She joined Thomas Sheridan's Smock Alley company in September making her Dublin debut in November 1752 as Monimia in *The Orphan*. She was a favourite with the Dublin audience and spent three years in the Smock Alley company, interspersed with summer seasons elsewhere in Ireland and Britain. She played at Newcastle from 12 September to 12 December 1753, transferring to Edinburgh until May 1754. She then appeared in Chester until late June, returned to Dublin in October and was with the Belfast company from November until March 1755. The spring of 1755 saw her appear at Waltham Abbey in Essex, in Birmingham in June, then return, by way of Glasgow, to Edinburgh and Lee's company, appearing as Mrs Sullen in *The Stratagem* on 25 November 1755.

In a complicated financial dispute (he had suffered severe losses as a result of tours to Glasgow, Dundee and Newcastle), John Lee lost control of the Edinburgh theatre, spent two months in gaol and finally quit Scotland. A Mr Callender was appointed business manager, and 'artistic policy' came under the control of West Digges, who rejoined the Edinburgh company in September. Ward and Digges were reunited on stage in *Romeo and Juliet* at the Canongate theatre on 28 September 1756, where, on 14 December, she appeared as Lady Randolph to his Norval in the premiere of John Home's *Douglas*. It was to prove one of her most popular and celebrated roles, her reputation in it eclipsed only by the great Sarah Siddons later in the century.

THE CONTROVERSY OVER JOHN HOME'S *DOUGLAS*

The production of the *Douglas*, a verse-tragedy by John Home, a minister of the Church of Scotland, was a watershed of remarkable and unprecedented proportions in eighteenth-century Scottish theatre, and the play itself has a stage history that is virtually continuous from its premiere until the mid nineteenth century. West Digges announced the *Douglas* in the *Edinburgh Courant* and the *Caledonian Mercury* of 4 December 1756:

> A *New Tragedy* called DOUGLAS, written by an ingenious gentleman of this country, is now in rehearsal at the Theatre, and will be performed as speedily as possible. The expectations of the public from the performance are in proportion to the known talent and ability of the Author, whose modest merit would have supposed a Dramatic work, which we think by the concurrent testimony of many gentlemen of taste and literature will be an honour to this country.

Rarely is a first-night audience aware that it is participating in history in the making but, while the significance of the *Douglas* certainly grew as its reputation, and the scandal associated with it, spun out of control, there can be little doubt that everyone in Edinburgh was fully aware that the night of 14 December 1756 at the Canongate theatre was going to be special. A further 'Notice to the Public about *Douglas*' was circulated explicitly suggesting that even members of the clergy would be welcome at the play and that tickets might be had 'at the Lodgings of D– H–, Esq', almost certainly the philosopher David Hume, a close friend of Home and himself intimately involved with the production of the play. Many of Home's literary friends had supported the project, to an extent that some might later have had reason to regret. One early rehearsal featured luminaries of the Scottish Enlightenment: the historian William Robertson read Randolph; David Hume played Glenalvon; Dr Carlyle, Old Norval; John Home, the Douglas; Adam Ferguson, Professor of Moral

Philosophy at the University of Edinburgh and himself a minister, Lady Randolph; and Hugh Blair, minister of the High Kirk, Greyfriars, and later Professor of Rhetoric at the University, Anna; and this before an invited audience, which included the Lords Elibank, Kames, Milton and Monboddo. The rehearsal was deemed all the more scandalous as the venue was Sarah Ward's lodgings.

John Home was born in Leith on 22 September 1722, son of Alexander Home, Leith's town clerk. He was educated at Leith grammar school and the University of Edinburgh, and ordained a minister of the Church of Scotland in 1745. Home completed his first play, *Agis*, in 1749, and offered it to David Garrick in London, only to have it rejected. His second play, *Douglas*, is an altogether more convincing tragedy, well suited to the demands of the eighteenth-century stage and particularly in tune with the patriotic mood of Edinburgh.

Douglas is based on a traditional Scottish legend and ballad 'Gil Morice', a bleak tale of a noble youth's bloody murder by a jealous and wicked stepfather. Home's play revises this material to fit with contemporary social and sexual morality, and to heighten the dramatic tension. In the ballad, Gil Morice is the illegitimate son of Lady Barnard. In the play, Young Norval is the legitimate son of Lady Randolph (originally named Lady Barnet) but his true identity has been concealed, almost by accident. In opposition to her father's wishes and in close secret Lady Randolph marries Lord Douglas and a child is born. Shortly afterwards Douglas dies a hero's death and the baby and his nurse are presumed drowned while escaping to a place of safety. Young Norval joins the Scottish army in an hour of great need and immediately proves a great hero. His identity as Lady Randolph's son is revealed and he then dies, nobly trying to protect her from the jealousy of Lord Douglas and the scheming machinations of his lieutenant, Glenalvon. Distraught, she throws herself from the highest tower of the castle. The play's sentimental and moral tones converge in the predicament of the mother and the nobility of her long-lost son. Actors knew both to be appealing and demanding roles and the piece entered the standard repertoire.

The published play's 'Prologue spoken at Edinburgh' is boldly patriotic, drawing an unembarrassed parallel between classical Athens and the renewed Athens of the North:

> In days of classic fame, when Persia's Lord
> Oppose'd his millions to the Grecian sword,
> Flourish'd the state of Athens, small her store,
> Rugged her soil, and rocky was her shore,
> Like Caledonia's; yet she gain'd a name
> That stands unrivall'd in the rolls of fame.

This nationalist tone was a great novelty, drawing enthusiastic support from the house and comment from the critics. 'Crito' of the *Caledonian Mercury* recorded the reaction of audiences and highlighted the particular contribution the acting of Ward and Digges made to the play's success:

> If the merit of a work could be ascertained by the general approbation it receives during its representation, and the ardour with which all ranks crowd to the Theatre, or the irresistable power it has of drawing tears from every spectator, we might safely pronounce the tragedy of *DOUGLAS* to be one of the most perfect works of genius that any age

Figure 2.4 John Home (1722–1808) author of Douglas *(James Tassie, 1791).* (Scottish National Portrait Gallery)

has produced ... The genius of the author, and the ability of the chief performers seem, by good fortune, to have been formed to illustrate each other in the highest degree; for we will venture to affirm, that as there is no other part that could have so fully shewn Mrs Ward's amazing powers in tragedy, so there is but one actress in Britain who could have performed the part of Lady Barnet as well as she has done, and we are far from certain that there is any actor at all who could have equalled Mr Digges in the character of Douglas.

The novelist Henry Mackenzie, in his biography *An Account of the Life and Writings of John Home*, recorded the affecting nature of the tragedy:

I was present at the representation; the applause was enthusiastic; but a better criterion of its merits was the tears of the audience which the tender part of the drama drew forth unsparingly.

The Rev. Alexander Carlyle, in his *Anecdotes and Characters of the Times*, provides a glimpse of the audience profile of the Edinburgh theatre in relation to *Douglas*. He recalls how, when houses were falling, Digges turned to him for advice:

Digges rode out one forenoon to me Saying, That he had come by Mr Home's Desire to Inform me, that all the Town had seen the Play, and that it could run no Longer, unless some Contrivance was fallen upon to make the Lower Order of Tradesmen and apprentices come to the Playhouse ... I Drew up what I Entitled, A full and True History of the Bloody Tragedy of Douglas, as it is now to be seen acting at the Theatre in the Cannongate. This was cried about the Streets Next Day, and fill'd the House for 2 nights more.

While *Douglas* itself has many strengths and is of some literary interest, the circumstances around its reception render it extraordinary. In Alexander Carlyle's version of the story:

The Play had unbounded Success for a Great Many Nights in Edinr. and was attended by all of the Literati, and most of the Judges, who, except one or two, had not been in use to attend the Theatre. The Town in genl. was in an uproar of Exultation, That a Scotchman had written a Tragedy of the First Rate, and that its Merit was first Submitted to their Judgement. There were a few Opposers however among those who pretended to Taste and Literature, who Endeavour'd to Cry Down the Performance in Libellous Pamphlets and Ballads (for they Durst not

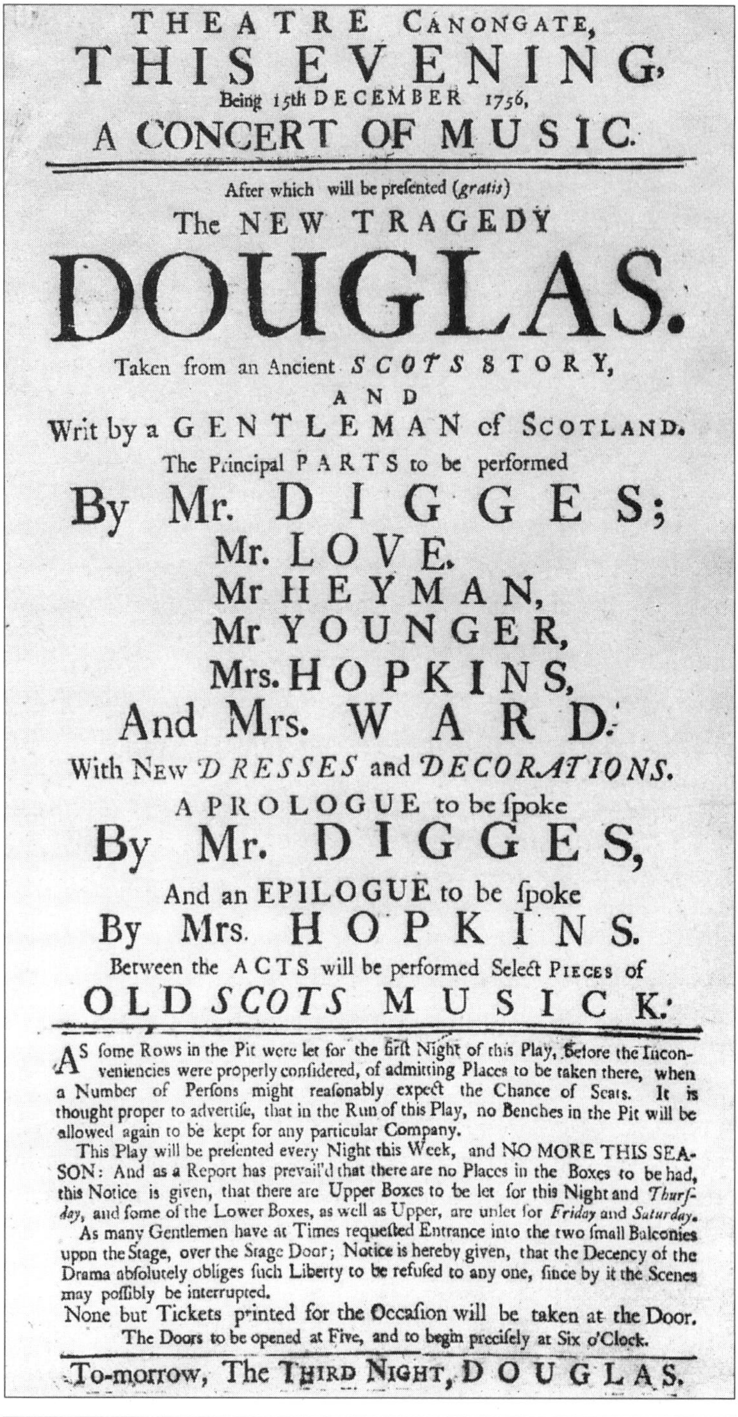

THEATRE CANONGATE,
THIS EVENING,
Being 15th DECEMBER 1756,
A CONCERT OF MUSIC.

After which will be prefented (*gratis*)

The NEW TRAGEDY

DOUGLAS.

Taken from an Ancient *SCOTS STORY*,
AND
Writ by a GENTLEMAN of SCOTLAND.

The Principal PARTS to be performed

By Mr. DIGGES;
Mr. LOVE,
Mr HEYMAN,
Mr YOUNGER,
Mrs. HOPKINS,
And Mrs. WARD.

With NEW *DRESSES* and *DECORATIONS*.

A PROLOGUE to be fpoke

By Mr. DIGGES,

And an EPILOGUE to be fpoke

By Mrs. HOPKINS.

Between the ACTS will be performed Select PIECES of

OLD *SCOTS* MUSICK.

AS fome Rows in the Pit were let for the firft Night of this Play, before the Inconveniencies were properly confidered, of admitting Places to be taken there, when a Number of Perfons might reafonably expect the Chance of Seats. It is thought proper to advertife, that in the Run of this Play, no Benches in the Pit will be allowed again to be kept for any particular Company.

This Play will be prefented every Night this Week, and NO MORE THIS SEASON: And as a Report has prevail'd that there are no Places in the Boxes to be had, this Notice is given, that there are Upper Boxes to be let for this Night and *Thurfday*, and fome of the Lower Boxes, as well as Upper, are unlet for *Friday* and *Saturday*.

As many Gentlemen have at Times requefted Entrance into the two fmall Balconies upon the Stage, over the Stage Door; Notice is hereby given, that the Decency of the Drama abfolutely obliges fuch Liberty to be refufed to any one, fince by it the Scenes may poffibly be interrupted.

None but Tickets printed for the Occafion will be taken at the Door.

The Doors to be opened at Five, and to begin precifely at Six o'Clock.

To-morrow, The THIRD NIGHT, DOUGLAS.

Figure 2.5 Playbill for second night of John Home's Douglas *at the Canongate Theatre, Edinburgh, 15 December 1756. (Scottish Theatre Archive)*

to oppose it in the Theatre itself) . . . The High Flying Set, were unanimous against it, as they thought it a sin for a Clergyman to write any Play, Let it be ever so Moral in its Tendency . . . The Zeal and Violence of the Presbytery of Edinr., who had made Enactments, and Declarations to be read in the Pulpit, provok'd me to Write this Pamphlet [*An Argument to Prove that the Tragedy of Douglas, Ought to be Publickly Burnt by the Hands of the Hangman* (1757)], which, in the Ironical Manner of Swift, Contain'd a Severe Satire on all our Opponents . . . This Pamphlet had a Great Effect, by Elating our Friends, and perhaps more in exasperating our Enemies. Which was by no Means Soften'd by Ld. Elibank and David Hume &c. Running about and Crying it up as the first performance the World had seen for half a Century.

Just two weeks after the premiere of the play the Presbytery of Edinburgh met and took the opportunity to begin proceedings against those connected with the *Douglas*:

A motion was made by one of the Members . . . that great offence had been lately given in this City by some of our Brethren, particularly by Mr John Hume [sic] Minister of Atholstonefoord in the presbytery of Haddington who had composed a Tragedy called Douglas and given it to the Stage players to be publickly acted by them in the head of the Cannongate, and that Mr Hume himself was often present at the acting there of.

The Presbytery minutes then list four other ministers known to have attended the play and record agreements to write to their presbyteries informing them of their ministers' wrongdoings and to set about drawing up a further 'Admonition and Exhortation' declaring playhouses immoral places. At a Presbytery meeting on 5 January 1757 the *Admonition*, having been prepared by a subcommittee, was approved and a further minister, Mr Thomas Whyte of Liberton, was accused of attending the play. The *Admonition* was to be read from pulpits on Sunday 30 January; it was also published and so reached a wider public. It made the position of the Presbytery clear:

The Presbytery taking into their serious Consideration the declining State of Religion, the open Profanation of the Lord's Day, the Contempt of public Worship, the growing Luxury and Levity of the present Age; in which so many seem Lovers of Pleasure, more than Lovers of God: And being particularly affected with the UNPRECEDENTED COUNTENANCE given of late to the Playhouse in this place, when the State of the Nation, and the Circumstances of the Poor, make such hurtful

Entertainments still more pernicious; judged it their indispensable Duty to express, in the most open and solemn Manner, the deep Concern they feel on this Occasion.

The Opinion which the Christian Church has always entertained of Stage Plays and Players, as prejudicial to the Interests of Religion and Morality, is well known; and the fatal Influence which they commonly have on the far greater Part of Mankind, particular the younger Sort, is too obvious to be called in question.

To enumerate how many Servants, Apprentices, and Students in different Branches of Literature, in this City and Suburbs, have been seduced from their proper Business by attending the Stage, would be a painful, disagreeable Talk.

They go on to catalogue the Presbytery's opposition to theatricals in Edinburgh in 1727, their support of the 1737 Licensing Act and their awareness of the ruse affected by the players in eluding the letter of the law 'by changing the Name of PLAYHOUSE into that of CONCERT HALL'. They continue:

This Presbytery, warmed with just Concern for the Good of Souls, do, in the Fear of god, WARN, EXHORT, and OBTEST, all within their Bounds, as they regard the Glory of God, the Credit of our holy Religion, and their own Welfare, to walk worthy of the Vocation wherewith they are called, by shewing a sacred Regard to the Lord's Day, and all the Ordinances of divine Institution; and by discouraging in their respective Sphere, the illegal and dangerous Entertainments of the Stage.

The Presbytery would plead with ALL in Authority, with TEACHERS of youth, PARENTS and MASTERS of Families, to restrain, by every habile Method, such as are under the influence, from frequenting these Seminaries of Folly and Vice. They would particularly beseech the younger Part of their Flock, to beware, lest, by Example, or from a Foolish Desire of appearing in the fashionable World, they be misled into such pernicious Snares; Snares which must necessarily retard, if not entirely mar that Progress in the respective Parts of their Education, on which their future Usefulness and Success depend. And, lastly, they would intreat and obtest Persons of all Ranks and Conditions, that, instead of contributing to the growing Licentiousness of the Age, they may distinguish themselves by shining as Lights in the World, being blameless and harmless, the Sons of God, without Rebuke.[6]

In such a context ministers who had attended performances of the *Douglas* were called to answer for their immoral behaviour. The Presbytery Records note that Mr White of Liberton duly confessed but added that he 'was very Sorry that he had been there at all, that he little considered that it might give offence to the presby: or any other good people, otherwise he would never have gone'. The Presbytery suspended the contrite minister for several weeks. More significantly they had issued a clear and unambiguous manifesto against the theatre and its increasing popularity. However, in her study of eighteenth-century theatre in Edinburgh Mary Susan Carlson has pointed out that 'there is no mention of *Douglas* in the town council's records', and this despite the magistrates' usual interventionist interest in the theatre life of their community.[7] It might not be overstating the point to suggest that the civil authorities were more or less resigned to the development of the theatre, while the religious authorities were determined to stage a final pitched-battle against the increasing irresistibility of theatrical entertainments.

The Presbytery's 'strong-hand tactics' resulted in a general backlash. The overt criticisms of the theatre, of the players, of audiences, and of otherwise respected members of the community like Home, Carlyle and, no doubt, the Reverend Mr Whyte and his theatre-going colleagues, inspired not outraged condemnation but widespread sympathy and encouragement for the offenders. It proved something of a catalyst in the general acceptance and rising respectability of the theatre. In his memoirs, *My Own Life and Times 1741–1814*, Thomas Somerville describes this quite clearly:

> The debates on the question of the unlawfulness of stage-plays, and the immoral effects of attending them, produced many interesting and eloquent speeches, both in the Synod of Lothian and Tweeddale, and in the General Assembly of 1757. The lay members of the Assembly – among whom were Lord Alemoor, Sir John Dalrymple, and Mr Wedderburn, – and the ablest of the moderator clergy, defending the conduct of the ministers who had been present at the acting of 'Douglas', some of them even going so far as to recommend the theatre as a school of moral improvement. It happened about the same time, that performers, of both sexes, of merit far superior to any who had before appeared, were introduced on the Edinburgh stage, making it the fashionable resort of public amusement; and as the clergy ceased to inveigh against this indulgence, the scandal of attending the playhouse was soon entirely done away with.

The Rev. Alexander Carlyle, who was himself persecuted for having attended the theatre and keeping company with the actors, wrote in his *Anecdotes and Characters of the Times* that:

> Altho' the Clergy in Edinr. and its Neighbourhood had abstain'd from

the Theatre, because it Gave Offence, yet the more Remote Clergymen when Occasionally in Town, had almost universally attended the Playhouse. And now that the Subject had been so Sollemnly discuss'd, and all men were convinc'd, that the violent proceedings they had witness'd were the Effects of Bigotry, or Jealousy, mixed with Party Spirit and Cabal, The More Distant Clergy Return'd to their usual amusement in the Theatre, when Occasionally in Town.

To this he added a famous anecdote, which suggests the tremendous changes the Church of Scotland underwent in the era after the *Douglas* scandal:

> It is Remarkable, that in the year 1784, when the Great Actress Mrs Siddons 1st appeared in Edinr. During the Sitting of the Genl. Assembly, That Court was oblig'd to fix all its Important Business for the Alternate Days when she Did not Act, as all the Younger Members Clergy as well as Layity, took their Stations in the Theatre on Those Days by 3 in the afternoon.

The outcry over *Douglas*, at times angry and bitter, revealed much of the prejudice and hypocrisy of the conservative forces in the Church and confirmed the dominance of the rising Moderates typified by Carlyle and his theatre-going colleagues. The Presbytery of Edinburgh never again attempted to intervene in the theatrical or cultural life of the capital. Indeed, the status of the theatre in Edinburgh was assured by the scandal and the Scottish theatre grew in popularity from that time.

As to its influence in inspiring an indigenous drama, the achievements of the *Douglas* are moderate. Home was not particularly interested in success in Edinburgh, what he wanted was a career on the London stage. In 1749 his first play had been rejected by Garrick, who also rejected his second play. It was only after Home had tried to get *Douglas* staged in London that he even offered it to Digges and Ward at the Canongate. Despite this early, local support by the Edinburgh house and the successful production they delivered, Home took all his subsequent dramas – *The Siege of Aquileia*, *The Fatal Discovery*, *Alonzo* and *Alfred* – to the London Patent houses rather than offering them first to the Canongate theatre. It still seemed impossible that an aspiring Scottish playwright would want to work for any but the London theatres. In a broader context, however, *Douglas* opened the theatre to a new section of the Edinburgh population and demonstrated the possibility of dramatising Scotland's stories on stage. It also hastened the decline of the Church's influence on theatre in Scotland.

La. Ran. Eternal providence ! What is thy name?
My name is Norval: and my name he bears.

Douglas

Figure 2.6 Mrs Wood, Mrs Siddons and Mr Sutherland in Douglas, *Theatre Royal, Edinburgh, 1784 (John Kay, 1784).* (Scottish Theatre Archive)

OTHER MID-CENTURY THEATRE ACTIVITY

The actress Sarah Ward, so successful as Lady Randolph, stayed on in Edinburgh until May 1758 when she left to appear in Newcastle and Liverpool. This period saw the abrupt disintegration of her relationship with Digges, who was forced to relinquish control of the theatre to Callender and his associates. Callender in turn lost control of the Edinburgh theatre to David Beat (or Beatt or Beatts or Bates), previously manger of the theatre in Newcastle.

Under Beat's management another Scottish play of some interest was produced. *The Coquettes; or, the Gallant in the Closet*, a reworking, by Eleonore Cathcart, the Lady Houston, of a play by Thomas Corneille, was played on 10 February 1759. Its production was primarily due to the efforts of her cousin, James Boswell, then a student at Edinburgh University. Boswell saw the play through rehearsals, penned a prologue and, when the production failed and its true author refused to acknowledge it, took responsibility for its authorship.

In Edinburgh, Beat, with Dawson as financial manger, formed a new company, including the actor and playwright Samuel Foote. When Callender left Edinburgh, Love entered into management with Beat. Digges and Ward were contracted by Beat to perform at the Newcastle and Edinburgh theatres. However, securing a contract with John Rich's Covent Garden company, Ward transferred to London. Upon Digges return to Edinburgh (on 8 November 1759) a vitriolic paper war was waged between the actor and the manager, who refused to engage Digges. Eventually, from 15 December, Digges was employed, although the engagement was somewhat short-lived; in 1760 he returned to Dublin where he appeared in the *Douglas* with Ward.

This season is of particular interest for a number of reasons. First, the Digges–Beat paper war signals the interest the public had developed in the stage and its characters. Second, it is the subject of perhaps the first sustained account of the theatre in Scotland, *A View of the Edinburgh Theatre During the Summer Season, 1759*. This invaluable work is generally attributed to James Boswell, despite the fact that the first edition gives the author merely as 'A Society of Gentlemen'. The book is dedicated to Boswell's favoured actor, West Digges:

> As to your *private Character*, into whatever Scenes of Folly and Impru-
> dence the World may imagine you have been hurried, through a too
> great Gaiety and Easiness of Disposition; yet, Sir, allow me to say, with-
> out Flattery, that if they know your many amiable Qualifications as
> well as I do, they would look upon your imperfections with the most
> favourable Eye; they would pardon, excuse and forget them.

Although Digges may have continued to enjoy Boswell's support, the actor's relationship with his most popular co-star, Sarah Ward, always stormy, was about to end. Around this time Digges seems to have met the rising star of George Anne Bellamy (1731?–88), with whom he began a new affair. Digges and Bellamy subsequently joined Beat's company in 1762 and Bellamy made her Edinburgh debut as the heroine in James Thomson's *Tancred and Sigismunda* on 2 May, going on to play Estifania in *Rule a Wife*. The *Edinburgh Courant* of 8 May was enthusiastic:

> The expectation of the public was never so highly raised, nor its plea-
> sures so truly gratified as they have been for some nights at the Theatre.
> The house has been generously filled by five o'clock, and crowds turned
> away for want of room.

Tancred and Sigismunda is important to the history of eighteenth-century Scottish theatre. Along with *The Gentle Shepherd* and *Douglas*, it became one of the century's most popular Scottish plays. It was revived by theatres in London and Scotland throughout the eighteenth and early nineteenth centuries and translated into both French and German.

James Thomson (1700–48) was both poet and playwright. As a poet he is notable for his collection of long poems *The Seasons*. His first theatrical success was *Sophonsiba*, which premiered at Drury Lane on 28 February 1730 and ran for ten performances. An allegory of contemporary British politics, showing Carthage (Britain) threatened by Rome (France), it was dedicated to Queen Caroline and, pointedly, featured a heroine active in the defence of her own country. Its overemphatic tone and rhetorical insistence drew parodic imitations which shocked the fledgling dramatist:

> This T[ragedy] raised such expectation, that every Rehearsal was dignified with a splendid audience, collected to anticipate the delight, which was preparing for the publick; it was observed however that nobody was much affected and that the company rose as from a moral lecture – the play has one feeble line – 'Oh Sophonsiba, Sophonsiba Oh!' – this gave occasion to a waggish parody 'Oh Jemmy Thomson, Jemmy Thomson Oh!', which for a while echoed through the town and then [was] burlesqued by Fielding in Tom Thumb.[8]

It was not until 6 April 1738 that Thomson's second play, *Agamemnon*, was premiered, also at Drury Lane, and also achieving a run of ten nights. By dedicating *Agamemnon* to Augusta, Princess of Wales, the playwright once more encouraged an allegorical reading of his work: Orestes suggesting Frederick, Prince of Wales; Clytemnestra, Queen Caroline; and Aegisthus, Robert Walpole. Such correspondences continued in Thomson's most controversial play, *Edward and Eleonore*, a tragedy set against a crusade and concerning Edward I, his consort, and several enemies. The Lord Chamberlain refused to permit the performance of *Edward and Eleonore* and although published it was never produced. Thomson then collaborated with fellow Scot, and already successful playwright, David Mallet (also known as Malloch), on *The Masque of Alfred*, played at Cliveden on 1 August 1740 (and now remembered for the song 'Rule Britannia').

Thomson's next play was *Tancred and Sigismunda*, undoubtedly his most successful. Set in Sicily, it is a melodramatic tale of true love denied by jealousy and ambition. Tancred is tricked by his guardian, the Lord Chancellor Siffredi, into marrying Constantia, sister of the dead king, despite the fact that he loves Sigismunda, Siffredi's daughter. Believing herself abandoned, Sigismunda agrees to marry Osmond, the Lord Constable, who duly murders his young bride and is himself killed by Tancred. Terence Tobin, in *Plays by Scots 1660–1800*, is cautiously enthusiatic about *Tancred and Sigismunda* arguing that:

Figure 2.7 James Thomson (1700–48) poet and playwright (John Vanderbank, 1726). (Scottish National Portrait Gallery)

The emphasis upon the sensational reduces the neo-classical coldness. The characters are less frigid than [his] previous heroes and heroines . . . Even in Thomson's most melodramatic play there is aloofness which results from exalted language and thematic priorities. Thomson valued philosophical expression above psychological motivation.[9]

Thomson's last play, *Coriolanus*, was premiered, posthumously, at Covent Garden on 13 July 1749 but did not achieve the success of *Tancred and Sigismunda*.

Mrs Bellamy, then, was being particularly politic in choosing *Tancred and*

Sigismunda for her first Edinburgh appearance in 1762. Not only was it a popular favourite but it had been written by a Scot.

Bellamy's first Scottish season ended when she played the title role in *Cleone* for her benefit night on 22 May (actors kept the profits after expenses on their benefit nights). The Edinburgh theatre's season ended on 29 May with *The Beggar's Opera* played for Digges's benefit. As James C. Dibdin noted in *The Annals of the Edinburgh Stage*:

> The long summer recess now set in, and it would have been strange indeed if an even less restless and enterprising mind than that of Mrs Bellamy had not turned its attention to the hitherto little-explored field of action that Glasgow offered. The city was, in fact, far behind Edinburgh in the matter of polite entertainments and, until the year under notice [1762], had not possessed anything approaching the dignity of a regular theatrical establishment.[10]

Four or five rich Glasgow gentlemen had decided to build and equip a simple theatre, to be managed by Beat and Love, at Alston Street in Grahamston just outside the city boundary, for the specific purpose of engaging the young star. The newly constructed theatre, along with Mrs Bellamy's wardrobe and properties, was partially destroyed by a fire set by religious fanatics on the very eve of her debut. Nevertheless, Mrs Bellamy was determined to fulfil her contract and satisfy her devoted fans. She appeared in *The Citizen* and the farce *The Mock Doctor* on a hastily repaired and temporary stage with costumes and properties lent by Glasgow's fashionable society. The venture was successful, indicating a developing appetite in Glasgow for theatrical entertainments. Bellamy was diplomatic in nurturing this. In her six-volume autobiography, *An Apology for the Life of George Anne Bellamy* (1785), she records that she was careful to include something 'Scottish' in her programme:

> Whilst I was at Edinburgh, I had prevailed upon a gentleman, who was possessed of some talents, to compose a little piece from the celebrated poem of Ossian; and I appeared in the character of Commela, there, with great success. But at Glasgow the applause I received was beyond all bounds. This little piece alone, tacked to an indifferent comedy, would fill the house, so that it was crowded every night . . .
>
> 'Macbeth' and 'Douglas' were much called for; but these pieces could not be performed, till clothes proper for appearing in them were made and brought from Edinburgh.

The Edinburgh theatre reopened on 4 September and Bellamy returned to lead the company along with one 'Mr Bellamy', that is, West Digges. In January

1764, with debts mounting, Digges was forced to quit Edinburgh. Tate Wilkinson (1739–1803) stepped in as leading man, was offered a two-month contract, and made his Edinburgh debut in *The Minor* on 13 February. Mrs Bellamy quit the Edinburgh theatre on 30 June 1764 and played another summer season in Glasgow before heading to England, appearing as Cleone at Covent Garden on 7 December 1764.

With Bellamy's exit from Scottish theatre, it is appropriate to complete both her story and that of Sarah Ward, the two actresses of particular significance in the story of eighteenth-century Scottish theatre. After twelve seasons at Covent Garden, Sarah Ward returned to Edinburgh for her last short season in Scotland in 1763. She died on 9 March 1771 at the age of 44. George Anne Bellamy continued at Covent Garden for another six years, earning slightly less than she had at the peak of her career. She was not retained at Covent Garden for the season 1770–1 but went into professional and social retirement.

In these middle decades of the century theatre in Edinburgh won a permanent footing, was increasingly and popularly accepted, and began to develop a strong and particular identity within the complex infrastructure of British theatre culture. The stage was set for the final push towards winning for Scotland its first letters of Patent.

LEGITIMACY ACHIEVED – EDINBURGH GRANTED A THEATRE PATENT

In the twenty years between its establishment in 1747 and the award of the Patent in 1767, control of the Edinburgh playhouse, known as the 'New Concert Hall' or the 'Canongate Theatre', in Skinner's Close, passed through a dizzying number of hands. Through Sarah Ward's early ambition, John Lee's reforming control, West Digges's periods as manager, Beat's tenure, Dawson's supervision, Tate Wilkinson's temporary stewardship and Samuel Foote's curtailed authority, the Edinburgh playhouse was at the centre of Edinburgh society and culture. None of the managements, however, was able to boast the legitimacy of the Patent and this, the final seal of social and cultural respectability, must sometimes have seemed an elusive grail. The award of a Patent was hastened less by theatrical success or lobbying by the Edinburgh literati than by architect James Craig's ambitious plans for the New Town. The Act of Parliament granting the city of Edinburgh the right to extend its boundary and build its modern neoclassical annexe also included a paragraph which would finally grant the city a Patent house.

The Patent was won by David Ross (1728–90) who was born in London of a Ross-shire family. Ross's acting career began at Smock Alley, Dublin, in 1749, matured under Garrick at Drury Lane (1751–7) and flourished at Covent Garden, where, in the 1760s, he began to venture into management during the closed summer season. Ross took companies to Manchester (1762 and 1763) and Edinburgh (1765) before becoming manager of the Edinburgh Theatre Royal. His appointment was not unopposed, particularly by the former managers Lee and Stayley, and something of a paper war ensued. Ross secured the Patent at a rental of £400 per annum and the first wholly legitimate play produced at Edinburgh's first Theatre Royal (the refitted Canongate Concert Hall) was played on 9 December 1767. The play was *The Earl of Essex* and James Boswell wrote a suitably patriotic prologue to be given by Ross:

> Scotland for learning and for arms renown'd
> In ancient annals, is with lustre crown'd,
> And still she shares whate'er the world can yield,
> Of lettered fame, or glory in the field:
> In every distant clime Great Britain knows,
> The Thistle springs promiscuous with the Rose.
> While in all points with other lands she vied,
> The Stage alone to Scotland was denied:
> Mistaken zeal, in times of darkness bred,
> O'er the best minds its gloomy vapours spread;
> Taste and religion were suppos'd at strife,
> And 'twas a sin – to view this glass of life!
>
> [. . .]
>
> This night the lov'd George's free enlighten'd age
> Bids Royal favour ev'ry bosom cheers;
> The Drama now with dignity appears.[11]

Three months later (on 16 March 1768) Ross laid the cornerstone of the new Edinburgh Theatre Royal in Shakespeare Square, at the east end of Princes' Street (now gone, Shakespeare Square was opposite Register House). Despite some opposition from religious quarters, the new theatre opened on 9 January 1769 with a performance of *The Conscious Lovers*. The construction programme was recklessly ambitious and Ross was plagued by debts. To make the situation worse, his company was considered inferior. Lee Lewes wrote in his autobiography *The Memoirs of Charles Lee Lewes* (1805) that:

Ross made no great stir to engage performers, but his perpetually drunken prompter, Heartley, kept on writing letters of proposed engagements to people, who regarded his letters, as they deserved, with contempt.

In the summer season of 1770 Ross joined Samuel Foote's Haymarket company in London and lost no time in completing a deal in which Foote (1721–77) would lease the Edinburgh Theatre Royal for a three-year period at a fee of 500 guineas per year. Foote planned to transfer his existing company, based at the Haymarket, a venue only licensed for the summer months when

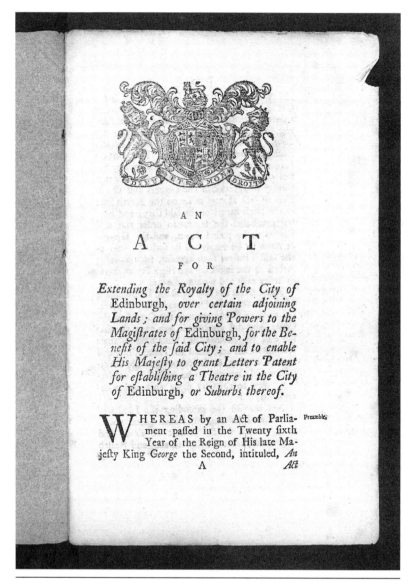

Figure 2.8 (above and opposite) Act of 1767 granting 'Letters Patent for establishing a Theatre in the City of Edinburgh'. (Edinburgh City Archives)

Covent Garden and Drury Lane were closed, to Edinburgh for the autumn/ winter season of 1770. Foote and his company opened at Edinburgh on 17 November with *The Commissary* and *The Lying Valet* while Ross remained in London and rejoined the Covent Garden company. Foote's scheme, to all appearances sound, was not successful enough to be repeated. Certainly Foote's company was large and highly paid and the new theatre only took £140, but his own stated view was that 'By the last advice from Scotland, the balance in my favour was £1022.6.3 which . . . closes the account.'

Foote sold his lease, at some loss, to West Digges, who opened as licensee on 23 November 1771. The following year Digges gained a partner in another actor, John Bland. During this period of tenure, in 1773 Digges simultaneously attempted to manage a season at the Glasgow theatre but found himself stretched too thinly and management of the Glasgow house passed to Ross. On 8 March 1773, during Digges's tenure, the Edinburgh Theatre Royal staged Henry Mackenzie's *The Prince of Tunis*, the first play written by a Scot to be staged there.

Believing her lover, the noble Arassid, dead, Zulima marries the powerful Barbarossa. Heli, one of Barbarossa's lieutenants, tells Zulima that Arassid is alive, but she then hears that he has died at Barbarossa's hand. Vowing

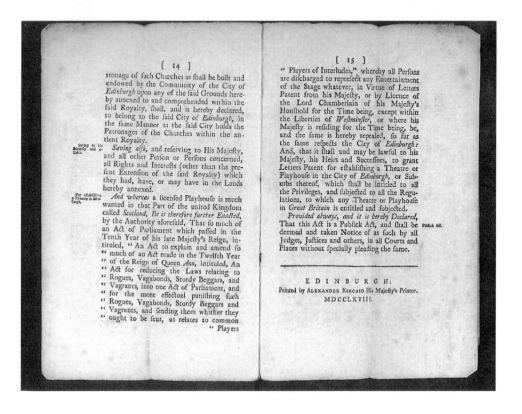

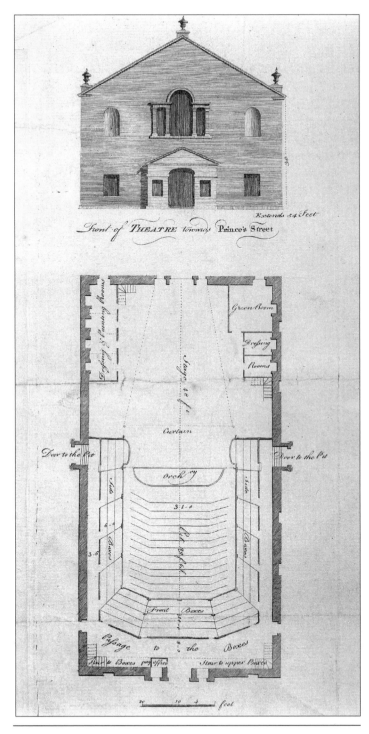

Figure 2.9 Plan of 1767/8 showing proposed internal layout and front elevation of Theatre Royal to be built in Shakespeare Square, Edinburgh. (Edinburgh City Library)

vengeance she sends poison to Barbarossa. In fact Arassid is alive and is re-united with his lover. In a tragic twist Zulima discovers that Heli is her long-lost father and that he has taken the poison meant for Barbarossa. In despair she takes her own life. Seeing the dying Zulima, Barbarossa falls into madness. The plot may sound the stuff of conventional melodrama but contemporary reviewers were enthusiastic about Mackenzie's play. The *Edinburgh Courant* of 9 March 1773 said:

> The play was received with very great applause. It is many years since a new play has been ushered into the world at our Theatre. It has been generally allowed that dramatic genius has been on the decline for several years in Great Britain, and we must give our assent to this opinion. We may affirm that if the testimony of a genteel and crowded audience may be credited, *The Prince of Tunis* will hold a distinguished rank among modern Tragedies. The fable is interesting, and the language

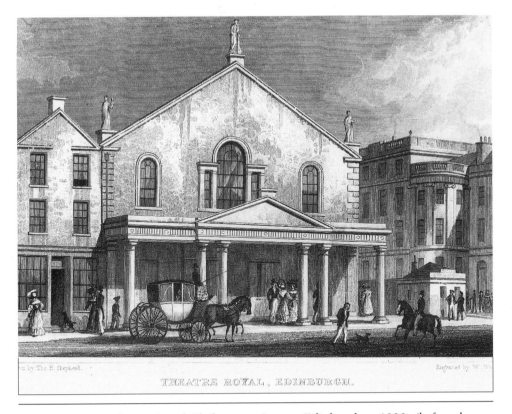

THEATRE ROYAL, EDINBURGH.

Figure 2.10 Theatre Royal, Shakespeare Square, Edinburgh, c. 1820s (before the front was remodelled in 1828). (Crown Copyright: Royal Commission on the Ancient and Historical Monuments of Scotland)

poetical, the sentiment just, and the catastrophe affecting. The play upon the whole was extremely well acted. Mrs Yates' powers were called forth and shone conspicuously in the unfortunate Zorlima [sic], and the unhappy fate of the virtuous Heli was fairly represented by Mr Digges. When the curtain draws up the audience are surprised with a most picturesque scene, when Mrs Yates appears as the Genius of Scotland, and speaks an excellent prologue.

However, in Dibdin's words, *The Prince of Tunis* was 'momentarily successful [but] never obtained a hold on the public'.[12] The play is too much a product of its own theatrical moment to have anything resembling an enduring stage history. It reads like an extended exercise in rhetoric rather than a drama and Terence Tobin is accurate in his criticism that 'The characters speak at, rather than to, each other in dialogue strewn with archaisms, similes and figures of speech that masquerade as aphoristic wisdom'.[13]

The Prince of Tunis was the first, but not the only one, of Mackenzie's plays to be produced. *The Shipwreck; or, Fatal Curiosity*, an adaptation of a tragedy by George Lillo, played for one night only at Covent Garden on 10 February 1784, and *Force of Fashion*, his first comedy, was premiered at the same house on 5 December 1789. Other plays, *The Spanish Father* and *Virginia; or, The Roman Father*, were published but not produced. *The Spanish Father* was rejected by Garrick as 'too horrid for the stage', containing as it does a filicide. *Virginia* was a juvenile piece, originally written in 1761 when Mackenzie was 16 years old, then rewritten and published privately in 1812 for distribution among friends.

At the Theatre Royal, debt haunted West Digges, just as it had Ross and Foote. On 25 January 1777 Digges was forced to quit the theatre. He voluntarily entered debtors' gaol but soon fled and 'accompanied by another man's wife set off for pastures new'. David Ross then attempted to sue Samuel Foote to recover two years' rent. On 26 May 1774 the case was found in Ross's favour. Foote must have rued the day he decided to move to Edinburgh. Tate Wilkinson again stepped in as leading man, performing between 15 February and 3 March 1777. Elizabeth Baker (née Clendon, later Mrs David Lionel Erskine Baker), with whom, in 1766, Sarah Ward had disputed over precedence in the Edinburgh theatre's billings, just missed out on becoming the second woman to adopt a managerial role in Edinburgh. She died in February 1778 shortly before she was due to acquire the lease from Bland. Bland carried on as manager until 12 March 1779, when Mr Corri, a musician who had been resident in Edinburgh for several years, very briefly held the position. On 15 May Corri's management ended and Wilkinson stepped in to operate the theatre for the subsequent winter and spring seasons. David Ross then returned to

Figure 2.11 A Watermill and a Bridge – Design for a Stage Set *by Jacob More (1740–97). More painted scenery for the new Theatre Royal in Edinburgh following its opening in 1769. He subsequently lived in Rome for twenty years, becoming the leading Classical landscapist of his time.* (National Gallery of Scotland)

active management of the Theatre Royal in partnership with Mr Heaphy, long manager of the theatre at Cork. Their first season opened around 6 January 1781. Ross oversaw another unsuccessful season which ended when he left Edinburgh in April. Wilkinson ran another summer season, during which John Philip Kemble made his Edinburgh debut (on 21 July in *The Toy Shop*). Finally, on 10 November 1781, Ross sold the theatre and the Patent to John Jackson for an unknown amount. Jackson, who had been an actor himself, became manager and opened a short season on 1 December 1781. (Jackson is the author of *The History of the Scottish Stage*, published in 1793.)

Meanwhile, on the west coast, the management of the Alston Street theatre in Glasgow passed almost seasonally through the hands of Digges, Wilkinson and Bland before the building burned down in 1780. On 9 January 1782 Jackson opened a replacement, the Theatre Royal, Dunlop Street, intending to operate this newly built theatre simultaneously with the Edinburgh house. Members of his company played both venues, and Jackson's time at these theatres was a period of relative stability for the Scottish stage.

THEATRE ACTIVITY IN THE LATE CENTURY

When the first Edinburgh theatre Patent expired on 29 September 1788, the Duke of Hamilton and Henry Dundas (later Viscount Melville) became joint Patentees and trustees of the interests of both the public and the proprietors. John Jackson continued as manager of both the Edinburgh Theatre Royal and the Glasgow Dunlop Street theatre until 1791, when mounting debts forced him out. Following disagreements over security and guarantees Stephen Kemble acquired a one-year lease on both houses.

Stephen Kemble (1758–1822) began his career at London's Patent houses but was considered not as fine an actor as his more celebrated older siblings, John Philip Kemble and Sarah Siddons. He turned to the provinces and summer seasons at the Haymarket in London to develop his career. He made his Edinburgh debut on 23 February 1786 playing Othello to the Desdemona of his wife, Elizabeth Satchell. He began his management career around February 1790 with a company numbering around sixteen, which played at Coventry almost every night until 5 June. On 7 March 1791 he won the management of the new Theatre Royal in Newcastle. From this base he bid for and won control of the Edinburgh and Glasgow houses when Jackson offered them for sale in November 1791.

Kemble took the lease at a rent of £1350 for one year. Jackson aimed to clear his debts in that period and then enter into joint management with Kemble. At this point another woman significant to the history of the Scottish stage enters the picture. In the pamphlet he subsequently issued to explain the case, Jackson claims that he would have preferred to lease the operations to the actress Harriet Esten (1765?–1865), a celebrated and popular performer whose Edinburgh career had begun in January 1790. However, delays or 'some mistake between Jackson and Mrs Esten's agent' made completion of the deal with Kemble more attractive. Lewes suggests that Jackson was particularly keen to see Kemble win the lease, fearing that if Esten won control he would lose it once and for all. Whatever the truth, when Jackson tried to negotiate the joint management deal with Kemble he was refused and was even denied entrance to the theatre itself.

In the meantime, Kemble had begun his first season as manager of the Edinburgh Theatre Royal with *The Beggar's Opera* on 19 January 1792. On 9 August, Henry Erskine, the Dean of the Faculty of Advocates, awarded Jackson half-profits of the theatre for the time Kemble rented it from his creditors. Kemble was also granted full rights as sole manager. But even while Erskine was making his judgement Jackson was persuading trustee Robert Playfair to lease the theatre to Esten for the subsequent season at a rent of only £1000.

Complex legal discussion continued about who had the right to the Patent attached to the Edinburgh house. Following the advice of the Lord Advocate,

Figure 2.12 Mr Henderson and Mr Charteris as Falstaff and Bardolph at Theatre Royal, Edinburgh (John Kay, 1784). (Scottish Theatre Archive)

Erskine and the Lord Provost gave their support to Kemble. The Duke of Hamilton supported Esten, with whom he was having an affair, which had begun by at least 1791 and was to continue until his death. Hamilon authorised her to use the Patent and awarded her the lease.

While Mrs Esten continued at the Theatre Royal in Shakespeare Square, Kemble transferred his operation to a venue in Leith Walk (at the junction of

Little King Street and Broughton Street), dubbed the 'Circus'. Kemble aimed to improve the 'Circus', refitting it as the city's new house.

Esten's season opened on 12 January 1793, Kemble's on 21 January. In his refitted venue, Kemble's season began strongly, enjoying stalwart support from the Kemble dynasty in the form of the Scottish debuts of Sarah Siddons's brother Charles Kemble and her son Henry. Nevertheless, he was forced to cease dramatic production on 6 February, being 'interdicted from exhibiting Plays and Farces' because he did not hold a Patent. Kemble lost some of his acting company to the rival operation at the Theatre Royal, where at least one significant production was under way – the Scottish premiere of Charles Macklin's *The Man of the World*, featuring the Scots character Sir Pertinax MacSycophant. Kemble continued to present concerts while he focused his attention on his Newcastle circuit. He was permitted to reopen the 'Circus' on 2 March but operations there were again curtailed while he opened theatres in Berwick Upon Tweed and Alnwick.

Having secured both the playhouse and the lease, Harriet Esten quit Edinburgh to play the spring season at Covent Garden. She appointed Williamson as manager and left her mother, Agnes Maria Bennet (d.1808), author of several popular novels but with no theatrical experience, to supervise the running of Scotland's only licensed theatre. The press commented on the 'absurdity of appointing, as the Manageress of the Edinburgh Theatre, a Lady, who, while she should be at her post in Scotland, is performing in London'. Esten was back, though, to appear as Indiana in *The Conscious Lovers* and Roxalana in *The Sultan* on 22 June 1793. She played till the season's close on 20 July when, despite some degree of success, she surrendered her lease on the theatre, and her claim to the Patent. Paying a fee of £200 per year to Esten for the use of the Patent and £1000 to Jackson's creditors for the theatre, Kemble now controlled both. While Esten returned to Covent Garden, Kemble returned to the Edinburgh Theatre Royal in January 1794 with a production of *Hamlet* with an all-star (all-Kemble) cast, including John Philip Kemble, Mrs Stephen Kemble, Henry Siddons and Charles Kemble. The Circus was left as a newly developed 'minor' house under Corri's management. (The Patent gave an exclusive right to perform 'legitimate' drama, hence the 'minor' houses – theatres without a Patent – were restricted to other forms of entertainment.)

Kemble ran the Edinburgh Theatre Royal until the end of the century, during which time his managerial ambition grew and his empire expanded. In early September 1795 he opened a newly built theatre in Aberdeen, then, in 1799, he won from Cawdell the Durham circuit, which included Scarborough, Sunderland, Stockton and North and South Shields.

Kemble's management of the Edinburgh Theatre Royal, though not wholly successful, did feature some notable performances, including a significant (not to say sensational) production of *Douglas* on 23 July 1794, when Henry

Figure 2.13 *Mr Clinch and Mrs Yates as the Duke and Duchess of Braganza at Theatre Royal, Edinburgh, 1785. The border features members of the audience.* (*John Kay, 1785*) (Scottish Theatre Archive)

Erskine Johnston played Young Norval in full Highland dress. When Johnston stepped on stage 'the whole audience rose and gave him a reception such as had seldom been heard within the walls of the building'.[14] The appearance on the Edinburgh stage of the heroic Highlander, the quintessential Romantic noble savage, dressed in the very plaid which Hanoverian politics had outlawed, was a breathtaking moment of iconographic excess. However, by that time, with Highland culture suppressed, the savage had effectively been neutered, and was safely cast within a heroic mythological past.

Johnston (1777–1845) became a fairly important figure in the subsequent history of the Scottish stage. He was born in Edinburgh and made his debut, as Hamlet, at the Theatre Royal, just a fortnight before his famous appearance as Norval. Johnston may then have played a summer season at the Crow Street theatre, Dublin, before returning to Kemble's company for 1795. In 1796 he played Belfast in March and returned to Edinburgh for April. He was already being billed as the 'Scottish Rosicus', after Garrick, the 'English Rosicus'. After appearing at the Crow Street theatre in 1796–7, he made his London debut, playing Douglas, at Covent Garden on 23 October 1797. He stayed in that company until September 1803 when he transferred to Drury Lane, making his debut there as Anhalt in *Lovers' Vows*.

Despite his London success, Johnston regularly performed in Scotland and he made an unsuccessful bid for the Patenteeship of the Edinburgh Theatre Royal in 1808 (he lost out to Henry Siddons). In 1814 he was manager of the Queen Street theatre, Glasgow, but lost the position when Irish creditors pursued him to Scotland.

Notwithstanding the early successes of the Kemble management of the Edinburgh Theatre Royal, the quality of the resident company deteriorated and

Figure 2.14 Henry Erskine Johnston (1775–1845) as Norval in John Home's Douglas *(Henry Singleton, 1802).* (Garrick Club, London)

the house's reputation waned. Failing seasons were artificially supported by the loyalty of the Kemble clan, visits by other London celebrities and the discovery of stars like Johnston, but, on 30 July 1800, Stephen Kemble's tenure as manager ended and he took leave of his, by then, disgruntled audience. Following a production of *Pizarro*, he addressed the house:

> After thanking the public for having generously supported him 'on many trying occasions', he said, 'though his followers might be more successful, they could not be more ambitious or anxious to please – he might almost take it upon him to assert he *had* given satisfaction' – At this point he was interrupted with considerable murmurs and some hissing; but he continued – 'I once thought to have left Edinburgh without a single enemy behind me' – the hissing then increased, but he proceeded. 'It is, however, not wonderful that I am disappointed, for even our great Redeemer had his enemies; and after his great example (at this phrase he clapped his hands on his great fat paunch) I will be meek and submissive'!! The row that ensued upon this was tremendous, and after again essaying to speak, Kemble had to retire in terror of being pelted![15]

After Kemble's departure, John Jackson, in partnership with Francis Aickin of Liverpool, assumed the role of manager. Kemble quit Scotland for his remaining northern circuits, but surrendered the management of the Newcastle circuit to Macready in 1806. He made occasional appearances on stages across Britain (including Covent Garden and Drury Lane) and in Dublin. He was temporary stage manager of Drury Lane in 1818–19, during which season his son, Henry Stephen Kemble (1789–1836), was brought forward in a number of increasingly inappropriate roles which were quite beyond his experience. Henry Stephen also collaborated with Kemble in the writing of *Flodden Field*, a Romantic drama based on Walter Scott's *Marmion*, which was premiered on 3 December 1818 and published the following year. Kemble retired from the London stage in April 1820 and died on 5 June 1822.

Beyond Edinburgh, theatre was flourishing across the whole of Scotland. Despite the early failures of Sarah Ward's companies to play in Aberdeen, that city had become the chief town of a northern touring circuit which also included Perth, Montrose and Dundee. It was also an important stop in a circuit operated by Corbet Ryder which covered most of Scotland, taking in Aberdeen, Glasgow, Edinburgh, Perth and Dundee. In 1768 the New Inn Theatre opened in Castle Street, Aberdeen, as a venue for such touring companies. In 1779 another new playhouse opened in Shoe Lane and, around 1780, yet another opened in Queen Street. However, Kemble's house was the first permanent theatre to operate in Aberdeen. Situated in Marischal Street it was modest in size, holding, according to its historian J. Keith Angus, an audience of just sixty-five.[16]

The end of the eighteenth century saw theatres open in some of the smaller Scottish towns. In 1793 a New Theatre was built in Arbroath, where theatrical performances also took place in the Trades Hall from 1812 onwards. In Dundee the Town Hall was available to touring companies between 1755 and 1767, and a more basic booth theatre was maintained in the second half of the century. The Yeoman Shore Theatre did not open until 1800, but when it did it paved the way for further developments in the new century.

Peter Baxter's book *The Drama in Perth* records that the Perth Guildhall was used for theatre from the early eighteenth century, but gives little indication of what was staged there, other than to mention that one visiting company was of a 'tag-rag description'. The Glovers' Hall, built in 1786, superseded the Guildhall as the main meeting place in Perth and, according to Baxter, was later 'fitted up in a temporary way as a regular theatre, with pit and gallery, but no boxes'. A company managed by Sutherland used the venue regularly and was responsible for the production of a play called *The Siege of Perth; or, Sir William Wallace* by J. MacLaren in 1792. Corbet Ryder's tours also used the Glovers' Hall for their performances, for the New Theatre (in the converted Grammar School) did not open until 1810.[17]

In Glasgow, as has been mentioned, the Alston Street theatre was superseded by the one in Dunlop Street, the foundation stone of which was laid by the man most closely associated with the venue, John Jackson, on 17 February 1781. The Dunlop Street theatre opened in January 1782 and was operated as a second house for Jackson's Edinburgh company. It established itself as an important part of Glasgow society and an essential venue for any tour of Britain by the age's leading actors. Among the notables who appeared were Dorothy Jordan, John Philip Kemble, Miss Farren, Stephen Kemble, Henry Siddons and Mrs Henry Siddons. Sarah Siddons finally made her Glasgow debut there in 1795. At its height John Jackson's empire included not only the Edinburgh and Glasgow houses, but also those in Aberdeen and Perth. When, in 1790, he lost control of Edinburgh and Glasgow to Stephen Kemble, it was only a temporary loss. Kemble managed the Dunlop Street theatre only until 1799, when Jackson, in partnership with Francis Aickin, regained control of Scotland's two Patent-holding Theatre Royals.

POPULAR ENTERTAINMENTS IN THE EIGHTEENTH CENTURY

This chapter has, inevitably, focused on the rapid advances made by theatre companies in Edinburgh and by the players, managers and playwrights whose work made eighteenth-century Scottish theatre such a dynamic force. But the tradition of the minor houses, of popular entertainment and strolling players,

Figure 2.15 Mr Moss at Edinburgh's Theatre Royal in the character of Caleb and with the song that he sung on stage (John Kay, 1787). (Scottish Theatre Archive)

which parallels and complements what was happening in the country's new theatres, must not be overlooked. The visit of a strolling company to Edinburgh in 1715 is significant not because it was the only one, but because it is the only one for which documentary evidence survives. Evidence of this kind of drama is rare and the sources are varied and sometimes unexpected. However, in their diversity they provide some of the most evocative descriptions of theatre in Scotland in this period.

By the end of the century there was a well-established network of fit-up stages in smaller towns. A string of touring companies worked this network, playing versions of Shakespeare and various 'Scottish plays', and providing entertainments in small temporary booth theatres, at markets, fairs and other impromptu venues. In *Annals of the Parish* (1821), John Galt's fictionalised account of life in small-town Ayrshire, the Rev. Balwhidder describes the visit of one such company:

> Another thing happened in this year [1795], too remarkable for me to neglect to put on record, as it strangely and strikingly marked the rapid revolutions that were going on. In the month of August, at the time of the fair, a gang of play-actors came, and hired Thomas Thacklan's barn for their enactments . . . Their first performance was Douglas Tragedy and the Gentle Shepherd, and the general opinion was, that the lad who played Norval in the play, and Patie in the farce, was an English lord's son, who had run away from his parents, rather than marry an old cracket lady, with a great portion. But, whatever truth there might be in this notion, certain it was, the whole pack was in a state of perfect beggary; and yet, for all that, they not only in their parts, as I was told, laughed most heartily, but made others do the same; for I was constrained to let my daughter go to see them, with some of her acquaintance, and she gave me such an account of what they did, that I thought I would have liked to have gotten a keek at them myself. At the same time, I must own this was a sinful curiosity, and I stifled it to the best of my ability. Among other plays that they did, was one called Macbeth and the Witches . . . But it was no more like the true play of Shakespeare the poet . . . than a duddy betherel [scarecrow], set up to fright the sparrows from the pease, is like a living gentleman. (Chapter XXXVI)

Such events were increasingly common and stimulated interest in some local communities in staging their own theatricals. Allan Ramsay's *The Gentle Shepherd* was performed annually by Pentland villagers well into the nineteenth century and the tradition of schools and colleges staging drama continued, spreading out of the academies into the professional and upper classes in the

Figure 2.16 The Guisers *by Alexander Carse, c. 1822, showing the Scottish folk play* Galoshins *being performed in a country cottage.* Galoshins *retained elements of medieval folk drama.* (National Gallery of Scotland)

Lowlands. However, this was all resolutely amateur. Professional players still tended to be English actors travelling north to find a new and ready market for their talents – as in Galt's suggestion that the leading man in the company described by the Rev. Balwhidder was 'an English lord's son'. A similar vagabond player is described in what is surely one of the most entertaining descriptions of Scottish theatre in the late eighteenth century. 'The Spouter' by Alexander Wilson, the radical weaver poet from Paisley, offers a more ribald account of touring players than that given by Galt's douce minister:

> Where is the place that mair o' life ye'll learn,
> Than 'hint the scenes in some auld kintra barn,
> Where two-three hungry, ragged, Spouter blades,
> – Wha'd better stuck through life to spools or spades, –
> Driven by stern want, the fell remorseless jaud;
> Mang kintra folk do ply their kittle trade?
> There ye may see a lang horn shottle chiel,   [shabby-like]
> On whose pale face, hunger is painted weel,
> As Dick the Third shout for 'a horse! a horse!'
> To meet young Richmond, an' the invading force:

Or else some sniftering, snivelling, ill-clad loon,
Wha wadna hae the heart a cat to droon;
As stern Macbeth, rampauging through his part,
An' for his crown stab Duncan to the heart.

Wilson continues by telling of a visit to a small village by a strolling player, one Mr Main 'come direct frae Drury Lane,/Where baith their Majesties,
the king an' queen,/Had aft wi' his performance pleaséd been', and his junior
colleague, a 'raggy laddie, ca'd Adolphus Sprat.' The pair take up residence in
a local barn and advertise a performance of 'Wondrous novelty'. Despite the
warnings of some god-fearing members of the community, the barn is filled and
the audience is entertained by the less than delightful musicianship of Master
Sprat, who is all but hissed off the stage, and the recitations and poems of Mr
Main. Wilson describes an excited, boisterous and very raucous audience, who
banter and gossip amongst themselves and are not averse to hectoring Adolphus
and passing comment on the subject and content of Main's stories, debating
their veracity or degree of implausibility and offering suggestions and potential
improvements: 'Stop that damn'd fiddle!', 'Save's! that's an awfu' bluidy tale',
'Think ye that's true?', 'Encore! encore! . . . Come, gie's that sang again!' and
'Wha threw that turnip! curse yer blood!' However, the next day while the
audience is still keen to talk over the merits of the players' tales, Main and his
assistant have disappeared, and in true vagabond tradition:

. . . (in their hurry) had forgot to pay
The debt they had contracted yesterday.
An' Willie Watson swore like any Turk
That it had been a thievish piece o' wark;
An' if he could the Spouter get, that he
The inside o' a jail wad let him see.
Although puir Willie said to us, –' I trow,
To sic a rascal 'twad be nothing new;
For weel-a-wat it isna his first trick,
Nor yet the first time he has 'cut his stick.'
But aff o' this, there's ae thing that I'll learn,
An' that's I'll ken again wha gets my barn;
An' mak' them always pay the cash before
They ever set a nose in at the door.'
An' then poor Will began an' swore again,
What he wad do when he got Mr Main;
When some auld wives said, 'Man, ye should think shame,
For ye hae nae ane but yersel to blame,

For they wha mak' an' meddle wi' sic crew,
Aye meet with something they hae cause to rue.'
An' Willie clawed his head an' said, 'Atweel,
They wad need a lang spoon wha sup kail wi' the deil.'

The kind of entertainment Wilson describes was, no doubt, the experience of theatre most familiar to the majority of ordinary people in Scotland; an experience of intimate and immediate performance in a fit-up venue.

Interestingly, both Galt and Wilson describe players who are English, again stressing the scarcity of Scots personnel and Scots language on the professional stage (although two of Mr Main's songs are in Scots, only one of his recitations is so, the others being in English). Alasdair Cameron focuses on this linguistic point arguing that:

> Scots had little opportunity to train as actors and the repertoire of most companies was overwhelmingly English. It consisted of either declamatory tragedy or verbal comedy, both of which put the Scot, with distinctive speech patterns, at a considerable disadvantage.[18]

Nevertheless, despite the repertoire problems, Scottish voices began to be heard increasingly in the legitimate theatres and in the fit-ups and geggies (travelling booth theatres). The rise to celebrity of Scottish actors such as Henry Johnston, Harriet Murray and W. H. Murray points to the fact that even in the legitimate theatres this was beginning to change. More general change was taking place too, with a new programme of theatre building going on across the country. By the end of the century not only were there two houses in Edinburgh but Aberdeen, Arbroath, Ayr, Dumfries, Dundee, Glasgow, Greenock and Paisley each had one. The expansion of the touring circuits into the countryside meant that a different type of audience, from a broader sector of the population and having different wants and needs from those of city audiences, was able to see theatrical entertainments.

Yet despite the expansion of theatre infrastructure and industry, despite the fact that Scots voices were occasionally to be heard, and despite the fact that the Church had become lenient and accepting, theatre managers in Scotland and, in particular, in Edinburgh, still found it hard to build a regular theatre audience. In his 1788 *History of Edinburgh* Hugo Arnot provides a useful corrective to the widespread notion that the fault lay solely with clerical disapproval. He also gives some idea of audience composition at the time:

> The fact is that Edinburgh does not give encouragement to the stage proportionable to the populousness of the city. This does not proceed

Figure 2.17 Mrs Henry Siddons (Harriet Murray) (1783–1844) actress and theatre manager (John Wood, n.d.). (Scottish National Portrait Gallery)

so much from the remaining leaven of fanaticism, as from the poorness of Scots' fortunes, the inconsiderableness of the trade and manufactures, or [sic] the smallness of the profits arising from them. These do not admit of ordinary gentlewomen, or the wives and daughters of shop-keepers and mechanics going often to the playhouse; therefore they keep their penny till some occasion, (no matter what), makes it reported that the house is to be throng, then everyone crowds the theatre, while, without such report the walls would be desolate. As for the gentlemen, the stage has not such attractions for them, as the social pleasures of the bottle, or the pungent emotions of the hazard table.

Mention of such diversions brings us to Robert Burns, for no account of the cultural life of late eighteenth-century Scotland would be complete without at least passing reference to him. Burns was an habitué of the theatre in Dumfries; his name, in fact, was on the theatre's free-list. He talked of writing a play and did write patriotic prologues for the theatre. In his letters, he provides enthusiastic sketches of the Dumfries theatre at the end of the century, praising a company stationed there and commenting on his own enthusiastic involvement. In a letter of 11 January 1790, to his brother Gilbert, he records that:

Figure 2.18 W. H. Murray (1790–1852) actor and manager of Edinburgh's Theatre Royal (Sir William Allan, 1843). (Scottish National Portrait Gallery)

We have gotten a set of very decent Players here now. – I have seen
them an evening or two. – David Campbell in Ayr wrote me by the
Manager of the Company, a Mr Sutherland, who is indeed a man of
genius & apparent worth. – On New-yearly I gave him the following
Prologue which he spouted to his Audience with great applause. –
>   No song nor dance I bring from yon great City
>   That queens it o'er taste – the More's the Pity.

This is probably the same George S. Sutherland who had been engaged as
an actor with John Jackson's company at the Edinburgh Theatre Royal in
winter 1781–2. Sutherland's company, which included his wife, toured across
the country, playing, for example, at the Glovers' Hall theatre in Perth in 1792.
In a letter of 9 February 1790, to William Nicol, an Edinburgh friend, Burns
gives more details of the successes of the players:

> Our theatrical company, of which you must have heard, leave us in a
> week. Their merit and character are indeed very great, both on the stage
> and in private life; not a worthless creature among them; and their
> encouragement has been accordingly. Their usual run is from eighteen
> to twenty-five pounds a night; seldom less than the one, and the house
> will hold no more than the other. There have been repeated instances of
> sending away six, and eight, and ten pounds a night for want of room.
> A new theatre is to be built by subscription; the first stone is to be laid
> on Friday first to come. Three hundred guineas have been raised by
> thirty subscribers, and thirty more might have been got if wanted. The
> manager, Mr Sutherland, was introduced to me by a friend from Ayr;
> and a worthier or cleverer fellow I have rarely met with. Some of our
> clergy have slipt in by stealth now and then ... I have given Mr
> Sutherland two Prologues; one of which was delivered last week.

The prologues Burns refers to are of particular interest. They are written in an
energetic Scots and are full of good humour about the theatre, while also making the point about Scotland's dependence upon London for theatrical fare:

>   What needs this din about the town o' Lon'on,
>   How this new play, an' that new sang is comin?
>   Why is outlandish stuff sae meikle courted?
>   Does nonsense mend, like brandy, when imported?
>   Is there nae poet, burning keen for fame,
>   Will try to gie us sangs and plays at hame?
>   For Comedy abroad he need na toil,
>   A fool and knave are plants of every soil;

Nor need he hunt as far as Rome or Greece,
To gather matter for a serious piece;
There's themes enow in Caledonian story,
Would shew the Tragic Muse in a' her Glory.
(From 'Scots Prologue for Mr Sutherland, on his benefit night,
at the Theatre, Dumfries')

SCOTTISH PLAYWRIGHTS IN LONDON –
THE MID AND LATE CENTURY

Throughout the century, despite the improved opportunities in Scotland, the London theatre remained an essential and influential market. Among the later Scottish playwrights who produced work of note for the London theatres and publishers are James Thomson, whose career has already been mentioned, Tobias Smollett, Lady Wallace and, at the end of the century, anticipating greater success in coming decades, Joanna Baillie.

Although Smollett's reputation as a novelist and essayist endures, he was also the author of several plays, some of which were produced. His first dramatic effort, *The Regicide; or, James the First, King of Scotland*, was written while he was a student at the University of Glasgow but was rejected by the potential patron Lord George Lyttelton and producer David Garrick. Smollett had it published privately in 1749. In 1750 *Alceste* was set to become Smollett's first play to be produced by John Rich at Covent Garden. However, when the production was abandoned, that honour fell to his only comic play, a two-act farce, *The Reprisal; or, the Tars of Old England*, which Garrick produced at Drury Lane on 22 January 1757. The play concerns the rescue of Harriet from the clutches of Champignon, a French commander in whose frigate the young girl is held. The rescuers are Harriet's devoted, if naive, fiancé Heartly and his capable servant, Brush. Their allies are two unlikely members of Champignon's crew; the Irishman Oclabber and the Scot Maclaymore. Smollett gleefully and wickedly satirises the foibles and stereotypical characteristics of each nationality, saving his venomous best for the Frenchman: rifling Champignon's ship the heroes uncover 'a very coarse canvas shirt, with very fine lac'd ruffles' and they conclude that 'This here is the right trim of a Frenchman – all ginger bread-work, flourish and compliment aloft, and all rags and rottenness alow.' It ran some six nights, was received warmly and later revived.

Towards the end of the century two Scottish women achieved different degrees of success with the drama. Lady Eglantine Maxwell Wallace wrote at least four plays, though only one comedy was produced, and Joanna Baillie made her reputation in tragedy and wrote an enormously significant piece of critical theory. Baillie could be said to be the most significant Scottish playwright of the nineteenth century (see Chapter 3).

Lady Wallace's first play, *Diamond Cut Diamond* was based on Dumaniant's *La Guerre Overte; ou, La Ruse Contre Ruse*, which was also the source for Mrs Inchbald's *The Midnight Hour*. While Mrs Inchbald's play won a Covent Garden production, Lady Wallace had to be satisfied with publication. Nevertheless, her next play, *The Ton; or, The Follies of Fashion*, was produced, with limited success, by Rich at Covent Garden on 8 April 1788. Her third play also seemed set for production but was refused a licence by the Lord Chamberlain and again was only published. Lady Wallace also wrote a tragedy, *Cortes*, which was neither played nor published.

Joanna Baillie wrote, published and had produced some of the key plays of the Romantic theatre, being universally celebrated as *the* playwright of her generation. Her first play, *Arnold* (1790), does not survive. Her earliest extant dramas are those in her essential volume *A Series of Plays in which it is Attempted to Delineate the Stronger Passions of the Mind, each Passion being the Subject of a Tragedy and a Comedy*, published in 1798. This first volume includes *Count Basil*, *The Trial* and *De Montford*, arguably her best plays. *De Montford* has a stage history unmatched by Baillie's later work. As *De Montford* was premiered on 29 April 1800 (at Drury Lane, with John Philip Kemble and Sarah Siddons in the lead roles) Baillie is an appropriate figure to lead the way from the eighteenth into the nineteenth century, when Scottish theatre achieved an economic and cultural maturity for which the perseverance and determination of eighteenth-century theatre practitioners and enthusiasts had paved the way.

The Nineteenth Century

BARBARA BELL

It would be impossible in so short a space to provide even a brief history of the close to 300 theatres which operated in Scotland during the nineteenth century, some open for much of the year for decades at a time, others open no more than a few days a year over a handful of years. Similarly, the many actors, managers and playwrights whose work enriched those theatres must remain largely unsung. What is important is that developments shaping a distinctive Scottish theatre during this period should be recorded and, where possible, examples given of major trends and common practices.

THE DROVE ROAD SOUTH?

Two versions of the same play, printed fifteen years apart, give some idea of the difficulties facing Scottish theatre at the beginning of the nineteenth century. Archibald Maclaren first published *The Highland Drover* in Greenock in 1790. At that time he seems to have been part of an itinerant company under the leadership of a Mr Ward. The character of Domhnul (Donald) Dubh, the Highland drover, was his own particular starring role. The title-page of the printed copy says that it was 'repeatedly performed at INVERNESS, ABERDEEN, PERTH, DUNDEE, and GREENOCK, with universal approbation', which gives some idea of Ward's route around Scotland; but the most interesting and unusual element of the piece is its extensive use of Gaelic.

In *The Highland Drover* the central character, the drover, understands no English and can speak a few words, 'yes,' 'no' and 'to be sure'. His exchanges with his fellow drover and with a maidservant are conducted entirely in Gaelic. Whereas in Maclaren's earlier piece *The Humours of Greenock Fair* (1789), the fun is derived from the ability of the Highlander to frustrate the Lowlander by switching languages in mid-sentence, here the comedy is rooted in the misunderstandings caused by the honest efforts of Domhnul Dubh and the

Englishman, Ramble, who wishes to engage Domhnul's help in an elopement, to hold a conversation. Both men latch on to the phonetic sounds of the other's speech and try to react accordingly, as in the extract below:

> *Ramble*: He does not understand me, if I thought he had a comrade that did, I would call him.
> *Domhnul*: Callum! an aithne dhuit fa Callum 'n donnas duille agum nach thu fhein Callum, oh laochain, thoir dhomh do lamh.
> ['Callum! do you know Callum? I don't think but you're Callum yourself, Oh my good fellow, give me your hand.']
> *Ramble*: You want to go to law! Well my friend who hinders you?
> *Domhnul*: Mata, 's duillich leam fhein nach'eil bearla agam air fon a ghille choir fo, 'on tha me creidsin gu'n do chail e a ghaelic, – s'urrin mi beagan a'radh, no agus yes, agus to be sure, agus a leite fin.
> ['Well, I'm sorry that I can speak no English upon this honest lad's account, for I believe he has lost all his Gaelic, – I can speak a little, such as no and yes, and to be sure, and the like of that.']
> *Ramble*: I'll tell you what it is friend, I have a little business to transact here, and I suppose you mean to prevent me.
> *Domhnul*: Ciod a their mi, nios? – yes.
> ['What shall I say now? – yes.']
> *Ramble*: Yes!

In order to make the printed text more saleable the Gaelic speeches were translated into English and marked with inverted commas; however, the full richness of the comedy and motivation of the characters would clearly only be available to audiences who understood both languages.

Despite his best efforts and periodic recourse to his original profession of soldier, Maclaren was never far from poverty. He eventually travelled to London, in the hope of preferment at the larger theatres, and republished *The Highland Drover* in 1805 'with alterations and additions' which render the original barely recognisable. The use of Gaelic has disappeared entirely and a quantity of two and three verse songs intersperse the greatly expanded number of scenes. New comic characters, such as a sweep Dickie White and Teddy O'Hump, an Irish barber, are added, along with a sentimental sub-plot in which the drover's Highland sweetheart, seduced from his side by trickery and the lure of London, proves to be the maidservant and confidante of the heroine. The drover's intervention on the side of the lovers is thus given a more conventional impetus than the Highland notions of clan loyalty displayed in the first version. When the heroine's outraged guardian tries to foil the drover by calling up a gang of drunken Irish labourers to rout the Scots, the two sides greet each other with cries of 'Dugald McCudgel!' and 'Teddy Shilelah' and refuse to fight. Maclaren has sacrificed the truth and individual characterisation of the original to pander to the stereotyped prejudices of a metropolitan audience. Sadly, even this compromise did not profit Maclaren much. He died around 1826, in poverty.

The Scottish theatre industry was too weak, fragmented and anglicised to offer any kind of future to a native talent. The few Patent houses operating were conscious of their legitimate status as satellites of the great London houses, whilst the travelling groups who made periodic attempts to open minor houses were hampered by the lack of a suitable repertoire with which to compete. Both camps were constrained by the zeal of the Lord Chamberlain's office and its official, the Stage Censor, who aimed to prevent any material with a 'national', which in Whitehall meant Jacobite, flavour from appearing on Scottish stages.

Yet there was a growing market for theatre. Attitudes had softened in the years since Allan Ramsay and John Home, a process described by *The Weekly Review and Dramatic Critic* in 1852:

> *The Gentle Shepherd* and Home's *Douglas* may be said to have produced quite a revolution in regard to theatricals in Scotland, and went far to negative [sic] the thunders of the Church. Douglas was the chosen character of every aspirant to the stage, and Patie and Roger found their way into the village barns, performed to groups of delighted rustics by rustics themselves. If a poor widow's rent was to be made up, or her winter's boll of meal and potatoes to be laid in – if a labourer or miner met with an accident – if any domestic calamity had occurred, calling upon the aid of the humane – forward stood the amateur dramatic club – and up went the curtain to *Douglas* and *The Gentle Shepherd*.

However, the professional theatre was staffed largely by incomers who could only meet the demand for Scottish pieces by endlessly repeating the limited repertoire at their disposal. As an added attraction, theatres occasionally brought in local amateurs to provide the authentic voices. On New Year's Day 1811, for example, at the Edinburgh Theatre Royal, the supporting pieces included 'favourite scenes' from *The Gentle Shepherd* with 'Patie and Roger by Gentlemen, Natives of the City'.

In essence, the 'Scottish' repertoire available to theatres at this time consisted of a handful of major works such as *Macbeth*, *Douglas* and Schiller's *Mary Stuart*, along with a larger number of plays in which individual Scottish characters, such as Charles Macklin's caricatures Sir Pertinax MacSycophant (from *The Man of the World*) and Sir Archy Macsarcasm (from *Love A-la-Mode*) appeared. These were primarily stereotypes – the tight-fisted Scotsman or the faithful Highlander. There were also a quantity of 'ballets of action', a species of balletic pantomime, with titles such as *Donald and Peggy; or Love in the Highlands* and *The Caledonian Lovers: or, the Gretna-Green Blacksmith*, featuring quaint Scottish peasantry. Finally, there were standard forms given a superficial local flavour, such as pantomimes with titles such as *Harlequin at Leith*.

There was very little in this range of pieces which could be considered controversial or political, but the vigilance of the Censor, which served effectively to stifle playwrights before they attempted national pieces, is more readily understood when one remembers that the theatres of Revolutionary France had proved hotbeds of political activity. Theatres were a rare arena of public assembly where frustrated and factional political feeling could all too easily become violent action. The authorities, anxious to leave the schisms of the 1745 Jacobite Rising well in the past, and to be sure of their Scottish regiments in the fight against Bonaparte, preferred to pre-empt trouble by banning Scotland's life and history from its theatres. Ironically, in this they were in complete agreement with Bonaparte, who banned Parisian audiences from seeing a play about Flora Macdonald on the basis that it was rather too sympathetic to dispossessed royalty.

With an obvious market for Scottish plays during the early years of the century, managements searched around for suitable material, and from England came stage adaptations, in the form of ballets, of works by Burns (particularly *Tam O'Shanter*) and Ossian. On 5 December 1812, the new Edinburgh Theatre Royal in Shakespeare Square presented, as guest artists, the dancers Mr Noble and Miss Luppino in a 'Scotch Ballet Pantomime' entitled *Mora's Love or the Enchanted Harp*, 'founded on the poem of the Harp, by Hector Macneil, Esq. and composed by Mr J. H. Egville of the Opera House'. The plays of Joanna Baillie (1762–1851) provided a brief dawn which served rather to emphasise the stagnation of the Scottish theatre than anything else. Baillie (as discussed later) was a serious commentator on the state of the drama but her plays, notably *The Family Legend*, could not on their own provide the breakthrough which would bring about change. Scottish material remained so rare that the Theatre Royal could consider it an additional draw to announce, in 1812, that the 'Melo-dramatic entertainment' of *Tam O'Shanter, and his mare Maggie*, 'taken from the tale of that excellent scotish [sic] poet', would be presented 'with a scotch overture – scotch music – scotch dresses – and scotch dances'. Overall, Scots could be portrayed as comic characters or as inhabiting an unspecified mythic country, but as little else. There was a dam of prejudice blocking the writing of Scottish plays, with pressure building up behind it from growing audience expectations. Some lever was required to loosen the log-jam.

Into this unsatisfactory state of affairs appeared the unlikely figure of

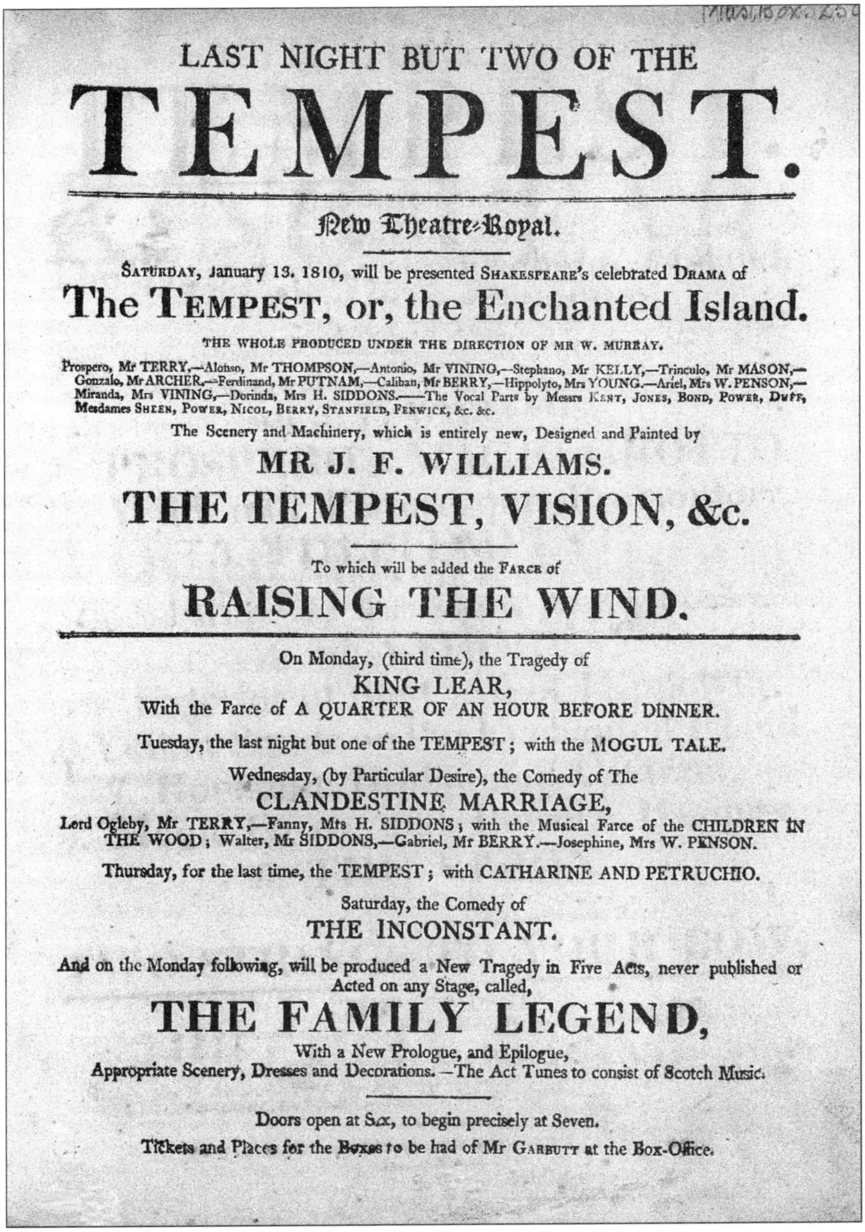

LAST NIGHT BUT TWO OF THE

TEMPEST.

New Theatre-Royal.

SATURDAY, January 13. 1810, will be presented SHAKESPEARE's celebrated DRAMA of

The TEMPEST, or, the Enchanted Island.

THE WHOLE PRODUCED UNDER THE DIRECTION OF MR W. MURRAY.

Prospero, Mr TERRY,—Alonso, Mr THOMPSON,—Antonio, Mr VINING,—Stephano, Mr KELLY,—Trinculo, Mr MASON,—Gonzalo, Mr ARCHER,—Ferdinand, Mr PUTNAM,—Caliban, Mr BERRY,—Hippolyto, Mrs YOUNG.—Ariel, Mrs W. PENSON,—Miranda, Mrs VINING,—Dorinda, Mrs H. SIDDONS.——The Vocal Parts by Messrs KENT, JONES, BOND, POWER, DUFF, Mesdames SHEEN, POWER, NICOL, BERRY, STANFIELD, FENWICK, &c. &c.

The Scenery and Machinery, which is entirely new, Designed and Painted by

MR J. F. WILLIAMS.

THE TEMPEST, VISION, &c.

To which will be added the FARCE of

RAISING THE WIND.

On Monday, (third time), the Tragedy of
KING LEAR,
With the Farce of A QUARTER OF AN HOUR BEFORE DINNER.

Tuesday, the last night but one of the TEMPEST; with the MOGUL TALE.

Wednesday, (by Particular Desire), the Comedy of The
CLANDESTINE MARRIAGE,
Lord Ogleby, Mr TERRY,—Fanny, Mrs H. SIDDONS; with the Musical Farce of the CHILDREN IN THE WOOD; Walter, Mr SIDDONS,—Gabriel, Mr BERRY.—Josephine, Mrs W. PENSON.

Thursday, for the last time, the TEMPEST; with CATHARINE AND PETRUCHIO.

Saturday, the Comedy of
THE INCONSTANT.

And on the Monday following, will be produced a New Tragedy in Five Acts, never published or Acted on any Stage, called,

THE FAMILY LEGEND,

With a New Prologue, and Epilogue,
Appropriate Scenery, Dresses and Decorations.—The Act Tunes to consist of Scotch Music.

Doors open at Six, to begin precisely at Seven.

Tickets and Places for the Boxes to be had of Mr GARBUTT at the Box-Office.

Figure 3.1 Playbill, 1810, Theatre Royal, Edinburgh, intimating at the bottom the premiere of Joanna Baillie's The Family Legend, *which was produced by Sir Walter Scott.* (The Trustees of the National Library of Scotland)

Walter Scott (1771–1832). Scott's 'unlikeliness' was not due to any failure to recognise and deplore the stereotyping of Scots, which had intensified so much since the 1745 Rising, nor to any lack of understanding of how the theatre worked. He had made a competent job of producing Baillie's *The Family*

Legend, with unusual attention to the details of costume and the placing of the supers (actors without speaking parts), although he plainly found the experience frustrating. He was also a good friend to and a conscientious trustee of the Edinburgh Theatre Royal and his correspondence was littered with sensible advice to the young playwrights who sought his aid. It was rather that the first adaptations of his works to appear on Scottish stages (versions of his poem *The Lady of the Lake*) served merely to reinforce the emphasis on the legendary at the expense of the actual.

None the less, it was a desire to deal with the actual, to present a truthful picture of various fast-disappearing groups within Scottish society, that prompted Scott to turn to the novel. The rounded, three-dimensional figures that he wished to portray, particularly those from Scotland's recent past, would simply not have been allowed on stage by the Censor. In novels Scott could deal, for example, with the full range of religious beliefs which had shaped Scotland's history and portray kings and politicians in a manner that did not seek to disguise shortcomings. Most importantly, he could use a range of language to do it, unlike on the stage where any kind of dialect was solely the province of comic characters.

Once Scott's authorship of the Waverley Novels was an open secret and adaptations of them filled theatres throughout Britain, he was often asked why he did not write for the stage. He had dabbled in the peculiar literary hybrid, the closet play, written to be read, without much success, but steadfastly refused to contribute more to the working theatre than the occasional song or address. Of course, the short answer was that Scott did write for the stage, but in an unusual form. Previously, a great failing had been the quality of the dialogue allowable in and available to the minor theatres. Scott was a fine mimic, who acted out, for the amusement of his friends, the scenes he intended to write, and his working methods forced him into a continual flow of improvisation. His dialogue was fresh and lively, bringing his characters, particularly the Scottish ones, immediately to life. In the case of a Scott adaptation the ideal dialogue could be lifted directly from the novel by any theatre manager who could obtain a copy. Nineteenth-century theatre professionals credited Walter Scott with hastening the abolition of the restrictive Patent in 1843, by immeasurably raising the standards of the minor theatres with this gift of a semi-legitimate repertoire with which they could challenge the supremacy of the Patent houses, with their exclusive right to perform legitimate drama.

The first Scott adaptation to enjoy major success was the version of *Guy Mannering* written for Covent Garden by Scott's friend, the actor Daniel Terry, in 1816. It was the first of a flood of dramas, melodramas, operas and horse-operas (dramatic entertainment performed on horseback) which saw Scott's major works reincarnated on every stage in Britain, providing many good actors with starring roles and many grateful managements with full houses. The 'Scott' dramas brought about a sea-change in the fortunes of the Scottish theatre and altered its relationship to the Scottish people, leading to the formation of a nineteenth-century dramatic genre that was Scotland's own – the 'National Drama'.

THE NATIONAL DRAMA

The progress of the National Drama can be viewed in four periods:[1]

1. 1800–1817   The restricted eighteenth-century repertoire was repeated with slight variations in the form of the works of Joanna Baillie and adaptations of poems such as Scott's *The Lady of the Lake*.
2. 1817–1835   The first wave of popularity of adaptations of Scott's Waverley Novels brought about a huge upsurge in the writing and performance of national plays.
3. 1835–1860   The National Drama established a unique niche in the Scottish theatre. Around 1850 the major theatres began to restrict and specialise their use of the National Drama.
4. 1860–1900   A split appeared in the kind of treatment accorded the National Drama in the major theatres as against on the popular stage.

There was, during the early years of the century, a real sense of frustration among many Scots at the perceived cultural and institutional drift towards reducing the status of their nation to 'North Britain', which was only partially halted by the work of Burns and Baillie. Dramatisations of the Waverley Novels began to effect a real change. These novels were read everywhere in polite society, at court and in Whitehall. Their comparative respectability, despite their setting in Scotland's recent past, allowed their transfer on to the stage, where they made Scotland's history an acceptable subject for representation. The dramatisations did not escape censorship entirely; any mention of religion, for example, was taboo. But, for the first time in many years, Scotland's actual history and character were considered serious subjects for plays and players. The 'Scott' dramas brought into Scotland's theatres thousands of her people who had never entered them before. Once the floodgates were open, the Scots, hungry to reassert their shared cultural identity in a public arena, returned again and again to see their national heroes and heroines portrayed in authentic Scottish settings by Scottish actors with Scottish accents.

The Edinburgh Theatre Royal, under the management of W. H. Murray, conducted a campaign to portray itself as the natural home of the National Drama, which has tended to obscure the true geographical spread and popularity of the genre. In fact, that theatre was slow to recognise the popularity of the new dramatisations of Scott's novels, leaving it to the minor theatres and travelling groups to pioneer the first stage adaptations of *Guy Mannering* and *Rob Roy*. The Borders saw a version of *Guy Mannering* by a travelling company before it was seen in Edinburgh, while Glasgow and the west, through the efforts of a Mr Mullender, and Aberdeen and Perth, through the work of Corbet Ryder (the most celebrated *Rob Roy* of his generation), all saw Bailie Nicol Jarvie's adventures long before the evening in February 1819 when *Rob Roy* opened at the near-bankrupt Edinburgh Theatre Royal.

That these Scott adaptations created pressure on the Theatre Royal to assert its independence can be seen in the way it dealt with *The Wanderer; or, the Rights of Hospitality*, Duval's play about Bonnie Prince Charlie and Flora Macdonald, which had already fallen foul of Napoleon's censors. The theatre had requested permission to play it in January 1819, but the Lord Chamberlain's office refused to licence the play unless it was set in another time and place. The piece that appeared was billed as taking place in Sweden during the sixteenth century. However, Murray, who had, as the grandson of the Pretender's secretary, a more than ordinary interest in the subject matter, included a precise account of the Lord Chamberlain's actions at the top of the playbills. Three weeks later the Theatre Royal produced *Rob Roy* for the first time.

By this time Charles Mackay (the 'real' Mackay), who was to figure prominently in the history of the National Drama, had transferred from Corbet Ryder's company to play Bailie Nicol Jarvie for W. H. Murray. This began a working relationship and a friendship which was to last over forty years. The Theatre Royal's historian J. C. Dibdin, in his *The Annals of the Edinburgh Stage*, described the effect of the production on the Edinburgh public, 'not only the play-going section, but hundreds who had never before been within the walls of a theatre', as 'marvellous'. A reviewer in *The Scotsman* of 20 February 1819 declared:

> He who is at once a man and a Scotsman must be delighted with *Rob Roy*. Why should we not be proud of our national genius, humour, music, kindness and fidelity? – *Why not be national*?

In an era when theatre programmes commonly changed nightly, *Rob Roy* began a run of forty-one consecutive nights. Murray cleared over £3000 and the theatre was saved. Indeed, over the years the play appears to have rescued so many managements that it became known as 'the managerial sheet-anchor' and the theatrical saying arose 'When in doubt – play *Rob Roy*.'

As each new Waverley Novel appeared it would be eagerly seized upon by

THEATRE, DUMFRIES:

LAST NIGHT but ONE of the Company's Performing here this Season.

FOR THE

Benefit of Mr MUNRO.

TUESDAY Evening, 16th November, 1819,

The Musical Drama of

Rob Roy Macgregor.

The Vocal Music selected from the National Melodies of Scotland, and arranged by BISHOP and DAVY.

Sir Frederick Vernon, Mr BROMLEY.—Rashleigh Osbaldiston, Mr C. MASON.—Francis Osbaldistone, Mr VINING.
Mr Owen, Mr BODDIE.—M'Stewart, Mr MACNAMARA.—Captain Thornton, Mr ROBERTS.—Major Galbraith, Mr EDWARDS·
Rob Roy, - - - - - - - - - Mr MUNRO.
Dougald, Mr BURNE.—Hamish & Robert, (Rob Roy's Sons) Master JOHNSTONE & Master ROBERTS.—Andrew, Mr HAZLETON.
Bailie Nicol Jarvie, Mr MACKAY, as performed by him, for 50 Nights, in the Theatre Royal, Edinburgh.
Host, Mr AITKIN.—Serjeant, Mr POINTER.—Corporal, Mr COLLIER.
Highlanders, Messrs Frome, Grant, Heath, Innes, &c. &c. &c.
Diana Vernon, Mrs LEONARD.—Martha, Mrs HAZLETON.—Mattie, Miss PENMAN.—Hostess, Mrs LACY.
Jean M'Alpine, Mrs BROMLEY.—Helen Macgregor, Miss LACEY.

ARRANGEMENT OF THE SONGS, GLEES AND CHORUSSES.

ACT 1st.	ACT 2d.
GLEE—" Soon the Sun will gae to rest."	SONG—" A Highland Lad my Love was born."
SONG—" Scots wha ha'e wi' Wallace bled."	The Words by Burns.
The words by Burns.	SONG—" A famous man was Robin Hood."
SONG—" Ah ! would it were my humble lot."	Words altered from Wordsworth.
DUET—" Tho' you leave me now in sorrow."	SONG—" Should Auld Acquaintance be forgot."
FINALE—" Hark ! Hark ! from St Mungo's Tower."	The Words by Burns.

ACT 3d.

Chorus of Highlanders—THE LAMENT—" O hone a rie ! O hone a rie !"
Chorus—" ROY'S WIFE OF ALDIVALLOCH."—Words altered from the Original.
Song—" O LIFE IS LIKE A SUMMER'S FLOWER."—THE AIR—" Sam my Johnny coming."
Song—" FORLORN AND BROKEN HEARTED."
FINALE—" Pardon now the Bold Outlaw, ROB ROY MACGREGOR.

NEW SCENERY:

CLACHAN OF ABERFOYLE.

Romantic Pass bordering on Loch Ard ; on each side precipitous rocks ; a track winding along the water's edge, under the base of the mountain, seen in the Perspective.

End of the Play,

" *The Dugald Creature's Account o' her sel',*" will be sung by Mr BURNE.

To conclude with, for the first time here, a Piece in three acts, taken from one of the most popular of the *Tales of Landlord,* and as acted in London upwards of one hundred successive nights, called

The Heart of Mid-Lothian

Or, *The Lily of St Leonard's.*

Duke of Argyle, Mr BROMLEY.   Staunton, Mr C. MASON.   Sharpitlaw, Mr HAZLETON.   Reuben Butler, Mr MACNAMARA.
Saddletree, Mr ROBERTS.   Davie Deans, Mr BODDIE.   Frank, Mr MUNRO.   Tom Tyburn, Mr VINING.
Officer, Mr COLLIER.   And the Laird of Dumbiedikes, Mr BURNE.
Caroline, Queen of England, - - - - - Mrs HAZLETON.
Effie Deans, - - - Miss HARRIOT LACY (her first appearance on this Stage).
Madge Wildfire, Mrs LEONARD.   Margery Murdockson, Miss PENMAN.   Mrs Glasse, Mrs BROMLEY.   And Jeannie Deans, Miss LACY.

Tickets to be had of Mr MUNRO, at Mr GLOVER's, English-street ; and of Mr SMITH, Perfumer, where places for the Boxes may be taken from twelve till two·

BOXES, 3s.——PIT, 2s.——GALLERY, 1s.

Dumfries :—Printed at the COURIER OFFICE.

Figure 3.2 Playbill, 1819, for two National Dramas at Theatre Royal, Dumfries, with Charles Mackay as Bailie Nicol Jarvie in Rob Roy, '*as performed by him, for 50 nights, in the Theatre Royal, Edinburgh*'. (Ewart Library, Dumfries)

managements and turned into a stage piece, regardless of its suitability for the theatre. The quality of the adaptations was variable and tended to be dictated by the needs of the individual theatres at which they appeared. Those Waverley

Novels set in Scotland, and which best transferred to the stage – *Guy Mannering, Rob Roy, The Heart of Mid-Lothian, The Bride of Lammermoor* and *The Abbot* – formed the core of the National Drama repertoire. This group of pieces, along with *The Fortunes of Nigel*, which contained memorable portrayals of James VI and the Edinburgh philanthropist George Heriot,

Figure 3.3 Preparatory sketches by Alexander Nasmyth in 1820 of six scenes for a production of The Heart of Mid-Lothian *at Theatre Royal, Edinburgh.* (National Gallery of Scotland)

encompassed a wide range of settings and regional voices. There was also a noticeable preference in Scotland for those Scott adaptations that most closely followed the originals in plot and language. Scottish audiences disliked a happy ending being tacked on to *The Bride of Lammermoor*. However, around the Scott pieces there now appeared many other works, for the most part historical in setting, which demanded from Scottish theatre professionals new performance standards and production values and which brought about a very general change in the attitude of the Scottish people to the material seen in their theatres.

Although the majority of the National Dramas were set in Scotland's past, it would be wrong to equate them simply with a tradition of Historical Drama. Government had made public access to and acknowledgement of Scotland's history a live political issue. The adjective 'Scotch' disappeared from the bills to be replaced by 'National' and managers were able to announce that 'a new National Drama' was in preparation, secure in the knowledge that they were advertising a popular and recognised type of work. Censorship relaxed, so that by 1828 the Edinburgh Theatre Royal could freely advertise a three-act 'drama' entitled *Charles Edward, or the Last of the Stuarts* written by 'a son of . . . Flora Macdonald'. There was now a far wider choice of Scottish material available to the Scottish theatre.

A measure of the change brought about by the rise of the National Drama can be seen in a visit made by J. H. Alexander's Glasgow company to Dumfries in 1830. In twenty nights, 7 October to 8 November 1830, they performed twenty different National Dramas or plays with Scottish connections, nine forming the main piece of the evening and five appearing more than once. The list below, compiled from playbills, is in order of appearance; the main pieces are underlined and repetitions noted:

The Highland Boy; or, the Castle of Glenalpine
Oscar and Malvina (repeated as a supporting work)
Jamie of Aberdeen
Macbeth
Tam O'Shanter and his Mare Meg
Wallace
Prince Charlie; or, the last of the Stuarts
The Family Legend
The Battle of the Inch of Perth or, for my ain hand
Guy Mannering
Rob Roy
Cramond Brig (twice)
The Bride of Lammermoor (twice)
Gilderoy

St Ronan's Well (twice)
Mary, Queen of Scots (from _The Abbot_) (twice)
Heart of Mid-lothian
English, Irish and Scotch
Love A-la-Mode
The Falls of Clyde

This list is worthy of close consideration for it represents a microcosm of the genre as a whole. The main pieces are a mixture of the new National Dramas, either from Scott or near relations like _Wallace_, and those earlier plays with substance, notably _Macbeth_. Joanna Baillie's _The Family Legend_ never achieved the popularity of the later works of the National Drama but its presence indicated a company that took its commitment to Scottish theatre seriously. _Wallace_ is impossible to identify positively from the bills, since there were at least three different works going the rounds on the subject of William Wallace and playwrights were rarely mentioned in advertising during this period.

The supporting works include lesser favourites from the National Drama, such as _The Battle of the Inch_, _Cramond Brig_ and _Gilderoy_, and a species of work much beloved by the minor theatres, best described as 'Covent Garden Caledonian'. The majority of the latter were English in origin and simply swathed old clichés in a new tartan dressing. The most successful and long lasting of them was Soane's _The Falls of Clyde: or, the Banditti of the Glen_. Some sixty years later, the memoirs of the Glasgow-based Glover family, published in the _Glasgow Evening Times_ of 3 October 1889, described it as a 'good old melodrama' which 'used to be a capital Saturday night piece'.

The Dumfries list represents the core of the national repertoire which would have been seen throughout Scotland. There were some regional variations which usually had local and/or scenic origins: Glasgow was particularly fond of _The Lady of the Lake_, which allowed her scenic artists full rein with views of Loch Lomond; the area around Perth had an affection for _The Battle of the Inch; or for my ain hand_. The larger cities, with the better equipped theatres, played the widest range of National Dramas, including adaptations of Scott's _The Pirate_, _Old Mortality_ and _The Antiquary_ (which needed considerable stage machinery to re-create its central scene of a storm raging around cliffs), but every Scottish audience of the period could expect to see the major pieces and whatever additional works were dictated by the tastes of the manager, guest artists or indeed the patrons.

An important feature of the National Drama was the way in which the new-found respectability of the theatre allowed a far wider range of groups to become involved through their patronage of particular nights, allowing their names to be printed at the top of the playbills. Previously, patronage had tended to be the province of powerful, socially secure groups such as the aristocracy or the military and those interested individuals who often patronised the benefit nights of favourite artists. The National Drama brought into the theatres groups as varied as the Aberdeen Junior Incorporated Trades, Golf Clubs, 'the ladies & gentlemen at Mr Seton's Hotel at Bridge of Earn', and the Border Lodge of Free Gardeners, for whose occasion in 1830 the theatre in Kelso was 'tastefully decorated with flowers'.

As the century progressed the National Drama carved out its own unique niche in the repertoire. It was used in ways which indicated the special status accorded it by theatre professionals and audience alike. In an age when a performer's economic survival often depended on occasional benefit nights (when they chose the pieces and took any profits after expenses), the National Dramas were repeatedly selected, in the first instance by managers or actors with starring roles, and, later, by minor performers and theatre servants, to assure a full house. National Dramas were used to open new theatres or seasons, being both straightforward to produce and regarded as benchmarks of good acting and management by audiences throughout Scotland. They were staged on occasions such as holidays and charity benefits to bring out the occasional, rather than the regular, theatre-goer, and aspiring actors chose national roles for their debuts. The National Drama literally became part of the fabric of Scottish theatres. In 1841 the Glasgow Theatre Royal, Dunlop Street, re-opened after re-decoration by William Dudgeon; the Lower Circle Boxes were decorated with 'subjects from Shakspeare's [sic] most Popular Plays', but

THE SECOND CIRCLE
[was] Embellished with Medallions in alto relievo,
and Vignettes:the subjects from the most
striking Scenes of the Dramatised Works of
Sir Walter Scott

The decoration of theatres went hand in hand with the most striking visual element of the National Drama on Scottish stages, the painted scenery created by some of its leading artists.

SCENE PAINTING IN NINETEENTH-CENTURY SCOTLAND

Changes in theatre lighting during the nineteenth century meant that scenery, particularly upstage, could be seen clearly for the first time, and the new repertoire provided opportunities for scenic artists to paint great landscapes and city views 'taken from the life'. Playbills made a point of listing new scenes, detailing locations and historical precedents for particular buildings or interiors.

For much of the period every theatre and company had its own team of scene painters of varying celebrity. An actress, Charlotte Deans, who toured widely in the Borders during the early part of the century, described in *A Travelling Actress in the North and Scotland* how in Melrose: 'two brothers, Messrs. McIntosh, painted us the best scenery I ever saw in a little theatre, they had judged so correctly of the distance for giving effect that it was admired by all'.

However, many better known artists also worked in the theatre. David Roberts, best known today for his paintings of the Middle East, began as a scene painter and actor for Bannister's Circus in Edinburgh. Roberts painted successfully for theatres in Glasgow and Edinburgh, before being lured to London and eventual employment at Drury Lane. Alexander Nasmyth, the celebrated landscape painter and portraitist of Burns, was for many years the principal scene painter at the Edinburgh Theatre Royal, where his scenery for the National Drama was widely renowned. The destruction by fire of the Glasgow Theatre Royal, Queen Street, was particularly mourned for the loss of an act drop, a view of the Clyde, by Nasmyth.

In Glasgow, Dudgeon provided not only scenery and interior decoration, but also made a speciality of moving panoramas which filled the whole proscenium arch of the stage with subjects such as Queen Victoria's visit to Scotland in 1843 (seven views including scenes of Edinburgh, Taymouth and Stirling Castles, and 7000 figures). Later scene painting in Glasgow was dominated for nearly a hundred years, from the mid century onwards, by the Glover family; the 1892 inventory of the Glasgow Grand Theatre made special mention of a 'Valuable Act Drop "Loch Lomond" by Glover'.[2]

The rise of the National Drama strengthened a practice among scene painters of choosing a national piece, for which they then provided new scenery, for their benefit nights. Scene painters built up followings by depicting those scenes Scottish audiences could recognise and therefore be confident of their ability to judge. If they approved, the play would be stopped while the gallery called for the 'penters' to come forward for applause. The National Drama raised the status and profile of Scottish scene painters and gave them far more of an opportunity to build up reputations and successful careers.

Many Scottish scenic artists began their training as nineteenth-century 'slab boys' learning to mix colours backstage, gradually working their way up to painting, first stock interiors, and finally reaching the heights of named localities. The hierarchy operating among scenic artists can be seen clearly in bills for the Glasgow Theatre Royal, Dunlop Street's 1864 production of Dion Boucicault's *The Streets of Glasgow*. The three painters named, along with an unspecified number of assistants, are F. C. Fisher, J. Brunton and, in large bold type, William Glover. All the scenes are described in the synopsis on the bill and the artist responsible for each is named alongside. John Brunton, the most junior of the trio, painted stock interiors such as 'Crawley's Office, Buchanan

St'. F. C. Fisher had charge of more complex scenes such as 'A Cottage near St Mungo's' and 'The Theatre Royal by Moonlight', while William Glover's principal scenes included 'The Trongate on a Snowy Night' and 'Park Terrace, West End'. It must be a matter for regret that none of Nasmyth's or Glover's

Figure 3.4 William Glover, 'the dominating figure in Glasgow theatricals in the 1860s and 70s'. Theatre manager and celebrated scene painter, whose family were the principal scene-painters in Glasgow from mid century on. (Scottish Theatre Archive)

theatre work survives. These, the largest nineteenth-century Scottish pictures ever painted, were all destroyed, mostly by fire.

Towards the end of the century scene painting began to be farmed out to specialist studios, particularly those in London. It was noticeable, too, that the decoration of theatres, however national in content, was increasingly entrusted to specialists from London. In 1872 when Her Majesty's Opera House, Aberdeen, opened for the season the bills announced that:

> The Decorations have been executed by Mr George Gordon of London, who has also painted the Act Drop, which represents that charming spot on Loch Katrine known as the Silver Strand. The Lunettes over the Private Boxes represent scenes from Sir Walter Scott's Poems, and have been painted by Mr W. Phillips, of London.

CHARLES MACKAY

Charles Mackay (1787–1857) has been associated with the National Drama more than any other actor. He was born in Edinburgh, but moved to Glasgow as a child and always considered the Saltmarket as his 'ain locality'. Mackay joined the Argyllshire Militia as a bandsman and first appeared, unsuccessfully, on the concert platform as a comic singer at the Assembly Rooms in Ayr around 1810. A position was found for him with Henry Erskine Johnston's company in Glasgow, where he began to learn his trade. He subsequently joined Corbet Ryder's company, where he first played characters from the Waverley Novels, and from there he transferred to the Edinburgh Theatre Royal, where he remained for much of his career.

In the 1840s Mackay began to tour Scotland as a solo guest artist. He would stay for around ten days at each theatre, playing all of his favourite national parts. Indeed, some theatres concentrated their use of the National Drama around Mackay's touring, so that once or twice a year they would play small seasons of national plays, up to three per night. Mackay had a round of characters which included not only figures from Scott – Bailie Nicol Jarvie, Dominie Sampson, Dumbiedykes, Poor Peter Peebles, Caleb Waterstone and Richie Moniplies – but also Jock Howieson from *Cramond Brig* and Sandy Macfarlane, who was added to *Mary, Queen of Scots* because there was no part for Mackay in the Scott original. Mackay was a talented singer and a versatile actor who was known for a fine *Richard III*, however, it was as a delineator of Scottish character that he excelled. His nickname became a universal byword for authenticity – 'the real Mackay'.

In the first flush of enthusiasm for the National Drama it had been common for plays to be 'compressed', cut down to the bare bones of the story, so that

Figure 3.5 Charles Mackay (1787–1857) actor (Sir Daniel Macnee). (Scottish National Portrait Gallery)

two or three could be played in a night. By this time audiences knew the mate-rial so well that it was no longer necessary to perform the whole piece. Plays became truncated, starting at the beginning of a second act, or playing acts one and three. It was not uncommon to see *Rob Roy* or *Guy Mannering* advertised as in two acts 'retaining all of [Mackay's] scenes'.

Very early on the National Drama had also spawned the phenomenon of characters who stepped out of their play settings to perform songs or mono-logues as individual acts, the forerunners of the well-loved characters created by Scottish variety artists. Mackay, for example, toured an 'Interlude' ostensibly from *St Ronan's Well*, which was a thinly veiled opportunity for him to sing 'There cam a young man to my Daddy's door' in character as Meg Dods.

Mackay retired in 1848, but financial difficulties forced his return to the stage and he worked up until 1852. On 12 February 1852 at the Glasgow Prince's Theatre Royal, West Nile Street, he was said to be performing Bailie Nicol Jarvie for the 'eleven hundred and thirty-fourth time'.

THEATRE COMPANIES, PROPRIETORS AND LESSEES

In the course of a century the theatre in Scotland changed out of all recognition. From being largely dominated by small family-run businesses, seasonal in the true sense of the word and frequently itinerant, following the social rounds of fairs, assizes, race meetings and cattle shows, by the beginning of the twentieth century it had followed the pattern of many Victorian industries, with chains of urban theatres presenting a standardised product in all their venues, achieving economies of scale and centralised managerial power.

During the early part of the century the size of establishments varied considerably. At one end of the scale were the small bands of performers, frequently members of the same family, doubling and trebling their roles within the organisations and working in whatever spaces could be contrived, occasionally a 'commodious room' in the local inn, which was then dignified with the name of 'Theatre'. Often the venue required some rearrangement for the occasion. The actress Charlotte Deans remembered a barn in Jedburgh where they

> covered the interstices of the roof with scenery to conceal the cobwebs that were abundant, [the] ceiling was a collection of variously grouped paintings of palaces, libraries, waterfalls, streets, &c.

This was a hard life. The title 'strolling player' was a cruel misnomer, implying a carefree ease, which was far from the lot of the common player. Whilst costumes and scenery travelled from place to place by carrier, there was rarely money enough for the actors to ride and Charlotte tramped the roads of Scotland with her husband and children in all weathers:

> We had to walk ten miles with the children, up to the knees in melting snow, and at every hundred yards Mr Deans had to bear us across swollen brooks; we must have perished at one place, but for the kindness of a traveller from Galashiels, the water taking his horse to the shoulders as he carried us across. It was dark long before we reached our place of destination; we had only one guide which was the volcanic-like blazing of Carron Iron Works.

Despite the hardships a number of little companies criss-crossed Scotland taking theatre to towns and hamlets alike, hoping for the patronage of the wealthy, who paid for their servants or farm hands to see the play and who provided some protection against scrupulous officials and clergy. One such company was the Fraser family. In February 1810 they were at the theatre in Inverness performing 'the admired TRAGEDY' of *Douglas, or the Noble Shepherd*. A decade later they were in the Borders playing *Rob Roy* on 12 January 1820 at the 'Theatre' in Galashiels. The company consisted largely of Mr Fraser, Messrs L. & D. Fraser and Miss P. Fraser. The bill was printed by 'D. Fraser of the Theatre' and L. Fraser was the company's scene painter.

In 1820 a 'Mrs Hay' is listed as one of the company. As we have seen, playing the principal works of the National Drama was a financial imperative for companies of all sizes during this period and if they were going to play *Rob Roy* and *Guy Mannering* they had to include all the well-loved music. The chances of such a small company having a good ballad tenor in their midst were remote and so women played romantic leads such as Francis Osbaldiston. *Guy Mannering* presented even more of a problem in that there were more singing roles. The Frasers solved that difficulty at the 'Theatre, Mason's Lodge, Selkirk' on 29 October 1819 by casting a juvenile, Master Fraser, as the equivalent character of Henry Bertram, thereby allowing Mrs Hay to play Julia Mannering.

If the Fraser's company was modest, Corbet Ryder's was considerable. Ryder's sphere of operations was for the most part north of the Central Belt. *The Dundee Advertiser* of 6 November 1819 carried an advertisement for 'His Majesty's Servants' at the Theatre, Arbroath, detailing performances on Monday, 8 November, under the patronage of the Lord Provost and Magistrates, and on Tuesday, 9 November, under the patronage of William Maule MP, when the company would play

The popular national musical Play of ROB ROY MACGREGOR
Already acted by the Northern Establishment
one hundred and eleven nights,

– a circumstance unprecedented in the annals of provincial theatricals.

Ryder added a list of the 'Northern Establishment', which illustrates well the hierarchy operating within a theatre company of the period:

Principal tragedians – Mr Young and Mr Ryder
Light comedian and juvenile tragedian – Mr Poer [sic]
First singing gentleman – Mr Dobbs
Second singing gentleman – Mr Bell
Hearty comedy old man and first Scotsman – Mr Williams
Principal low comedy old man – Mr Chippendale senior
First country boy and eccentric – Mr Berriman
Sentimental father and second Scotsman – Mr Leech

First heavy business – Mr Brown
Irishman – Mr Atkins
Walking gentleman – Mr Denham
Second heavy business – Mr Henry
Second country boy – Mr Chippendale junior
Frenchman, German, Jew &c., – Mr Amherst
Actors generally useful – Mr Taylor, Mr Power, Mr Melmoth, Mr Wright, Mr Rory, Mr Patterson, Mr Leggit, &c.
Orchestra. First violin – Mr Mackenzie
                    Second violin – Mr Power junior
                    Flute – Mr Miller
                    Bass – Mr Macleod
Leading actress in genteel comedy and juvenile tragedy – Mrs Dobbs
First singing lady and general actress – Mrs Ryder
Heavy tragedy and sentimental business – Mrs Henry
First old woman – Mrs Young
Second old woman and Scottish character – Mrs Power
Chambermaid – Mrs Berriman
Second singing lady and dancer – Miss Atkins
Third old woman, &c., – Mrs Atkins
Dancers – Misses Ryder
Stage-manager, Mr Amherst, Prompter, Mr Power, Scene-painters, Messrs Atkins and Henry. Principal mechanist Mr [blank]. Assistant-carpenters, stage-keepers, scene-shifters, wardrobe-keeper, lamp-lighter, bill-sticker, door-keepers, &c.

Here is a self-contained world of theatre – a company capable of playing a huge variety of pieces out of its own strength and relying on each new locality for no more than perhaps a party of the local militia to fill up the background in battle scenes and the occasional guest artist who usually travelled alone.

Most of the theatres on Corbet Ryder's circuit would not have been owned by him, but would be leased, one season at a time, from the proprietors. Dundee City Archives contain Thomas Watt's Account Current Book for the Theatre Royal, Castle Street, for the years 1816 to 1826.[3] Watt was one of a group of businessmen who owned the theatre and his book combines letters to lessees and prospective lessees with end-of-year accounts and correspondence about the range of shops on the ground floor of the building. One interesting aspect of the book is the way in which Watt's circle of correspondence widened over the years, making clear that just as the National Drama began to offer some kind of financial security to the established managers like Corbet Ryder, Henry Johnston, W. H. Murray and Charles Bass, who tended to anchor themselves in major cities, it also encouraged a growing number of individuals prepared to try their luck in an expanding area of business, touring the smaller towns and country areas.

In 1816 Watt wrote to only two managers: W. H. Murray in Edinburgh and Dundee, and Henry Johnston in Glasgow. By 1819 Corbet Ryder was writing to Watt from Inverness and Montrose and Watt was also writing to S. W. Ryley in Cupar, St Andrews and Glasgow; A. Louis was negotiating for the theatre from the Pantheon Theatre in Edinburgh and from Aberdeen, as was a Mr Chalmers from Dundee, and an F. McRoy was being pursued for non-payment of the rent. In fact, collecting the rent became a considerable problem for Watt; the final set of letters, written in 1827 to Corbet Ryder, then occupying the Caledonian Theatre Edinburgh, are all concerned with efforts to make the 'bold outlaw' pay up.

THE POPULAR THEATRE IN TOWN AND COUNTRY

The world of popular theatre in nineteenth-century Scotland encompassed a wide variety of entertainment ranging from the cheapest, frequently unlicensed, theatres in towns, known as 'penny gaffs' from the cost of admission, to the travelling booth theatres, called in Scotland 'geggies', some of which were sizeable affairs with more than competent companies.

The repertoire of the geggies and gaffs seems to have consisted of burletta, melodrama, pantomime, Covent Garden Caledonian and, occasionally, Shakespeare, if the theatres were licensed or lucky enough to avoid detection. They also played the major pieces of the National Drama. Historians of these most basic of theatres have sometimes concluded that they often dispensed with scripts; however, a distinction has to be made between ordinary visits to localities, when the geggies operated a similar timetable and repertoire to the permanent theatres, and fair days, when a shortened programme was played as often as the geggie could be filled. In the case of the National Drama the scripts utilised in gaff and geggie may have been more substantial than usual. The original Scott novels might have been out of the reach of the poorest players, but the short chapbook versions of them were not and many of the widely available chapbooks of the Waverley Novels were in fact drawn from the National Drama, following the changes in plot and dialogue made for the stage.

Unfortunately very few playbills survive for these theatres, but Dundee City Library holds two fine examples. What appears to be the earlier of the two is an undated bill for 'Scott's Royal Licenced Shakespearian Pantheon Open during the Fair In the Meadows with a Dramatic Company 45 in Number!' The playbill lists pieces for Thursday, Friday and Saturday, 'The doors to open at 12, each day, during the Fair.' Thursday's programme features a 'Grand Scottish Melo-Drama, entitled the *SCOTTISH CHIEFTAINS; or, the Haunted*

Tower!' followed by a song, a dance and a 'Comic Pantomime, called *DUNMOW REVELS; or, Harlequin and the Flitch of Bacon!*' A comparison of this with the second bill illustrates the difference between the types of entertainments offered by geggies. The other is for the same theatre on Monday and Tuesday evenings, 12/13 September 1836. Both evenings began with 'the New Romantic Drama' of *The Bear Hunters; or, the Man with Seven Wives!*, followed by a series of turns, concluding with *Lochinvar; or, the Bridal of Netherby*, 'received on the last Three Nights with unbounded Applause, and to Crowded Houses'.

   Not all geggies were laid out like regular theatres. Mr Ord, of Ord's Circus, along with Pablo Fanque, Andrew Ducrow and others, specialised in work in a ring or 'amphitheatre'. Whilst nineteenth-century popular entertainment encompassed circuses, which would still be recognisable as such, the more interesting companies, from the point of view of the theatre, were those formed around equestrian actors, a breed quite unknown today, despite the survival of the occasional 'Hippodrome'. The general dependence on horsepower at the time meant that there was great interest in fine horsemanship; artists toured the country with troupes of horses and trained dogs, performing a mixture of feats of skill, melodramas and pantomime stories while standing on the backs of horses cantering around a ring. For example, Ord's Royal

Figure 3.6 Glasgow Fair, c. 1825, showing a variety of stages and popular entertainments. (Scottish Theatre Archive)

Sketch of the RUINS of the CITY THEATRE, Glasgow.
as they stood on November 20th 1845

Figure 3.7 Ruins after fire of City Theatre, Glasgow, 1845. (Scottish Theatre Archive)

Amphitheatre 'Front Of The Green, Glasgow' in August 1831 featured Mr Ord's new character of 'Bailie Nicol Jarvie on Horseback!' These performance spaces were built with a circle at pit level and often a stage at one end.

Much of the surviving evidence about the popular theatres comes from official efforts to control or suppress them, sometimes for reasons of safety but more often in the name of public morality. They were said to have a pernicious effect on the morals and industry of the working class and young people who attended them, and they were therefore the targets of employers, politicians and clergy alike. A Glasgow Dean of Guild Report for 6 July 1849 noted sourly that a Mr Calvert 'of the wooden Hibernian Theatre' had obtained:

> authority to erect a new brick edifice in Greendyke Street immediately to the east of the Episcopal Chapel, and adjoining the Model Lodging Houses for the working classes. Now that the Adelphi Theatre, the City Theatre and Cook's Circus have been all swept off the Green by fire in less than four years, we have no doubt that this Hibernian will have 'ample room and verge enough' for dishing up the penny drama for the delectation and improvement of the canaille and young Red Republicans of the Bridgegate, the Wynds, Saltmarket, High Street, the

Vennels and the Havannahs. Since the house is to go up the Court wisely resolved to look to its security.

This was the Queen's Theatre, and the Dean of Guild despatched a structural engineer to ensure the proper construction of the building. However, not all popular venues were so thoroughly checked; enquiries into the fatal panics at Springthorpe's Music Hall, Dundee, in 1865, the Star Theatre of Varieties, Glasgow, in 1884, and the fire in the People's Palace of Varieties, Aberdeen, in 1896, concluded that all three venues were structurally unsafe.

There was, overall, rather more emphasis on the morality than on the safety of popular entertainments. In 1863 the pages of the Dundee press were occupied for weeks by reports and correspondence about the supposed evils of 'penny theatres' and one particular gaff in Lindsay Street which was causing concern among the unco guid. On Friday 24 July, *The Dundee Advertiser* printed the text of a petition set before a meeting of the Police Commissioners deploring

> the existence in Dundee of what are generally known by the name of 'Penny Theatres' which, by all former experience have proved the source of vice and crime wherever they are permitted . . . a vast amount of profligacy has been occasioned in this town by entertainments of the above description, and . . . every means should be adopted to prevent the continuance of an evil so demoralising to the young of the lower classes.

When the petition was presented, Mr O'Farrell of the Watching Committee promised their careful consideration and added that he also 'knew' that

> the very boys who went with lamps to awake workers in the morning were so vitiated by their love for these amusements that one broker had been sold no less than 30 and 40 of the lamps, in order that the proceeds might procure them admission to the penny theatre.

The following Tuesday (28 July) *The Advertiser* printed an indignant letter from Charles Fitzball, the manager, who refuted O'Farrell's many complaints point by point:

> To say that immorality can be carried on in the hall is simply absurd . . . the place is a large open room – a blaze of light. There are men stationed to enforce order, and their task is an easy one. No intoxicated person is admitted; no smoking is allowed; the least attempt at disturbance is followed by immediate expulsion. The utmost order and quiet is kept

during the performance; and the audience for decorous behaviour and attention would bear favourable comparison with audiences of a much higher class. As to the stage itself, the pieces put on are just the same as are performed in Theatres Royal. No piece of an immoral or questionable tendency is ever permitted . . . My company is the one your Magistrates licensed under the management of Miss Goddard. They are all respectable men to whom I pay high salaries . . . It humbly appears to me, Sir, that, instead of blame, I deserve the thanks of your town for providing a comfortable place of rational amusement for the class who generally attend. Do the petitioners think they would better be left on the streets? Do they think that their homes are attractive enough to entice them to remain in them? Does not the fact that my place is filled night after night throughout the year show that some amusement is wanted; that hard unvarying toil and sleep alone does not satisfy the 'lower classes', as the petition calls them?

THEATRE MANAGERS AND THE LAW

Theatre managements had always to be careful not to overstep the bounds of local licensing regulations, but in the years before the abolition of the Patent the legal position of theatres could be very awkward indeed. The most usual sources of friction were instances where the managements of the Theatres Royal felt the minor theatres to be infringing on their Patents; however, in 1825, the citizens of Glasgow were treated to the lively spectacle of two rival managers of minor theatres fighting over the same building. The Caledonian Theatre in Dunlop Street (the old Theatre Royal), which had been superseded by the new Queen Street Theatre, was leased by a Mr Seymour, who just secured the licence ahead of J. H. Alexander. 'Alick' was not a man to accept such an imposition and so he leased the cellar beneath the Caledonian, rechristened it the Dominion of Fancy, and opened up as a rival house. This would have been provocation in itself, but for the fact that there was only a set of floorboards between the establishments:

On nights when a quiet romantic drama was planned for one theatre the other would hire a brass band; if the theatre in the cellar . . . was producing a play with special firework effects . . . then the occupants of the theatre above would pour water down through the floorboards and extinguish the flames. Eventually the Glasgow Magistrates insisted that the theatres played on different nights, but the Glasgow public, anxious not to miss the fun, came in their thousands and the more illustrious Theatre Royal in Queen Street lost heavily.[4]

A far more serious dispute occurred between the Edinburgh Theatre Royal and the Caledonian Theatre, Edinburgh, under Corbet Ryder, highlighting the place of the National Drama in the rise of the minor theatres. The economic importance of the National Drama to the Theatre Royal meant that any rival company which looked like making a name for itself with national plays was seen as a threat, and Ryder's company was known for its confident production of national pieces. During a brief season at the Caledonian in 1823, Ryder had largely ignored warnings from the Patent house that he should desist from playing 'regular' pieces. In 1825, faced with his continuing success on a return visit, the Theatre Royal applied for an interim interdict against him in the Court of Session.

At first sight it seemed as though Ryder had laid himself wide open to legal action. His company had always played the legitimate drama in those towns and cities where he held the Patent, but once in Edinburgh, Ryder had continued to perform, for example, *Richard III*, renaming it, *The Battle of Bosworth Field*. However, when the case came to court he hardly argued the point, as it soon became clear that the real target of the Theatre Royal's actions was the National Drama.

Every theatre in Scotland and every travelling company played *Rob Roy*. Most used Pocock's popular adaptation and all regarded the National Dramas as 'plays' or 'operas', not falling within the legitimate repertoire proper, but definitely a cut above the 'melodramas' and 'burlettas' previously allowed in minor theatres. Ryder was playing *Rob Roy* at the Caledonian, but calling it a 'melodrama', and so now the Theatre Royal were attempting to prevent him from playing any piece that a Patent theatre had ever staged or had licensed, legitimate or otherwise, from Shakespeare to the most illegitimate pantomime. Ryder insisted that he sought only to perform those pieces seen in minor theatres throughout Britain. The Theatre Royal replied that as soon as a Patent house applied to perform any piece, thereby automatically triggering a licence from the Lord Chamberlain's office, that play became the exclusive property of the Theatres Royal, regardless of whether they ever actually performed it. Since *some* melodramas had been licensed, *no* melodramas could be performed without a licence. Dibdin's *Heart of Midlothian* might have been written for a minor theatre in London, but the Edinburgh Theatre Royal had received a licence to play it and it was therefore now the Theatre's property, despite the fact that it actually preferred to use a version by W. H. Murray, manager of the Theatre Royal.

Legal argument raged back and forth about the exact meaning of the word 'melodrama' and the provisions of the original statute. Finally, the interdict was granted, and the effect on the Caledonian was immediate. It was cut off from a large and lucrative part of its repertoire and Ryder lost no time in acquainting the wider public with the real target of the Theatre Royal's actions.

On the evening of 26 February 1825, the bills announced the 'Independent National Melo-drama' of *Robert the Bruce, or Liberty Restored* – a shrewd choice of work. The trial had been followed avidly in the press, and once the verdict was known, letters for and against the judgement filled the columns of the theatrical journals. Many resented the apparent restraint on trade, feeling that Scotland's capital ought to be able to support more than one theatre. Finally, regardless of the ruling, Murray's was a hollow victory. He could not stop Ryder playing *Rob Roy*, he could only ban the use of certain versions of it, and the novel, with its invaluable dialogue, was firmly in the public domain. On 30 March 1825 the *Edinburgh Dramatic Review* reported from the Caledonian Theatre that:

> A new version of Rob Roy was produced . . . last night with decided success. The language is almost *Verbatim* from the novel and where the incidents require to be filled up, a complete variation may be observed from the text of Mr Pocock, or from that of the Theatre Royal version.

Alongside 'new' National Dramas, Ryder fought back by instituting a half-price policy, which the Theatre Royal was then obliged to copy. Murray, by his actions, had also made his own repertoire a matter of vociferous public debate. On 23 April 1825 the *Dramatic Review* declared roundly that:

> The excessive run of Scotch pieces in this theatre is rather provoking . . . The Theatre Royal management is now more imperiously called upon than ever to provide the public with variety, and the most classical pieces, having obtained a monopoly of such pieces; and the public, which grudged this monopoly at all times, will not passively endure any attempt virtually to extend it by competing with The Caledonian upon the only ground which remains to it.

In 1829–30 Murray finally resolved the nagging problem of the Caledonian by managing it himself. He was granted the lease on condition that he open the theatre for an agreed number of days per year; however, he largely ignored this, opening only when the Theatre Royal was closed for the summer. The building was as much a drain on the Theatre Royal's coffers when empty, as it had seemed to be when occupied.

THE EDINBURGH THEATRE ROYAL – THE NATIONAL THEATRE

The Theatre Royal's long-running dispute with Corbet Ryder was symptomatic of the difficult position in which it found itself. It could not seem to find a balance between its perceived role as the premier Patent theatre in Scotland and the demands of the box office. When Murray played the legitimate repertoire he found the treasury all too often emptying at an alarming rate, his company criticised for lack of classical experience and his productions for parsimony. Yet when he spent money on spectacles to which audiences flocked, thunders rained down upon his head for debasing public tastes and wasting the rights conferred on him, so exclusively, by the Patent. However, there is no doubt that the nineteenth-century Scottish theatre was headed, certainly in the minds of those who worked in the industry, by Edinburgh's Theatre Royal, and that theatre was dominated by its manager, W. H. Murray, for nearly forty years.

When Henry Siddons died in 1815, leaving a young wife and family loaded with debt, his brother-in-law, Murray, took over the management of the theatre and thereafter devoted his life to it. All the surviving accounts of Murray's management speak loudly of his bustling energy and commitment to detail, his emphasis on the disciplined running of every department of the house, and the affection in which the majority of the actors, many of whom stayed with the theatre throughout their careers, held him. Although a small man he was not above climbing into the boxes himself and bodily ejecting troublemakers, while his aristocratic antecedents and friendship with many of the leading figures in Edinburgh society did much to raise the status of the theatre.

The autobiography of the Victorian actor-manager John Coleman devotes considerable space to his experiences as a young actor training in various Scottish theatres. One chapter, recounting his time in Edinburgh, begins: 'The National Theatre of Scotland occupied a position so unique and so dignified that nothing like it now remains in existence.' Coleman describes the day-to-day workings of the Edinburgh Theatre Royal towards the end of Murray's career:

> During my apprenticeship the routine of business proceeded with the regularity of clockwork. Our rehearsals commenced daily at ten and terminated at or about two . . . The principal members of the company had been together for years; hence a large and comprehensive repertoire of pieces was always ready for representation. The old stagers had few new parts to study, but whether new or old, every play was carefully rehearsed; hence everything was completely and admirably done. Newer works Murray invariably super-intended himself, and it was most interesting to see the finesse, the variety, and completeness he imparted to them.[5]

From the first Murray's management was characterised by the kind of rigorous application and attention to detail, which included an insistence on proper rehearsals. By sheer hard work, he kept the Theatre Royal open for much of the year, year after year, using every wile to coax, cajole and bully audiences into coming. When a play taken from Southey's poem 'Mary, the Maid of the Inn' was produced in 1823, Murray had the original ballad printed on to posters, which were plastered all over the city. When Charles Mackay retired in 1848, Murray created a furore around the possible consignment of the National Dramas 'to the tomb of the Capulets' and the subsequent search for a new 'Bailie', which was nicely calculated to draw the curious.

Combined with this tireless energy Murray displayed a single-minded devotion to the interests of the theatre, which could lead to his acting ruthlessly with employees. J. H. Alexander left the Theatre Royal in 1821, after an acrimonious argument with Murray, and published his own account of a salary and contract dispute which hardly reflected well on the manager. Also around this time, when the Theatre Royal was perceived as making a good deal of money from the National Drama, the theatrical press engaged in a sniping war over the modest salaries paid at what was supposed to be Scotland's premier theatre. In 1823 the *Edinburgh Dramatic Review*, after a very two-edged appeal to support Murray's impending benefit, published a letter from a group of dismissed actors; it speaks volumes about the conditions under which the

Figure 3.8 Scotland's 'National Theatre' – the Theatre Royal, Shakespeare Square, Edinburgh, after remodelling carried out in 1828 (John Le Conte, c. 1854). (Crown Copyright: Royal Commission on the Ancient and Historical Monuments of Scotland)

lowliest members of the company worked and about the iron hand with which Murray ruled (the original spelling and grammar are preserved):

Sir this is to let You Know about Something that Past in the Theater the Time George Herriot Came out the Play Was Rehersed 3 Days Tuesday Wedensday and Thursday Julles Cecere Was Rehersed on the Monday and the Ware 12 Super[-] numers On it and Mr Murray Picked 6 of the Oldest Hands Out fore George Herriot and We all Attended the 3 Days for 6d the Night and the Solders 1s the Night and We had a Grait Deal More to Do in it then the had and We asked Mr Murray if he Would Give us a Shilling the Night fore that Pice as We had So Much to Do and he said is Was a Damd insult on A Gentlemen and Put us all to the Door and Told us Never to Show Your Faces Within the Door agan and he Ordred 6 Solders On and the Would Not Come fore a Sixpence the Night and he had to Send to Mr Callam Tin Smith Leith Walk fore 6 of his Men At 5oClock that Night of the Play and Mr Murray had to Reherse them that Night and he Told us he Could Get Lads to Come for Nothing after We had Ben there fore 3 or 4 years. Please Sir to insirt a Little about it in your Paper Will Much Oblige us all

THE SUPERNUMERS

Murray's one serious artistic failing was that he viewed the profession of playwright as hardly meriting the dignity of the name. He consequently had a very uneasy relationship with playwrights, which kept the Theatre Royal short of new material. It also meant that Scotland's 'National Theatre' provided no kind of refuge or proving ground for native playwriting talent. Whilst the National Dramas which appeared under his name, either finely crafted novel adaptations like the five-act *The Heart of Mid-Lothian* or the smaller original pieces *Gilderoy* and *Cramond Brig*, provided much of the core of the genre, once Scott stopped writing Murray produced no more, certainly nothing with the nationwide appeal of *Mary, Queen of Scots*. Finally it was Murray's refusal to pay a modest fee to the playwright J. R. Planché, and his subsequent piracy of the play in question, *Charles XII*, which occasioned the formation of the first authors' rights society.

The precise role within any society to be played by a National Theatre has always been a contentious one. Under its previous manager, Henry Siddons, the Edinburgh Theatre Royal began to contribute to the theoretical debate surrounding the drama through Siddons's writings on the art of acting and through the theatre's championship of the plays of Joanna Baillie. Under William Murray, if it did not contribute to any long-term flowering of Scottish playwriting, it indubitably provided a home for one of the most talented and truly Scottish companies ever to appear on the Scottish stage, and since graduates of

Murray's hard school travelled far and wide, it was also a training ground for a generation of actors and so benefited the whole of the country.

W. H. Murray retired in 1851, worn out by the unending struggle to make the theatre viable. He had maintained the Theatre Royal's monopoly on Edinburgh audiences, but by mid century the Edinburgh press and audiences had begun to demand more variety to their amusement, almost literally, and Murray decided that it was time to go. His forty-two years before the Edinburgh public represented a unique and hard-won achievement but at the last, despite the many plaudits which accompanied his retirement, he seems to have been so disheartened that he burned every piece of paper connected with his career, including twenty-two years of carefully kept diaries. He died less than a year later in St Andrews.

SCENE CHANGES: THE NATIONAL DRAMA, 1850–1900

After Murray retired, the Theatre Royal was taken over by the comedian H. F. Lloyd, while Robert Wyndham opened the Adelphi (the former Caledonian) after alterations. Lloyd barely lasted a season before his expansive style of management brought him to bankruptcy. Rollison and Leslie, who followed him, did no better. Meanwhile Wyndham was persevering at the Adelphi. On 4 September 1852 Miss Vining stepped before the curtain with an address that declared that:

> Old Shakespeare ever and anon peeps forth,
> 'Never say die' his motto i' the north: –
> And ever welcomed fresh, with one accord,
> Your bold Rob Roy can never be outlaw'd!
>
> [. . .]
>
> Guy Mannering – Mid Lothian and the Bride
> Of Lammermoor in favour still abide:
> Your hearts, like Prince's [sic] Street, with truth declare
> Scott's Monument exists for ages there.[6]

However, there was no doubt that the relationship between the major Scottish theatres and the National Drama was beginning to show signs of strain. On playbills the adjective 'Scotch' began to reappear, and there was a resurgence of the 'Scotch Ballet'.

By mid-century, economic considerations demanded that the major urban theatres woo back the middle-class audiences, who had largely deserted them except for opera and the annual pantomime. Throughout the second half of the century managers refurbished their houses, eliminating the rowdy pit benches in favour of cushioned individual stalls seats. Middle-class audiences wanted what they perceived to be more sophisticated entertainment than the old National Drama. Their national identity was at once more secure and more fragmented, in that middle-class economic hopes and aspirations were often irrevocably bound up with the expanding fortunes of the British Empire. There was, therefore, a temptation on the part of managers to cater for that 'elevated' taste with productions bought in from London. As far as the National Drama was concerned, those elements of Scottish history and character which appealed to the exile, and to those patrons at home who saw their Scottish identity as something nostalgic, were emphasised.

The major works of the National Drama were now being placed carefully by managements for maximum return. Theatrically conservative play-goers, to be found in major theatres only on occasions such as Christmas, were charmed by lavish productions of the National Drama. National pieces were often chosen to accompany Juvenile Nights, when the usual order of performance was reversed and the pantomimes that normally came at the end of the bill, being aimed largely at adults, were placed first. The Fair Holidays also found many large theatres balancing the budgetary security of the winter pantomime with a summer production of a National Drama.

The major theatres developed a two-pronged strategy to deal with national materials in this changed climate. The first approach involved taking new theatrical forms and employing them on Scottish subject matter. Forty years

Figure 3.9 Playbill heading, 1845, Theatre Royal, Dunlop Street, Glasgow.
(Scottish Theatre Archive)

after the publication of the Waverley Novels, playwrights no longer had to work within the constraints placed on them by audience expectations of a faithful representation of the originals; they had a new freedom to work with the materials. An example of this type of writing can be seen in the work of one of the most prolific nineteenth-century playwrights, Irish-born Dion Boucicault, who dramatised *The Heart of Mid-Lothian*, re-creating it as one of the new 'sensation' dramas, *The Trial of Effie Deans*. It appeared at the Prince's Theatre Royal, Glasgow, in 1863. Nevertheless, it was noticeable that the new plays were not considered to be or advertised as true National Dramas. There were also home-grown attempts at working with the new forms, such as E. W. Gomersal's 1853 play *The Flax Spinners of Dundee! Love, Jealousy and Revenge!* Written for Gomersal's own Theatre Royal, Dundee, it was a tale of murder and suicide set in a mill, with a headline on the bill that read: 'Oh! could but the Wealthy see, instead of hear of, one-half of the misery and want that exists, they would shudder at the sight.' Unfortunately, these pieces rarely ran for more than a handful of performances in a single theatre.

Certain sections of the industry responded to changing audience expectations by treating National Dramas with a new reverence. Scottish managers sought to emulate the spectacular Shakespearian productions being put on by Charles Kean at the Princess's Theatre in London, which were proving so popular with middle-class audiences. Some material lent itself more readily to this type of treatment, notably Scott's long poems, hence *The Lady of the Lake* came into its own on stage once again, produced in a quasi-operatic style. One of the pioneers of this lavish production style was the Glasgow manager Edmund Glover, who staged a series of Shakespeare plays but soon turned his attention to the National Drama as a more realistic financial proposition.

The centenary of Scott's birth in 1872 was marked by most of the theatres in Scotland and provided a further impetus for this type of production, often in new adaptations. In April 1872, A. D. McNeill's 'Waverley' company appeared at the Theatre Royal, Dundee, 'For Twelve Nights only' . . . 'for the production of his [McNeill's] Popular adaptations of Sir Walter Scott's beautiful Romances of Redgauntlet and St Ronan's Well Which achieved an uninterrupted run of Nine Consecutive Weeks when originally produced in Edinburgh' (*The Dundee Advertiser*, 30 April 1872).

In 1878 a production of *Rob Roy* at the Theatre Royal, Dundee, by J. B. Howard's Edinburgh company, was described in the programme as 'on a scale of magnificence hitherto unattempted. New scenery, including a real waterfall, elaborate accessories, appropriate music, costumes, &c'.

By this time, programmes had replaced the miniature playbills formerly sold inside theatres and several Edinburgh theatres included the legends and devices of the National Drama on their covers, giving the genre equal weight with 'Tragedy', 'Comedy', 'Opera' and 'Farce.' However, the major theatres,

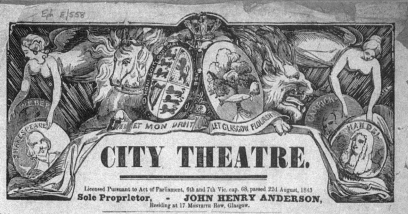

CITY THEATRE.

Licensed Pursuant to Act of Parliament, 6th and 7th Vic. cap. 68, passed 22d August, 1843

Sole Proprietor, - JOHN HENRY ANDERSON,

Residing at 17 Monteith Row, Glasgow.

By the Regulations of the Licensing Magistrates, the Performances at this Theatre will terminate at or before TWELVE o'clock every Evening, with the exception of SATURDAYS, when the Curtain will fall at or before Half-past ELEVEN, P.M.

Doors will be open at Half-past Six, and the Performance commence precisely at Seven.

Immense Houses! Hundreds turned unable to gain admission.

Mr J. H. ANDERSON feels great pleasure in announcing to the Nobility, Gentry, and Public of Glasgow, that on THIS EVENING, MONDAY, September 22, will be performed, for the first time at the City Theatre, and in a style unparalleled in the Annals of Theatricals in Glasgow, the immortal bard of Avon's beautiful Tragedy of

HAMLET!

With Gorgeous Scenery, Appropriate Costumes, Splendid Paraphernalia, Properties, &c. &c.

Hamlet, Prince of Denmark, - - - - - - by Mr JAMES BENNETT.

His First appearance in Glasgow in that Character.

Gertrude, Queen of Denmark, - - - by Mrs DYAS.

Her First Appearance in that Character in Glasgow.

First Night of the GRAND BALLET of ACTION, produced under the entire direction of

MONSIEUR LE CLERCQ,

OF THE

WOODMAN PRINCE!

Mario, Monsieur Le CLERCQ, his first appearance. - Carilda, Mademoiselle Le CLERCQ, her first appearance.

First Night of the Laughable Afterpiece, never acted in Glasgow, of

Mr & Mrs WHITE.

Peter White, - - - by Mr H. BEDFORD.

This Evening, MONDAY, Sept. 22d, 1845,

Will be performed, for the First Time, Shakspere's Tragedy of

Hamlet!

Hamlet, Prince of Denmark, Mr JAMES BENNETT

King, Mr SIMPSON—Ghost, Mr HAE—Polinus, Mr J. JAMES—Laertes, Mr M. SMYTHSON

Horatio, Mr BIRCH—Rosencrantz, Mr ROYSTON—Guildenstern, Mr OSBORNE—Osric, Mr WILLIAM MONTAGUE—Marcellus, Mr DYAS—Bernardo, Mr STODDART

Figure 3.10 Playbill, 1845, City Theatre, Glasgow. (Scottish Theatre Archive)

while retaining the icons of the National Drama on their fitments and its legend on their programmes, had begun to rework national material to reclaim it for a cultural élite.

A side-effect of this reverence was that the burlesques of Scott dramatisations, so popular in English theatres, were frowned upon by the Scottish critics. One commentator, shortly after a visiting company had played *Robbing Roy; or Scotch'd and Kilt* in Glasgow, complained that:

> [The] Arabian tale of 'The Forty Thieves' is a much fitter subject for burlesque than is our Scottish National Drama. Somehow I never can thoroughly enjoy a burlesque of a serious piece. There is a sort of vandalism in the very act of laughing that, for me, at any rate, blunts the point of every witticism. (*The Quiz*, 2 September 1881)

The National Drama had become a kind of valuable antique, to be treated with respect but kept immobile, behind glass, on the picture-frame stage.

THE POPULAR STAGE AND THE 'NATIONAL' REPERTOIRE

During this period a percentage of the population seems to have been excluded from the major theatres not merely by market forces but almost by statute, as audience attendance was manipulated by official bodies. In 1887 (27 August), *The Chiel* reported the reopening of the Glasgow Theatre Royal under the management of W. T. Rushbury and noted that:

> The gallery boys were very well behaved. In charging only threepence for admission to this part of the house, Mr Rushbury has played a trump card, but it will revive an old controversy. The other caterers for the amusement of the public already complain that their licence does not permit them to follow suit, and I shall not be at all surprised if Mr Rushbury's experiment does not lead to a revision of the local laws governing theatres. The old Dunlop St Theatre had a threepenny gallery, and surely we are as orderly now as then.

In fact, solicitors for the other Glasgow managements had already complained to the Lord Chamberlain's office that under regulations set down by the local Justices they were obliged to charge a minimum of sixpence for admission. The Examiner of Plays had replied to the effect that the Lord Chamberlain was unable to interfere with the old Patent, which did not include any such ruling.[7] With the major theatres priced out of their range, working-class audiences were increasingly directed towards the cheaper and, coincidentally, more flexible environs of the popular stage, such as the penny geggies, working-class theatres, circuses and music halls, which retained their commitment to the old 'National' pieces. In Dundee on 29 September 1885, the Adelphi Theatre, Old Cattle Market, whose bills were proudly headed, 'The Only Theatre at People's Prices', offered a version of *The Heart of Mid-Lothian* in a week of attractions which included *Hamlet*, *Pizarro* and *The Octoroon*. Walter Baynham, in *The Glasgow Stage* (1892), regretted the passing of the national repertoire at the leading theatres in favour of 'slangy leg-pieces' and noted that:

> Since the epoch when travelling companies became the fashion the old Scotch melodramas have found their city of refuge only in the shows. Our only chance now of having our boyish theatrical recollections revived is at Vinegar Hill during the Fair holidays. To canvas-covered Temples of the Drama – the plays have fled, and also many of the players, and some very good actors will still be found at Collins's at the Fair time.

The popular stage had fewer inhibitions about working with, even subverting, the traditions of the National Drama, and it is possible to see here the survival of traditional performance techniques which have been exploited so successfully by twentieth-century playwrights and performers. The popular theatre differed from the 'legitimate stage' in its treatment of the National Drama in the flexible use of performance space and the continued exchanges between audience and performers. The latter had been largely eliminated in the legitimate theatres by the actors' gradual retreat upstage into the midst of increasingly complex scenery. The flexible use of space was nowhere more obvious than in the circles of circus and geggie. Military spectacles were standard fare in mid Victorian theatres; theatres in Glasgow and Edinburgh both, for example, staged versions of *The Battle of the Alma* during the Crimean War. Managements and audiences at the popular end of the market also took delight in large-scale national spectacle, particularly *The Gathering of the Clans*. This was a form, like pantomime, in which numbers of children were employed. Certain managers, notably Mrs Allford in Dundee, made a speciality of training the 'Infant Armies' for these occasions. The Alhambra Theatre, Dundee, in May 1866, presented *The Gathering of the Clans*, featuring 'upwards of 100 persons . . . including Highland Dancers, Pipers, Vocalists, and the Infant Army of 50 Dundee Children' (*The Dundee Advertiser*, 11 May 1866).

When national material was reworked by the popular stage it was usually to add a populist slant to the Victorian passion for spectacle. Almost twenty years later *The Gathering of the Clans* had mutated into a Christmas offering

Figure 3.11 Playbill, 1850, Edinburgh Adelphi Theatre. The mixed programme features an adaptation of a Shakespeare comedy alongside a troupe of 'histrionic dogs and monkeys', demonstrating the uninhibited nature of the popular stage. (The Trustees of the National Library of Scotland)

at Newsome's East End Hippodrome (Circus) in Glasgow. *The Quiz* reviewer of 30 December 1881 announced that it was:

> Mr Newsome's extra treat for the holiday season. It takes the shape of a Royal Review at which Her Majesty the Queen watches with patriotic pride the warlike manoeuvres of her Highland lads. The children are cleverly drilled, and the whole thing is, in its way, most effective.

Newsome's Hippodrome would have attracted a Christmas audience that included a fair percentage of middle-class spectators. At the same time the Royal Princess's, in the Gorbals, was giving its own characteristic twist to the same materials, making the spectacle at once more fantastic and more down to earth. The Princess's pantomime was *Aladdin*, containing a *Gathering of the Clans* in which Widow Twankey replaced Victoria on the reviewing stand. The army of children were dressed in the uniforms of local regiments.

The amateur societies which flourished throughout Scotland played their part in preserving the repertoire, as they had done a hundred years earlier, and in going some way to replacing the training ground for young performers which had been lost with the demise of the stock system. Participation in theatrical societies was a leisure activity which cut across class lines. Amateur theatricals brought a number of performers on to the professional stage; the Scots actor and comedian, James Houston, described the 'The Shakespeare', a Glasgow working-class club he joined while an engineering apprentice:

> We had a nice little hall at the foot of Brunswick Street, well furnished, with every thing necessary for a dramatic performance. There would be about twenty members – young trades' lads, clerks, and shop-keepers . . . Mr Wright, the highly respected lessee for the last quarter of a century of the Theatre Royal, Greenock, was a member; also Mr James Craig, now an eminent actor.[8]

'The Shakespeare' was an all-male affair, as were most clubs. Professional actresses were engaged to play the female parts. Houston also describes performances by the club in large professional theatres hired specially for the evening.

There were regular performances of National Dramas, particularly *Rob Roy* and *Guy Mannering*, by amateur companies throughout the rest of the century. They were felt, quite apart from their popularity, to be well suited to amateurs, having large casts and choruses which allowed a good number of members to participate in productions. *The Quiz* of 8 December 1892 commented on a production of *Rob Roy* by the Dramatic Club of the 1st Lanark Rifle Volunteers at the Glasgow Grand, declaring that it was the play of plays of Scotch amateurs. The business is so well known and so easily learned by capable players, that a first-class performance of the old fashioned work is by no means uncommon.

One other area of amateur involvement, which was to have more of an effect on the Scottish drama during the first half of the twentieth century, emerged in embryo during this period, in the socialist Sunday schools, whose teaching plays, performed by the children on special occasions, sought to convey the messages of the socialist movement. Whilst the nineteenth century had seen isolated incidents of workers' groups employing theatrical forms to convey, for example, their position in labour disputes, there had been an overall tendency for political and trade organisations to regard dramatic readings and performances simply as good ways of fundraising. Particularly in Glasgow and the west, however, the turn of the century saw the beginnings of a blending of political theory with theatrical practice.

MUSIC HALL

No account of the Scottish theatre at the end of the nineteenth century can omit some mention of two of the most flourishing forms of popular entertainment: music hall and pantomime.

Music halls developed out of a number of different types of venue as a result of legislation designed, primarily, to control theatres. The origins of music hall can be seen in entertainments as diverse as the geggie theatres, burletta houses and pleasure gardens, the largely amateur free-and-easies and the singing saloons attached to public houses, all of which catered for the burgeoning urban populations with money wages in their pockets and little inducement to spend their free time in cramped and uncomfortable homes.

The Act of 1843, which allowed the minor theatres to play the legitimate drama, also took away from them the right to sell alcohol and tobacco within the auditorium during the performance. The new music halls, which retained this valuable concession, imitated song-and-supper rooms. These haunts of urban upper-class men often determined the shape of a theatre. They were mostly oblong in shape with a single gallery and a stage at one end, and a flat floor at pit level for the drinkers' tables and the chairman who controlled the proceedings. The auditorium audiences were a cross-section of the urban working class and included a surprising number of children and groups of young women. Certain halls, such as the Star Theatre of Varieties in Glasgow, made special provision for women with babes in arms.

The north of England and some areas of Scotland retained a tradition of 'free halls', where admission was gained by purchase of a refreshment ticket which was then exchanged for drink. Glasgow had a particular fondness for 'bursts', temperance concerts so-called because the audience would blow up and burst the paper bags which had contained the bun accompanying their cup of tea in the interval.

Now that the sale of alcohol and tobacco during the performance was prohibited, theatres became concerned about the way the music halls impinged on their province by playing sketches and regular plays. There were repeated skirmishes between rival managements and the licensing authorities. It is doubtful how successful the theatres were at eliminating competition through legislation, particularly when the same managements sometimes ran both venues. Certainly the Dundee Theatre Royal and the Dundee Music Hall appear at times to have run almost parallel programmes. In January 1872 the Scottish actor-playwright William Lowe was appearing at the Music Hall as 'Dougall McDougall' in *The Orphan of Glencoe* while the Theatre Royal was preparing for a series of Scott dramas as part of its centenary celebrations. The Theatre Royal played *Jeanie and Effie Deans*, *Rob Roy* and Andrew Halliday's *The King O' Scots* in succession over the next few weeks. Meanwhile the Music Hall catered for the national tastes of its audiences with Lowe's *Tam O'Shanter*, *The Thistle and the Rampant Lion*, and the farce *The Dundee Weaver*.

The artists who appeared in the new music halls, selling their own individual short turns, rather than appearing in something longer chosen by the management, were if anything, more mobile than the ordinary run of performers. They could appear at several halls in a single night and rarely stayed in any one locality for long. Wages, in comparison to those in the 'legitimate' theatre, could appear high, but variety performers were responsible for their own travelling expenses, lodging, costuming, band parts and so on. The Scots who worked in the halls were mainly dancers and singers whose material and style of performance were largely unaffected by changes of venue, or actor-comedians who used skills learned in the theatre and on the concert platform and condensed their work into a format suitable to the occasion. The time allowable to performers other than those at the top of the bill was very short, sometimes no more than five minutes, and it was essential that audiences were gripped immediately by familiar or intriguing images. Perhaps it was this pressure of time that brought about a reliance on the kind of Scottish icons and symbols, notably the use of tartan, which led to criticism of the Scottish popular stage as 'presenting a debased image of the country to audiences, at home, in the South and abroad'.[9] The very mobility of music-hall performers made it even more important that their material was readily understood in different localities. Many, like Harry Lauder, developed a language, basically English spoken with a Scottish accent and a smattering of Scots words, which gave the suggestion of a cultural identity without becoming bogged down in local dialect.

As the century drew to a close the distinctions between the programmes played in theatres and music halls became more pronounced. Theatres increasingly presented a single play per evening, giving up the small turns which had appeared between pieces. The variety stage reduced its presentation of small-scale drama but retained the short dramatic sketch. Albert Mackie's study *The Scotch Comedians* sees the influence of 'Kailyard drama' in sketches 'such as

HARRY LAUDER.   J. M. & CO.

Figure 3.12 Harry Lauder. (Scottish Theatre Archive)

The Concealed Bed and *The Wash-House Key*, which presented the humours of Scottish working-class life'.[10] Many of the original characters created by Scottish variety performers, such as Will Fyffe's pathetic Daft Sandy, were as strongly developed as characters from any 'legitimate' work and they owed much to the National Drama tradition of figures who stepped out of their play settings. Variety performers moved easily between variety stage, concert platform, pantomime and roles in the National Drama. When Mrs Fyffe recounted Will's life to *The Glasgow Evening Citizen* in June 1955, she recalled Sir Harry Lauder visiting Fyffe backstage during the panto season:

> *Rob Roy*, one of Bill's old favourites, was a play they often discussed during these dressing-room visits. How wonderful it would be, they would say, to play it together – Sir Harry as Bailie Nicol Jarvie, and Bill as Rob Roy.

The Scottish music hall also gave rise to one of the great theatrical organisations in Britain, consisting, at its height, of thirty-three music halls all over the country, controlled by Horace Edward, later Sir Edward, Moss. As a young man Moss played the piano for his father's moving diorama show. In the 1870s when Moss Snr became the proprietor of the Lorne Music Hall, Greenock, Edward Moss began to gain experience in management. At the age of 25, he decided to start up on his own account and, in 1877, became the manager of the tiny Gaiety Theatre in Chambers Street, Edinburgh, where he soon made a name for himself. Moss began to look further afield. In 1884 he opened his first music hall in Newcastle, employing the Edinburgh firm of Messrs Dobie and Sons to decorate the interior. That venue was so successful that, in need of larger premises, Moss had designed and built the first of his Empire theatres, which opened in 1890, with scenery by William Glover of Glasgow.

In Scotland, Moss's energy and business acumen led him to acquire interests in a number of music halls in Glasgow and Edinburgh. The Empire Palace Theatre, Edinburgh, opened its door to the public in November 1892. By this time, the old pattern of music hall, based on the original supper rooms, had disappeared in favour of a conventional theatre auditorium, often decorated with great magnificence. Moss employed the premier theatre architect of the day, Frank Matcham, to design many of his Empires, including the Edinburgh house, which had a movable proscenium arch and a sliding roof for extra ventilation. The new chains of venues now required business skills from their managers, who were coming increasingly from the commercial, rather than the artistic, side of the industry.

Middle-class audiences came only slowly to the music halls and once again they ventured in response to changes in the layout of venues which offered

Figure 3.13 Auditorium of the 1892 Edinburgh Empire Palace Theatre. Lavishly decorated and seating 3000, it suffered a disastrous fire in 1911. (Edinburgh Festival Theatre)

more exclusivity and security. *The Chiel* of 3 September 1887 congratulated the manager of the Glasgow Gaiety on recent alterations to his house:

> Every week brings additional proof that Mr D. S. McKay acted wisely in making the alterations he did . . . The appearance of the house is infinitely improved, and the new orchestral stalls are growing in popularity. Indeed, generally business has been wonderfully good, and the class of people who frequent this house would scarcely enter any other house of variety entertainment in the city.

The Gaiety lasted until 1896, by which time it was under Moss's management and deemed too small and old fashioned. It did, however, occupy a good site in Sauchiehall Street and so was demolished to make way for the celebrated Glasgow Empire, which opened its doors at Easter, 1897.

Music hall offered Scottish artists a new national and international stage, but one which expected a very particular vision of Scotland and the Scots. As part of the popular 'theatre', music hall educated the next generation of Scottish performers, playwrights and audience. The commentator in *The Chiel* who had congratulated McKay on his alterations shrewdly observed:

> The combination of the dramatic with the variety entertainment has been slowly but surely growing in public favour for some time. As is usual in all tastes theatrical, the feeling has come upward from the masses and has not travelled downward from the cultured ... The music-hall is always taking something from the theatre, and the theatre from the music-hall.

PANTOMIME

Pantomime came from a long tradition, which went through a period of evolution during the nineteenth century resulting in a form of theatre which would be largely recognisable today.

During the first half of the century, in part as a result of the licensing laws which prohibited many minor theatres from using the spoken word, there was a strong tradition of 'mime'. The characters of the Harlequinade had come down from the improvised comedy of the Italian *Commedia dell'arte* (and Greek and Roman comedy before that). Productions such as the Edinburgh Theatre Royal's 1811 *Harlequin in Leith* took the strongest comic characters from the *Commedia* – Harlequin, Colombine, Punch, Pierrot, Pierrette, Pantaloon – and set them loose in familiar settings to cause mayhem with a host of tricks, illusions and physical knockabout (an echo of which survives in the slapstick scenes, such as baking a cake in Widow Twankey's kitchen, of our modern pantos). These pantomimes, like the *Commedia* before them, were aimed at adult audiences. They could appear at any time during the theatrical season, although they were more common around holiday times, and they were placed at the end of an evening's entertainment. This was a very specialised type of performance and it became the province of highly trained groups of actor-acrobats, often members of the same families of Italian origin, who were engaged by theatres specifically to work out the tricks and machinery for the pantomime.

At the beginning of the period the pantomimists played the central characters in the story who then 'became' Clown and Harlequin. Gradually during the course of the century, with the introduction of literary scripts, often based on European fairy tales, the figures of the Harlequinade became more and more marginalised. Eventually the pantomimes acquired a storyline with a separate cast, which would be almost at an end before the characters of the

Harlequinade appeared. The plot would then go off on a detour into their dizzying fantasy world where nothing was ever what it seemed. Finally the plot line would loop back in an improbable sweep to a grand finale with all the gorgeous spectacle that limelight, tinplate spangles, gilding, cut glass and cheap labour could effect. Theatres spent very large sums of money on their pantomime scenery and costumes because they expected large returns. However, the individual chorus dancers and children employed, literally in their hundreds, were not so well paid for what was, admittedly, steady work over several weeks.

Alongside the reworkings of European fairy tales there also appeared a number of pantomimes which drew on Scottish literature and legends, anticipating twentieth-century productions such as *The Tintock Cup* at the Glasgow Citizens' and the *Jamie* series. The most home grown of pieces seem to have appeared mainly in urban, working-class theatres and to have been primarily the work of the actor-playwright William Lowe. The survival of some of Lowe's pantomime scripts is largely due to the fact that the theatres would publish and sell them for a penny. They were written, like most pantos, in rhyming couplets, employed a lot of topical references and puns, and tended to reserve dialect for the comic characters. In 1869 Lowe wrote *Edina and the White Hart of the Lothians or, Prince Edwin and the Fairies of the Thistle*, for the Southminster Music Hall, Nicolson Street, Edinburgh. This tale, based on the legend of the founding of Edinburgh, featured 'the Tartan Twins', Lankytartan, played by Lowe himself, and Servingstartan, played by D. B. Young, who were the faithful retainers of the principal boy, Prince Edwin. The tyrant Feudalfond seeks to gain sway over the Lothians but is foiled in his plans by the Immortal Edina, who, protected by a 'charmed wand', the gift of St Giles, enlists Edwin to fulfil the prophecy about a young prince who shoots and then tames a white hart. Various Edinburgh personalities are mentioned, for example Professor Syme, holder of the Chair in Surgery at Edinburgh University. When they appear, the Tartan Twins, captured by Feudalfond's henchmen, play on the exhibition of Siamese Twins in freak shows and drop their dialect to mimic English-speaking showmen.

Lanky: Hoo dae ye find yersel', my brither?
Serving: I fin' we're stuck tae ane anither.
            The folk a' here seem wondrous ceevil.
Lanky: For me they may gang tae the deevil.
            Hoo are we draggit here like thieves?
            My brither here and I hae nieves,   [fists]
            An' faith we'll fecht – we wear the tartan.
            Noo brither, mind nane o'yer scartan.
Feudal: We mean you well.

Serving: Weel, that is funny.
Lanky: At fairs he wants a little money.
              Hi! hi! come up, the show begins,
              Come up and see the Tartan Twins.
              They've never been surpassed by any.
Serving: The charge is only but one penny.

By contrast, a collection of pantomime scripts for the Edinburgh Theatre Royal 1887–96 are based on the traditional stories, such as *Aladdin*, *Dick Whittington* and *Babes in the Wood*. Specifically Scottish material is restricted to topical references, to some rather incongruous Scottish settings, and to two appearances by the Scottish comedian W. F. Frame, whose characters of Cook in *Dick Whittington* and the villain Abanazer in *Aladdin* are written in a form of dialect.

Figure 3.14 Pantomime character in thistle costume, from Ali Baba, *Edinburgh Theatre Royal, 1869/70*. (The Trustees of the National Library of Scotland)

Figure 3.15 W. F. Frame. (Scottish Theatre Archive)

The traffic in performers and materials between variety stage or concert platform and the pantomime stage was a two-way street. Frame's celebrated female character, Maggie Mucklemou, who stayed with him for the rest of his career, made her first appearance at the Princess's Theatre in the Glasgow Gorbals, in December 1890, when Frame played her in the pantomime *Goody Two Shoes*. The Princess's was one theatre which tried to combine the traditions of universal fairy stories with more local materials, in productions such as its 1880 'People's Pantomime' *Babes in the Wood, or Harlequin Rob Roy, the Merrie Men of Borderland, Virtuous Vesta, and Vulcan the Venomous*. In fact the whole of Glasgow provided particularly fertile ground for pantomime. The mixture of familiar stories, comedy, sentiment, spectacle and music presented in lively fashion across the footlights appealed strongly to Glasgow audiences.

Pantomime was an area where the critics found themselves at variance with popular tastes. In December 1892 *The Quiz* noted with satisfaction that the

Glasgow Theatre Royal's cast for *Dick Whittington* contained no 'Scotch Pantomime Comedian' because 'the character has more often than not been a distinct frost'. The following year 'Our Cantankerous Critic' was finally driven to protest by the seasonal takeover of the theatres:

> Why our Theatres should be converted for a couple of months into first class Music Halls; why enormous sums of money should be expended on gaudy scenery and costly dresses, on ballets and banners; why there should be a public which does not care to support the best and cleverest pieces of the year, performed by the most talented artists on the stage, but which can go nightly to the Pantomime . . . are questions to which I am aware many conflicting answers might be given . . . There appears to be a great mass of the public which has little or no understanding or appreciation of dramatic work, and to which Pantomime appeals as the highest theatrical achievement of the year, the production which *must* be seen.

The article also considered the previous year as 'one worth remembering' for Glasgow play-goers and listed, among other attractions: five different renditions of Hamlet, by Wilson Barrett, F. R. Benson, Hermann Vezin, Osmond Tearle and Beerbohm Tree; 'several new comic operas and burlesques [which] found their way to Glasgow'; and 'Mr. J. L. Toole came on the scene with *Walker, London*, J. M. Barrie's fresh and novel comedy'. While the same columnist had given regular and often enthusiastic notice of the music halls, none rated a mention in this end-of-year summing up. There is evident in this article both a devaluing of popular theatre forms and an expectation that novelty or innovation, if they should appear on the legitimate stage, will inevitably come from London.

THE THEATRE INDUSTRY IN THE LATE CENTURY

The shape of the theatre industry had changed as the century progressed, the old provincial circuits gradually disappearing along with the stock companies. However, whilst this period was felt to be the era of the great actor-managers, several of whom, like Henry Irving, trained in Scotland, it also saw the rise of the commercial manager and of organisations like the Moss Empire and the Howard & Wyndham partnership. Scotland had her own Victorian actor-managers, notably J. B. Howard, the Wyndhams, father and son, A. D. McNeill in Edinburgh, Bruce Norton in Dundee and the Glovers in Glasgow. Howard, at first alone and then in partnership with F. W. Wyndham, and McNeill, operated 'Waverley' companies, sending productions out from their bases in Edinburgh to tour the country with National Drama pieces. Howard in particular criss-crossed Scotland starring as Roderick Dhu and Rob Roy with his own company and as a guest artist.

There was a period during the 1870s when the two systems, of stock companies and commercial managements, co-existed uneasily. Some of the pressures on proprietors to dispense with potentially unreliable actor-managers in favour of proven commercial successes can be seen in the papers of Alexander Hannay, proprietor of the Prince of Wales' Theatre, later the Glasgow Grand Theatre, in Cowcaddens. This theatre went through the hands of a series of lessees during this period and Hannay's correspondence with them is littered with complaints about the quality of their resident companies, the unsuitability of their repertoire and the lack of big-name artists to compete with those theatres operating largely as receiving houses.

The terms and conditions of the early agreements between proprietors and lessees seemed simple in comparison to the complex arrangements now operating. In April 1878 Alexander Hannay wrote to a prospective lessee dividing up the responsibility for the various departments of the theatre:

[The manager] to find dramas, entire company, supers, Pictorial Posters, Leader of Band, Scenic Painters and Assistants, Ballet, Authors etc. all to be first class & License. I found [sic] Theatre, Gas, Taxes, Gasman, Stage Carpenters, Property man. Band, Hall Keeper, Money & Cheque takers, advertising in two papers, any bills & bill stickers.[11]

The 'entire company' referred to in this letter was of a different shape to the one Corbet Ryder had run earlier in the century. The size of companies had reduced and the categories of performer were now less specific. In 1873 Hannay wrote to a correspondent in Leeds, who had asked about the exact definition of an 'entire company', explaining that it included:

Leading [Man]
Juvenile Lead & Light Comedian
1st Low Comedian
2nd do.
1st Walking Gentleman
2nd do.
2 Gentlemen for responsible business
And 2 for General Utility
Leading Lady
Juvenile do.
Chambermaid
2nd do.
Old Woman

Utility Ladies
Ladies for Responsible Business
<u>any Ladies to play in Burlesque if required</u>, the Ballet, or Lady dancers
do not come under the definition of entire company unless specially
applied for, neither do Stage Manager or Prompter, or Supers.[12]

This type of company would have been anchored in a theatre in a major
city with access to a large pool of artists available for casual work. It is also
symptomatic of the changes in the repertoire, whereby the bill, featuring two
or more pieces changing nightly, gave way to the single piece, possibly with a
slight curtain raiser beforehand to allow the latecomers to arrive, which ran for
a week at a time and frequently longer.

Proprietors gradually came to see the financial returns from visiting companies who arrived with reputations ready made and their products tried and
tested as more reliable than supporting a resident company. Touring companies
were graded by their celebrity, repertoire and by the type of venue they visited.
D'Oyly Carte, who thrilled Dundee audiences in 1879 with *HMS Pinafore*,
was very definitely a 'number one' company, employing the most celebrated
artists and visiting the largest theatres, usually for a minimum of a week at a
time. Lower down the scale came 'number two' or 'three' companies who had
correspondingly less well known artists and played smaller venues. At the
bottom of the ladder were the fit-up companies, who changed venues nightly,
and who carried with them the minimum of scenery and perhaps a false
proscenium arch for performances in halls which did not have one.

Some of these companies faced punishing schedules often only made possi-
ble by the greatly improved transport system of the period. In January and
February 1895, W. J. Lancaster's company toured a production of Charles H.
Hawtrey's *The Private Secretary*. After an introductory week at the Theatre
Royal, Greenock, they progressed on to:

January	28	Dumfries	Theatre Royal
	31	Kilmarnock	Corn Exchange
February	6	Dumbarton	Burgh Hall
	7	Hamilton	Victoria Hall
	9	Airdrie	New Public Hall
	11	Dunfermline	St Margaret's Hall
	12	Kirkcaldy	Corn Exchange
	13	St Andrews	Town Hall
	15	Arbroath	New Public Hall
	18	Montrose	Assembly Hall
	19	Brechin	City Hall
	20	Forfar	Reid Hall

	21	Falkirk	Town Hall
	23	Alloa	Town Hall
	25	Stirling	Arcade Theatre
	28	Perth	City Hall
March	4	Aberdeen	Her Majesty's
	11	Glasgow	Royalty
	18	Edinburgh	Lyceum

To undertake such a tour in winter would have been impossible before the spread of the railways.

Upon arrival at a station large companies who were travelling their own sets were met by Wordie's, the Scottish railway carriers, who transferred the flats into horse-drawn scene waggons for the trip from the railhead to the theatre, as, for example, in Edinburgh:

> The carriage of theatre scenery demanded a high-sided 'monkey' [a type of pole wagon with an adjustable rear axle] long enough to take the light but unwieldy flats from the King's or the Lyceum in Edinburgh to Lothian Road. This was always Sunday work, after the last performance on Saturday evening but ready for the next billing on Monday. It was the same in Dundee and other cities.[13]

Theatres' advance publicity appeared increasingly focused on named companies identified by current or previous London hits. However, the idea that the Scottish theatre industry was wholly dominated at this time by the travelling companies from London is one which should be approached cautiously. The title 'company' could be a misleading one. On 14 August 1878 the management of Drury Lane wrote to John Coleman, then manager of the Glasgow Grand, about a forthcoming engagement:

> Mr Chatterton is willing to send you his 'Peep O'Day' Company representing the following characters viz. 'Barney O'Toole' 'Father O'Cleary' [indistinct] 'Harry Kavanagh' 'Black Mullin', 'Mary Grace' & [sic] 'Kathleen Kavanagh' also to supply you with . . . 'Peep O'Day' bills on the following terms viz. Mr Chatterton is to receive one clear third of the nightly receipts for the remaining two thirds you are to provide remainder of company – proper scenery etc – Band & all other local expenses with *not less* than 40 supers and 20 ballet . . . Mr Chatterton also sends a man to superintend the production.[14]

The engagement was for eighteen nights and there was work here for Glasgow artists, but it was all at a comparatively low level, chorus and bit parts. There was also a limited amount of work available in curtain raisers and afterpieces, if the travelling company were not filling the entire evening. Sometimes there was a single vacant night between engagements, when some of the old small-scale National Drama favourites such as *Mary, Queen of Scots*, *The Two Drovers*, or *Cramond Brig*, easy to cast and costume, made their appearance. But these occasions were comparatively rare.

As the Drury Lane letter makes clear, a 'company' could at this time consist simply of half a dozen leading actors and a 'man to superintend the production'. One undoubted result of this shift was that it became necessary for Scottish actors to journey south to gain experience and regular employment in anything other than small parts or specialist Scottish roles. The latter were increasingly being filled by 'part-time' actors – theatre managers and comedians – and, in a return to a tradition active at the beginning of the century, talented amateurs. The only other real alternative was to join the geggies.

GAS LIGHT ON THE SCOTTISH STAGE

As early as December 1820 the Edinburgh Theatre Royal gave details on the bottom of its bills of the new gas lighting in the auditorium:

> The New Central GAS LUSTRE and those over the Private Boxes, [was] designed by Messrs RANKIN and Co. Leith Walk, and executed by them and Mr JOHN MILNE, Brass Founder... The GAS LUSTRE round the Front of the Boxes [was] designed by Mr JOHN MILNE ... The New VENTILATORS, and Alterations in the Pit and Boxes under the entire direction of Mr RONADDSON [sic].

The last mentioned were essential not only to carry away fumes from the gas jets, but also to give some relief from the heat generated by the lighting, which in poorly ventilated theatres, before the era of dimming the lights during performances, could lead to temperatures in the nineties in the Galleries. There was no doubt that the considerable trouble and expense incurred by lighting theatres with either candles or oil lamps were greatly reduced by the introduction first of gas and then limelight into Scottish theatres. They permitted effects which had previously been impossible, but they brought with them their own challenges and hazards.

Many stage gasmen and carpenters became skilled in building advertising devices for the fronts of theatres, while other managements bought such illuminated signs ready made from specialist workshops. William Glover remembered how, in 1855, the Theatre Royal, Dunlop Street, advertised the Crimean War spectacle *The Battle of the Alma* with 'a large gas device, having the word

"Alma" encircled by hearts' which 'made the entrance to the theatre as conspicuous as need be'. Auditoriums were lit by a combination of individual gas jets, with globe covers, spread throughout the house, and large multi-jet 'gasaliers', or modified gasaliers called 'sun-burners', which replaced the central chandeliers. The stage was normally lit by various gas devices around the front and behind the proscenium, though as early as 1847 a theatre in Greenock was fitted with an experimental rig which tried to do away with this system in favour of light directed by reflectors on to the stage from a central fitting in the auditorium roof. Since this was before the age of readily focusable light, the experiment failed to catch on, which was a pity as it might have cut down on the number of theatre fires.

A large number of nineteenth-century Scottish theatres, in common with those in other parts of Britain, were destroyed by fires attributable in some way to the gas.[15] The problems arose from a combination of technical difficulties with the new medium and human error. Certainly the backstage arrangements then common to most theatres appear to have been potentially lethal.

The normal method of lighting the stage was via a combination of footlights running around the edge of the stage; battens (pipes with gas jets at regular intervals running the width of the stage and hung in the flies among the scenery); 'side-lights' or 'wing lights' (a form of vertical batten hidden from view behind the scenery wings); and 'bunch-lights' (jets at the top of long poles set into portable stands). All of the light sources at stage level were connected to the central gas plate, located near the prompter, by hundreds of feet of rubber tubing snaking across the floor, which constituted a hazard in itself in the darkness backstage. An article in *The Builder* of 1849 described the gas fittings for the Prince's Theatre Royal, West Nile Street, Glasgow:

> Two 1½ inch pipes extend round the stage, with Argand [fishtail] burners, chimney and shades to each; the burners in each pipe are six inches apart, but those in one row placed alternately, in relation to those on the other: the lights on the outer pipe have green glass chimneys, for moon-light scenes; those on the inner one, colourless chimneys for ordinary use . . . [The theatre was] . . . also fitted with gas-battens extending the width of the proscenium. These were about one foot broad and a quarter-circle in section, lined with galvanised sheet iron. To prevent the borders or anything inflammable from coming into contact with the jets, the battens were hooped over at intervals.

The framework over the battens was primarily to keep the mediums – strips of coloured cloth pulled in front of the jets to give coloured effects – from catching alight, but the heat generated by the battens made everything in the fly-space, ropes, wood and canvas scenery, tinder-dry. The necessity for venting away the fumes caused a stiff breeze to stir all about. It took only a loose thread or frayed edge to poke through the protective framework for scenery to catch fire. The stage crew, many of them ex-sailors, would then use their experience aloft to walk out along the battens with a knife and cut the ropes supporting the scenes, which fell to the stage where they could, hopefully, be extinguished.

Before the introduction of automatic ignition, pilot lights on all the gas jets had to be lit by the gasman, using a lighted spirit torch on a long pole. It was the gasman of the Edinburgh Theatre Royal who inadvertently destroyed the building in 1865. *The Times* of 16 January reported that:

> The fire originated it would appear, in the top shifts of the scenery, which were so badly protected that, on several occasions, they had taken fire . . . the men had been able to extinguish the flames promptly by cutting away the drapery. In the present case the gas-man, named Cassey, who had just been putting in the lights . . . had succeeded in lighting the second row of top lights, and was lighting the first when the drapery caught fire . . . The flames spread so rapidly that Cassey was unable to get the border down in time.

Later in the century, the introduction of the brilliant and focusable lime-light, necessitating tanks of oxygen and hydrogen gas, was another technical innovation which required careful handling. The rebuilt Theatre Royal burned down again in 1875 after an explosion in limelight equipment being used for the pantomime. Three Glasgow theatres actually burnt down on the last night of pantomimes, a circumstance which Walter Baynham attributed to the backstage staff's traditionally being very drunk on that night.

Nineteenth-century production values emphasised the use of 'coloured fires' and 'fireworks' in pieces like *Der Freischutz*, which was playing on 18 November 1845 when the Adelphi on Glasgow Green burnt to the ground. Melodramas featuring burning buildings were commonplace and it is a wonder that more people were not killed or badly injured. The 1892 inventory of the Glasgow Grand lists various precautions such as an electric fire alarm, fire buckets, water hydrants and hoses at stage level, firemen's axes and blankets, and a windlass used for the 'asbestos curtain'. However, these measures came towards the end of a century during which the authorities were slow to lay down guidelines, let alone regulations, for fire safety at public performances. Occasionally financial considerations overrode safety. Alexander Hannay, of the Prince of Wales' Theatre in Glasgow, sent an urgent note to his then lessee Sidney on 13 December 1873:

As there is <u>danger</u> & much risk of <u>fire</u> in the Gas Plott [sic] handed to my Gas Man only this forenoon I must wash my hands from all responsibility arising from a desire to substitute ground Rows (very dangerous on a stage at any time but more so at a pantomime) to save your share of the <u>expense</u> of the <u>Lime Light</u>. Had your plot been given in time I would have submitted to the <u>Fire Insurance Office</u> in the <u>meantime all risk & Responsibility rests on you</u> and as I am noways bound to supply or work veregated [sic] Lime Light you had better find men & appurtenances for yourself.[16]

Ground rows were movable battens laid on the floor. They presented particular risks to elaborate costumes during the pantomime when there might be upwards of one hundred artists onstage at any one time.

Once alight, theatre fires could spread rapidly, especially if the gas was conveyed in cheap 'white-metal' alloy pipes which melted in contact with flames. Panic, caused by the fear of being trapped, resulted in the greatest loss of life in a Scottish theatre. Disaster overtook the Glasgow Theatre Royal, Dunlop Street, on 17 February 1849 when the house was packed to see *The Siege of Calais* followed by the pantomime. Walter Baynham, in *The Glasgow Stage*, gives a harrowing account of the panic which resulted in the deaths of seventy people, crushed or suffocated in a rush for the gallery stairs. He ends with some telling details: 'Nearly all were lads. Only six females were amongst them, and one of these was a little child of three years old. The money found on the bodies amounted in all to only 17s 1d.' Other exits were available in the Dunlop Street theatre, but fear had gripped the crowd. Panics, and ways to avoid them, and the design of exits and crush barriers, became matters for long-running debate within the industry.

THE PLAYWRIGHTS

The story of nineteenth-century Scottish theatre appears at first sight to be somewhat divorced from nineteenth-century Scottish drama, being bound up instead with social history and the development of a modern industry, its fortunes in the hands of actors, managers, patrons and those, like Sir Walter Scott, who were not known as working playwrights and yet who exercised great influence over it. Commentators have tended to approach the plays in literary terms, looking for them in the literature section on library shelves. This approach has been inadequate on two counts. First, it has failed to appreciate the material as the raw stuff of theatre, as

something to be measured, not just by the quality of its language and ideas, but by its popularity with audiences, its national significance, its

appeal to actors, its interest for historians, its reflection of social attitudes and so on . . . though there are few masterpieces, Scottish drama
between 1800 and 1900 offers a cornucopia of riches.[17]

Second, some of the most successful stage plays were not published, and
those that were available were all too often the dilettante products of keen
amateurs, closet plays, which now read badly to an audience which judges
playtexts by their fitness for the stage. The amateurs ranged from such literary
luminaries as Walter Scott, James Hogg and John Galt, to comparative
unknowns. Many of the closet plays are frankly depressing attempts to copy
forms drawn from Shakespeare, written in laboured blank verse in stilted
English.

Part of the problem was that many Scottish amateurs sought to emulate the
style of the playwright, Joanna Baillie, who had a clearly thought-out theory
of the drama, without themselves possessing her vision. Baillie, born in
Glasgow in 1762 and educated in Scotland, was a daughter of the manse whose
mother came from a medical family. In due course Joanna's brother inherited
a prestigious London practice and she lived with him in England for most of
her life. She was without doubt the best-known Scottish playwright of her
time. Her volumes of plays were as eagerly awaited and enthusiastically discussed as any being written, yet her stage career was diminished by the fact
that she was a woman and by certain aspects of her personality.

The first of her plays to come to general notice was *De Montfort*, which
appeared in a volume of three plays published anonymously in 1798. The book
also contained a long 'Introductory Discourse', in which the author criticised
current playwriting and set forth her own plan for a series of *Plays on the
Passions*. These were to emphasise rounded, and therefore potentially contra-
dictory, characterisation, which would determine plot, rather than complicated
plotting which seemed to lead to one-dimensional, stereotyped characters. As
the (anonymous) book took hold in literary circles the clarity and authority of
the commentary prompted great discussion. Both Walter Scott and John Philip
Kemble were put forward as possible authors. When, the day after the opening
of *De Montfort* at Drury Lane in 1800, the playwright was revealed to be a
maiden lady living in Hampstead, many commentators were taken aback, the
more so since there was a growing feeling that women were fundamentally
incapable of writing tragedy. The opinion of many was summed up by the poet
Byron, a keen supporter of Baillie's:

When Voltaire was asked why no woman has ever written even a tol-
erable tragedy [he replied] . . . 'the composition of a tragedy requires
testicles'. If this be true, Lord knows what Joanna Baillie does – I
suppose she borrows them.

Figure 3.16 Joanna Baillie (Mary Ann Knight). (Scottish National Portrait Gallery)

Over the years Baillie received repeated and blighting criticism, and she once wrote bitterly to Scott that 'John Any-Body would have stood higher with the critics than Joanna Baillie.'

De Montfort was a good first effort, prompting the actress Sarah Siddons, who recognised Baillie's particular talent for writing parts for women, to request from her 'another Jane Montfort'. But the script required some reworking for the stage and J. P. Kemble, the Drury Lane manager, was unwilling or unable to provide the dispassionate practical advice Baillie needed. This became a recurring problem. Unable to get her plays performed in London, in part because of her sex, other theatres would not take them up. She acquired the reputation of being a fine poet who did not understand the theatre, yet the 'Introductions' which prefaced each new volume of her plays contained perceptive analyses of subjects such as stage lighting and blocking. Baillie keenly felt the want of opportunity to see her work performed:

> The chief thing to be regretted in this failure of my attempts is, that having no opportunity of seeing any of my pieces exhibited, many faults respecting stage effect and general impression will remain to me undiscovered, and those I may hereafter write be of course unimproved. (Preface to *Miscellaneous Plays*, 1804)

Unfortunately, in the absence of such experience, her serious aspirations for drama, that it should teach and inspire as well as entertain, led her increasingly towards laborious imitations of Shakespeare. The situation was not helped by the fact that Baillie absolutely refused to attend rehearsals. The prospect filled her with dread. She was naturally shy and, in truth, the Regency stage remained a dubious milieu for a gentlewoman. A measure of what might have been achieved by judicious reworking can be seen in *The Family Legend*, a tale of Scottish clan feuds and the most neatly crafted and frequently performed of her plays. She turned over the 1810 production of it at the Edinburgh Theatre Royal to her friend and 'champion', Walter Scott. As he wrestled with the practicalities of staging it, she readily agreed to every script change he suggested.

Joanna Baillie was not immune from the prejudices of her day, reminding readers of her play *The Martyr*, which dealt with the conversion of a Roman centurion to Christianity, that the subject of the piece was 'too sacred, and therefore unfit for the stage'. Nevertheless, her talent for characterisation, particularly of women, continued unabated. It is evident in one of her last stage works, *Witchcraft*, published in 1836 when she was over 70 years old. In *Witchcraft* Baillie explored the psychology of those who mistakenly believed themselves to be witches, to their peril. The range of women she brings to life is impressive, from the crazed and ultimately dangerous Grizeld Bane, and the innocent heroine, Violet, who begins a little blandly but acquires real dignity as her burning approaches, to the villainness, the naive, spoilt society beauty, Annabella, whose jealousy sets events spiralling out of control. There is a somewhat contrived sub-plot about a father falsely accused of murder, but it is the women who hold centre stage. In this play, Baillie cast off the burden of blank verse, describing the language 'both as regards the lower and higher characters' as being 'pretty nearly that which prevailed in the West of Scotland about the period assigned to the event'. There is real power in the outraged cries of the mob, surrounding the piled faggots in Paisley Market Square when they discover that witchburning has been banned by Act of Parliament:

> *Voices*: My certes! The deil has been better represented in the House of Parliament, than a' the braid shires in the kingdom. Sic a degree as that in a Christian land – To mak Satan triumphant! – There'll be fine gambols on moors and in kirkyards for this, I trow – Parliament forsooth! We hae sent bonnie members there, indeed, gin these be the laws they mak.

Other nineteenth-century professional playwrights can be divided roughly into those who were primarily performers and those who were paid wordsmiths, writing to order. The actor-playwrights are in many ways the most interesting, though a great deal remains to be discovered of their lives and work. The only one of their number about whom much is known is W. H. Murray. Others are more shadowy; foremost among these, if only for the apparent number of his plays and his unusual use of Gaelic with Scots and English, must be the soldier-playwright, Archibald Maclaren (see the start of this chapter). Most writers like Maclaren were writing their own material, at least in the first instance, as a novelty, perhaps for a benefit or as an added attraction for a guest visit. Charlotte Deans tells us that Mr Deans adapted James Hogg's tale *The Brownie of Bodsbeck* into a very successful play in this way, and the actor-manager Charles Bass seems to have written 'National Dramas' and to have been an able adaptor of Scott for his own company. Unfortunately, most of these plays do not appear to have got into print. Similarly, Corbet Ryder's company performed 'National Dramas' that survive only as names on the bills.

The rarity of surviving manuscript materials is due largely to the habit of actors copying out not the whole play, but only their own parts with cue lines. Unless a copy was lodged with the Lord Chamberlain's office for licensing there might only be one full script in existence, held by the manager of the company. The loss of that copy was a disaster. Not surprisingly, hardly any material from the geggie repertoire survives at all.

Around mid-century there were individuals who seem to have written one or two plays but then no more. Notable among these were A. D. McNeill, author of *The Gloamin and the Mirk* (1869), and James Ballantine. Ballantine was one of the 'Whistle-Binkie' poets, whose verses attracted criticism for their narrow provincialism and sentimentality. His stage works tended to reflect his training as a poet. *The Provost's Daughter* (1852), produced at the Edinburgh Theatre Royal, was described by Dibdin in *The Annals of the Edinburgh Stage* as having a 'simple' plot 'composed of the lives and escapades of two students', and was largely a vehicle for some ballads with music by Mackenzie. In *The Gaberlunzie* (1858), Ballantine was more ambitious, adapting his own novel, *The Gaberlunzie's Wallet*, for Wyndham's company. The *Edinburgh Evening Courant* of 8 June 1858 congratulated Ballantine on the stage version:

> Mr Ballantine has been very successful in reducing his novel to a three-act play, and in bringing out its various points and dramatic situations . . . the spirit of the scene often evokes the enthusiasm of the audience.

The plot concerns the restoration of a forfeit Jacobite estate to its rightful heirs, and Ballantine takes the opportunity to introduce figures from Edinburgh's past and to create set-pieces in historic settings, such as a grand ball in the 'Auld Mint'. The text reveals a writer still coming to terms with stage action and the dialogue ranges from the easy to the mechanical, thus a fond father bids his daughter goodnight with: 'My love, Phemie, it is now your hour of retirement; and, as usual, we'll sing the evening hymn, in which your maidens will join you.' The *Evening Courant* gave special praise to the 'most admirable and faithful delineation of Scottish character' by Miss Nicol in the role of Matty Hepburn. Her task had undoubtedly been made easier by having some of Ballantine's livelier dialogue to speak.

Professional playwrights came into their own later in the century, when changes to the structure of the industry, the copyright laws, and the repertoire, made full-time playwriting a more attractive proposition. One thorough-going professional, much in demand for the London stage, was Robert Buchanan, the author of several successful stage adaptations of novels, notably *Tom Jones*, *Joseph Andrews* and *Crime and Punishment*, and melodramas such as *The Sailor and his Lass* and *Storm-Beaten*. Andrew Halliday, author of a string of Scott adaptations, might have achieved more if he had not died in 1877 at the age of 47. His *The King o' Scots* (1868) provided several leading actors with a starring role as James VI and was described by the *Edinburgh Evening Courant* as affording 'ample scope for the gratification of the modern thirst after realism'.

Whilst stage settings, blocking and, to an extent, acting were becoming more realistic, the content of plays seen on the British stage continued to be constricted by convention and censorship. Playwrights who sought to tackle serious subjects, especially contemporary social concerns, found it necessary to compromise their thinking and adopt conventional dramatic forms in order to see their work performed. Three Scots, William Sharp, William Archer and J. M. Barrie, were in the vanguard of change. They returned to the British stage a strand of Scottish influence which had affected the drama of Continental Europe throughout the nineteenth century. Walter Scott was called the first 'European' novelist and the inspiration he provided playwrights could be seen in the myriad foreign-language stage adaptations of his work, many of which were subsequently translated back into English to appear on the British stage. However, Scott's influence, and that of his friend the artist David Wilkie, went much further than mere adaptation; it affected fundamentally the way playwrights, designers and the new breed of stage directors approached the task of representing reality onstage.

As the century drew to a close, on the Continent the spirit of enquiry, given artistic shape by the domestic realism of Wilkie's paintings allied with the historicism and psychological realism of Scott's novels, and scientific legitimacy by the observations of Darwin, resulted in work which sought to turn an analytical as well as an artistic gaze on the human condition. Gerhart Hauptmann's *The Weavers* (1892), for example, was a landmark of European naturalism, which charted the terrible hardships faced by Silesian weavers during a period of famine. Conceived as a series of genre paintings brought to life, with a huge cast of characters, it presented ordinary working people illuminating history through their experience, and speaking in their own dialect. It owed a great deal to Scott and to Wilkie's paintings such as *Village Politicians* (1806) and *The Rent Day* (1807).[18]

Avant-garde European playwrights and their supporters battled government and industry disapproval by forming their own theatre societies, such as Antoine's Théâtre Libre in Paris, to circumvent the censorship which dogged public entertainment. A desire to create conditions which would allow such theatrical experimentation in Britain prompted William Sharp and William Archer to become involved with some high-profile, certainly contentious, schemes. Both men were already well known, Sharp as a journalist, novelist and poet, Archer as a highly respected theatre critic who, for as long as he had written about the theatre, had been pressing for a publicly funded National Theatre.

William Sharp was born in Paisley in 1855 and educated at Glasgow University. A life-long world traveller, he settled in London around 1879 and began work as a journalist. As well as his own poetry, Sharp wrote extensively on contemporary European poetry but became best known for his 'Celtic' tales, plays and romances, published under the name 'Fiona Macleod'. He was, until his death in 1905, engaged in the development of what he called 'Psychic Drama', which would concentrate on the inner processes of the human mind at the expense of the 'lesser emotions'. Sharp had been planning a seven-play cycle to be called *The Nature of the Soul*; in the event, he only completed two pieces, *The House of Usna* and *The Immortal Hour*, before he died. Both pieces plainly show the influence of the Belgian Symbolist playwright, Maeterlinck.

Sharp was more than a closet playwright. He became practically involved in the foundation, in 1899, of The London Stage Society, established to present 'plays of artistic merit which are not likely to be performed in the theatre'. The

Stage Society was the latest in a series of attempts to form a theatrical organisation which would enable interested parties, both within the profession and
from the wider community, to produce work by such inflammatory playwrights

Figure 3.17 William Sharp (Daniel Albert Wehrschmidt, 1898).
(Scottish National Portrait Gallery)

as Ibsen, Hauptmann and George Bernard Shaw. It was in many ways the most successful of such societies and certainly the most securely funded, having almost 400 subscribers, who attended Sunday evening 'meetings' (so-called to evade the attentions of the Lord's Day Observance Society). Sharp was the Society's President and *The House of Usna* had its premiere during the Society's opening season in a triple bill with two Maeterlinck plays.

A notable non-member of the Stage Society was William Archer, who had been closely involved in the workings, first of J. T. Grein's Independent Theatre in 1891, and, in 1897, with the short-lived New Century Theatre, of which he was one of the founders. Archer can be accounted a major influence on the British theatre of his day: a vigorous critic of those evils, such as the censorship system, that he felt were stifling serious experiment; a translator, primarily of Ibsen, whose work he promoted on the British stage; an innovative director of Ibsen plays – a role for which he is largely unknown due to his refusal to have his name on the programmes; a champion of publicly funded training for the theatre; and a tireless commentator on all aspects of the drama, notably the psychology of acting in his study *Masks or Faces?* (1887). George Bernard Shaw credited Archer with having been largely responsible for his early career, and Archer was a friend to a host of playwrights, including the Scots, Robert Louis Stevenson, whose *Admiral Guinea* was produced by the New Century Theatre, and J. M. Barrie.

William Archer was born in Perth in 1856 into a family spread internationally from Scotland to Norway to Australia. A major influence on his later career came from the family home in Norway, for the time the young William spent there enabled him to translate Ibsen with comparative ease. Graduating from Edinburgh University, Archer trained as a lawyer, though he never practised, preferring to spend his time in London at the theatre, or in the Reading Room of the British Library, writing innumerable reviews, articles and books of criticism about his first love, the stage.

As a young man Archer wrote a handful of unsuccessful melodramas before a wider acquaintance with contemporary playwriting persuaded him that his work as a critic, translator, director and agitator for reform could contribute more to the development of the British theatre. An intensely private man, characterised by many as a 'cold fish' but revealing great warmth and humour to his friends, Archer was never afraid of either robust comment or confrontation. It was a strength which became essential once he took up the cause of Ibsen's work, for the Norwegian's challenges to conventional mores, and daring representations of many topics hitherto considered unfit for the stage, brought howls of protest from conservative critics. Although wholly committed to Ibsen, Archer's healthy sense of humour enabled him to enjoy a one-act parody, *Ibsen's Ghost*, which appeared in London in May 1891. Archer urged readers of *The World* to see this 'piece of genuinely witty fooling

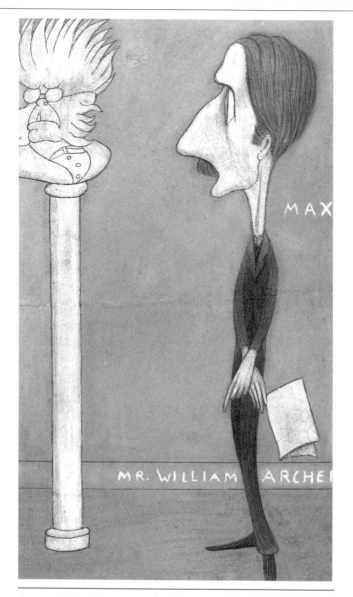

Figure 3.18 William Archer by Sir Max Beerbohm. Archer is facing a bust of Ibsen, whose work he translated and championed. (Department of Printed Books & Manuscripts, Sotheby's, London)

which ought not to be missed'. The anonymous author was J. M. Barrie, who later wondered how he could have stooped to deride someone he recognised to be a truly great playwright, and refused to allow *Ibsen's Ghost* to be included in collections of his work. However, it was not the only omission; almost his entire nineteenth-century dramatic output, his 'apprentice work', was excluded.

Barrie came to playwriting with an established reputation as a journalist and novelist. Born to a working-class family in Kirriemuir in 1860, he had received a broad education: first at school, where his enthusiasm for the travelling companies who visited Kirriemuir and for productions at the Theatre Royal, Dumfries, led to his first forays into playwriting, then at Edinburgh University, where the young student supplemented his income working as a theatre critic for the *Edinburgh Evening Courant*. The necessity to earn his living had taken Barrie to Nottingham to work as a journalist, briefly back to Scotland and then, in 1885, to London and the heart of a theatre industry in which playwrights were once more coming to the fore. The new-found respectability of the theatre and the financial rewards to be obtained from a successful play made playwriting a far more attractive proposition for the serious writer than it had been for a long time. Barrie wrote:

> Plays and novels require quite different construction, but the story-writer who is dramatic [can] become sufficiently theatrical by serving a short apprenticeship to the stage. There are such prizes to pluck for those who can stand on tiptoe.[19]

After a couple of false starts, followed by the modest success of *Ibsen's Ghost*, Barrie set himself methodically to work to learn his craft, producing in turn a farce *Walker, London* (1892), a comedy *The Professor's Love Story* (1892), a mythic romance *The Little Minister* (1897), and a problem play *The Wedding Guest* (1900). The first two had successful runs in Britain and America, while *The Little Minister* was a 'smash hit' on both sides of the Atlantic. Barrie became a wealthy man on the proceeds and in the process gained a grounding in the work of the theatre, which would enable him not merely to 'stand on tiptoe' but to fly.

The key to Barrie's understanding of the theatrical process came through his prolonged attendance at rehearsals, during which time he learned what was involved in translating his work from the page to the stage. Like Joanna Baillie, J. M. Barrie was shy, but theatre professionals found him to have definite ideas about how his work should appear. Stories abound about the slight Scotsman who quietly insisted, for example, that experienced comic actors did not add in their own particular gags to dilute the world of the playtext. This was not to imply that Barrie was rigid, for once he saw the text being brought to its feet, he would readily rewrite unsatisfactory dialogue; he was still handing revisions to the cast of *Walker, London* as it reached the 300th performance of its London run. It was simply that he was acquiring the skill to balance the demands of the production process with his own vision.

The materials for all Barrie's plays were contained in a series of notebooks, a hangover from his journalist days. In fact, by 1900 Barrie had planned, or had the outline materials for every play he wrote. From the first, his imagination was fired by pictorial images and visual effects, his understanding of the potential of which was evident in *Walker, London*, for which he envisioned a complex, multi-levelled set on a houseboat. The original notebook jottings included the spare but intriguing image of a 'Flirtation scene [seen] through blinds in [a] houseboat/ (Shadow pantomime)'. This would eventually form part of the climax to the play. Barrie developed a sophisticated and flexible single setting for the finished piece:

> Scene: A house-boat on the Thames. The blinds are down. Time: morning. A canoe and punt on bank at the bow are tied to house-boat. Someone in distance is playing a penny whistle. W. G. is lying on plank lazily writing a letter. Presently he sleeps. Nanny is on deck fishing. Mrs Golightly is seen pulling up the blind in opposite saloon. The table is set for breakfast on deck. The opposite blind is also going up, giving a view of the river and towpath. Mrs Golightly sits at window and knits. Andrew is seen in the saloon with no coat, waistcoat or collar. Bell is in the cabin. Nanny raises the line. She has her hair only partially done.

The actors were initially horrified by the apparent complexity of the setting, but as the work progressed Barrie explained where each character spoke from. The attention to detail and feeling for atmosphere, which included the penny whistle in the opening, also extended to the periodic sound of crashing crockery from below decks.

The plot of *Walker, London*, a slight confection of tangled love, misunderstanding and audacious impersonation, was taken variously from Barrie's earlier prose works, including *When a Man's Single*. The cast of characters included a Scots medical student, Andrew MacPhail, and a lively Irish girl, Nanny, and Barrie used one of their opening exchanges to acknowledge and gently mock the stage stereotyping of the Scots and Irish:

> *Nanny*: I can see you're a Scotchman now, and I used to doubt it.
> *Andrew*: Why?
> *Nanny*: Because you never say 'Bang went saxpence whatever', and then you don't wear the national costume.
> *Andrew*: What national costume? [Nanny points to her skirts and to his legs.] Oh, it's only the English tourists that wear that; besides you're not national either, for though you're an Irish girl, you don't flirt!

Barrie uses stereotypical character traits for comic effect, but the characters' actions are based on very individual motivation; for example, Andrew's fear that he will fail his final medical exams.

When the play reached Scotland the Scottish press found *Walker, London* 'fresh and novel'. Unfortunately, their reaction to the long-awaited adaptation of *The Little Minister* was far less favourable. The Scots had great expectations of stage adaptations of Scottish novels which the play failed to fulfil. A reviewer in *The Scotsman* of 8 November 1897 declared that the hope engendered by Barrie's career so far was now 'replaced by disappointment in the hearts of those who think seriously about our national drama'. Even the playwright himself grew to dislike it and excluded it from his *Collected Works*.

Barrie's dislike of *The Little Minister* may have been based on a realisation

Figure 3.19 Sir J. M. Barrie (Sir William Nicholson, 1904).
(Scottish National Portrait Gallery)

that the commercially successful work, which earned him £80,000 in ten years, could have been a much better play. His most ambitious dramatic experiment to date, it had been undermined by a combination of inexperience, in that Barrie had not been able to handle the effects he wanted with the delicacy they required, and interference. The young playwright had broken his own rules and allowed himself to be swayed by others into changing the emphasis of the finished adaptation for what appear to have been largely commercial reasons. He found himself under pressure, from the American play-brokers and managers for whom the play was intended, to provide a star vehicle for Maude Adams in the lead role of Lady Barbara (Babbie), the free-spirited changeling girl who disguises herself as a gypsy and captures the heart of the young minister.

Barrie greatly admired Maude Adams and spent his customary long hours at rehearsal, shaping the work to suit her. At the same time he was endeavouring to extend his dramatic technique by stripping down the lengthy novel to focus on and develop the mythical and allegorical aspects of the tale. It was natural that the process of dramatisation should have simplified a rambling plot and decreased the number of characters; however, in order to accommodate the allegorical, Barrie also stripped away much of the original historically based, and therefore fatally realistic, Chartist background to the action. Many of the characters who survived the translation were simplified, and the chorus of Auld Licht elders, whose appearance at the back of the scene like jack-in-the-boxes in stove pipe hats caused *The Scotsman* critic great offence, were divorced from their original role and became at least partial figures of fun.

Barrie's vision of the world of the play was, on the evidence of the note-books and the early draft versions of the script, considerably darker than the sentimental romance which finally appeared. He wanted to use the gypsy characters to explore the idea of a return to 'savagery'. There are repeated jottings on the theme of dominance turning into slavery, set against which Babbie's final submission to a tame future as the dutiful minister's wife, who will dress up in her gypsy clothes only when they are alone, assumes an altogether more ambiguous tone. The draft ending for the American production used this idea of submission to the full:

Rintoul: Don't be alarmed, Mr Dishart. It is only her way of trying to get round the pair of us. [*Lifting cane*] If you would just let me bring this about her shoulders for once, I think I might forgive her in time.
Gavin: [pleasantly] Ah, Lord Rintoul, no one has the right to punish her now except her husband.
Babbie: [Startled] Oh! [*He's unaware he has said anything disgusting. Gavin opens the door for Lord Rintoul who goes into manse, leaving door open.*]
Gavin: [*Returning to Babbie gloriously*] Babbie – my wife!

Babbie: Yes, but what was that you said just now to father?
Gavin: [*Seriously*] I have forgotten – what was it about?
Babbie: [*rather breathless*] If you have forgotten – it doesn't matter.
[*She looks around and a fit of shivering seizes her – this should go on till every bit of her is shivering.*]
Gavin: [*putting arms round her*] Beloved, you are shivering – why?
Babbie: I don't know why – you lovely, fussing husband! [*sweetly*] Gavin you will always be kind to Babbie won't you in case she doesn't last!
Gavin: [*He is lovingly drawing her to Left away from the house as if to sit at wall – she is warmer now*] No, dear, let's go in by the door.
[*They enter manse hand in hand – The head of Nanny alone rises over dyke watching them with beaming face*][20]

A watered-down version of this scene was also prepared for the Lord Chamberlain's perusal. In the event the ending which appeared reduced the action to near farce.

With every new edition of *The Little Minister* Barrie seems to have tried to repair some of the damage done to his reputation by the suggestion that he was holding Scotland and the Scots up to ridicule. He inserted little passages in the dialogue designed to bolster national pride, but the compromises he made resulted in a piece which fell well below his own expectations and angered those Scots who felt that the torch of national theatrical pride, the National Drama, had not been adequately taken up by its rightful bearer. Nevertheless, as the century came to a close, Scotland found in J. M. Barrie a writer of international stature, whose eventual mastery of playwriting would enable him to manipulate the mechanics of the process and ultimately to push back the boundaries of the art with a skill so unobtrusive and apparently effortless, that the full measure of his artistic achievements has only really become clear with hindsight.

The nineteenth century was a time of great expansion for the Scottish theatre. There has never been another period when so many Scots have gone to see live theatre; and the emergence and heyday of the National Drama was one of those rare instances when the theatre captured the mood of a nation rather than of one class or interest group. However, towards the end of the period critics and commentators bemoaned the loss of the stock companies which had provided both training and a career structure for Scottish actors. J. C. Dibdin, in *The Annals of the Edinburgh Stage*, described an Edinburgh actress, Miss Nicol, as:

one of the last of the class of provincial actors . . . who, having a comfortable home and engagement in the country, were content to remain there in the full confidence and respect of their managers, and regarded by the audience as friends. There were many such throughout the country at one time; but they have all passed away, and the class is dead, never to be revived.

He also complained that 'in the present age [1888] and for many years past, our theatres have been nothing more nor less than buildings with resident manager, orchestra, scenepainter (sometimes), carpenters, and money takers, in which performances are given by companies from London'. Scottish critics wrote nostalgically of a time past when Scotland's literary figures had both attended, and contributed to the life of, the theatre. They could not seem to address the issue of the integral part the repertoire, and its relationship to the audience, had played in creating that community of spirit, and they saw no contradiction in slanting their current criticism towards the output of the London West End. This reluctance to express a commitment to an independent theatrical voice was an expression of changing attitudes among both audience and practitioners. While Scottish politics and cultural identity were outwardly more secure, and trade, particularly with the Empire, was booming, it was much harder to discern a role for a Scottish theatre industry, increasingly riven by class divisions – as seen in differentiated audiences, venues and forms of entertainment – as an expression of a unified national identity.

4   *1900 to 1950*

DAVID HUTCHISON

The theatre industry in Scotland entered a period of remarkable expansion at the beginning of the twentieth century, as the following figures demonstrate:[1]

Table 4.1 *Number of theatres in Scotland in 1900 and 1910.*

	Total	Aberdeen	Dundee	Edinburgh	Glasgow
1900	32	2	3	5	10
1910	53	3	6	7	15

The upsurge in theatre building was particularly marked in Glasgow: the King's opened in 1904, the Pavilion the same year, the Alhambra in 1910, the Lyceum in 1900, the Palace in 1904, the Coliseum in 1905 and Hengler's in 1905. The King's, Pavilion and Alhambra were large theatres in the centre of the city while most of the others were music halls serving their immediate localities. In the event, music halls suffered most as a consequence of the advances of the cinema. But that transition was yet to come. In 1906 the Glasgow *Evening Citizen* could inform a curious reader that the total seating capacity of the city's theatres was 29,000.

Elsewhere in the country, theatres were also being opened: the Gaiety in Ayr (1902), the Grand (1903) and the Electric (1910) in Falkirk, the Empire (1903) and King's (1909) in Dundee, the King's (1906) in Edinburgh, the Empire (1903) in Greenock, the Hippodrome (1907) in Hamilton and the King's (1904) in Kirkcaldy. The confidence of the managements of the time can be seen in the architecture of the buildings they erected. Those that are still extant, for example the King's in Glasgow and the King's in Edinburgh, are substantial and attractive edifices. When they opened, press comment emphasised their sumptuousness, comfort and pleasing decor. However, like the Victorian playhouses that preceded them, these theatres were heavily dependent on touring productions which originated south of the border. The Scottish element in their repertoire consisted largely of pantomimes, variety and very occasional dramatic pieces.

THE GLASGOW REPERTORY COMPANY

Drama in Britain in the early years of the twentieth century was becoming a more serious affair than it had been for much of the nineteenth century. In London, through the Sunday-night presentations of the Stage Society and the Vedrenne-Granville-Barker seasons at the Royal Court, and elsewhere in the country through the work of other ventures, an audience for more demanding plays than were generally available was developing. Against this background a company was established in Glasgow whose work, though short-lived, is of great importance in the history of Scottish theatre. This was the Glasgow Repertory Company. Its progenitor was an Englishman called Alfred Wareing.

Wareing was born at Greenwich in 1876. He gave up a career in the book trade for the theatre, beginning as an advance agent for F. R. Benson's company. From there he moved on to work for several other eminent actor-managers and, while company manager for Beerbohm Tree on a visit to Dublin in 1906, he became interested in the work of the Abbey Theatre. Wareing was so impressed by the performances he saw that he arranged a tour for the Irish Players in Britain, which took in Aberdeen, Edinburgh and Glasgow, as well as several venues south of the border. His involvement with the Irish Players and with Miss A. E. Horniman, who financed the Abbey, and later the Gaiety company in Manchester, led directly to his developing the scheme for the establishment of a Repertory Theatre in Glasgow, of which venture he was to be managing director for most of its existence.

In 1909, as a result of the efforts of Wareing and several prominent Glasgow figures, the Glasgow Repertory Theatre was established. A meeting was held on 19 February at which Wareing explained his proposal to start a citizens' theatre – one owned by those members of the public who subscribed to its foundation – and thus make the city independent of London for drama provision. The enterprise was to be initiated with a capital of £2000, one thousand of which would be called up. By the middle of March plans had been announced for a first season, which was to commence at the beginning of April, and the prospectus for Scottish Playgoers Ltd was issued:

> The objects of the company include the establishment in Glasgow of a Repertory Theatre . . . the organisation of a stock company . . . and the encouragement of the initiation and development of purely Scottish drama by providing a stage and acting company which will be peculiarly adapted for the production of plays national in character, written

by Scottish men and women of letters. (*Glasgow Herald*, 19 March 1909)

The directors of the company were drawn from the city's business and cultural élite: Professor W. MacNeile Dixon, the distinguished Professor of English at Glasgow University; Deacon Convenor Andrew Macdonald, a leading businessman who acted as chairman; Neil Munro, the journalist and writer; Professor J. S. Phillimore, who held the chair of Humanity at the university; J. W. Robb, an accountant; and Wareing himself. They decided to start the company with a capital of £3000 in £1 shares, £1000 more than had originally been announced, of which £2000 were offered for subscription. In point of fact only 1000 of these had been taken up when the company began operations in April 1909, in the Royalty Theatre in Sauchiehall Street (later known as the Lyric). The theatre had been leased for £80 per week from Howard and Wyndham, with all the profits from bars, cloakrooms and programme sales remaining with the proprietors.

It is clear that those who worked for the establishment of a Scottish theatre throughout the first half of the twentieth century had constantly before them

Figure 4.1 The Royalty Theatre, Glasgow, from the back of the pit, September 1910, drawn by Muirhead Bone. Onstage the last act of George Bernard Shaw's Man and Superman *is being performed by the Glasgow Repertory Company.* (Scottish Theatre Archive)

the example of the Abbey Theatre in Dublin, where a distinctive Irish drama was in the process of being created. The achievements of that drama were constantly invoked, for example, in much that was written about the Glasgow Repertory Company: on the death of J. M. Synge, the *Glasgow Herald* (26 March 1909) commented that the country was moving towards 'the establishment of a Scottish theatre equal to the Irish one in national spirit and possibly superior to it in breadth of artistic horizon'. Whether it was wise to regard what was happening on the other side of the Irish Sea in a largely non-industrialised society on the verge of a war of independence as an exemplar for Scotland is another matter altogether. In practice this tended to encourage not political engagement but an emphasis on the rural and the quaint at the expense of the urban and the modern. Aiming for the Abbey's level of aesthetic attainment was eminently sensible, but in other respects the Irish experience was to prove a problematic model for Scottish theatrical enterprises, particularly during the inter-war period.

During the first six weeks of the Glasgow Rep's existence Shaw's *You Never Can Tell*, Ibsen's *An Enemy of the People*, Galsworthy's *Strife* and Arnold Bennett's *Cupid and Commonsense*, along with plays by other writers, were produced. The season did not make a profit and capital was absorbed to cover the operating loss. The company continued to lose money until the last year of its existence when it moved into the black. The figures for the five years are as follows:

    1909–1910: £3019 loss
    1910–1911: £1539 loss
    1911–1912: £322 loss
    1912–1913: £125 loss
    1913–1914: £790 profit

The final season took place in the spring of 1914, under the directorship of Lewis Casson. Colonel F. L. Morrison, the chairman, remarked at the AGM in May 1914 that he thought the company had at last turned the corner and reached a self-supporting stage. He made the point, however, that the margin of profitability was narrow, since average weekly receipts were only £9 higher than two years previously when a loss of £322 had been sustained. It was decided that the name of the organisation should be changed to the Scottish Repertory Company, a change symbolic of the bolder policy that was to be followed in future, particularly with regard to the production of modern and Shakespearian plays, despite the expense of mounting these. Sadly, the company had little chance to put its aspirations into practice, for the outbreak of the First World War in the summer of 1914 swamped its efforts.

The work of the Glasgow Repertory Company was at an end, and although

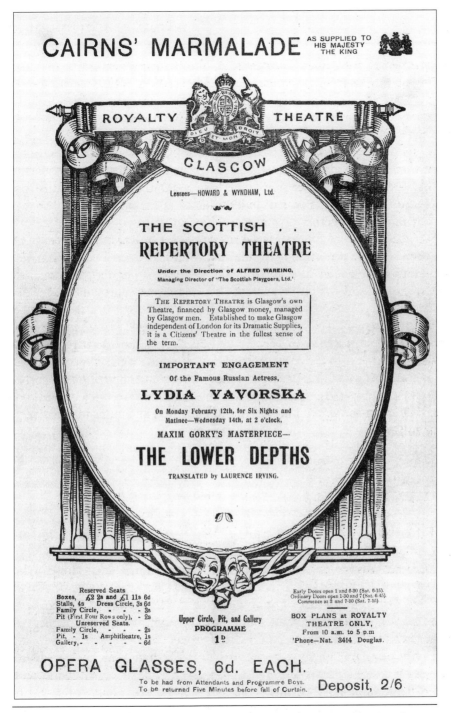

Figure 4.2 Playbill for Maxim Gorki's The Lower Depths *at the Royalty Theatre, Glasgow, 1914, starring Russian actress Lydia Yavorska. The Glasgow-based Scottish Repertory Company's aim was 'to make Glasgow independent of London for its Dramatic Supplies'. (Scottish Theatre Archive)*

the remaining funds were transferred to the St Andrew Society of Glasgow, under whose aegis the Scottish National Players were formed, the nature of the work of the Players was so different from that of the Glasgow Repertory Company that the tradition started by the latter was not properly restored until the growth of professional repertory theatres in Scotland. It is wrong, however, to look upon the Glasgow Repertory Company as a failure. Although it had to struggle for the five years of its existence, by 1914 it had reached a semi-secure position as a serious repertory theatre without benefit of public funds (and had just secured the 'patronage' of Glasgow Corporation, though it is not clear what the financial implications of that development would have been). Admittedly the company received private subsidy from its shareholders, who did not gain, nor expect to gain, any return for their investment, but the fact that a profit was made in 1914 does indicate that the venture had so established itself in the city that thenceforth it could have been financially viable. It was the first repertory theatre in Scotland, one of the first in Britain (though it never played strictly in repertoire), and the first citizens' theatre in the English-speaking world. In five years it presented over one hundred plays, thirty-three of which were new to the stage, and sixteen of which were new Scottish plays. The company performed work by some of the leading writers of the day – seven plays by Shaw, two by Ibsen, four by Bennett, three by Galsworthy and three by Granville-Barker. It could not be regarded as a thorough-going art or avant-garde theatre, but although lightweight material was presented, the proportion was no higher than that found in the programmes of many subsidised theatres today.

As just noted, a third of all the plays presented were entirely new to the stage, a remarkably high proportion. The company scored a few notable coups, in particular with the presentation in 1909 of *The Seagull*, the first production of a Chekhov play in Britain. Encouragement was given to Scottish authors and although no masterpieces were produced and there was no upsurge comparable to the Irish one, a start was made to building a native modern dramatic tradition. Crucially, the context in which new Scottish work appeared – an eclectic mix of quality contemporary plays – was the one most suited to stimulating indigenous writers to be ambitious. Among the Scots who wrote for the Glasgow Repertory Company were Neil Munro, best known as the author of the Para Handy stories; J. J. Bell, the creator of Wee MacGreegor; Anthony Rowley and G. J. Hamlen, who both tackled contemporary urban themes; and Donald Colquhoun and J. A. Ferguson. The two best Scottish plays produced were Colquhoun's *Jean* and Ferguson's *Campbell of Kilmohr*.

Jean (1910) is set in a farmhouse in Lanarkshire and, despite a rather melodramatic plot, has the great merit of honesty in its presentation of the hard life of the small farmer as he tries to establish a position of security for himself.

The remarks old Milroy makes to his son about his dead wife ring true, and the Scots dialogue employed is effective without being quaint:

> *James*: Afore ye kent yer mither an' me, we wis by wi' the worst o't, we wis kinna weel aff, and easy like . . . But ye should have seen us when we started. Man, it was a fair wrastle, day an' nicht – nicht an' day. I widna like ye to hiv yon tae dae.
>
> *Sandy*: It couldna be as bad for me – noo.
>
> *James*: Mind ye, it's no' every woman wad hiv turned oot like yer mither. She got on rael weel. There was a wheen years there, afore she deed, ye widna hiv kenned her for the same woman – she wis that sensible and wise-like. But there's no' mony lassies turns oot like her. The maist o' them gangs intae their graves wi' nae mair sense in their heids than the first day they stairted courtin'.

The play follows the course of an argument between the old farmer and his son, Sandy, over Sandy's proposed marriage to the farm maid – the Jean of the title. The argument ends with the revelation by Milroy that Jean has previously had an illegitimate child, the counter-revelation by Sandy that he has already married the girl, and the consequent fatal seizure which kills Milroy.

Campbell of Kilmohr (1914) is set in the Highlands after the 1745 Jacobite Rising. Ferguson is concerned to contrast the integrity of the Highlander with the dishonesty and roguery of the Lowlander. It is a new experience for Campbell, a government official, to find that his wiles in seeking to prise information about the Pretender's whereabouts from Highlanders are unsuccessful. His ideas on human nature up to this point in time have been straightforward:

> Now, I've had a lairge experience o'life, and I never saw yet a sensible man insensible to the touch of yellow metal. If there may be such a man, it is demonstrable that he is no sensible man. Fideelity! quotha, it's sheer obstinacy. They just see that he wants something oot o' them, and they're so damned selfish and thrawn they winna pairt. And with the natural inabeelity o' their brains to hold mair than one idea at a time they canna see that in return you could put something into their palms far more profitable.

Campbell, however, is forced to change his views in the face of Highland obstinacy, and to resort to the trickery of a young girl in an attempt to secure the information he requires. Having gained it, he cynically goes back on an undertaking not to execute the girl's cousin. The final irony is that what he had been told about the Jacobites is misleading, and he is no further forward in his hunt for them. *Campbell of Kilmohr*, which was presented during the company's last season under Lewis Casson's directorship, and has been much revived, particularly by the amateur movement, is a slight play. Its merit is that, like *Jean*, it rings true to life, though the aftermath of the failed rising had a barbarity scarcely hinted at by Ferguson. It is a dramatically effective piece and does not lean too heavily on what has in recent years been described as the discourse of tartanry; that is to say, the presentation of the Highlands as a land of charm and romance peopled by noble, but canny, pre-industrial men and women.

JAMES BARRIE

The work of J. M. Barrie (1860–1937) ought to be discussed at this point, though it made only a brief appearance in the programmes of the Glasgow Repertory Company, which is a little surprising, given that he was the only contemporary Scottish dramatist of note. Indeed Barrie was, and remains, the most financially successful Scottish dramatist to date, although that success has not been accompanied by universal critical acclaim. R. D. S. Jack in his major reassessment of Barrie's dramatic art, *The Road to the Never Land* (1991), argues forcibly that Scottish critics are too quick to dismiss Barrie, and have done so on dubious extra-textual grounds.[2] That is not the position of this writer, for whom Barrie has always seemed to be an extremely able creator of well-made plays, in which the action is usually lively, the characters varied, and the wit pleasing.

Born the son of a handloom weaver in Kirrriemuir, he was in many ways the archetypal lad o' pairts celebrated in the work of the so-called Kailyard writers such as S. R. Crockett, Ian Maclaren and Barrie himself. After studying at Edinburgh University, he went south to work as a journalist and produced the prose sketches, *Auld Licht Idylls* (1888) and *A Window in Thrums* (1889). After several unsuccessful forays into the theatre, he began to make his mark with *Walker, London* (1892), as discussed in the previous chapter. From then on he enjoyed considerable success.

In *The Admirable Crichton* (1902), one of the two full-length plays the Glasgow Repertory did present (the other was *Walker, London*), Barrie's wit is deployed to explore the case in favour of an aristocracy of nature, as opposed to one of birth, when Lord Loam's butler, Crichton, takes command of the situation after his master's family and entourage are marooned on a desert island. Loam is a man given to egalitarian tokenism, a stance which Crichton thoroughly dislikes. As he says before the shipwreck occurs:

> I am the son of a butler and a lady's maid, perhaps the happiest of all combinations; and to me the most beautiful thing in the world is a haughty, aristocratic English house, with every one kept in his place.

Yet Crichton is something of an enigma, for he is not slow to suggest that on the desert island things must be ordered differently:

> *Lord Loam*: Well, well. This question of the leadership; what do you think now, Crichton?
> *Crichton*: My lord, I feel it is a matter with which *I* have nothing to do.
> *Lord Loam*: Excellent. Ha, Mary? That settles it, I think.
> *Lady Mary*: It seems to, but – I'm not sure.
> *Crichton*: It will settle itself naturally, my lord, without any interference from us.

Although Crichton appears to slip back easily into the hierarchical social order of England after the party is rescued and normal relations are smoothly resumed as if they had never been interrupted, the play does subtly undermine the legitimacy of a hereditary class system without setting out a radical critique of that system.

Figure 4.3 The Scottish National Players performing J. M. Barrie's The Admirable Crichton *in the 1920s.* (Scottish Theatre Archive)

A similar point can be made about *What Every Woman Knows* (1908). Barrie presents us in this play with a very believable picture of the dour Scotsman on the make. John Shand is dull, without humour, and so lacking in self-perception that he fails to understand that his success as a Member of Parliament is due to the efforts of his supposedly plain, uninspiring wife, Maggie, whose 'rough womanish' suggestions turn plodding speeches into polished rhetoric. What is not clear is whether the play can really be regarded as feminist before its time. Despite the acknowledgement of Maggie's intellectual superiority to her husband, there is no suggestion from Barrie that Mr and Mrs Shand should reverse their positions. But, as with *Crichton*, the conventional view of the social order has been deprived of some of its credibility.

If there is one aspect of Barrie's talent which stood out in a theatre dominated by naturalism, it was his interest in the supernatural. His most successful venture in this area is of course *Peter Pan* (1904), which continues to hold a special niche in the repertoire; it is probably the most commercially successful play ever written by a Scot. In it Barrie is able to give free rein to his deeper feelings about the tragic loss of childhood. He explores his obsessive interest in the boy–mother relationship, which in a more conventional, naturalistic piece would have had to be contained, and indulges his pleasure in whimsy. The fantasy world of the Never Land, however, is no paradise, but has its own very real terrors which threaten destruction. It is these terrors, and the essential sadness of Peter's plight, which give the play its resonance.

In *Dear Brutus* (1917) and *Mary Rose* (1920) Barrie's attraction to a world beyond the material one is most clearly expressed. *Dear Brutus* is set in the country house of a rather mysterious gentleman called Lob – the name is a variation on Puck – on Midsummer's Eve. Lob has brought together a disparate collection of individuals who have in common the desire for a second chance in life. Outside the windows a strange wood appears, as if from nowhere, and the characters do indeed dally with what might have been, before returning to the present with its unavoidable complications. The allusion to Shakespeare and the implication that we, not circumstances, are responsible for our fates, lurk behind the action. *Dear Brutus* is a play of considerable wit and some pathos, but it does lack depth. Barrie goes so far and no further in his presentation of emotional and sexual conflict; he is a dramatist who often hovers on the edge of powerful feeling but appears reluctant to allow himself to be immersed in it.

Mary Rose focuses on the experiences of a girl whose life is arrested when she steps on to a remote Hebridean island. The first time her parents 'lose' her for a few days, but on the second occasion she disappears for twenty-five years, leaving behind her young husband and their baby son. When she returns she has not aged at all – and Barrie does not quite know what to do with her. At the end of the play she reappears as a ghost to her son, now a young man, and seems to be regressing even further back into childhood as she expresses the wish to 'go away and play'. As the curtain falls, she is summoned to her final rest and walks into the night. For all the rather cloying quality of some of the dialogue, Barrie does succeed in creating the sense of a world beyond the rational. *Mary Rose* still has the ability to send shivers down an audience's spine.

Both *Mary Rose* and *Dear Brutus* were written after the demise of the Glasgow Repertory Company, so it can hardly be criticised for not presenting them! As to the long-term impact of the Company on the development of Scottish drama, that is difficult to measure. The existence of a theatre presenting new Scottish plays clearly encouraged potential dramatists to write for the stage and thus to begin learning their craft, though very few of them appear to have continued in the profession. However, it is known that the young James Bridie (discussed later) was encouraged by what he saw at the Royalty to try his hand; indeed he actually submitted a play to Wareing, although it was never performed. Like so many of his countrymen, during the years immediately following the disbandment of the Glasgow Repertory, Bridie served in the armed forces, and it was only in the 1920s that he was able to pursue his interest in the theatre again.

THE INTER-WAR PERIOD

Culturally the inter-war period was dominated by the consolidation of cinema and the arrival of broadcasting. Picture houses began to appear in Scotland in the early years of the twentieth century, often in makeshift premises. Their number climbed steadily after the First World War, as can be seen from the following figures:[3]

Table 4.2   *Number of cinemas in Scotland in 1920 and 1930.*

	Total	Aberdeen	Dundee	Edinburgh	Glasgow
1920	557	15	22	25	94
1930	634	15	27	39	127

A vast popular audience had come into existence and grown at a remarkable rate. Whereas in 1920 there were over five hundred cinemas, twenty years previously there were no buildings that would have been recognised as such.

Regular broadcasting came to Scotland in 1923 when the British Broadcasting Company's Glasgow station was opened; other stations at Edinburgh and Aberdeen followed. In 1924 all UK stations were linked by landline to allow simultaneous broadcasting. The growth in the number of licence holders was steady throughout the inter-war period and, by 1939, of a UK total of nine million, just under eight hundred thousand lived north of the border.[4] Early on, the BBC in Scotland began to broadcast drama: an adaptation of *Rob Roy* was mounted a few weeks after the Glasgow station opened and, in 1932, the Scottish service organised its first Radio Drama Festival.

These two developments had many consequences. As far as theatre is concerned, the rapid decline of the music hall, which had enjoyed a boom before the war, can be attributed to the rise of the cinema. Several music halls and variety theatres became cinemas: for example, Glasgow's Britannia, later the Panopticon, became the Tron Cinema in 1920; the Savoy opened in the same city in 1911 as a variety theatre and was a cinema by 1916. In Dundee, the Palace was a cinema by 1911 (though during the Second World War it reverted to variety). In Edinburgh, the Grand became a cinema in 1920. Elsewhere in Scotland theatres were converted: Greenock's Alexandra in the mid 1920s, Kirkcaldy's King's in 1924, and Falkirk's Grand in 1934.

The extent to which the theatrical expansion of the first decade of the century had been halted can be seen by looking at the relevant figures:[5]

Table 4.3   *Number of theatres in Scotland in 1920, 1930 and 1940.*

	Total	Aberdeen	Dundee	Edinburgh	Glasgow
1920	45	3	3	6	16
1930	30	3	0	4	12
1940	32	3	1	6	11

The decline from the 1910 position was most marked, among the cities, in Dundee and Glasgow. Elsewhere in Scotland there was a steady slide, so that by 1940 there were over a third less theatres in Scotland than there had been in 1910.

While cinema provided little extra employment for Scottish writers and actors, radio began to open up new opportunities. Neither development had, however, quite as striking an effect on live theatre as television was later to have on the cinema. Theatre survived, but as a minority interest, for the mass audience did not give it much support. Whereas previously that audience had mainly patronised the music hall, now, vastly increased in numbers by reason of higher incomes, it gave its allegiance to the cinema and wireless, a loyalty later transferred to television. However, something of the music hall survived north of the border in the work of Scots comedians such as Harry Gordon, Tommy Lorne, Tommy Morgan and Dave Willis, in both variety and pantomime. Indeed the popular theatre tradition, whose origins were discussed in the previous chapter, remains an important one from which many performers and some playwrights have drawn sustenance.

London-originated tours of plays, musicals and variety shows occupied many stages in Scotland throughout the inter-war period. There were also a small number of repertory companies based in Scotland. These companies cooperated closely with the theatrical management of Howard and Wyndham, the Edinburgh-based organisation formed in 1895 by two of the leading theatrical figures of the day, J. B. Howard and F. W. Wyndham. The first of the repertory companies to establish itself in this period was the Masque Theatre, which was founded in 1928 under Robert Fenemore, and alternated between Glasgow and Edinburgh for the next five years. In late 1932 a plan for the establishment of a permanent repertory theatre building in Edinburgh was announced, but it came to nothing and the company effectively ceased to exist. Its place on the Howard and Wyndham circuit was taken by the Brandon-Thomas Players, which had been formed in 1930 and had given its first performance in Newcastle. Thereafter it toured throughout Britain and came north to Edinburgh for a fourteen-week season in 1933. This season and a subsequent one in Glasgow were deemed so successful that the company stayed in Scotland until, in 1937, it decided to try its fortune in London. Sadly, the transfer to the capital was not a success and the company was disbanded early in 1938. Among its actors was Wilson Barrett, whose own repertory company was established shortly after the Brandon-Thomas one disappeared. Barrett's company was to come north permanently in 1941 and to provide regular repertory seasons until 1955. In 1938 Howard and Wyndham filled the gap left by the departure of the Brandon-Thomas Players by sponsoring a repertory company of its own, which performed until the outbreak of war in 1939.

Collectively, all the ventures described above were a forerunner of the modern repertory theatres. They represented a retreat from the position of the Glasgow Repertory Company, for their programming was less adventurous, but they kept professional theatre alive in Scotland and continued the important work of audience-building: the Brandon-Thomas Players claimed patronage latterly of 10,000 persons per week in each of the two theatres in which they performed, although they had a lean period during the very worst years of the Depression. Scottish drama found a very small place in these companies' programmes: Bridie's *The Anatomist*, for example, was given its premiere by the Masque Theatre, but this was the exception rather than the rule.

A more permanent repertory theatre was successfully established in one Scottish town during the period: Perth Repertory was a joint venture by Marjorie Dence and David Steuart, who had met at London University. Steuart's ambition to found a repertory in Perth was realised when a theatre was advertised for sale there. Perth's first regular theatre opened in 1810 and, although it was destroyed by fire in 1824, another theatre, the Royal, opened in 1820, and continued to operate until mid century. Perth Theatre opened in 1900 and housed a variety of travelling companies until it was put up for sale. Marjorie Dence's father assisted in the theatre's acquisition and it opened again in

September 1935 with a production of Clifford Bax's *Rose without a Thorn*. By 1939 it felt secure enough to organise a theatre festival, for which Bridie wrote *The Golden Legend of Shults* and at which performances of *Romeo and Juliet* (with Alec Guinness), Chekhov's *Three Sisters* and Shaw's *Caesar and Cleopatra* were also given.

Persistent attempts to found a professional theatre in Edinburgh were unsuccessful, as were efforts, towards the end of the 1930s, to establish a similar venture in Glasgow, under the auspices of a Theatre Society of Scotland, which clearly had 'national' aspirations. The various little theatres which opened – at Dundee, Glasgow and St Andrews, for example – were for the use of amateur groups.

THE AMATEUR THEATRE AND
THE SCOTTISH NATIONAL PLAYERS

The development of indigenous drama during this period took place largely in amateur clubs, rather than in the professional theatre. Members even of leading companies, such as the Scottish National Players and the Curtain, normally received no, or only nominal, payment for their work, apart from fees for radio broadcasts. None the less, they found themselves charged with the onerous responsibility of creating a national drama.

The amateur theatre movement in Britain began in the middle of the nineteenth century, essentially as a pursuit of the upper and middle classes. By the turn of the century it was firmly established. By the end of the First World War it was such a significant activity among all social classes that associations of amateur clubs came into being; the British Drama League was founded in 1919 and the Scottish Community Drama Association (SCDA) in 1926. The sudden rise to popularity of the amateur theatre in Scotland can be seen by comparing the number of entries for the SCDA's one-act festival in 1926–7 (35), 1928–9 (88) and 1930–1 (243); by the 1932–3 season the entry had reached 307. By 1937 there were more than one thousand amateur clubs in Scotland.

It is difficult for people who did not live through the boom period in amateur drama to realise how extensive the activity was. A perusal of the press of the time makes it clear that this was no coterie pursuit. The Scottish newspapers of the 1930s, for example, all had regular weekly columns on the amateur scene and reviews of productions. The development of the play festivals, whatever it may have done for artistic standards – and this is a matter very much open to debate – certainly appears to have aroused public interest. For example, the fortunes of the Ardrossan and Saltcoats Players, who were successful on a national and international scale, were followed locally like those of a football team.

The upsurge in amateur theatre in the twentieth century can be attributed to the general increase in leisure time, the expansion of education, and the realisation, particularly in areas relatively far from large centres of population, and hence from professional theatres, that this activity not only provided an opportunity for large-scale community involvement but also a clear way of participating in and gaining access to the arts. Beyond a certain point amateur drama became a fashion, if not a craze, and it was inevitable that when some other fashion came along the less dedicated clubs would die, as in fact has happened since the advent of television. In 1951 the SCDA's one-act festival could still attract 500 entries, but by the early 1960s that number had halved.

What was the effect of all this activity on the growth of Scottish drama? As anyone who has had any dealings with the amateur movement in Scotland will confirm, the self-expression of the Scottish nation on the stage is not always very high on its list of objectives. However, there were two groups of amateurs based in Glasgow who rather courageously took on the role the vast majority of their colleagues had little interest in.

The scheme for the formation of the Scottish National Players was initiated before the First World War under the auspices of the St Andrew Society of Glasgow, and was aimed at the 'production of plays dealing with Scottish life and character'. The war, however, led to its postponement, and it was not until January 1921 that the Players gave their first performance in the Royal Institute, Glasgow, when three one-act plays were presented and favourably received by the press. Several other performances were given that year and, in February 1922, the Scottish National Theatre Society was formed with the following objectives:

1. To take over the assets and liabilities of the Scottish National
    Players Committee of the Saint Andrew Society (Glasgow).
2. To develop Scottish national drama through the productions by the
    Scottish National Players of plays of Scottish life and character.
3. To encourage in Scotland a public taste for good drama of any type.
4. To found a Scottish National Theatre.

Throughout their existence, the Players gave short seasons in Glasgow, spread out over the year, and toured at other times. This was deliberate policy, as the Players sought to be a national rather than a regional group, but it was a policy which attracted some criticism from those who felt that their efforts should be concentrated in Glasgow rather than dissipated wandering the Highlands. In addition to their regular performances at the Athenaeum, and afterwards the Lyric, two of the city's smaller theatres, the Players appeared at other Glasgow venues. In 1925, and again in 1926, they performed Robert Bain's *James the First of Scotland* at the Theatre Royal; in 1923 and 1926 they presented John Brandane's *The Glen is Mine* at the King's.

Figure 4.4 The Scottish National Players on tour in the 1920s. (Scottish Theatre Archive)

The Players performed in London on three occasions, and also toured the Stoll music-hall circuit, one of the chains of variety theatres which operated venues throughout Britain. Several visits were paid to Edinburgh, and a number of broadcasts were undertaken; the Players made a substantial contribution to broadcast drama in the early days of the BBC in Scotland. In an analysis of the development of radio north of the border during the inter-war period, Adrienne Scullion has explored the relationship between the BBC and various amateur companies, including the Players.[6] She demonstrates not only that there was the obvious dependence, in the reliance on actors, but that on occasion an evening of two or three one-act pieces, such as the Players offered to their live audiences, would be transferred intact on to the air waves. It is also clear that although there was a little experimentation, radio drama in Scotland drew heavily for its subject matter on those aspects of the nation's life to which the amateur movement in general, and the Players in particular, was attracted.

By far the most important side of the Players' activities, apart from their seasons in Glasgow, were the country tours and one-night stands, to which the company itself, and others, attached great significance. *The Glasgow Herald* of 22 January 1926 reported on one such tour:

> It has been said that the work of a national theatre cannot properly be restricted to one centre of activity; it must carry its work to the small town and village as well, and this it should do consistently and thoroughly. Recognising this, as well as the educational and social value of good drama worthily presented, the Carnegie United Kingdom Trust has generously guaranteed this tour against financial loss. This guarantee is part of a considered scheme by the Trust for bringing good drama within the reach of the smaller communities which cannot hope to support it on a purely commercial basis.

Local communities were exhorted to give all their support to the company, which it was claimed was 'the country's movement to establish a National Drama'. Among the many places visited were Oban in 1922; Bridge of Allan, Perth and Dunoon in 1924; several towns and villages during a three-week tour, in summer 1927, of Perthshire; Aberdeenshire and Fife (during which the company slept under canvas); and the Border towns in the course of another tour in 1929.

Despite the efforts of some members of the governing board to change the situation, the actors who worked with the Players were amateur or semi-professional (although a good many later turned fully professional and had successful careers). The governors, among them the dramatists James Bridie and John Brandane, believed that if the company was ever to be properly established it would have to become completely professional. The idea was to take the Athenaeum by the season, but the majority of governors did not care for this proposal, nor did most of the actors, who were understandably nervous about giving up their jobs. A policy of two-night runs was adopted instead, and in that year, 1932, the Players gave only four programmes. Operations were formally suspended two years later, although the company did carry on mounting performances – largely of lightweight material – until the outbreak of war. The Scottish National Players finally petered out in 1947.

Unlike the actors, the principal producers were engaged throughout on a professional basis. Among them were A. P. Wilson, Frank D. Clewlow, Elliot Mason, W. G. Fay, and the young Tyrone Guthrie. Wilson, who was a Scot, came to the Players from the Abbey Theatre, Dublin, and when he left them he went into film production. Clewlow came from Birmingham Rep and went to broadcasting in Australia, Elliot Mason was later to become an actress of some note in comedy, and W. G. Fay was another recruit from the Abbey. Guthrie was the most distinguished producer the Players employed. He stayed for two years, leading the first summer camping tour in 1927 and directing *The Sunlight Sonata*, the first of Bridie's stage plays to be performed, in 1928. He went on to establish himself as a director of the first rank in England, particularly at the Old Vic in the 1930s and 1940s, in Europe and in Canada, where he was largely responsible for the creation of the Shakespeare Festival Theatre in Stratford, Ontario. Late in his life he wrote that some of his happiest professional memories were of his time in Glasgow.

Guthrie's connection with Scotland was renewed periodically. In particular he directed *Ane Satyre of the Thrie Estaitis* in the Assembly Hall during the 1948 Edinburgh Festival, the first occasion on which that venue was used for drama. It was an inspired choice of acting space for the presentation of Sir David Lindsay's masterpiece, and fitting that, in that landmark production, Guthrie should have employed a number of actors who began their careers with the Scottish National Players. Guthrie's relationship with James Bridie continued, and he was responsible for the first presentation of a Bridie play in London when *The Anatomist* was staged in 1930. His last visit to Scotland, in 1968, was to direct a production of *The Anatomist* at the Glasgow Citizens' Theatre by way of tribute to the actor Duncan Macrae.

The Scottish National Players presented 131 full-length and one-act plays, half of them premieres. Enough of the texts have survived for some general judgements to be made about their quality.[7] As can only be expected of a situation where dramatists are learning their job, many of the plays lack theatricality. Not all of the writers, however, fail in this respect. John Brandane, who specialised in light comedies set in the West Highlands, was always conscious of the need to keep an audience interested in what is happening on stage; and the growth of theatrical craftsmanship can be seen in a writer like George Reston Malloch. Malloch's early plays are static, whereas *Soutarness Water* (1926), a grim piece about a young couple who marry without knowing they are siblings, has real dramatic momentum despite long discussion passages. On the whole, the one-act pieces are better constructed; although the subject matter is often trivial and they are often more music-hall sketches than plays, the audience's attention is held throughout. On the other hand, the strain of attempting to sustain interest over two hours is clear in many full-length pieces.

An examination of these plays shows not so much a predominance of historical settings as of rural ones, whether in the Highlands, the Lowlands or the Southern Uplands. The dramatists seem to have gone to great lengths to avoid contemporary urban milieux. Glasgow, the centre of the Players' activity, scarcely makes an appearance, and the First World War, the traumatic effects of which were keenly felt during the period, is hardly dealt with at all. There is throughout these plays an obsession with the Highlands, and the discourse of tartanry is regularly employed. However it is not the case that the view of the Highlands offered is universally romantic or escapist; realistic notes are occasionally sounded. The real failure is in the plays concerned with the rest of Scotland, which is seen as a non-urban backwater, apparently unaffected by the twentieth century. What is worse, it is only rarely that there is any penetration below the surface of rural life. Obviously, this cannot be expected of light-hearted comedies, but it would be good to have more plays like *Soutarness Water*, which, whatever its deficiencies, conveys a sense of actual lived experience. The eight plays by Bridie presented by the Players, four of them premieres of his early work, are the exception that proves the rule in this case: his interest in contemporary Glasgow bourgeois mores was not generally shared by his fellow dramatists, nor were his plays very popular with the Players' audiences.

Writers for the Scottish National Players also tended to avoid the language issue. The inter-war renaissance in Scottish poetry was bedevilled by arguments about whether to write in English, Lallans or some other form of Scots. The difficulty was not likely to be so acute in the drama, for the simple reason that it is a convention of the naturalistic theatre that the characters speak for the most part in a fashion approximately like that employed by their real-life counterparts. As most of the plays were naturalistic in form and set in non-urban areas where regional dialects were still spoken at the time of writing, it was possible to use Scots without producing the uneasy situation where contemporary characters use archaic language. However, while there was nothing to prevent a writer from rendering the Glasgow working-class dialect on the stage, as Unity Theatre's writers were to do in the 1940s, that option seems not to have appealed to the dramatists who wrote for the Players.

John Brandane and Joe Corrie

Among the Scottish National Players' writers who still have some claim on audiences' attention, and rise above the general level of mediocrity, are John Brandane and Joe Corrie. John Brandane (real name John McIntyre) (1869–1947) was born in Bute. While working as a clerk in Glasgow, he studied part time and qualified as a doctor. Thereafter he practised in various parts of the United Kingdom before settling in Glasgow. Brandane made a two-fold contribution to the work of the Players: he took a leading part in running the company's affairs, and he wrote a number of one-act and full-length plays performed by them. He was, in a sense, the house dramatist.

Brandane's view of the Highlands is rather a superficial one. Most of the characters who people his plays are flat, hackneyed caricatures, drawn from melodrama and farce rather than from life. They are predictable and not very interesting. *The Glen is Mine* (1923) is an exception to this stricture. Angus MacKinnon, the central character, although falling into the loveable Highland rascal stereotype, has greater intelligence than his author's other creations and can turn his mind to more than avoiding paying bills or screwing money out of people (although he does a fair amount of this, too). MacPhedran, the rapacious, sycophantic village trader, with his obsequious 'Take care of yourself – Good people are scarce', also has more individuality than most of Brandane's other characters.

The *dramatis personae* of *The Glen is Mine* gain substantially from the fact that the play has a recognisable theme, which is more than can be said for most of its author's other works. That theme is quite simply the future of the Highlands: should they remain an unspoilt (and perhaps depopulated) paradise or should they be industrialised? Colonel Murray, the proprietor of Ardsheilach and Coillemore, has handed over his estate to his son Charlie in order to avoid death duties. Charlie, unknown to his father, has hired an iron prospector who has found a seam which could be profitably worked. Charlie proposes to start an iron mine and makes this clear to the Colonel when the latter discovers his plans. It then emerges that Charlie proposes to use water power in his scheme, and this involves the eviction of an old crofter, Angus MacKinnon, from his land. The scales of sympathy are by now a little bit weighted against Charlie. The Colonel is concerned to emphasise the social price of industrialisation, and this is taken up by Angus with his prospective son-in-law, Murdo. Angus feels the ironworks will ruin the countryside, whereas Murdo sees them as bringing 'life', 'knowledge', 'science' and opportunity:

> I ken I'm fit for something better than an odd-man's job at Torlochan Hotel. Driving, fencing, sheep-shearing, peat lifting. Tach! The life of a slave!

Murdo's problem is the young Highlander's perennial problem: how can he find a job for which his abilities fit him? When Morag, Angus's daughter, objects that the iron mine would destroy the old ways, Murdo replies:

> The good old Highland ways! Three o'clock of a cold morning and up the hill to the lambing. Bringing the mails over Kellan cliffs when the snow's drifted yards deep. Driving the Doctor to Moy, thirty mile and back, when the North wind's skelping down the sound. That's the good old ways for Murdo Mackay!

Unfortunately Brandane fails to resolve the dramatic conflict he has set up, evading it by means of a series of contrived *dei ex machina*, so at the end of the last act Angus can go off 'into the sunlight and the breeze' rather banally playing 'The Glen is Mine' on his pipes. Nevertheless the play is a skilful and entertaining piece of theatre.

Only two plays by Joe Corrie (1894–1968) were performed by the Players.

This is surprising, for he was a prolific writer, producing over fifty one-acters and a number of full-length pieces, in addition to a novel and several volumes of verse. He began writing while earning his living as a miner in Fife, and that background shows in his work for the Scottish National Players. *The Shillin' A Week Man* (1927), a one-acter, deals with the efforts of a Mrs Paterson to avoid the 'Shillin' A Week Man' to whom she owes money. There is in the piece a sense of poverty, brought out in small things such as the borrowing of tea,

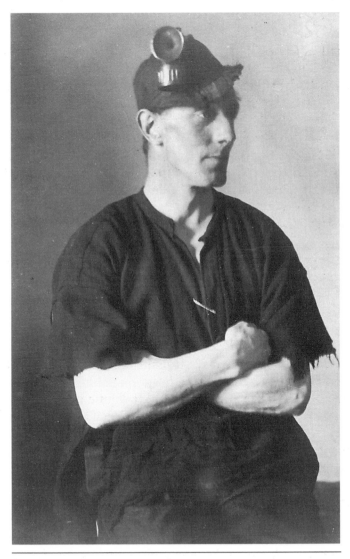

Figure 4.5 Miner and playwright Joe Corrie. (Scottish Theatre Archive)

and in larger matters such as redundancy, strikes and the shillin' a week system itself.

This sense of poverty is also found in a more deliberately humorous play, *The Poacher* (1926), and comes across, for example, when the hero tries to coax money from his wife and when he makes a speech about the injustices of society. Unfortunately, Corrie displays in *The Poacher* a fatal tendency to aim for laughs at all costs, a tendency which continually stunted his growth as a dramatist. It is clear that Corrie's later development took him away from his own aim, as articulated in the *Scottish Stage* magazine of August 1932:

> The drama should deal with life, and the state of our environment has so much to do with life that we cannot ignore it on the stage. We must show the worst that is in us to bring out the best that is in us, which means being ruthless and cruel and offensive.

In some of his work Corrie does reflect the hard and bitter struggles of ordinary working people, most obviously in *In Time o' Strife* (1928), which is set during a miners' strike. Corrie's first full-length play, it was written shortly after the General Strike of 1926 and explores the dreadful hardships imposed by the miners' dispute which precipitated it. The amateur club which presented it, the Bowhill Players, toured the production throughout Scotland to considerable acclaim. Although Corrie's own political sympathies are very clear, he avoids, for the most part, stereotypes and caricatures. However he does at times allow his ability to secure easy laughs to get the better of him. This was a harbinger of things to come, for most of Corrie's later output is of the Scots comedy variety; indeed his name has come to be identified with a particular kind of play, set in rural Scotland, with couthy characters who speak the Doric.

Corrie was writing for the amateur market and his plays went down well at one-act festivals, women's guilds and similar gatherings. But, in truth, Corrie was ruined by the amateur movement, for it limited him formally and encouraged him to resort to facile humour and neat solutions. It is hard to disagree with James Bridie's verdict on both Corrie and T. M. Watson, author of *Bachelors are Bold* and *Beneath the Wee Red Lums*. Watson was another dramatist who, after making brave statements about 'plays which kick orthodoxy in the pants and sail as near to the blasphemy and obscenity laws as possible',[8] proceeded to turn out amusing but empty Scots comedies. Bridie wrote:

> If I am asked whether I admire Messrs Corrie and Watson, I reply that I do; and that I continually mourn over them and pray that they may see the light. It is as if Dickens and Thackeray, knowing themselves to be masters of the anecdote, had written nothing but magazine stories

till the greater constructive virtue went out of them. If I were in the mood for casting blame, I should blame the SCDA Festivals for robbing Scotland of two rare dramatists. They are not the only ones.[9]

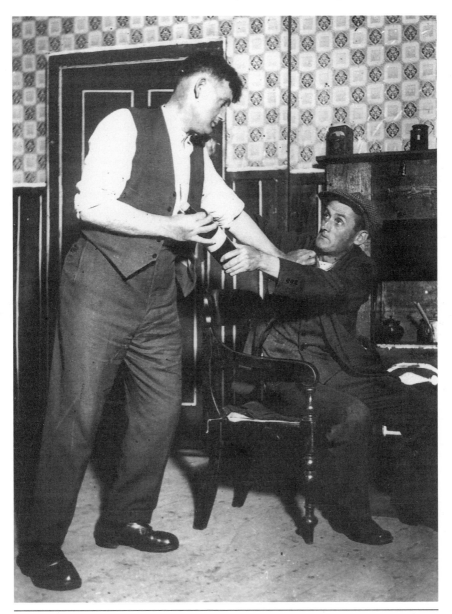

Figure 4.6 Fife Miner Players (formerly the Bowhill Players) – a group of local miners and their wives – in their 1929 production of Joe Corrie's In Time o' Strife *which toured Scottish music-hall theatres.* (Scottish Theatre Archive)

THE CURTAIN THEATRE AND ROBERT MCLELLAN

The Curtain Theatre, the other amateur group which sought to advance the cause of indigenous drama, was a more modest venture than the Scottish National Players. It was started by a group of enthusiasts led by Grace Ballantine, who, with a mere £100 in capital, hired a large L-shaped drawing room in a house in Glasgow's Woodside Terrace and turned it into an auditorium with seating for sixty-five people. The aim was to provide a stage where practising playwrights might see their work being rehearsed or performed. Starting in 1933, about six programmes a year were given to an audience of subscribers in the tiny Curtain Theatre itself. Between 1935 and 1940 they took place in the Lyric Theatre.

Of the actors who worked with the Curtain, Molly Urquhart, who later founded the Rutherglen Repertory Theatre and then joined the Citizens' Company, and Duncan Macrae are best known. Macrae learnt his craft with the Curtain, attracting much attention for his performances, particularly for his creation of the title role in Robert McLellan's *Jamie the Saxt* (1937). He was born in 1905, the son of a Sutherland crofter who had, like many Highlanders, migrated to Glasgow and joined the police force. After briefly studying engineering at Glasgow University, Macrae took up school-teaching and acted in his spare time. He joined the Citizens' Company on its inception in 1943 and went on to exploit his marvellous and grotesque comic talent in pantomime as well as in the straight theatre. He was the most talented Scottish actor to emerge from the amateur movement and his death, in 1967, was a great loss to both theatre and television.

Although its aim was to encourage Scottish plays, the Curtain had difficulty attracting enough worthwhile native material and in making the material it did attract commercially viable. Despite this problem, its record was creditable. George Malcolm Thompson, Robins Millar and Paul Vincent Carroll, best known for *Green Cars Go East* (1937), were among the dramatists whose work was performed there. *Green Cars Go East*, premiered not by the Curtain but by another amateur group, the Glasgow Players, depicts the efforts of a young schoolteacher to escape her grim background, and is an all too rare example of urban naturalism. The Curtain's most important dramatist, however, was Robert McLellan, the leading exponent of Lallans plays.

McLellan (1907–84), who supported himself by his writing for most of his life, spent his early years on a farm where he heard Scots dialect used. The Scots he employs in his plays is based on spoken language and is not a synthetic construct. After the controversy which arose out of Hugh MacDiarmid's use of Jamieson's Scots dictionary to cull words with which the poet himself was not familiar, McLellan resolved that he would never resort to this device. That he has a fine grasp of Scots dialect is the first thing that strikes the hearer

Figure 4.7 Robert McLellan, playwright, 1946. (Courtesy
John McLellan)

about McLellan's work. The dialogue moves vigorously and naturally; that it
is a living language, not some anachronistic artefact, is evident in this exchange
from *Toom Byres* (1936):

> *Sir Robert*: Weill, I propose, Sir Andra, to let ye keep the stock ye hae
> liftit frae the Hanginshaw, for I conseeder ye less to blame for the affair
> nor Wat here.
> *Wat*: Eh!
> *Sir Robert*: Juist haud yer tongue the noo, sir! I was sayin, Sir Andra,
> that I propose to let ye keep the stock ye hae liftit frae the Hanginshaw,

and I hae entert a clause in the bond to that effect. Ye may regaird it as
a jeynt tocher o the twa Hanginshaw lassies, wha are to mairry yer
sons.
Wat: Hae my byres and stables to bide toom?
Sir Robert: Sir Andra will doutless let ye hae yer stock back gin ye mak
him a guid offer in ready siller.
Wat: And has there to be ane tocher wi his dochter?
Sir Robert: I hae made nae proveesion in the bond for ony sic thing.

On the other hand, McLellan, who recalled with great regret that every
time he wrote a successful play in Scots he was encouraged from all sides to
write in English, did not have the same facility with that language. Using it, he
produces dialogue that is often limp and lifeless, quite lacking the theatricality
of his Scots.

McLellan's plays are almost all set in the past – in eighteenth-century
Edinburgh, in the Borders of the early seventeenth century, at the courts of
Mary Queen of Scots or James VI – but his approach to history contrasts
sharply with that of many other Scottish writers. Whereas they often view the
past through romantic spectacles, McLellan presents a harsher and more
believable world, even though he is writing comedy. Sudden death comes
uncomfortably close to Archie Armstrong in *The Changeling* (1935) when he
steals one of the Elliots' sheep, and to Will Scott in *Jeddart Justice* (1934) when
he refuses to marry one of Sir Gideon Murray's daughters as recompense for a
similar misdeed. The laird of *Torwatletie* (1946) inhabits a world of unattrac-
tive scheming rascals, while James Boswell is presented in *Young Auchinleck*
(1962) without any attempt to hide his excesses, or the venereal disease which
ensued in consequence. Samuel Skinner in *The Hypocrite* (1967) is a bigot,
supported by a legion of other bigots, while *Jamie the Saxt* (1937) finds himself
in the midst of intriguing lords, and only survives by consummate deviousness.

Given the strong tendency running through Scottish culture to sentimen-
talise the past, this aspect of McLellan's work must be emphasised. None the
less, it is disappointing that he never felt able to tackle large contemporary
themes. *The Road to the Isles* (1954), set on a Scottish island in recent times,
attempts to deal with the regeneration of the Highlands, but unfortunately
the play's energies are dissipated as McLellan tilts at a variety of irrelevant
windmills. Only two of his historical pieces, *The Hypocrite* (1967) and *The
Flouers o Edinburgh* (1948), can be directly related to the modern world.

The Hypocrite, set in eighteenth-century Edinburgh, centres on the activities
of a minister, Samuel Skinner, who successfully prevents an exhibition of
'obscene' Italian engravings from being staged. Skinner is shown to be a las-
civious hypocrite whose obsession with nakedness is far from innocent, a man
who will happily sleep with a married woman to advance his son's career.

Skinner is surrounded by clergymen and burghers as dishonest as he is. McLellan obviously intended the play as a satirical comment on the civic reaction to the Edinburgh Festival 'happening' in 1963 when, on the last day of a rather unexciting drama conference, as a way of livening up speakers and audience, a naked woman was pulled momentarily across the balcony above the speakers' platform. The next day's newspapers (appropriately, it was a Sunday) carried the headline 'NUDE AT FESTIVAL'. Most of them did not explain the context in which the event occurred. The Lord Provost issued an inane statement, lamenting the fact that 'three weeks of glorious festival should have been smeared by a piece of pointless vulgarity', and refused to surrender 'to the irresponsible actions of a few people sick in heart and mind'. The model was summoned on an indecency charge, of which she was later acquitted. In *The Hypocrite*, historically placed beyond libel action, McLellan renders the reactions to these events ridiculous, and suggests that they are not as innocent as they might appear.

The Flouers o Edinburgh (1948), again set in the capital in the eighteenth century, has as its main theme the conflict of mind felt by the gentry of that time about whether they should speak Scots or English, and McLellan has a great deal of fun at the expense of one of his characters who has abandoned his 'barbarous' native tongue. The play can be taken as a contribution to the discussion on the use of Scots today. McLellan, it is clear, is in favour of using Scots in literature and, perhaps even, in daily life.

Searching McLellan's plays for themes is not a very profitable exercise. He once said that in his drama he was more interested in character than in theme. Historical personages, for example, interested him for their own sakes. He was also concerned to present individuals he knew in his own life as a way of 'fixing' certain components of Scottishness which he felt had been ignored by Scottish dramatists. Thus McLellan's best play, *Jamie the Saxt* (1937), is notable mainly for the strength of its characterisation. It is set during the period 1591–4 when the young King was struggling to assert himself amid a web of conspiracy woven by dissident lords, the Church, the burghers of Edinburgh and the English government. The picture of James as a much-tried young man, who survives not by a display of heroics but by using his wits to play one faction off against another, is very appealing. McLellan's Jamie is no fool, but a canny individual whose qualities see him through till the end of the play, when he is able to look forward confidently to claiming the throne of England:

The King: Oho, but fortune's favoured me the day! There's naething in my wey! Aa that I hae wished for is promised at last; Bothwell on the scaffold, the Papists houndit doun, the kirk in my pouer, England ahint me, and then, in the end the dream o my life come true! It gars my pulse quicken! It gars my hairt loup! It gars my een fill wi' tears! To think hou

the two puir countries hae focht and struggled. To think o the bluid
they hae shed atween them, the touns they hae blackent wi fire, the
bonnie green howes they hae laid waste. And then to think, as ae day
it sall come to pass, that I, Jamie Stewart, will ride to London and the
two countries sall become ane.
(*Mistress Edward can be heard off calling 'Nicoll! Nicoll! Come for yer
supper!'*)
Maitland: (*Coming out of his trance and reaching for the bottle*) Ay, yer
Grace, it's a solemn thocht. But the auld bitch isna deid yet.
(*He places the bottle before the King. The King fills his glass.*)
The King: (*Raising his glass high*) Jock, here's to the day. May the
mowdies sune tickle her taes.
(*Mistress Edward appears at the door of the dining room*)
Mistress Edward: Yer Grace, the supper's ready.
(*The King and Maitland eye each other and drink the toast*)

Figure 4.8 Duncan Macrae (centre) in rehearsal for Robert McLellan's Jamie the
Saxt, *Citizens' Theatre, 1947.* (Scottish Theatre Archive)

When it was originally performed, the piece served as a vehicle for a highly individual performance by Duncan Macrae, though the author was not in complete agreement with Macrae's interpretation of the character, which rather prophetically revealed the gift for pantomine that the actor was later to exploit.

Robert McLellan demonstrated considerable theatrical talent and skill; none the less it can only be a matter of regret that he was unable to find substantial contemporary themes attractive enough to engage him. Perhaps the problem was a linguistic one; while his Scots is neither archaic nor incomprehensible, it is a variety with which many, perhaps most, modern Scots are unfamiliar. In a sense the language McLellan uses is a signal that, as a playwright, he is not very comfortable in the modern world.

JAMES BRIDIE

McLellan is one of two writers of substance the amateur movement could claim to have nurtured through their apprentice period; the other is Osborne Henry Mavor (1888–1951), who wrote under the pen-name 'James Bridie'. Bridie, by far the most distinguished man of the theatre Scotland has yet produced, apart from Barrie, was born into a respectable and reasonably prosperous Glasgow family, his father being an engineer. He was educated at Glasgow Academy (where he suffered the tribulations that often attend the non-athletic boy) and at Glasgow University, from which he graduated in medicine. Apart from a period of war service, which took him to Europe and the Middle East, he spent the rest of his life in the city or in the surrounding area. Although in his early years he was not without financial worries, success as a doctor came with his appointment as consultant at a Glasgow hospital, and then as a playwright, for which career he was able eventually to abandon medicine.

As noted earlier, Bridie's interest in the theatre had been stimulated by the work of the Glasgow Repertory Company. After the First World War he sent *The Switchback* to Alfred Wareing, then in Huddersfield. Wareing commented that the play was too clever for any manager to present, though it was, in fact, presented by Sir Barry Jackson at Birmingham in 1929. Some years after its formation, Bridie joined the board of the Scottish National Players and was one of the directors most determined that they should turn professional. When the Players chose not to do so, he left the board. The formation of the Citizens' Theatre in Glasgow during the Second World War marks the start of the period in Bridie's life when he made his greatest contribution: he was chairman of the Citizens' from its inception until his death; he played the main role in the establishment, in 1950, of the Glasgow College of Drama as an extension of the Royal Scottish Academy of Music; he was a member of the Council for the

Figure 4.9 James Bridie, playwright. (Scottish Theatre Archive)

Encouragement of Music and the Arts, the forerunner of the Arts Council, and at one point its Scottish chairman; and he was adviser on drama to the Edinburgh Festival.

Bridie's contribution to nurturing the theatre in Scotland was matched by a substantial output of dramatic works. Not every one of his plays has something of very great importance to say, for he was, as he often emphasised, an entertainer, diverting an audience for a couple of hours. But it would be foolish to accept completely Bridie's own judgement of himself. Many of his plays do comment on human experience, often wryly and ironically, at the same time as they divert or amuse. His constant reluctance to make claims for his work is significant, and it could be argued that this was Bridie's way of protecting himself against a society whose response to artists is often indifference or derision. As Christopher Small has commented:

> No-one is more exposed to the uncomprehending laughter of his fellows than the artist, and nowhere more, perhaps, than in the solidly, one may say almost impenetrably Philistine society of middle-class Glasgow when Bridie was young. He was an artist, he couldn't help it; but he could ward off laughter by getting his laugh in first, both at others and at himself.[10]

That man as a species should accept his cosmic limitations and individual men should accept their personal shortcomings is the main theme which recurs constantly in Bridie's drama. It is easy to see how a society which derides claims to anything better than the humdrum produces this attitude in a writer. In a sense it is a reflection of that society's own attitude, but it also offers a refuge to anyone foolish enough to have aesthetic pretensions; at the same time it can easily become a restraint on ambition and risk taking.

The limitations of the human species are explored in several of Bridie's plays which have biblical backgrounds. *Tobias and the Angel* (1930), for example, is based on the Apocryphal Book of Tobit. It tells, with considerable wit, the story of Tobias, son of the blind Tobit, who travels to Hamadan accompanied by a servant Azarias, who is the archangel Raphael in disguise. After surviving, with Azarias's help, several dire perils, Tobias marries Sara, a wealthy young woman. On Tobias's return to Nineveh, Raphael/Azarias restores old Tobit's sight, and all look set to live happily ever after. But unfortunately Sara has fallen in love with Raphael, to whom she insists that she has grown impatient with the ordinary run of men; however the angel refuses to listen to her plea that she is dissatisfied with mere mortals:

> You must cease to be so. Often at odd times in the future, you will see me looking out of Tobias's eyes. But you must look the other way and busy yourself with your household tasks.

In *Susannah and the Elders* (1937) the tone is much harsher. The play's opening scene, which, like *Tobias* is adapted from the Apocrypha, demonstrates the grim inflexibility of Babylonian law, which Bridie clearly feels takes inadequate account of human weakness. The elders, or judges, of the title, Kashdak and Kabbittu, are presented sympathetically, but the mistake they make is to forget that beneath their respectable ageing exteriors the fire of lust still smoulders. Soon they find themselves in a position of the most base hypocrisy, so attracted are they to the beautiful young Susannah. There are hints, as the play progresses, that they are beginning to sense the gap between appearance and reality, but that does not prevent the catastrophe. Lust and hypocrisy combine to bring about their downfall. Exposed, they accept their fate with resignation and, in his last speech before judgement is delivered, Kabbittu admits his false-seeming:

> All the world has known me as a kindly, just, respectable man. And so I thought myself. For I forgot how the exalted Anu had made us all. What you saw was the head of a man, uttering discreet things, above the robes of a grave and seemly magistrate. Beneath these robes was the body of a goat. The head ensures and cherishes honour, justice, pity, shame and a good conscience; the beast can be tamed, but he knows nothing of any of these things.

Alongside Bridie's emphasis on the fallibility and limitations of humankind goes an insistence on the worth of apparently insignificant people. The best expression of this is to be found in *Mr Gillie* (1950). The eponymous hero, a part originally created on the stage by Alastair Sim, with whom Bridie had a long and close working relationship, is a village schoolmaster on the west coast of Scotland. A failed man of letters himself, he has none the less encouraged many young people to trust the talents he discerns in them, only to see them come to grief in the outside world. The play is set within a heavenly framework in which the Procurator and the Judge are discussing whither it would be appropriate to consign Mr Gillie, who has died after being knocked down by a pantechnicon. The Judge, ignoring the Procurator's insistence that Gillie's life was a useless one, places him between Lincoln and John Wesley. 'Let us honour the forlorn hope,' declares the Judge: the obscure life, even when apparently a failure, can be as significant as other lives lived in the midst of public acclaim.

Bridie's championing of the ordinary man's integrity and importance has a counterbalance in his somewhat ambivalent admiration for superman figures who override the demands of decency and morality; figures such as Doctor Knox, the recipient of the body snatchers' victims in *The Anatomist*. Knox is presented by Bridie as a man contemptuous of lesser mortals, so dedicated to the pursuit of medical science that he is apparently unconcerned when told that one of his anatomical subjects may have been murdered:

> The life of this poor wretch is ended. It is surely a better thing that her beauty of form should be at the service of divine science than at the services of any drunken buck with a crown in his pocket.

The Queen's Comedy (1950), arguably Bridie's best play, is much more ambitious. Set during the Trojan Wars, it is concerned with the relationship between men and gods and the impact of the latter's actions on the lives of the former. The action opens at the bottom of the sea where the immortals are arguing peevishly over the support being given to Greeks and Trojans by different members of the supernatural fraternity. Jupiter reflects on the morality of using men as playthings in heavenly quarrels:

> There are quarter of a million men in the Dardanelles all made more or less in my image and capable of rejoicing and suffering, of foresight and afterthought. Sometimes up there in Mount Ida, when I cannot sleep, I try to put myself in their places and wonder what they are thinking.

The play develops the idea that men are made to suffer needlessly as a result of divine whim, and conveys a bleak view of the human lot. The mortals are represented not by the generals, who are very closely involved with the gods, but principally by an orderly, an infantryman, and Hecamede, a nurse. In their first scene both the orderly and the infantryman take a roughly similar view of the gods, namely that they have a 'touch of class' denied the ordinary person. As far as the war is concerned, the orderly is in favour of pressing on and defeating the Trojans:

> We've got to show them what we're made of. We canna let a lot of Trojan baskets put it across the Greeks. We got an ideal to fight for, see.

The infantryman has his doubts, particularly when he looks at the casualties:

> It all come of a bit of square-pushing. One of them there Trojan Gussies pinched a General's Judy. What's you and me and that poor write-off over there got to do with that smooth Cissie and his little bit of Oojah. We never seen either of them!

When they next appear, the infantryman shows little sympathy for the orderly's view that the gods are on the Greek side. The orderly, however, has had a vision of 'A popsy about ninety feet high' (Juno) who had assured him that the Greeks enjoyed her protection. Several scenes later, the debate about the gods continues between Hecamede and Captain Machaon. Machaon adopts a pious attitude towards them, but Hecamede insists that it would be better to have human replacements who would at least show sympathy for the plight of ordinary mortals. The present gods are not merely indifferent to human suffering, they appear to relish it:

> They want to make more birds and stags, flowers and people to be trapped and trampled and torn. That's really what they want. That's what it means. What do they care?

In the last scene Bridie brings immortals and mortals together in Olympus, where the gods are chatting wittingly to each other and Vulcan is telling unfunny stories. The shades of those killed in battle pass through, *en route* to Hades, and Mercury catches a few, including Machaon, Hecamede, the orderly and the infantryman, in a butterfly net. The gods are embarrassed, particularly

Figure 4.10 James Bridie's The Queen's Comedy, *Citizens' Theatre, 1950.* (Scottish Theatre Archive)

Juno when she is reminded by the orderly of the promise she gave him in his dream. He insists on telling the gods what he thinks of them:

> Well . . . There you are. You're the push we've been praying to. 'Bless Daddy and Mummy and make Jack a good boy.' Now I seen you I know what's wrong. You sit up here in your gold settees with a noggin of nectar at your elbows, tearing on us poor devils like we was terriers and rats. You great, stupid, lazy, good-looking sticks of barley sugar! They say you send us the rain and the sunshine and the wheat in the fields. Well, get on with it and leave us alone!

It is clear that Bridie's sympathies are with the orderly and Hecamede. The gods have behaved abominably. Their only supporter, Machaon, is an ass. But Bridie does give Jupiter the chance to defend himself:

> *Jupiter*: I soon found that it was easier to make a universe than to control it. It was full of mad, meaningless, fighting forces. I got most of them bound and fixed and working to rules and all of a sudden I felt lonely. I felt that I would rather my mother had given me a puppydog or a kitten. But I should not have made the puppydog or the kitten, so I thought of something else. I found that if I arranged the forces in a certain way, I got a thing called Life. Life is very interesting, I am still working on its permutations and combinations . . . But our poor Shades have long ago missed their convoy. I shall make them into three Stars, I think. I shall call them the Rebels. They will be very interesting to astronomers in a few thousand years.
> *Hecamede*: You have not answered us.
> *Jupiter*: Were you asking questions? I am afraid I shall have to refer you to somebody who understands such matters. I don't pretend to understand them myself.

There are, Bridie is implying, no answers to the problem of human suffering, just the reality of suffering itself, in the face of which stoicism is the only possible defence.

There can be no question about the value of James Bridie's general work for the development of the theatre in Scotland. About his own writing it is difficult to be so certain. Bridie was an extremely prolific dramatist, and that often leads to a thinness of texture. Plays which suffer from this, although they demonstrate their author's ability to divert an audience with witty dialogue or interesting turns of plot, lack depth and have little claim on posterity. On the other hand there are a few plays, *The Queen's Comedy* and *Susannah and the Elders* among them, in which Bridie's gifts as an entertainer are combined with an intense concern for his subject matter. These plays are of permanent value. However, they, too, have a characteristic which modern audiences can find off-putting: Bridie uses too many words. His dialogue is rarely lean or sparse; too often it is repetitive and diffuse. In a theatre where there is little taste for rhetoric or philosophical speculation, this is a serious handicap.

Bridie was, commercially, the most successful Scottish dramatist there has yet been (after Barrie, whose base was England and the English theatre). Although for much of his life he combined writing with medicine, latterly he was able to write full time and earn a good living from it. He could do so because he did not target an exclusively Scottish market. He aimed at the British or English market and many of his plays had their premieres in London. Bridie was an astute man and must have realised early in his career that the way to recognition and financial success was to please the metropolitan audience first and foremost. Of Bridie's full-length stage plays, almost two-thirds were premiered south of the border, mostly in London but sometimes elsewhere. *The Anatomist* was his first play to appear in London, in 1930, after the Masque Theatre had presented it in Edinburgh; *Jonah and the Whale* was his first to be premiered in London, in 1932. Although *Jonah and the Whale* lost money, Bridie's plays continued to be presented in the West End. *A Sleeping Clergyman*, after its premiere in Malvern in 1933, ran for 230 performances in London. His most successful London presentation was of *Daphne Laureola* in 1949. North of the border four of his plays were premiered by the Scottish National Players and a number by other companies, particularly Glasgow Citizens' towards the end of his career. Bridie's artistic concerns, unlike those of some of his Scottish contemporaries, were well suited to metropolitan audiences seeking wit, diversion and a dash of philosophy, so the London route did not necessitate many compromises. No writer can escape his background, however, and, as has been argued here, and elsewhere,[11] Bridie's most fundamental attitudes and themes stem directly from his native land.

One of Bridie's merits lies in the fact that his imagination is able to inhabit a variety of milieux: Apocryphal, Trojan, English and Scottish. Scotland does predominate however, but it is in the Lowlands, not the Highlands, that he sets many of his plays. Bridie seems to have been well aware of the traps which writing about the Highlands posed, and to have avoided them. Watching and reading those of his plays which are set in the north, one is never overly conscious of locale. The same cannot be said of his Lowland plays. They are anchored firmly in the world Bridie knew and lived in all his life, the world of the Glasgow middle classes, people wealthy enough to own a substantial residence in the West End, and to have a house on the Clyde coast, taken for the season or owned outright. It is perhaps a rather insular world, but it is one from which Bridie never escapes. Indeed, as has been argued, it represents his fundamental problems as an artist and a man. But Bridie never wrote about Lowland bourgeois Scotland in such a way that his plays became impenetrable to the outsider. The world he explores may have been a parochial one, but Bridie was not a parochial man. Although his imagination takes flight most effectively when he leaves Scotland behind – hence the choice of plays discussed in detail here – when he is writing about his own country he usually avoids hackneyed characterisation and offers his audiences a gallery of Lowland Scots which ranges across social class and dialect.

This might seem of little account, but, to reiterate, Bridie is the first modern *Scottish-based* dramatist with any claim to international attention. That he earned this attention to a significant degree by presenting an accurate contemporary picture of his fellow countrymen on the stage seems a remarkable achievement when it is remembered how little effort was given to the task at the time. As far as Scottish drama is concerned, this is the most encouraging aspect of Bridie's career; the most discouraging aspect is that, despite his achievement, and largely because of his cultural environment, he was not as good as he should have been.

SECOND WORLD WAR AND BEYOND

The Second World War did not have such a profound effect on the development of the theatre in Scotland as the First. Whereas in 1914 the most promising venture, the Glasgow Repertory Company, came to a sudden end, throughout the Second World War, after the brief period of general closure ordered by the government in 1939, existing ventures for the most part continued and others were initiated.

In Perth, the players continued running the theatre themselves on a non-profit-making basis. The actors did all the work and some of them even slept in the building. At the end of a week, after theatrical and living expenses were deducted, the residue, varying between a few shillings and a maximum of £3, was divided among them. Despite these privations, in 1941 a Perth Theatre Pageant, which included a visit from Bristol Old Vic, was mounted, and a tour of the west and the Highlands organised. Just as the war ended, another drama festival opened in Perth, this one under James Bridie's patronage.

In 1939, Robert Thornley, an English producer, looked up a gazetteer in order to find the largest town in the United Kingdom that did not have a theatre. As a result, he brought his company of actors to Dundee, and live drama to a city that the touring companies had bypassed for ten years, leaving it to be content with variety, pantomine and the occasional professional dramatic production. Dundee's first regular theatre had been opened almost a hundred and fifty years previously in 1800, and by 1909 the city had two substantial playhouses and a number of music halls. However, the onslaught of the cinema was severe in Dundee, and by 1930 there was no stage for the legitimate drama.

Financial backing for Thornley came from the city itself, in the shape of a £2000 guarantee fund which was raised principally by the efforts of two local businessmen. A non-profit-making company was formed and, while negotiations went on to acquire the Foresters' Hall for transformation into a theatre, plays were performed in the local amateurs' Little Theatre. Foresters' Hall opened as a theatre in December 1939 with a production of *Hassan*. In the course of the next few years the company required more money, but by 1945 all loans and guarantees had been paid off. Thornley had been succeeded as producer by Anthony Hawtrey, then, in 1942, by A. R. Whatmore, who did much to consolidate the position of the Dundee venture. Whatmore regarded his theatre in many respects as an English repertory that happened to be in Scotland, and consequently showed little interest in Scottish plays: he believed the Scottish public shared his view.

The Byre in St Andrews, which, as the name implies, started life as a cow-shed, was let by the Town Council in 1933 to the amateur St Andrews Play Club, whose members converted the building into a tiny theatre. During the war, for the first time the Byre, which held only seventy-four people and had a stage twelve feet square, was occupied by a small professional company led by Charles Marford, who had been stage director at the Old Vic when Lilian Bayliss was running it.

In the Glasgow area, although the Curtain closed in 1940, a small repertory theatre opened in Rutherglen in 1939 and, in 1940, John Stewart, who later founded the Pitlochry Festival Theatre, opened the little Park Theatre next door to the Curtain's West End premises. The Rutherglen theatre lasted until 1944, the Park till 1949.

The two most important new ventures in Glasgow during the war were the Citizens' Theatre and Unity Theatre. The Citizens' was formed with aspirations very similar to those which inspired previous projects: 'with a view to founding the theatre and encouraging a national drama through the production of plays of Scottish life and character'. Bridie himself put it in a more practical way:

> If we are going to have Scottish plays, or plays by Scottish writers, the Scottish playwright will have to be encouraged. In Scotland today there are many novelists, poets and short story writers, and we want to see them turning their attention to the theatre. But unless there is a chance of their plays having a reasonable run in Scotland, they cannot be expected to take a real interest in writing for the theatre, and no one can blame them.[12]

Glasgow Citizens' Theatre

The story of the founding of the Citizens' has been told in great detail by Winifred Bannister in her book *James Bridie and the Scottish Theatre* (1955). Suffice it to say here that Bridie assembled a directorate, with himself as chairman and, having raised £1500 in donations, secured a guarantee against loss from the Council for the Encouragement of Music and the Arts. The Athenaeum Theatre in Buchanan Street, then part of the Royal Scottish Academy of Music, where the Scottish National Players gave many of their early performances, was chosen as the only suitable and available hall in which to launch the venture. The name Glasgow Citizens' Theatre, with its allusion to Alfred Wareing's earlier Glasgow Repertory Company, was intended to be a purely temporary measure.

Bridie decided to seek directorial talent outside Scotland and approached nineteen different producers before he found one, Jennifer Sounes, willing to come north. The theatre opened in Ocotber 1943 with a production of the chairman's own *Holy Isle*, a play which starts well but fizzles out. Neither it, nor the second production, Goldsmith's *The Good-Natured Man*, was very popular; but with the third presentation, Paul Vincent Carroll's *Shadow and Substance*, the theatre began to establish itself. By the end of its first season the company had broken even.

The second season included three Scottish plays: a revival of John Brandane's *The Treasure Ship* and premieres of Joe Corrie's *A Master of Men* and Bridie's *The Forrigan Reel*. The inclusion in the programme of these plays, and in the company of a number of actors who had previously worked with one of the smaller amateur or semi-professional groups, indicates clearly the debt the Citizens' owed to the ventures of the inter-war period: Duncan Macrae and Molly Urquhart were both formerly with the Curtain and Rutherglen Theatres, Gordon Jackson had been at Rutherglen, and James Gibson had worked with the Scottish National Players.

As the popularity of the Citizens' grew, a better venue was required. By an extremely fortunate coincidence, Harry McKelvie, the owner of the 1000-seater Royal Princess's Theatre, situated near Gorbals Cross, was finding that his health was no longer up to the ardours of running the pantomine seasons for which the theatre was famous. He offered the building on a ten-year lease to the Citizens' company at an annual rent of £1000, provided the total ten-year sum was guaranteed. A gift from a leading industrialist, Sir Frederick Stewart, met these conditions and, in March 1945, the last performance was given in the Athenaeum. The Citizens' opened in the Gorbals the following autumn.

Unity Theatre

In complete contrast to what might be regarded as the 'bourgeois' Citizens', the committedly proletarian Unity Theatre was established in the city, initially

on an amateur basis. It came into being in 1941, under the impetus of the
Unity Theatre movement elsewhere in Britain, and was formed by members of
various Glasgow clubs, the Workers' Theatre Group, the Clarion Players, the
Transport Players and the Jewish Institute Players. These organisations had
stood rather apart from the mainstream of the amateur movement and had
presented material which was aesthetically and politically more challenging
than the norm. The members of Unity, for their part, sought a more socially
involved theatre than existed at the time, and aimed to attract working-class
audiences. The company included some communists and Marxists, but it would
be wrong to assume that Unity was a highly doctrinaire body more interested
in politics than theatre. A dozen productions were mounted during wartime,
but it was in the post-war period that Unity made its bid for permanence.

In an attempt to put the venture on a firmer footing, and possibly mindful
of the failure of the Scottish National Players to grasp a similar opportunity,
Unity decided to form a professional company, as London Unity had done.
Thereafter there were two Unity companies, one amateur, whose productions
were mainly directed by Donald McBean, formerly of the Transport Players,
and one professional, under the directorship of Robert Mitchell of the
Glasgow Players. The professional company, which made its debut in April
1946 with Sean O'Casey's *Purple Dust*, had ten members, in addition to the
director and stage staff, which meant that a considerable income was necessary
to sustain operations. Although Unity had played in the Athenaeum Theatre
during the war, that venue's availability was restricted after 1945 and the
professional company performed wherever it could in Glasgow, and toured
throughout Scotland, playing regularly in Edinburgh and other centres. Several
visits were made to London towards the end of Unity's career. The part-time
company's activities were more intermittent, but it too was peripatetic.

As might be expected, Unity Theatre's main problem was finance. When
the professional company was formed, Unity had only a few hundred pounds
in the bank – a comfortable position for an amateur club, but hardly a firm
basis for a venture of the kind being undertaken. Throughout the professional company's existence the amateur, or part-time, company as it was
known, continued to provide a subsidy. Other revenue came from the box
office, principally from Robert McLeish's *The Gorbals Story*, Unity's best
money-spinner. For a time Unity received funding from the recently established
Arts Council, but this was withdrawn as a consequence of what Bridie, who
had a hand in the withdrawal, called its 'scatterbrained finance'. This charge
appears to have had substance: Unity did not apparently show much business
acumen, though for a time under the supervision of Oscar Loewenstein, who
was employed for a year as business manager, an orthodox approach to financial
matters was adopted. But neither Loewenstein, nor the income from amateur
activities, nor the royalties from a film of *The Gorbals Story* could save the

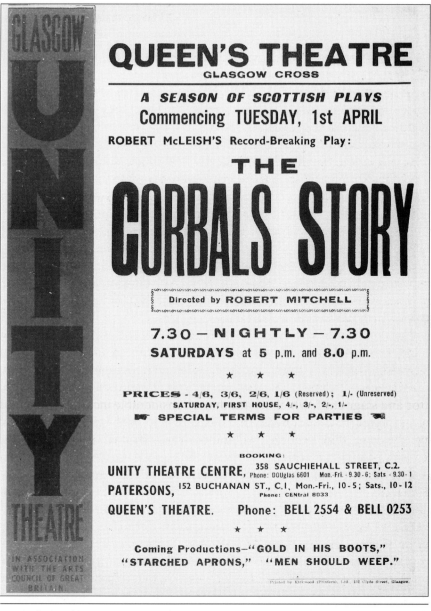

Figure 4.11 Playbill for Glasgow Unity Theatre's hugely successful The Gorbals Story *(1946), by Robert McLeish, which transferred to London's West End. Here revived as part of 'A Season of Scottish Plays' by Unity at the Queen's Theatre, Glasgow, along with George Munro's* Gold in His Boots *and Ena Lamont Stewart's* Starched Aprons *and* Men Should Weep. *(Scottish Theatre Archive)*

venture. Unity petered out, rather than stopped, at the end of the 1940s, and some of its debts have never been cleared. The amateur company continued for a time, but it too disappeared in the 1950s.

Despite its sad demise, Unity made an important contribution: it helped keep theatre alive during the war and extended the range of drama available to the Glaswegian and Scottish publics after the war; it attracted working-class audiences to serious plays; it could claim to have founded the Edinburgh Festival Fringe, since it performed McLellan's *Torwatletie* and a Scots version of Gorki's *The Lower Depths,* without official support, at the first festival in 1947; finally, and crucially, it introduced a new dimension to Scottish theatre. The Scottish National Players were criticised above for the fact that much of the drama they presented bore little relationship to the lives of the people of the country, particularly the lives of the urban population. Unity deliberately sought to make up for this failure. The evidence lies in the programmes presented, in which Clifford Odets, Sean O'Casey and Maxim Gorki feature prominently; furthermore, the work of these writers was usually given a Scottish context in production. Unity also sponsored a visit to Glasgow by the then young Theatre Workshop in 1946. Most importantly, Unity presented a number of new Scottish plays with important social themes.

Robert McLeish's *The Gorbals Story* (1946) portrays the appalling housing conditions in Glasgow. While not a particularly impressive piece of writing, for McLeish is clearly learning his job, it is carried along by the author's concern for his characters. In *The Lambs of God* (1948) Benedick Scott offered the first homosexual character in the modern Scottish drama and was told by the *Glasgow Herald*'s reviewer that his dialogue was 'unnecessarily frank'. George Munro, who later had plays performed by the Citizens', began his career when Unity presented *Gold in his Boots* (1947), about a young man's attempts to escape poverty via professional football; James Barke wrote about the shipyards in *Major Operation* (1941); Ena Lamont Stewart explored the realities of life in the nursing profession in *Starched Aprons* (1945), and the impact of poverty on family life in *Men Should Weep* (1947).

What is very striking about *Men Should Weep* is its author's even-handed approach. Maggie Morrison's life is awful: her husband is unemployed and has only just managed to curb his alcoholic excesses; one of her children has tuberculosis; an older son has married a worthless wife. There is ample evidence of the unending struggle women like Maggie have:

John: Ma Goad! Whit a hell o a hoose tae come hame tae!
Maggie: It's no ma fault! I've din a hale copper-fu o washin and scrubbed three floors an the hale lot o yous had naethin tae dae but lie in yer beds! Ye couldna even wash up a dish for me. It's me that aye has tae dae twa jobs when you get the sack!
John: Aw, shut up harpin on that string. It's no ma fault. I've been oot lookin for work.
Maggie: Aye, I've seen yous men lookin for work. Haudin up the street

corners, ca'in doon the Government . . . tellin the world whit *you'd* dae
if you wis rinnin the country . . .
John: Shut yer mouth or I'll shut it for ye!

But Stewart does not suggest that Maggie's problems can be blamed completely
on men; indeed some of the nastier characters in the play are women. It is also
clear that Maggie's husband, John, although of little use to his wife, does make
some effort to find work, and that Maggie is still in love with him.

For a short period in 1946–7 Unity published a magazine, *Scots Theatre*.
Each issue bore on the front cover a quotation from Gorki: 'The theatre is the
school of the people – it makes them think and it makes them feel.' The edito-
rial in the first issue declared:

Today we have Unity Theatre established as the most vital native cultural influence in Scotland. Its actors, playwrights and technicians have

Figure 4.12 Glasgow Unity's production of Ena Lamont Stewart's Men Should
Weep, *1947.* (Scottish Theatre Archive)

been drawn from the ranks of ordinary working people, whose background and everyday life is identical with the masses who form its
audiences.

Clearly many people in Unity were convinced they were moving the Scottish
theatre in a radical new direction with their vision that it should be a 'people's
theatre':

> In the new Scottish theatre there are two divisions: primarily middle-
> class repertories and writers whose art is seen in Perth, the Glasgow
> Citizens' Theatre and elsewhere; and the tougher working-class drama
> and performances to be seen at Glasgow Unity Theatre.[13]

Like so many Scottish theatrical enterprises, Unity looked to the Irish
example, but from a left-wing viewpoint: 'we pray for the time when a
Scotsman will emulate the great Irishman [O'Casey] and produce such plays
of the people'.[14]

The political orientation rouses mixed feelings. On the positive side, Unity
attempted to make the theatre meaningful to ordinary folk and seems to have
succeeded for a time in doing so. Working people came, though not in the
numbers Unity would have liked, and watched plays that they could relate to
their own lives. On the negative side, the left-wing commitment of Unity would
in the long term have proved a limitation, for, to judge by some of the writing
in *Scots Theatre*, it might well have blinded its members to the merits of drama
without obvious political content. But perhaps this is to carp. It is quite wrong
to think that all Unity members were committed socialists, adhering slavishly
to the kinds of opinions and views expressed in *Scots Theatre*; many were
simply interested in drama.

Several of Unity's actors joined the ranks of the professionals, among them
Archie Duncan, Russell Hunter, Andrew Keir, Roddy McMillan and Marjorie
Thomson. A proletarian vitality has been clear in the later work of these
artists. It was said of Unity that its techniques were those of Stanislawski, but
in practice they were based on those of the British stage at the time, with an
infusion of a strong feeling for contemporary urban Scotland. Reviews of their
productions often used such terms as 'sincerity' and 'conviction', sometimes, it
must be said, in a rather patronising way. The company did, however, find
writers of talent who, had they been given the opportunity to develop their art
more fully, could have achieved far more than they actually did. (A revival, in
the 1980s, of a number of plays by Unity writers re-emphasised the value of
their work.)

It would be foolish to pretend that Unity's contribution was a great one,
but it was important. Lack of money, financial mismanagement and the

absence of a permanent home all prevented the company from realising its full potential. Its enduring achievement is the progress it did make towards its self-declared objectives of presenting socially aware plays and bringing working-class people into the theatre. That it was unable to achieve these aims completely is a loss the Scottish theatre has yet to make up, though the 7:84 Theatre Company (Scotland) and Wildcat have pursued similar objectives in more recent times. It could be argued that it was naive of Unity to expect to break down the social and educational barriers that divide the mass of the population from the arts and that its approach sometimes had too much of the battering ram about it, but before people can begin to appreciate the subtleties and complexities of art they must be excited by it. Unity for a time provided that excitement. It also offered the 'bourgeois' Citizens' useful competition in both programming policy and vision of what Scottish theatre should ultimately be about. Each venture clearly aspired to be national; and if there is ever to

Figure 4.13 1948 Edinburgh International Festival production of Sir David Lindsay's Ane Satyre of the Thrie Estaitis. (Scottish Theatre Archive)

be a genuine Scottish National Theatre, in whatever form, its repertoire would have to take account not of one or other of these two visions, but of both of them.

The optimism which lay behind ventures like Unity and the Citizens' found its most remarkable expression in the inauguration in 1947 of the Edinburgh International Festival – the most significant artistic development in the immediate post-war period. The 1948 and 1949 Festivals featured, to great acclaim, Tyrone Guthrie's production of Scotland's major pre-twentieth-century drama, Sir David Lindsay's *Ane Satyre of the Thrie Estaitis*. These Festival presentations provided an international showcase for the native Scottish dramatic tradition and seemed to herald a confident new era for Scottish theatre.

By 1950 Scottish theatre looked as if it was on firm foundations at last, with professional repertory companies established, or about to be established, throughout the country. Artistic policies varied considerably, but there appeared to be a chance that indigenous writers would be able to develop their talents on Scottish stages, and would not have to rely on overworked amateurs. Furthermore, many of the performers who had come through the amateur movement were now able to join the ranks of the new breed of Scottish professional actors and could see the chance of making a reasonable living through live performance, supplemented by broadcasting and the cinema. For writers, performers and everyone who believed in the importance of indigenous Scottish theatre the future looked far brighter than it had done fifty years previously.

5   *1950 to 1995*
DONALD SMITH

Between 1950 and 1955, theatre in Scotland seemed to be enjoying a golden age. Established professional companies served the cities of Glasgow, Dundee and Perth, while Pitlochry Festival Theatre, the Gateway Theatre in Edinburgh and the increasingly professional Byre Theatre in St Andrews demonstrated vigorous new growth. The Wilson Barrett Company was active in Edinburgh, Glasgow and Aberdeen, providing well-produced, commercially successful repertory; and variety theatre continued to be a staple of popular entertainment throughout Scotland.

Only since the late 1930s could Scotland boast the beginnings of a modern theatre profession outside variety. In 1943, it took courage, James Bridie's persuasion and the founding of Glasgow Citizens' Theatre for Duncan Macrae to give up teaching for the stage. The formation in 1951 of a drama school within the Royal Scottish Academy of Music in Glasgow vindicated the pioneers by providing the vital nursery in which future talent could be trained and validated. Professional status was gained, as Bridie had intended, in parallel with the growth of Scottish-based companies, offering a regular diet of theatre tailored to the needs of each city or region, and employment for the new breed of actors trained north of the border.

However, this situation did not mean that Scotland's theatre culture was transformed within a generation. For the majority of people, theatre meant variety, the direct heir of the techniques, entertainment values, commercial acumen and buildings of the music hall. Despite gloomy predictions, variety had survived the challenge of the cinemas, albeit with a reduced number of outlets. In 1950 cinema in Scotland was at its peak with over six hundred premises, some of which had taken over variety venues. But early cinemas often imitated the foyers, decor and customer facilities of theatres because they felt they were offering a similar night out to the same popular audience. Variety lived on and in the 1950s was given new vigour by the *Five-past-Eight* shows, which played to capacity audiences in Edinburgh, Glasgow and Aberdeen. Even the later development of television failed to repress variety, which invaded the new medium's Light Entertainment schedules.

The amateur movement also remained vigorous during this period. Until the founding of the Drama School in 1951, the Scottish Community Drama Association was the training ground for professional and amateur talent. Each decade up to the 1950s saw significant growth in the number of amateur clubs throughout Scotland and, since the professional companies produced the same kind of theatre as the amateurs, the re-emergence of a professional sector increased rather than diminished local enthusiasm. Both produced plays, though each Christmas, pantomimes were a clear reminder that plays did not necessarily reach the popular audience that theatre could still command.

A review of theatre seasons in the early 1950s shows fairly similar tastes among play-goers throughout Scotland. Perth, Dundee, Glasgow Citizens',

Figure 5.1 Theatre-goers leaving Edinburgh's Royal Lyceum on a rainy night in the early 1950s. The Wilson Barrett Company was playing The Philadelphia Story. (Scottish Theatre Archive)

Pitlochry, Edinburgh Gateway and the Byre offered a mix of popular classics, West End successes and a generous diet of new Scottish plays and adaptations. However, the mix does vary significantly in emphasis at the Citizens', perhaps the theatre most committed to Scottish work at this period, followed by the Gateway. Perth, Pitlochry, the Byre, in its professional seasons, and Dundee were more inclined to the English repertory pattern. The larger theatres were producing a remarkable twenty-plus plays each season and employing companies of twenty to thirty actors. Weekly or fortnightly turnarounds of plays were still the norm.

Equally significant is the blend in these early companies of Scottish and 'British' actors. Among the Scots, many of them graduates of the amateur movement, were Duncan Macrae, Molly Urquhart, Russell Hunter, Ida Schuster, Andrew Keir, James Gibson, Una McLean and Walter Carr. But the pioneering condition of the acting profession in Scotland and the demands of the repertoire programme meant that for many actors the Scottish theatres were simply an extension of the English repertory system. All the producers, later to be called directors, were products of the longer-established English theatres.

This situation deserves careful exploration since, even though the acting profession gradually came to achieve a natural dominance in Scottish theatres, the mix of plays in the main houses has remained, despite important variations, remarkably constant. To read this as an issue of English domination is to over-simplify, since the roots of Scottish taste lay in a dual identity – Scottish and at the same time British – which originated in the eighteenth century. Within this often uneasy combination of loyalties at least three different approaches to theatre production can be identified.

First, theatre in Scotland was viewed as a legitimate expression of international cultural citizenship. In this approach, plays, actors and production styles with little or no tradition in Scotland were espoused as an antidote to the perceived narrowness of native culture. Inevitably these styles were often associated with English theatre. Second, there was theatre for Scotland, which involved a conscious translation of texts and styles to suit specifically Scottish contexts. In the 1950s many original plays by Robert Kemp, R. J. B. Sellar and Moray MacLaren were effectively such acts of translation, seeking to make the repertory ethos relevant to Scotland. Third, there was the quest by playwrights, such as Robert McLellan, Alexander Reid and Alexander Scott, who wrote mainly or exclusively in Scots, for a theatre distinctively Scottish in language and form. Given Scotland's dual cultural identity during most of the twentieth century this has inevitably remained an elusive ideal, though none the less influential. Characteristically, in modern Scottish theatre all three approaches have had some play, even within the same theatre institution, though usually a combination of two has worked to secure a viable audience. Remarkable organisations have survived on only one, making a virtue of their single-mindedness, but they are the exception. In the early 1950s, the main producing houses were presenting theatre in and for Scotland.

THE EARLY 1950s

This alliance of tastes, which sustained Scottish theatre through a period of relative success and stability, cannot be understood in isolation from the post-war climate of reconstruction and national consolidation. A key expression of this mood was the government-funded Festival of Britain in 1951, through which theatres received generous subsidies towards special productions. Perth, Dundee and the Citizens' exchanged their productions in a successful model of cooperation, with Perth contributing *Twelfth Night*, Dundee a new adaptation of Goldoni's *The Liar*, and Glasgow Alexander Reid's *The Lass wi the Muckle Mou*.

In the Festival of Britain, regional identity, as expressed in the work of a J. B. Priestley or a James Bridie, was an accepted part of Britishness. In much the same spirit, the Edinburgh International Festival of 1950 mounted the premiere of Bridie's *The Queen's Comedy*, as one of three Citizens' productions. Bridie is the master mixer of styles, acutely conscious and sometimes manipulative of the different strands of Scottish taste. In *The Queen's Comedy* he clearly devised a tract for the times – a British theatre work which utilises a common European mythology and is also shrewdly tailored to a Scottish audience. Yet at the same time Bridie's focus on unmerited suffering profoundly questions the post-war optimism of the Festival of Britain. I cite this not in praise of Bridie but to underline the ways in which Britishness and Scottishness were closely intertwined.

Significantly, this is equally true of the radical socialist drama of the Unity theatres, which in many other respects has been contrasted with Bridie's theatre. Their appeal to working-class solidarity was as much British and international as Scottish. By the early 1950s this tradition was struggling for even amateur survival, partly because it had not been accepted by the emerging system of state subsidy. None the less, in 1952, Theatre Workshop based itself for a brief period in Glasgow and toured with Ewan McColl's *Uranium 235*. This powerful anti-nuclear drama played to an audience of 2000 people in Glasgow's St Andrew's Hall.

The only serious challenge to British cultural, if not political, consensus during this period came from the playwright Robert McLellan's unswerving devotion to a Scots community of language, and from Duncan Macrae's *Scottishows* of 1952–5. As a direct challenge to what he saw as the anglicisation of Scottish theatre and the lack of 'native drama', Macrae, in Priscilla Barlow's phrase from her biography of him, *Wise Enough to Play the Fool* (1995), 'barnstormed round Scotland', reviving the tradition of the actor-manager. The

Figure 5.2 Rehearsals for Roddy McMillan's All in Good Faith, *Citizens' Theatre, 1953–4 season.* (Scottish Theatre Archive)

Scottishows covered most of the country in a gruelling three-month schedule, which included a three-week season in Edinburgh during the Festival. Looking to the theories of R. F. Pollock, Macrae desired a theatre that was Scottish in style, form and content. To achieve this he drew on both the popular and artistic strengths of Scottish writing, producing T. M. Watson's *Bachelors are Bold* and *Johnny Jouk the Gibbet*, Alexander Reid's *The Warld's Wonder* and Bridie's *Gog and Magog*. Central to the enterprise was Macrae as actor who, despite his close association with both McLellan and Bridie, tended to bypass the ideas of art theatre and even plays, in order to connect with the working-class variety audience and 'steal the show'. The *Scottishows* operation was entirely commercial, extremely successful and outside the Arts Council's developing subsidy system with which it was often seen, particularly at the Edinburgh Festival, to be in competition.

In theatre terms the most important symptom of post-war reconstruction was the principle of public subsidy. Begun as a wartime expedient through the Committee for the Encouragement of Music and the Arts (CEMA), subsidy

was institutionalised by the foundation of the Arts Council of Great Britain
(ACGB) in 1946. Like CEMA, the Arts Council formed a Scottish Committee
with its own guaranteed proportionate budget, though, until 1952, the
Edinburgh Festival received its funding from the British allocation. The ACGB
report for 1952–3 strikes a characteristic note:

> The principle of collective patronage, like many other principles of British
> behaviour, has become accepted in a piece-meal, almost absent-minded
> fashion. There have been milestones, of course, in its development, such
> as the creation of the Arts Council, by Royal Charter, in 1946 and the
> inclusion in the Local Government Act of 1948 of a brief but significant
> clause empowering local authorities to devote up to a 6d rate (4½d in
> Scotland) on entertainment and the arts.

However piecemeal the principle, the strategy of the Scottish Committee in
the early years was founded on the main producing or repertory theatres and
on the style of programming to which I have referred: play-goers, not theatre-
goers, were the target. While consistently proud of the number of new plays by
Scottish authors, the ACGB report of 1954–5 observes:

Figure 5.3 Duncan Macrae in Gog and Magog *by James Bridie, Citizens' Theatre,
1951–2 season.* (Scottish Theatre Archive)

The genre of the play varies according to the needs of the city; in Glasgow and Edinburgh where the commercial theatre caters for a wider public, the repertory theatres tend to concentrate on works by Scottish playwrights, whereas in Perth, Dundee and Pitlochry the repertory programme is broader in scope and includes a greater proportion of good repertory and classical plays in addition to Scottish ones.

Though it overstates the difference between the theatres, this statement reveals the extent to which the early policy of the Arts Council was based on a mixed economy of subsidised and commercial theatre. Even the play policy of the principal Scottish houses only makes sense when set alongside the work of the popular Wilson Barrett Company and the touring sector. In 1950 Edinburgh's commercially managed Lyceum Theatre was host to the Old Vic Company's *Hamlet* with Michael Redgrave as the Prince, the Swedish actress Signo Hasso in Ibsen's *Rosmersholm*, and Evelyn Laye and Frank Lawton in Daphne du Maurier's *September Tide*. It also presented a full season of Wilson Barrett's weekly repertory, in which Bridie was the only Scottish presence. In 1951 Wilson Barrett contributed Beaumont and Fletcher's *The Knight of the Pestle* to the Festival of Britain.

As Donald Campbell points out in *A Brighter Sunshine* (1983), his perceptive history of the Royal Lyceum, it was the Wilson Barrett Company which, while playing Aberdeen and Glasgow seasons, maintained its identity as Edinburgh's principal producing theatre and met the challenge of the cinema at its peak by keeping attendances at a viable level week after week. The company was responsive to Scottish sentiment and thus extremely popular with Scottish play-going audiences, but the production of Scottish plays for their own sake or in order to create a distinctively Scottish theatre was no part of their concerns. Yet without this commercial repertory and touring sector and the audience expectations it created, the maintenance of the Scottish repertory companies on the basis of the small percentage subsidies provided at that time by the Arts Council would not have been financially viable, and so limited in its impact on the total population as to have been almost inconceivable as a stand-alone initiative. The alternative way to reach a wide Scottish public would have been to support the popular and indigenous theatre of Duncan Macrae's *Scottishows*, but the Scottish–British ethos of the Arts Council, and its securely middle-class concept of culture, precluded such a radical departure from the norms of collective patronage.

WINDS OF CHANGE: THE LATE 1950s

The 1960s was a decade of crisis for theatre in Scotland, with decisive shifts of artistic regime, high death and birth rates among theatres, mounting subsidies, dwindling audiences, and a ferment of creativity. The prologue to these rapid social and cultural changes is to be found in the late 1950s.

In 1955 Wilson Barrett announced his retirement and advised his company to leave the theatre business. In the same year, Duncan Macrae wound up the still highly successful *Scottishows* operation. The television age had begun. Between 1952 and 1962 the number of television licences in Scotland increased from 41,699 to 1,119,824. However, it was not just this alternative entertainment that hit the theatres but the social changes that accompanied it. With television came a new domestic lifestyle in which entertainment was confined to the home, which had become increasingly comfortable as a result of improved incomes and advances in domestic technology. At the same time populations were dispersing from city centres to housing schemes and suburbs. People did not suddenly abandon the theatre, but the old habit of regular weekly theatre- and cinema-going gradually evaporated.

Commercial theatre was the first to feel the draught, with touring houses and the variety stage both hit. Between 1950 and 1970 over twenty theatres in Scotland closed,[1] while the surviving tour-receiving houses passed one by one into local authority ownership. The Arts Council-subsidised companies also suffered despite increased state subventions, experiencing a 15 per cent drop in weekly attendances between 1957 and 1960.[2] These figures conceal more severe periodic falls at the Glasgow Citizens' and in Dundee, and more stable audiences at Perth and Pitlochry, but the overall effect on theatres which still earned between 60 and 90 per cent of their income from the box office was life threatening.

The changes between 1955 and 1960 threw much more responsibility on to the subsidised sector in general and the Arts Council in particular. Despite the brave and successful experiment of Henry Sherek's Scottish Repertory Season in 1956, when two companies, one led by Duncan Macrae, the other by Stanley Baxter, interchanged a programme of Scottish plays between Edinburgh and Glasgow over twelve weeks, the commercial theatre outside London and the pantomime season was being rapidly undermined. Within five years the strategy of modest subsidy to theatres, for which the Arts Council was not directly or even principally responsible, was overtaken by events.

As problems began to loom the Arts Council's first line of defence was spelt out in its 1955 annual report:

> If the living arts are to hold their own in the face of competition their strategy must be to consolidate and not to diffuse. To deplore without discrimination the closing of theatres in so many towns is to beg the whole question of theatre provision. The fewer theatres for the time being the better; the better, that is to say, for building a strong network of repertory theatre in Britain.

Figure 5.4 Gateway Theatre's Look Back in Anger *by John Osborne, 1958–9 season.* (Scottish Theatre Archive)

The aim was to achieve 'a selected number of well-based, well-manned and well-equipped playhouses with a devoted [i.e. regular] audience and a prospect of economic survival'. In 1955 thirty theatres, five of them in Scotland, were regarded as fulfilling these criteria, though it was acknowledged that some 'theatreless towns' would probably add to the total in due course. The main problem was seen as providing these repertory, later 'regional', theatres with backstage facilities conducive to high production standards, and front-of-house facilities which would compete with Britain's increasingly comfortable restaurants and pubs. The policy was as much social and economic as cultural.

The 1955 strategy did not foresee the collapse of the commercial touring circuit and the subsequent pressure on large-scale venues which variety alone could not sustain, even in Scotland. If the problem had affected only drama it might not have compelled the Arts Council to action, but the large-scale theatres were also key venues for opera and ballet. Consequently the Arts Council had to subsidise and even, on occasion, to initiate tours. The New Scottish Touring Company was one such venture, offering Wilson Barrett's style of theatre, but the Scottish Committee's preferred option was to give increased grants to the repertory companies for touring.

Perth already had a long-established touring operation, serving medium-scale venues in the Highlands, Angus and sometimes the Borders; while Dundee, the Gateway and Glasgow Citizens' had also toured from time to time. Planning began for a Festival of Scottish Repertory Theatre, which would involve the principal companies in exchanging productions in order to raise the companies' overall profile and form the basis of a more systematic method of providing major tours. In the background to this plan was the Arts Council's desire to pave the way for the National Theatre, the foundation stone of which had been laid in London, by supporting a National Theatre Company, supplemented by a 'National Provincial Theatre' of producing companies throughout Britain. The Scottish Committee wanted to keep Scotland in the picture.

The relative failure of the Festival, which, after planning delays, took place in 1958, prefigured the repeated frustration of later plans to establish a national framework for Scottish theatre. Four companies took part: Dundee Rep with Sartre's *Crime Passionel*, Perth Rep with Shaw's *Antony and Cleopatra*, Glasgow Citizens' with *The Cherry Orchard*, and Edinburgh's Gateway Company with Robert Kemp's *The Penny Wedding*. The contrast with *Scottishows* and Henry Sherek's Scottish Repertory Season of 1956 was marked; Kemp's play was the sole representative of theatre in Scotland and of Scottish theatre. The key influences on the choice of plays were the Arts Council's desire for something artistically worthy and significant, and the ambitions of the directors, not box-office appeal. In the event, *The Penny Wedding*, a Scots comedy centred on the folk custom of the guests paying for the wedding party, was a kind of triumphal progress to which audiences turned out in force. Otherwise business was barely respectable. Perth declined to support any of the other plays and in Dundee an outstanding performance by resident director Raymond Westall in *Crime Passionel* failed to raise the city's temperature even a notch. The experiment was never repeated despite considerable good will on the part of all concerned and a respectful press.

Apart from the obvious gap between audience taste and artistic provision, the Scottish Repertory Festival failed to address the problems of audience loyalty and the different expectations of each city. In 1957 an attempt to merge the Perth and Dundee repertory theatres, in response to growing financial pressures, also failed because of civic identification with the local theatre and distrust of imported and perhaps alien policies. It seemed that the repertory system would not in itself serve all the needs of theatre in Scotland.

TURBULENT DECADE: THE 1960s

If the 1950s left Scotland's theatres a legacy of unsolved problems, the 1960s brought a volatile social mood which theatre immediately reflected. In *The Traverse Theatre Story* (1988), Joyce McMillan describes a sharp generational change in audience expectations:

> By the end of 1962 the whole of British society had reached a strange, tense condition with the mood of timid conservatism and suburban apathy that had characterised the 50's about to be blown sky-high by the attitudes of a post-war generation that was young, healthy, well-educated, well-heeled and historically speaking, exceptionally fearless – unafraid of poverty, disease, unemployment, and as the pill era dawned, increasingly unafraid of sex.

The Scottish theatres were exceptionally ill prepared for this climate of social revolution. In Britain as a whole, the initiative was passing from the middle-class theatre of the repertories to the expression of working-class experience. But in Scotland the subsidised theatres had eschewed working-class experience and cut themselves off from the popular theatre traditions, which might have offered new lines of development. The post-war Scottish playwrights were suddenly left high and dry in an apparently provincial regionalism, while, despite the rise of a new generation of acting talent, few Scottish directors were available to interpret the fresh situation in Scottish terms. Consequently, in addition to the long-running economic crisis and a forthcoming management crisis, theatre in Scotland was hit by an artistic crisis as well.

In Glasgow, a decisive shift came in 1960–1 when, in the Arts Council's phrase, the Citizens' 'went experimental', producing Durenmatt, Giradoux, Ionesco, Wesker's *Roots*, and *Breakdown* by Stewart Conn, one of the few Scottish playwrights to emerge during the 1960s. The big success of the season, however, was a bold *Hamlet* with John Cairney in the lead. Thereafter the pace hardly slackened through the decade, with eight changes of artistic director. In 1965 under the leadership of chairman Michael Goldberg, the Close Theatre was developed alongside the main house, to accommodate a new, intimate and experimental theatre which absorbed the influences of television while maintaining vital artistic and intellectual freedom.

In Dundee the 1962 spring and autumn seasons shifted away from the 1950s repertory style, introducing Harold Pinter, Shelagh Delaney, Keith Waterhouse and even Machiavelli's *Mandragola*. However, before 1962 was out, the long-serving administrator John Henderson and the recently appointed production director Piers Haggard moved on, leaving the theatre caught between the increased pace of artistic change and Dundee's verdict on the new ethos. Audiences liked *A Taste of Honey* but otherwise stayed away. In 1963, Dundee Rep was gutted by fire, stared extinction in the face, but then found a 'temporary' home in a converted church in Lochee Road, where gradually the lost ground was regained.

The theatres in Perth, Pitlochry and St Andrews were insulated from the harshest effects of these artistic changes by their resolutely bourgeois audiences. None the less, each theatre cannily adjusted to maintain its artistic credentials without alienating its patrons. Perth occasionally looked to London for contemporary writing to produce along with its ration of West End successes. Audience loyalty was crucial in Perth, since the play-goers' club raised an annual sum three times the theatre's local authority grant. Throughout the 1960s Pitlochry maintained a skilful mix of classics, including some rare British and European revivals, with popular comedies and a continuing Scottish contribution from Barrie, Bridie and the occasional contemporary premiere. The Pitlochry company could shine artistically in a production of Pirandello's *Henry IV* without resorting to Wesker, Arden, Pinter or Osborne.

Edinburgh experienced the worst turbulence. In a well-nigh disastrous season in 1960–1 the Gateway managed to lose its home audience and manifest the ethos of the, by now, stale 1950s by producing Robert Kemp's less-than-inspired *Master John Knox* and Bjornson's *Mary Stuart in Scotland* at the Edinburgh Festival. The audience situation was stabilised in the next year but the *floreat* of the mid 1950s, when the Gateway was the focus of a school of Scottish dramatists including Robert McLellan, Alexander Reid and Robert Kemp, was never recovered. In 1965 the Gateway company was absorbed into the larger enterprise of Edinburgh's new Civic Theatre Company at the Royal Lyceum.

While the Gateway trod water, the new spirit of restless dissatisfaction gave birth, in 1963, to the Traverse Theatre in Edinburgh's Lawnmarket. The original impulse would have been inconceivable without the existence of the International Festival, and reflected the trend towards small-scale experimental spaces. But the Traverse was also the result of an intense desire on the part of a small but significant section of Edinburgh's professional classes to break away decisively from the city's Presbyterian ethos. Only this pioneering spirit can explain the quasi-religious fervour with which the members of the Traverse Theatre Club sustained and supported their theatre through the precarious early years, when the only public subsidies available were one-off guarantees towards the costs of individual new plays. The young Traverse was that rare phenomenon – a theatre that changes social attitudes.

Given this impetus for change and the increasing importance of the Edinburgh Festival to the city's economy, the Corporation reluctantly agreed, in 1963, to buy the Lyceum Theatre to safeguard an emerging scheme for the development of an ambitious Civic Centre, which was to include an Opera

House, on Castle Terrace. Characteristically it took a property deal to push the Corporation towards supporting a repertory theatre equivalent in scale and artistic ambition to the Citizens' Company, which Glasgow had enjoyed since 1943. The Edinburgh Civic Theatre commenced operations at the Royal Lyceum in 1965.

The Lyceum development was only one example of the way in which the

Figure 5.5 Pirandello's Henry IV, *Pitlochry Festival Theatre, 1962.* (Pitlochry Festival Theatre)

state, in the form of central and local government, moved in the early 1960s from being the subsidiser of theatre to being its principal patron. To some extent this was merely an extension of the philosophy about the role of government and the arts which had been established in the post-war period. In reality the balance had shifted decisively in favour of corporate management and direction, albeit the corporations were public ones. What policies would direct this new exercise of power?

In 1960 the Scottish Committee of the Arts Council convened a conference of theatre practitioners and funders which was designed to achieve a new policy. The result was a firm majority in favour of 'going for youth' and an abandonment of the patterns of compromise which had sustained the repertory programme thus far. The policy was accompanied by a new scheme of bonus grants for 'plays of good quality', to be paid at the end of each season. These initiatives led directly to the programme changes and attendant financial traumas already described, and could not have been ventured without a 25 per cent hike in core Arts Council grants in 1961–2, which was passed on from government, through ACGB, to the Scottish Committee and then to individual theatres. The paradox of simultaneously increasing grants and implying that the bulk of the repertoire did not qualify as 'worthwhile', seems to have escaped the notice of both the grateful dispensers and recipients of the much-needed government largesse. In 1962–3 a pleased Scottish Committee was able to report that 76 per cent of plays were now 'worthwhile', though by 1964 this had fallen to a 'majority' of plays. During the same period, the total number of Scottish plays premiered by the repertory companies plummeted to one or at most two a year. Audiences stabilised, though at a lower level, since the number of older play-goers lost due to the new programmes exceeded the numbers of new theatre-goers attracted by them.

Local-government funding was also on the increase and vital to another plank in the national strategy. In the Arts Council's view, to make play-going more attractive and exciting, new 'civic theatres' were required in Glasgow, Edinburgh and Dundee. In due course Pitlochry and the Byre would also require new model theatres. Studio spaces and opera houses featured on the shopping list, too. Progress on this front was in reality painfully slow, and Kirkwall, Motherwell, Glenrothes, Dumbarton and Lerwick were all to anticipate the cities in achieving new or upgraded theatres. In 1967 the Arts Council launched a 'Housing the Arts' fund to spearhead the drive towards civic theatres and cultural centres, and to coax local councils into action. Consequently, even as commercial developers were demolishing older theatre buildings, a new wave of theatre construction had begun and would gather pace over the next two decades.

If any confirmation of the prevailing trends was required, the election of Labour governments in 1964 and 1966, the granting of a new Royal Charter to the Arts Council in 1967, and the appointment, in the same year, of Jennie Lee as Minister for the Arts, accelerated the dominance of state patronage. In 1967–8, theatre grants lurched upwards in response to a national economic crisis. In 1966–7, the proportion of self-earned income dropped below 50 per cent at Dundee, Edinburgh (Lyceum Theatre and Traverse) and Glasgow. Perth earned 56 per cent. Only Pitlochry and the Byre continued to be principally self-supporting. Between 1964–5 and 1968–9, Arts Council grants rose by 300 per cent, leaving staff and committee members of the Arts Council somewhat fazed over the exercise of their hugely increased power. The 1968–9 report tentatively raised the question of how the Arts Council itself should be organised since 'quasi-governmental bodies' were a newish phenomenon among impresarios and patrons of the arts. Power without any direct means of accountability has remained a feature of 'arm's length' state funding of the arts since its inception.

The crisis of management was not confined to quasi-governmental bodies. Until the early 1960s, the most powerful and stable figure in the theatre hierarchy was the manager; producers or production directors came and went along with everyone else on a 'hire and fire' basis. The simple benchmark of success was the box-office returns. With the switch to subsidy and then state patronage, Boards of Directors now included Councillors and other public appointees whose concerns and responsibilities extended to the ethos, purpose and programme of the theatre. At the same time, public patronage enabled ambitious production directors to persuade committees to back their artistic ideas. The concept of the artistic director was born.

In 1962 Iain Cuthbertson was appointed to run Glasgow Citizens' administratively and artistically, but by 1964 he was centre stage with an acclaimed performance in the lead role in John Arden's *Armstrong's Last Goodnight*. When he left for the Royal Court in 1965 his job was split between a general manager and an artistic director. But if this new situation allowed the rise of the artistic director, it could also engineer his or her fall. In 1966, after less than a year as artistic director of the Edinburgh Civic Theatre at the Lyceum, Tom Fleming resigned in protest at the Board's creation of a subcommittee to scrutinise programming. In the same year, Jim Haynes, a co-founder of the Traverse, was ousted as artistic director by a committee grappling with the problems of institutionalisation. In 1968 it was Iain Cuthbertson's turn to resign, in this instance from Perth, when his bold season of Scottish work, combined with Arden and Brendan Behan, left the city's play-goers disgruntled and disaffected. In 1968, after featuring as a playwright at Dundee, Cliff Hanley defined the 'civil war in the Civic Theatres' as a battle between local worthies ('drapers') and artistic directors.[3] Quite correctly he saw this as a struggle to reconcile financial viability, accountability to funders, and social responsibility, not to mention the normal forces of prejudice and egotism.

Another factor in the 1960s' maelstrom was the diminishing effectiveness of the Lord Chamberlain's office as theatre censor, a role finally abandoned in 1968. As far back as 1957 the Citizens' had circumvented the Chamberlain, with the Arts Council's approval, by presenting Arthur Miller's *A View from the Bridge* for members of the Citizens' Theatre Society, thereby substantially increasing its membership. This was the route followed by the Traverse and then the Close in order to allow a new wave of theatre writing and, at the same time, charge the theatre space with a sense of excitement and risk. In this way a greater responsibility was placed on directors and committees of management, as demonstrated by the rumpus at the Close Theatre when, in 1965, Charles Marowitz's experimental *Dr Faustus* was held to insult the Queen. The management committee stepped in and the first-night performance was replaced by an impromptu argument between Marowitz, as the production's artistic director, and the Close's committee. The production went ahead on the second night with modifications, but Michael Goldberg, who had inspired and facilitated the Close, never fully recovered as chairman of the Citizens' from that traumatic evening. In 1968, the Citizens' Board, now minus Goldberg, fell out with their artistic director Michael Blakemore, when they blocked his plans to premiere Tennessee Williams's *Sweet Bird of Youth* and opted instead for a revival of Bridie's *The Anatomist*.

Audiences were usually on the sidelines of these debates. The ultimate power of the box office remained but its immediate effect was muffled by the new, complex power structures. Without the funding these power structures controlled, theatre could not survive and develop, but there was also a real danger of leaving the audience behind. The regionally influential Dundee press betrays an undercurrent of resentment throughout the 1960s at the changes in theatre policy. Why, readers' letters asserted, should Dundee be blamed for not supporting 'the right kind of play'. In 1963, in *The Dundee Courier*, journalist and theatre historian Alec Robertson questioned the new play choices: 'Is the criterion of value to be that they carry the hallmark of the avant-garde Royal Court Theatre, or that they are considered likely to appeal to the particular taste of the inhabitants of Dundee?' This may be a more metaphysical question than Robertson intended, but it had a practical dimension. In 1967, for example, Arden's *Sergeant Musgrave's Dance* received 'only light applause' from a loyal but bemused rump audience. In the same year, the City's annual grant to the theatre was challenged on Council by a demand for less 'highly cultured shows'. A predictable criticism perhaps, yet, in 1967, public opinion was a factor in blocking the conversion of the Caird Hall into a civic cultural centre and theatre at a cost of £600,000. The Rep was to remain in the hurriedly converted church in Lochee Road for another twelve years.

Despite these problems the 1960s was a decade of achievement for Scottish theatre. Even the crises were fuelled by an upbeat mood of underlying economic optimism and social change. A wave of fresh acting talent came through the Royal Scottish Academy of Music and Drama, including Hannah Gordon, John Cairney, Alex McAvoy, Bill Paterson, Phyllis Logan, Gregor Fisher, Tom Conti and Jack Shedden, to name only a few. Scottish directors, though still in an overall minority, counted Calum Mill, Tom Fleming and Iain Cuthbertson among their number. The skills base of the profession was broadening and embraced designers, stage managers and technicians, while the actors retained the loyalty and the responsiveness of a wide Scottish public, even when the play was considered obscure.

Production triumphs in the 1960s included Pirandello's *Henry IV* at Pitlochry (1962), Tom Wright's *There was a Man*, performed by John Cairney (1966), Tom Fleming's production of Brecht's *Life of Galileo* at the Edinburgh Civic Theatre (1966), the Citizens' premiere of Peter Nichol's *A Day in the Death of Joe Egg* (1967), Leonard Rossiter in Michael Blakemore's Edinburgh Festival production of *The Resistable Rise of Arturo Ui* (1968), which featured back projections of Soviet tanks rolling into Czechoslovakia, and Jay Presson Allen's adaptation of *The Prime of Miss Jean Brodie* at the Lyceum (1968).

Scottish writers were not a dominant feature of 1960s' theatre, partly because the indigenous school of the 1950s was not ready for the pace of change.[4] None the less, the Traverse's 'resident' playwrights, C. P. Taylor and Stanley Eveling, brought new political, social and philosophical perspectives to Scottish playwriting. Jack Ronder, Joan Ure, Stewart Conn and Eddie Boyd emerged as 1960s' voices without as yet commanding a wide audience, except through the broadcast media. For all these writers the techniques of radio and television drama were a potent influence, reshaping the form of stage writing and establishing a more complex relationship between audience and performance. Their cultural reference points are European and international as well as Scottish and British, but their plays, whether implicitly or explicitly, are informed by an urgent awareness of contemporary issues and a desire to engage the audience intellectually and imaginatively.

THE RESURGENCE: THE 1970s

If the 1960s brought turbulence and inspiration in equal measure, the 1970s saw a theatre resurgence in Scotland. Despite, perhaps because of, the quality of drama now offered on radio and television, live theatre reaffirmed its complementary identity and its very special capacity to respond flexibly and quickly to social and economic change. In terms of audience numbers the size of the live-theatre space had shrunk, but it was still a precious area of freedom. There was a reaction against the often vapid internationalism of the previous decade and a new emphasis on the importance of cultural difference and identity. There was also a wave of generational energy, later in Scotland than in

England, which brought new areas of class experience into theatre, and an impetus towards theatre's involvement in education and community development. Equally significant was the political temperature, with investment in North Sea oil, economic growth in some industries combined with fierce resistance to the decline of traditional labour-intensive heavy industry, and a sharp rise in nationalism. Whatever political disappointments lay ahead, the 1970s began a cultural shift in which Scottishness reshaped and reasserted itself against both external forces and its own stereotypes.

The resurgence took different forms according to the institutions and personalities involved. These contrasts ensured that the overall effect was to broaden the range of theatre, strengthening Scottish theatre, and theatre in Scotland, while retaining a commitment to the international contexts. There were, of course, tensions and disagreements, but it would be a mistake to interpret the 1970s as a time of conflict between Anglocentric and indigenous influences in which the natives gained the upper hand. Each strand of theatre production was aware of and influenced by the others, while contrasting perspectives co-existed within the same theatre institutions. In the 1970s, Scottish playwrights staked their claim to a share of the theatre space and, whatever the production context, Scots actors became increasingly confident in speaking with their own voice. The ground rules had shifted.

Resurgence was led by the existing theatres, including the Traverse and the Close. In one sense this was a vindication of the Arts Council's consistent support over two decades, though, ironically, a 1970 report, *Theatre in Scotland*, is weighed down with a late 1960s' pessimism about the main producing houses and their perceived failure to show the way forward creatively. This important report will be discussed in due course.

After his appointment as director of Edinburgh's Lyceum Theatre in 1966, Clive Perry pursued a shrewd, pragmatic policy, building audience confidence and acknowledging a necessary compromise between artistic ambitions and public taste. In this he proved himself a successor to Wilson Barrett as well as Tom Fleming. The success of *The Prime of Miss Jean Brodie* pointed the way towards a specifically Scottish dimension in this policy, which was fully realised in the 1971 production of Stewart Conn's *The Burning*, directed by Bill Bryden. In its choice of subject (James VI and I) Conn's play has one eye on Robert McLellan's comic masterpiece *Jamie the Saxt*, but in reaction. In a series of short scenes played on an open stage, *The Burning* deploys a powerfully realistic and poetic form of non-naturalistic Scots, challenging superficial readings either of Scottish history or of stage naturalism. In Donald Campbell's view, the play can be read as 'the first attempt to apply a truly modern consciousness to the Scottish drama'.[5]

The Burning was followed by a string of popular Scottish plays at the Lyceum, where Clive Perry gathered a team of outstanding directors, including

Bryden and Richard Eyre, and a company of Scottish actors which included
Rikki Fulton, James Grant, Roy Hanlon, Eileen McCallum, Fulton Mackay,
Roddy McMillan, Clare Richards, Jan Wilson, James Cairncross and Paul
Young. Among their successes were Roddy McMillan's *The Bevellers*,
McLellan's *The Flouers o Edinburgh* and Bryden's own *Willie Rough*, in addition to the full range of the classical repertoire. Much of this work was not as
technically innovative as Stewart Conn's contribution and featured stage naturalism in a Scottish guise, but there is no denying the creative energy which
spilled over into the formation of the Young Lyceum Company and into the
audiences, which responded enthusiastically to the range and the quality of the
work presented.

North of the Tay, resurgence came to Dundee – still in its temporary home
– with director Stephen MacDonald. New Scottish plays, combined with a

Figure 5.6 Roddy McMillan's The Bevellers *(with McMillan centre), Royal Lyceum,
1973.* (Scottish Theatre Archive)

revival of interest in older work, the classics and occasional productions with
a local angle, offered Dundee a way out of its 1960s' dilemmas, and MacDonald
brought real talent to the task. Notable among Dundee's successes were the
1973 and 1974 productions of Hector MacMillan's *The Rising* and *The Royal
Visit*. Both plays focused on key political events in early nineteenth-century
Scotland and set contemporary politics in a radical perspective, but it was
MacMillan's use of folk music, played by the McCalmans in *The Rising*, which
increased its impact. At the same time MacMillan's *The Sash* caused a considerable stir in Edinburgh and Glasgow by putting the uncomfortable, and to
many insupportable, issues of Scotland's religious bigotry and conflict centre
stage.

At Perth, Pitlochry and the Byre the pace was more measured and the
continuity through each decade more marked. None the less, encouraged by
the Arts Council, which had abolished its approved plays scheme in 1967 in
favour of commissions to playwrights in Scotland, the other Tayside theatres

Figure 5.7 Hector MacMillan's The Rising, *Dundee Rep, 1973.* (Alex Coupar)

supported work by James Kennaway, William Watson and Tom Gallacher. Kennaway's *Country Dance* and Gallacher's *Schellenbrack* and *Revival* set a high standard of new writing and added another seam to the repertoires, which were carefully nurtured by Joan Knight at Perth and Kenneth Ireland at Pitlochry.

In Glasgow discontinuity continued to be the main theme as Giles Havergal arrived at the Citizens' closely followed by Philip Prowse and Robert David MacDonald. The 1970 production of *Hamlet*, with David Hayman in the lead, was calculated to shock, and generally succeeded. More importantly, it announced that something new had arrived, and that a bold contemporary theatricality would now take precedence over both literary notions and bourgeois expectations of repertory theatre. 'I'm like the Madame of a Brothel,' Havergal told *The Guardian*, 'I have my girls on the one hand and my clients on the other and the delicate art is to bring them together.' Glasgow Councillors huffed and puffed but soon realised that they had a potentially international success on their hands and backed it with hard cash.

Among the Citizens' successes in the 1970s (the Close was, sadly, destroyed by fire in 1973) were a series of Jacobean resurrections by Philip Prowse, Robert David MacDonald's *De Sade Show* and *Chinchilla*, and Havergal's bravura rendering of *The Importance of Being Earnest*, as well as his magnificent Christmas pantomimes. The key to the Citizens' phenomenon was, as in the early 1970s' flourishing of the Lyceum, the complementary strengths of an artistic team. The difference was that the Citizens' triumvirate stayed in post.

The Citizens' regime was criticised for its failure to support the new Scottish dramatists; though in MacDonald himself they fostered a one-man dramaturgical act unequalled in modern British theatre, and the theatre was a supportive host venue to other Scottish companies in its summer seasons. Argument will continue about the Citizens' offences against the literary canon, but as Michael Coveney points out in *The Citz* (1990) – an excellent account of the triumvirate, though cavalier in its treatment of Scottish theatre as a whole – the Havergal initiative belongs to Glasgow just as the Traverse in the 1960s was a product of Edinburgh's particular cultural chemistry. The flamboyant artistic policy was a defiant and affirmative affront to the post-industrial devastation of Glasgow, and to the philistinism and cultural snobbery of its middle classes. The repertoire had unfamiliar reaches but it did get across to its audience, who were not just repertory theatre-goers. By maintaining low ticket prices and a uniquely welcoming atmosphere in its bars and front-of-house operation, the theatre made itself accessible to the people of Glasgow. It would be foolish to deny that the extremes sometimes depicted on the stage did not echo aspects of Glasgow and Scotland's experience. In theatre artifice holds its own kind of mirror up to life.

As if to demonstrate how the different strands of Scottish theatre competed

GLASGOW CITIZENS THEATRE
PRESENTS THE CITIZENS COMP
ANY IN LOOT BY JOE ORTON NO
VEMBER 4–NOVEMBER 26 GOR
BALS GLASGOW 041 429 0022

Figure 5.8 Citizens' Theatre poster for Joe Orton's Loot, 1971, *with posing Gorbals' boys.* (Citizens' Theatre)

and interlocked, the Traverse began the 1970s with one of its most successful world-theatre regimes under Michael Rudman, and ended the decade under the direction of Chris Parr, whose local writers' policy turned the Traverse into the dynamo of new Scottish theatre between 1975 and 1980. Rudman's successes included C. P. Taylor's *The Black and White Minstrels*, with Tom Conti, Alan Howard and Patti Love, and Stanley Eveling's *Caravaggio Buddy*, with Ian Holm. Rudman's predecessor was Max Stafford-Clark, whose Workshop Company continued to contribute to the programme. Rudman's successor

Mike Ockrent presented neglected work by Brecht, Fassbinder, Handke and Kroetz, though his most memorable production was a reworking of Sternheim's *Burger Schippel*, in which the actors, including Simon Callow, revolted during rehearsals, recast the play, and went on to achieve a company hit.

It was Chris Parr, originally Ockrent's associate, who caught the national mood and, as the political debate on nationalism gathered pace, responded to the shift in Arts Council policies towards a more Scottish orientation. The continuity between Rudman and Parr lay in their shared faith in a writers' theatre and the primary role of texts rather than performance or production styles, a belief that, as much as any issue of Scottishness, put clear water between Havergal's Citizens' and Parr's Traverse. But Chris Parr was passionately committed to the development of Scottish writers and his investment was richly rewarded.

Figure 5.9 Citizens' Theatre's Troilus and Cressida, *1973.* (Diane Tammes/Citizens' Theatre)

Parr's first season at the Traverse, in 1976, featured three Scottish premieres: Tom Gallacher's *Sea Change*, Hector MacMillan's *The Gay Gorbals* and Tom McGrath's *Laurel and Hardy*. In the same year the Traverse extended into the Old Chaplaincy Centre (now the Bedlam Theatre) at Festival time, where it co-promoted The Heretics' premiere production of Donald Campbell's *The Jesuit* and Borderline Theatre's *An Me Wi a Bad Leg Tae* by Billy Connolly. The poet and jazz musician Tom McGrath represented a modern theatre of improvisation and experiment. Donald Campbell's virtues in *The Jesuit* were those of a mainhouse dramatist employing authentic spoken Scots with a powerful sense of dramatic and poetic form. Billy Connolly, building on the spectacular success of *The Great Northern Welly Boot Show* on the expanding Festival Fringe in 1972, was recasting the variety tradition as a contemporary dramatic and musical vehicle which would take live theatre back to a popular audience via new touring companies such as Borderline. Together these talents constituted a modern theatre renaissance which transcended naturalism in a variety of styles. The Traverse was at the centre of the action.

A remarkable flow of productions was maintained, including George Byatt's *The Silver Land*, Tom McGrath and Jimmy Boyle's *The Hardman*, John Byrne's *The Slab Boys* trilogy, C. P. Taylor's *Walter*, Donald Campbell's *Somerville the Soldier*, Michael Wilcox's *Rents*, Marcella Evaristi's *Hard to Get*, the first version of McGrath's *Animal* and John Hale's *The Case of David Anderson QC*. Later critics have detected an overall bias towards Scottish, male, working-class experience in this phase of writing or, as Joyce McMillan more positively expresses it, 'a high energy, strongly physical culture with a powerful undercurrent of aggression and suppressed tenderness'.[6] Elizabeth MacLennan, co-founder of 7:84 Theatre Company, was less kind in her analysis:

> The success of 1972, the most 'progressive' piece of new Scottish theatre, was *The Great Northern Welly Boot Show*. It starred Billy Connolly in his most triumphal machismo, anti-granny, anti-mammy, anti-wifey mode, and our own Bill [Paterson], Alex [Norton] and John Bett in small parts, enthusiastically within the same tradition. The women were definitely stereotypes and no two ways about it. The audience loved it . . . Scottish theatre was, and remains, in many respects stubbornly male chauvinist.[7]

Both descriptions fairly characterise individual productions, but as a retrospect on Scottish playwriting in the 1970s it is in danger of itself becoming a stereotype, as Joyce McMillan points out. McGrath's exploration of sexual roles widened with the decade, and was focused on and through women in *Sisters*, anticipating his later Traverse play *Kora*. Donald Campbell's *The*

Figure 5.10 Tom McGrath and Jimmy Boyle's The Hardman, *Traverse Theatre, 1977.* (David Liddle: Scottish Theatre Archive)

Widows of Clyth was about female solidarity, while Michael Wilcox wrote about the gay scene in Edinburgh. In the 1970s Scottish playwrights opened up a wide range of social, personal and political issues in the theatre. Most importantly, they kept live drama creatively and technically abreast of the broadcast media, investing their art with an edge of contemporary significance. This vehicle was then available for others to explore new concerns and perceptions in evolving patterns of form and language.

These social and artistic developments were not confined to the existing theatre companies and venues. In 1971, 7:84 Theatre Company began with the production of *Trees in the Wind* on the Edinburgh Festival Fringe. At first 7:84 was in the Unity and Theatre Workshop mould of British socialism, but, in 1973, a separate Scottish company began with John McGrath's *The Cheviot, the Stag and the Black, Black Oil*, which sent shockwaves through the Scottish theatre scene. The originality of *The Cheviot* lay in the directness of its political message, in the circuit of clubs, community centres and halls to which it toured, and in its harnessing of popular theatre forms by a first-class professional company, which included Bill Paterson, Elizabeth MacLennan, John Bett and

Figure 5.11 John Byrne's The Slab Boys, *Traverse Theatre, 1978.* (David Liddle: Scottish Theatre Archive)

David MacLennan. To some extent *The Great Northern Welly Boot Show* had made these connections, taking as its starting point the sit-in at the Upper Clyde Shipbuilders. But 7:84 was also tapping into the Highland tradition of ceilidh, and from the start its approach was disciplined, concerted and driven by intellectual and emotional commitment.

Moreover, 7:84 went back to its new-found audience. The criticism that in the 1970s 7:84 Scotland repeated itself, with shows such as *The Game's a*

Bogey, *Little Red Hen*, *Blood Red Roses* and *The Catch*, misses the point. The company had discovered a method of working and an audience to which it remained stubbornly loyal through the decade. This was a different achievement from that of the Traverse, the Lyceum or the Citizens', and even from the later successes of the touring companies such as Borderline and Wildcat, who consolidated and diversified the new touring audience. While Arts Council

Figure 5.12 John McGrath's The Cheviot, the Stag and the Black, Black Oil, *7:84 Theatre Company (Scotland), 1973.* (Scottish Theatre Archive)

committees talked about making theatre accessible to a wider public, 7:84 showed how it could be done, though in a way which challenged accepted notions of cultural value. This implicit conflict was submerged in the 1970s as the Scottish Arts Council swam with the Devolution tide, but resurfaced in the 1980s to muddy the theatrical waters.

Mention of the Arts Council is a salutary reminder that, despite a recovery in theatre attendances from 1970, the growth and development of Scottish theatre throughout the decade was dependent on public subsidy. Despite the new scourge of rampant inflation, Arts Council grants more than matched inflationary pressures, though subsidy increases were reactive rather than proactive to financial crises, leaving theatre managements perpetually on the brink of insolvency. The idea that public subsidy through the Arts Council was more cushioned than the older commercial disciplines is a fallacy; each year the public expenditure round became more politically complex and unpredictable, with two general elections and, at the end of the decade, a minority government. Furthermore, 'arts inflation', which reflected the labour-intensive theatre business, consistently outran price inflation. Against this background the drive to provide new civic theatres became a race against time. The Mac-Robert Arts Centre, in Stirling, opened in 1971, and the Eden Court Theatre, in Inverness, in 1976, significantly extending the medium-to-large-scale touring circuit. Other smaller theatre arts centres, including the Crawford Arts Centre in St Andrews and Theatre Workshop in Edinburgh, were developed, while, in 1974, Scottish Opera converted the Theatre Royal, Glasgow, into a large-scale performance base. Ominously for the finances of the Scottish performing arts as a whole, cost inflation consumed the endowment which was to have met the theatre's operating costs.

On the downside, Dundee and Pitlochry struggled unsuccessfully in the 1970s to secure urgently needed new theatres, while Perth, the Lyceum and the Citizens' were all scheduled for substantial upgrading. Demand outstripped financial supply. The Arts Council maintained its support for the vision of major new civic cultural centres, but public opinion in Dundee, the Fine Art Commission in Glasgow, inflation and, finally, local government reorganisation frustrated the grand design. The saga of Edinburgh's Opera House and the 'Hole-in-the-Ground' in Castle Terrace requires a publication to itself, but the harsh reality was that when the scheme finally collapsed in 1975 (latest price tag £19.5 million), Edinburgh was left with no new theatre and two old buildings, the Lyceum and the King's, badly in need of improvement. In 1976, the newly formed Lothian Regional Council stepped in to help save the Playhouse Theatre in Greenside Place, principally as an opera venue, but the Arts Council was unwilling to accept this as anything other than a stop-gap. By the end of the 1970s, institutional consolidation lagged significantly behind the achievements of Scotland's theatre artists.

MODERN THEATRE ANATOMY: THE SUPPORTING ACTS

In 1967 the Scottish Committee of the Arts Council of Great Britain became the Scottish Arts Council (SAC). Though enjoying a greater measure of independence and profile the SAC was still part of the UK Arts Council, reporting to government through the Office of Arts and Libraries. In 1994 a further devolution was effected when responsibility for a now independent Scottish Arts Council was transferred to the Scottish Office. During the 1970s, the SAC broadened its responsibilities by supporting theatre in education, small- and large-scale touring, the development of new theatre venues and community theatre. The drama budget was still principally devoted to the network of producing regional or repertory theatres, but its scope was now much wider. During the 1970s, many of these wider responsibilities found some form of institutional expression.

Outwith the Scottish Arts Council, the Royal Scottish Academy of Music and Drama (RSAMD) continued to provide the backbone of professional theatre training, offering diploma qualifications for both actors and speech and drama teachers. The methodology of the drama school was eclectic rather than philosophically driven, and was responsive to the needs of the profession. Hence, in 1962, television studies were introduced in association with BBC Scotland and, in the 1970s, Received Pronunciation gradually ceased to be the dominant speech mode. A Speech and Drama diploma was also developed, after 1973, at Queen Margaret College in Edinburgh and, in the 1980s, the emphasis shifted towards acting, providing an alternative to the RSAMD. In the 1980s, some colleges of Further Education introduced Foundation and Certificate courses in Theatre Studies.

From its inception the RSAMD drama school enjoyed a close relationship with Glasgow University. The University formed a department of Theatre Studies (now the Department of Theatre, Film and Television Studies) under James Arnott in 1966 and, to date, Glasgow remains the only fully-fledged theatre department in a Scottish university, though others offer theatre-course options. In 1981 the Scottish Theatre Archive was established at Glasgow University with the initial support of the SAC. It is now part of the University Library's Special Collections and has grown to be the most important theatre research resource in Scotland. The relationship between the RSAMD and Glasgow University was altered in 1994 when the Academy was granted its own degree-awarding powers, but cooperation continues with the proposed development of postgraduate courses in scenography, playwriting and direction. These are important initiatives, since the overall weakness of professional theatre training in Scotland to date has been its almost exclusive focus on acting.

Also outside the Scottish Arts Council umbrella, the amateur movement has continued to be serviced by the Scottish Community Drama Association

(SCDA), with modest support from the Scottish Office towards an advisory or tutoring service. To some extent this is an accident of history attributable to the fact that the SCDA predates the Arts Council. None the less, the Arts Council's Royal Charter clearly embraces the amateur arts, and the 1993 *Charter for the Arts in Scotland* affirmed the place of the amateur movement in Scottish theatre. Community theatre, which brings together the professional and amateur sectors is an active concern of the SAC. A similar mixed system of support applied to the vigorous youth theatre movement that sprang up in the 1970s. The Scottish Youth Theatre was begun in 1977, with funding from both the Scottish Office Education Department and the Scottish Arts Council. Its role in serving professional theatre by feeding in new talent, and education by offering access to professional skills and experience, has proved invaluable.

The community theatre movement has, by its nature, been the least institutionalised branch of Scottish theatre, though none the less influential in reaching new audiences and redefining the relationship between artistic product and creative process. The longest-running community event is the Craigmillar Arts Festival in Edinburgh, which was already celebrating its tenth anniversary in 1970, but many others followed. Equally significant in theatre terms was the way in which professional companies, led first by TAG (Theatre about Glasgow) and 7:84, worked with local people in community projects and productions. These became more ambitious in scale and artistic conception in the 1980s and 1990s. Theatre Workshop, which began life as a children's drama centre, broadened its remit in the early 1970s to provide a community service for all ages. In 1974 the Workshop secured its first SAC revenue grant and, in 1976, it moved to its present premises in Edinburgh's Stockbridge. Robert Palmer, the first director of the new building, went on to become drama director of the SAC, and the influence of the Workshop philosophy can be seen on Arts Council policies as well as on the work of other theatre companies in the 1980s.

Children's theatre, or more narrowly professional theatre for children, was relatively late in achieving a coherent development in Scotland. Theatre Workshop made a pioneering contribution but, until 1968, the main provider outside the pantomime season was Bertha Waddell's Children's Theatre, which was founded in 1927. Her approach was firmly child-centred and her company was immensely successful in reaching a wide audience due to its small scale and mobility. Though touring companies, such as Borderline and TAG, and venue-based companies produced some work for children, after the close of Bertha Waddell's heroic marathon the mainstay of touring theatre for children was puppetry, until the emergence in the 1990s of companies such as Visible Fictions and Hullabaloo dedicated to children's work. This process was given a major boost by the establishment, in 1991, of the Scottish International Children's Festival by Duncan Low, who drew particularly on Canadian models to provide a benchmark of quality in this important field. During the same period, Stuart Paterson developed from his early beginnings with TAG into a major writing talent, whose skilful original plays, crafted as classic adaptations, offered a real alternative to pantomime treatments. Puppetry achieved its own parallel developments with the annual Puppet and Animation Festival in the Lothians and the work of the Mask and Puppet Centre in Glasgow but, despite attempts to place this theatre art form in its European and international contexts, the Scottish public continued to regard puppetry as a medium exclusively for children.

Figure 5.13 Stuart Paterson's The Snow Queen, *Dundee Rep Theatre, 1990/1.* (Anthony Brannan/Dundee Rep)

In 1967 TAG became the Citizens' Theatre for Youth, performing for schools but also for the wider community. In its early years TAG was less differentiated than it later became from a clutch of educationally orientated companies (including Theatremakers at the MacRobert Arts Centre, TIE-Up in Inverness and Theatre-in-Education offshoots at Pitlochry, Dundee and Edinburgh) which were created between 1967 and 1971. In fact, the boundary between professional performances for children and young people, and theatre as part of a curricular learning process was blurred. The first wave of professional TIE (Theatre in Education) in Scotland collapsed due to funding pressures on the Scottish Arts Council and to the way work in schools hovered uneasily between education authorities and the centralised mechanisms for professional arts support. This uncomfortable situation was made more uncomfortable by local government reorganisation in 1976, in which theatre support became a District Council responsibility and education a Regional Council function. It took a decade for arts organisations and Councils to establish working patterns of cooperation and support and to create the conditions which would allow new growth in theatre for children and young people in and out of schools. In 1996 local government was reorganised once again into unitary authorities; the long-term consequences for the theatre remain to be seen.

In 1977 the Young report *Drama in Scottish Schools* recommended that all children should have an experience of live theatre, without fully articulating the financial means by which this might be achieved. The report, produced to some extent in response to the TIE collapse, was a mark of theatre's increasing academic respectability in Scotland, which was finally sealed in 1993 when Drama was made an examinable subject at Standard Grade. This was followed, in 1994, by Higher Grade Drama, which included a major component specifically on Scottish theatre. Issues of artistic form and literary analysis are curiously absent from the Scottish component, which favours themes such as popular theatre, gender studies and the treatment of history. None the less, it was a valuable beginning and created a need for access to Scottish theatre texts which has not yet been satisfactorily met.

A NATIONAL THEATRE?

The catalogue of theatre development in Scotland between 1950 and 1995 is remarkable, yet to theatre practitioners there has often seemed to be a lack of overall coherence and progression. Is this simply a product of chronic funding problems and of Scotland's geographical and cultural diversity, or has there been a failure of consistency in the growth of theatre policy and institutions? Throughout this period there has continued to be a steady loss of professional theatre talent from Scotland, even among those who would have preferred to centre their career development on Scottish theatre, film and television. Is there an elusive cohesion and economic integration still to be sought, and is it right that a single organisation – the Scottish Arts Council – should be the policy maker, the support mechanism for existing theatre organisations and the agency which implements new development? These questions and, to some extent, frustrations have informed discussion and debate in Scotland since the arts began to be subsidised. They have tended to gravitate, not necessarily in a helpful way, around the issue of whether Scotland should have a National Theatre.

One root of this argument is cultural and relates theatre, as a public art form, to language and identity. This was clearly the impulse behind the formation of the Scottish Actors Company in 1970, which is described by Andrew Cruickshank in his autobiography:

> A group of us, Fulton Mackay, Roddy McMillan, Una McLean, Alex McCrindle and Cochrane Duncan, faced with the great diversity around us, thought a space should be found for a Scottish, distinctive voice. It was really born out of a particular enthusiasm provided by Bridie and the Citizens' Theatre. We were aware of the fragments of society broken up by the appeal of the new range of entertainment, radio, film, television, theatre. And acutely conscious of language, as between English, Scots, Lallans. And ultimately the roots of identity... The closeness of England had through the centuries created an ambivalent attitude to the language... Yet when our actors used English they revealed an idiosyncrasy (as in Duncan Macrae and Alastair Sim), and toughness that was not natural to the English character. It was something of this that we wanted to present.[8]

The same cultural and artistic motives underlay the conference convened at Edinburgh University in 1986 by the Advisory Council for the Arts in Scotland, a voluntary body which inaugurated a decade of fitful campaigning for a National Theatre Company.[9]

The Scottish Actors Company folded in 1973 but its sense of the Scottish identity as a challenging and, to a large extent, unexpressed vehicle for theatre art lay behind the early 1970s success of the Lyceum and Chris Parr's work at the Traverse later in the decade. The argument had, it would seem, been vindicated in the work of a new generation of Scottish playwrights and by the positive responses of the public that came to see the plays, pushing up theatre attendances in the first half of the decade. But the resurgence was led by actors, directors, designers, technicians and critics, and therein lay the source of its creative strength, and its institutional weakness. Personnel and policies at both the Lyceum and the Traverse changed, just as the Glasgow Citizens' changed in the 1960s from the theatre most concerned with Scottish writing to one determinedly unconcerned. Moreover, throughout this period the producing theatres continued the pragmatic, mixed programme policy which had weathered the storms of the 1960s largely intact at Perth, Dundee, Pitlochry and the Byre. By the end of the decade the resurgence began to look increasingly homeless.

One early response to the problem of continuity was the formation, in 1973, of the Scottish Society of Playwrights (SSP). The SSP could not, by definition, do the whole job, but it did undertake a support and representation service for playwrights, organising rehearsed readings, conferences and the duplication and publication of scripts. In 1981 the excellent *Scottish Theatre News* was launched, picking up from where Kenneth Roy's pioneering magazine *Scottish Theatre* had left off in 1973. These publications provided a vital, independent forum for discussion and debate. In the words of Hector Mac-Millan, one of the moving spirits, 'the writers just sensed there was much to be done, and it could be done'.[10]

Much was achieved over ten years but, in 1985 the SSP lost its Arts Council grant, principally because it did not fit into the 1980s' regime of management accountability, sponsorship and the maximisation of earned income. Cultural purpose and achievement were not, in the end, sufficient, and the SSP was left to undertake the narrower but necessary task of defending playwrights in negotiation with theatre managements. Perhaps the SSP should have been more realistic about the funding climate, but in this case the wider ongoing role and vision was lost primarily because of a change in the Arts Council's priorities. Weaknesses in the SSP's own structures could have been remedied had that been the real issue.

The cultural case for theatre development is seen at its clearest in Gaelic theatre, which, on the one hand, echoes the National Theatre argument while at the same time challenging the meaning of 'national', given Scotland's linguistic and cultural diversity. In this area the Scottish Arts Council was prepared to undertake a large grant commitment through the formation, in 1978, of Fir Chlis, a professional Gaelic touring company. Unfortunately, Fir Chlis folded traumatically in 1981, leaving considerable deficits and a sense of failure and disappointment. Gaelic drama still had its lively amateur clubs, which might have offered a better starting point. In the mid 1980s the formation of Comunn na Gàidhlig, followed by significant Scottish Office funding for Gaelic broadcasting and the emergence of the National Gaelic Arts Project, provided new forums and possibilities for development. In 1995 SAC funding was earmarked for a new professional Gaelic touring company, TOSG, whose debut production in 1996 was *Taighean na Mara* by George Gunn.

The Gaelic situation has remained a special case. The main policy developments in Scottish theatre have not been driven by cultural arguments concerning language and identity. This is clearly demonstrated by the way the Scottish Arts Council handled the National Theatre issue from 1970 onwards. As previously indicated, the Arts Council was forced, in the late 1950s, to modify its almost exclusive commitment to regional theatre development, based on the producing theatres, because of the collapse of the commercial theatre circuit and the crisis in the large-scale touring theatres which ensued in the 1960s. In 1970 the now Scottish Arts Council undertook an internal review, which was published as *Theatre in Scotland* and described itself as 'less a report than a working paper'. The starting points of this influential document are the problem of the large-scale theatres and what the authors (staff members and selected committee members of the Council) see as the inadequate return on investment in the regional repertory companies. This deficit is measured in terms of box-office figures, programme quality, commitment to artistic development and the poor state of many theatre buildings consequent on the failure to date to construct new civic cultural centres.

As always with reviews of Scottish theatre, the problems are easier to list than the solutions. Options aired in the 'working paper' included a national touring agency, a theatre investment fund and a national touring company. The last could be either a completely new organisation, an extension of an existing building-based repertory company (probably the Lyceum), or the transplant of Bristol's Prospect Theatre Company to Scotland (in the same way the Western Theatre Ballet had moved to Glasgow to become Scottish Theatre Ballet). Whatever its origin, the aim under this option was a national drama company able to stand alongside Scottish Opera and the Ballet. What clinched the argument, albeit in a tentative manner, was the promise of a new Opera House and Lyric Theatre in Edinburgh, which in combination with the Lyceum would provide an adequate base with national status and an appropriate three-masted flagship.

This policy vision is far removed from the cultural purpose articulated by the founders of the Scottish Actors Company and the Scottish Society of Playwrights. As if to emphasise this point, *Theatre in Scotland* pushes the logically opposite standpoint:

> What Scottish theatre-goers want by and large is to be able to see a range of plays and players, and a company of Scottish actors is hard-pressed to fulfil properly the requirements of this kind of audience. We believe indeed that theatre directors in Scotland must be free to employ a company of foreign actors should this be appropriate to their season of plays and to public taste.

In this context, the majority of the Scottish population, which was still devoted to popular theatre and variety, did not count as either theatre-goers or as a constituent of public taste; a glaring example of the state-subsidised arts at their paternalistic worst. But the vital point is the contrast between the perspective of the cultural planners, and the energies which were actually to breathe new life into the existing theatres within months, rather than years, of the report's publication. The Scottish Arts Council's 'national theatre' was to be *The Cherry Orchard* (with Russian actors?), not *Willie Rough*, *The Hardman* or *The Widows of Clyth*.

Remarkably the 'working paper' of 1970 was translated into action, and over the next few years the Lyceum received substantial enhancement funding in preparation for its flagship status. Ironically the scheme came to feed off the resurgence of Scottish theatre in which the Lyceum company played such a prominent role, but when the plans for Edinburgh's international Lyric Theatre stalled and then failed, so did the SAC's policy. Paradoxically, the planners' vision turned out to be more insubstantial than the cultural one. As the 1970s progressed, Scottish Arts Council thinking was altered by the political climate and the build-up to devolution towards a more Scottish and populist policy, but this was fulfilled through the existing theatres and funding for the new touring companies.

It could be argued that Scottish Theatre as a whole did not lose out from the failure of the policy makers, but was, in fact, saved from a top-heavy centralising institution. This, however, is rationalisation after the fact, since what occurred was not the triumph of some higher wisdom but a disturbing disjunction between the gurus of state patronage and the realities of cultural change. Between 1967–8 and 1991–2, the proportion of the Scottish Arts Council's budget expended on drama plummeted from 33 to 17 per cent, because there was no national structure to compete with the Scottish National Orchestra, Scottish Ballet and the subsidy-consuming Scottish Opera. Some will argue that this is a simplistic view, but the actualities of resource politics are often crude. Repeatedly, Scottish Opera's flagship status for the Scottish arts gained it a share of available resources quite disproportionate to its audience or its relationship to Scottish social and cultural life. This situation was camouflaged in the 1970s by the large overall increases in arts funding, which outstripped inflation at 20 to 25 per cent. But in the 1980s Scottish Opera continued to receive increases beyond inflation when the major theatre companies were squeezed by a reduction in real terms of SAC support. During the same period, Scottish theatre companies as a whole increased their audiences and self-earned income, but struggled to maintain and improve their artistic standards or to gain any recognition of their national cultural role. Institutionally, it was as if the artistic gains of the 1970s had never been, and the battles were all to be fought again in the more difficult circumstances of the succeeding decade.

THEATRE IN THE 1980s

Theatre is, of necessity, a social art; consequently it is political. In the 1950s, Scottish theatre was part of the post-war reconstruction of British society, though, outside the emerging subsidy system, dissenting Scots voices spoke with a popular accent. In the 1960s, social values were challenged and theatres struggled to find new directions on which artists, audiences and patrons could agree. The 1970s brought an underlying sense of artistic purpose because, regardless of differing cultural tastes, there was a shared mood, as opposed to an agreed agenda, that Scottishness had a future which was better than its past. In 1979, Devolution was disallowed by Parliament, despite a referendum majority vote in Scotland in favour of it. In the same year, a new Conservative administration under Margaret Thatcher began its move to the political right, which increasingly alienated even Unionism's natural supporters in Scotland. As Scotland's Conservative MPs dwindled in number at each succeeding British election victory, Scotland became a managed rather than a governed society, dependent on its local authorities, the broadcast media and its artists for its sense of social cohesion.

If the media were already recognised as the fourth estate, in the 1980s the Scottish arts became a fifth estate. Everything theatre did in this situation was political by implication, and the Scottish Arts Council was left on a knife edge, managing the arts on behalf of the political administration while caretaking a vital area of political freedom. As the decade proceeded and public expenditure was cut, the knife edge became sharper.

It is in accord with this analysis that the dashed hopes of the 1979 Devolution referendum were accompanied by an upsurge, and not a downturn, in theatrical endeavour, though at the time the immediate impact of the new administration was financial constraint. Notwithstanding, in 1979, 7:84 toured *Joe's Drum*, a typically direct political response; TAG began their series of small-scale, high-energy Shakespeare productions under Ian Wooldridge; Wildcat Stage Productions burst into music–theatre action with *The Complete History of Rock 'N Roll*; and Winged Horse Touring Productions was formed by John Carnegie. Cumbernauld Theatre and the Brunton Theatre in Musselburgh opened in 1979, and planning began for the conversion of the Tron Church into a home for the newly founded Glasgow Theatre Club, which aimed, in some respects, to take up where the Close had left off.

In the next three years, Communicado, Theatre Alba and, in the north-east, Guizers Theatre all began operations as touring companies, devising and producing innovative work, while Theatre Workshop launched a small-scale touring company with Tom Lannon's *Year of the Cabbage*. In this period Borderline built on its established reputation for touring popular Scottish and children's work with a commitment to the theatre of Franco Rame and Dario Fo, so securing another important Scottish author-by-adoption. Just as audiences in previous decades had seen themselves in the frequent Scottish productions of Molière, so audiences in the 1980s saw their new situation in Fo's political theatre. In the early 1980s Cumbernauld Theatre began to tour its productions, and the Netherbow in Edinburgh began to function as a small-scale venue for new Scottish writing. Also in Edinburgh, the Festival Fringe, which had experienced major growth in the 1970s under full-time administrators John Milligan and Alistair Moffat, increased exponentially in size, if not always in quality, through the decade. In Glasgow, in 1982, 7:84's 'Clydebuilt Season' of Scottish popular theatre from the 1920s, 1930s and 1940s paved the way for the foundation of Mayfest in 1983. At the heart of this new festival was a commitment to popular Scottish and international theatre.

The new touring wave followed where 7:84 had led in taking theatre to unestablished venues and fresh audiences. The number of small- and medium-scale theatres also began to increase. The new companies offered actors, writers, directors and designers the chance to experiment and develop in a way the older theatres could not allow for reasons of economic safety. The 1970s had

Figure 5.14 Robbie Coltrane in Dario Fo's Mistero Buffo, *Borderline Theatre Company, 1990.* (Brian Lochrin)

made Scottish theatre a goal to aim for, and a generation of new talent, too numerous to list, needed outlets. Some of the new companies, such as Gerry Mulgrew's Communicado, reacted against the explicit politics of 7:84's earlier work, seeking to express their politics through a low-cost theatre of the imagination, which evaded the class-bound conventions of naturalism without falling back on the techniques of music hall and variety. A more physical style of acting also developed, with music and movement and less emphasis on text. In effect, this was a new wave of National Theatre development, which was diverse and eclectic in method but motivated by a common impulse to engage audiences in an artistic experience that would change perceptions and constitute an imaginative community of resistance to prevailing economic and social trends. The Fringe and Mayfest provided arenas in which this kind of work could reach a wide audience and gain media attention.

Something of the same impetus lay behind the formation in, 1981, of the Scottish Theatre Company (STC), which was to provide a parallel layer of larger-scale touring theatre. Ewan Hooper's SAC-funded 1979 study, *A New Scottish Theatre*, which was the catalyst for STC, leans heavily on the cultural case for a company devoted to performing and developing a Scottish repertoire. An initial turnover of £600,000 was envisaged, with a Glasgow base and regular performance dates at the Theatre Royal alongside Scottish Opera and Scottish Ballet. In 1980 the Scottish Theatre Trust, the legal progenitor of the Scottish Theatre Company, was formed and funds were provided by the SAC to commission new plays from Marcella Evaristi, Billy Kay and Tom McGrath.

What counted in this process, however, was not Hooper's report but the decisions and announcements of the Scottish Arts Council. A decade earlier, in 1971, when the initiative to give the Lyceum international status was conceived, the SAC had said:

> The Council and the Board of the Royal Lyceum Theatre have agreed in principle to establish gradually over a three year period a Scottish Theatre Company comparable to Scottish Opera and Scottish Theatre Ballet, to provide for audiences in Scotland and elsewhere an international repertoire of drama at the highest standard, and within this concept to explore Scottish Traditions by encouraging substantially but not exclusively Scottish playwrights, directors, players, designers, technicians and administrators.[11]

A decade later both the tone and the scale had altered:

> At the beginning of a new decade, SAC has welcomed the establishment of the Scottish Theatre Company, founded to build a repertoire consisting of Scottish plays and of Scottish adaptations of the major world

classics . . . One of the aims of the new company will be to take a varied programme of plays to theatres which do not have a permanent company.[12]

Initial grants from the SAC's drama department to STC were £50,000 and then £75,000, which was much less in real terms than the Lyceum had received in enhancement funding towards its new role a decade before. But additional subsidies were made available through the SAC's separate touring department to enable 'a substantial tour of the major touring theatres in Scotland'.

From the begining, there was a fatal ambiguity in the aims and intentions of the SAC in funding the Scottish Theatre Company. If the purpose of the venture was primarily repertoire development, then the company needed to operate on a medium-scale basis to interact with existing theatre networks and maximise its touring circuit within Scotland. Instead, the fledgling company was schizophrenically co-funded by another committee to undertake semi-commercial touring to the large-scale theatres, which no one else in Scotland could fill apart from TV stars and the surviving heroes of variety and pantomime such as Stanley Baxter and Jimmy Logan. Moreover, the large-scale Scottish theatre circuit was too small by itself to sustain the number of weeks required to recoup a reasonable proportion of the investment needed to mount a large-scale production in the first place.

Ewan Hooper fulfilled his repertoire remit with a bold programme which included Bill Bryden's *Civilians*, Robert Kemp's Scots Molière *Let Wives Tak Tent* and an outstanding reworking of Tom McGrath's *Animal*, but the financial outcome of the initial progammes left the company in severe deficit. Tom Fleming was brought in to save the day, and the extraordinary thing was not that he ultimately failed but that he nearly succeeded, with some substantial help from the Edinburgh Festival. Fleming's Festival revival of *Ane Satyre of the Thrie Estaitis*, the Mayfest production of *Waiting for Godot* with Walter Carr, John Grieve and Phil McCall, and the triumphant tour to Poland in 1986, came close to fulfilling something of the 1971 vision as much as that of 1981. But much else in between was underfunded, sometimes artistically backward looking, and always hamstrung by the attempt to fulfil two conflicting remits. In the end, the large-scale touring theatre managers effectively ended STC's five-year existence by withdrawing their support. After a pause for review, the SAC followed suit with a measure of relief.

The hurt and embarrassment surrounding the troubles and demise of the Scottish Theatre Company reflected the significance of the company's cultural aims and a degree of dismay at the way they had been frustrated and mishandled. In particular, STC had displayed the strength and range of Scottish acting in the talents of Ron Bain, Edith McArthur, Gerda Stevenson, Iain Cuthbertson, Alec Heggie, Vivien Heilbron, Robert Urquhart, Anne-Louise Ross and many more. It is no insult to the achievements of either Ewan Hooper or Tom Fleming and their companies to say that the SAC should either have initiated a properly resourced, large-scale touring venture, capable of reaching beyond the Scottish circuit as the other national companies already did, or have devoted available funds to the strengthening of Scottish repertoire through the existing venue-based and touring companies, backed up by a revamped Scottish Society of Playwrights or Scottish Theatre Institute to provide some necessary continuity. Between 1976–7 and 1985–6, attendances at subsidised theatres had risen from 570,000 to 700,000, excluding the expanding community sector.[13] Earned income had also increased significantly in real terms. Scottish theatre did not need, or deserve, a high-profile failure at this time. It is revealing that during the same period which included the STC initiative, the SAC's overall support for theatre, in marked contrast to its treatment of Scottish Opera, fell in real terms, leading the Drama Committee of 1987 to state that 'the current funding level for theatre was no longer adequate to maintain the standards of existing drama companies'.

It is against this background that the struggles and achievements of the established building-based companies in the 1980s must be measured, since, in effect, they were being squeezed to pay for developments elsewhere and to satisfy the new Arts Council emphasis on management, marketing, sponsorship and self-earned income. Programmes were severely constrained as small casts became the norm, and ticket prices were forced upwards. Despite these circumstances, the theatres adapted and, in most cases, did much more than just survive. The situation was eased by local authorities coming to support the cause of improved theatre facilities. Between 1980 and 1992, long-awaited new theatres at Dundee and Pitlochry were built; the Citizens', Perth and the Royal Lyceum were refurbished; large-scale touring theatres such as His Majesty's in Aberdeen and the Edinburgh King's were upgraded; and new theatre spaces were developed at the Tramway, the Arches and the Tron in Glasgow, the Lemon Tree in Aberdeen, and the new Traverse in Edinburgh. As the relative value of the SAC central budget declined, there was more emphasis on partnership with local authorities, but this would have fallen on deaf ears had there not been political will. To some extent, arguments about the economic and social benefits of the arts had proved effective, as tourism and the service industries seemed to offer a post-industrial lifeline, but culture was also one of the few areas left in which local councils had any freedom of political manoeuvre. Between 1982–3 and 1992–3, local-government expenditure on the arts in Scotland increased in real terms by 128 per cent, to £35.5 million.[14] During the same period the SAC budget increased in real terms by 23 per cent to £23 million. In addition, drama and theatre accounted for 40 per cent of local-government arts expenditure compared to 4.5 per cent on opera, a remarkable inversion of the SAC position, and a clear indication that theatre had a broad cultural base in Scotland. Without this local-authority investment the building-based regional companies could not have survived the 1980s.

Perth and Pitlochry reacted to the new decade with highly professional marketing, enhanced visitor facilities and safe programming. Joan Knight's Perth Theatre was held up as the exemplar of the 1980s, with 90 per cent of seats sold by subscription, consumer loyalty, and a careful commitment to one or two serious dramas each season. Pitlochry had to fight harder for local-authority support, but compensated with its 'theatre-in-the-hills' tourist appeal. After an inevitably unsettled period under Sue Wilson, following Kenneth Ireland's retirement in 1988, Pitlochry secured the services of Clive Perry, who brought his own distinctive flair to the art of safe programming while managing to retain one of the few large acting companies to survive the decade. The Byre, meanwhile, was compelled by the modest size of both its auditorium and its grants to play very safe, until the 1990s brought a sense of adventure to St Andrews in the shape of Maggie Kinloch and then Ken Alexander.

Dundee's modern theatre space invited a different kind of development under Robert Robertson, with theatre, community drama and dance advancing together. Successes such as Billy Kay's *They Fairly Mak Ye Work*, based on Dundee's jute industry, a revival of John Byrne's *The Slab Boys*, Stuart Paterson's plays for children, and the epic community drama *Witch's Blood* forged a new relationship between the theatre and the city. At the same time Joanna Lumley's appearances in Ibsen and Chekhov provided the kind of leading-lady glamour which Dundee's public and Councillors still relished. After a fallow period at the turn of the decade, Robertson's 1990s' successor Hamish Glen revived the spirit of creative endeavour which had characterised the theatre since its time at Lochee Road.

In Glasgow, the Citizens' company continued to flourish, undaunted by its growing artistic status. Ahead of the Royal Shakespeare Company and London's National Theatre, the Citizens' pioneered, in its own inimitable style, the kind of large-scale adaptation of novels which was to dominate the next fifteen years of British theatre. *A Waste of Time* (*A la Recherche du Temps Perdu*), *The Last Days of Mankind* and *Anna Karenina* provided only one strand in the eclectic international dramaturgy, and the determination to create theatre rather than the acting of texts. When Glasgow received the accolade of European City of Culture in 1990 the Citizens' was not the least of the reasons, and a powerful *Mother Courage*, designed and directed by Philip Prowse, with Glenda Jackson in the lead, topped the theatre's achievements.

Glasgow in the 1980s, however, was a changed city in search of new theatre metaphors. The Tron began life in 1981–2 as a writers' theatre. Its early programmes featured established 1970s' names such as Tom McGrath, Hector MacMillan, C. P. Taylor and John Byrne, as well as a wave of up-and-coming playwrights including Marcella Evaristi, Alan Spence, Liz Lochhead, Robert Forrest, Sue Glover, Peter Arnott and Rona Munro. The Tron's biggest impact, however, came at the end of the decade with a series of Scottish translations of the Québécois playwright Michel Tremblay, notably *The Guid Sisters*, produced at the Tron in 1989 and subsequently successfully toured to Toronto and Montreal. This story of a family that 'hits the Jackpot' with the equivalent of its Green Shield or Co-op stamps struck chords in Glasgow. But the real chemistry was one of language linking two minority cultures and simultaneously making an international artistic statement.

This upping of scale and artistic ambition owed much to the growth of Mayfest and to the European Year of Culture in 1990. The Tron reacted directly to the changing face of Glasgow with plays such as Iain Heggie's *Clyde Nouveau*, the Tremblay translations and, later in the 1990s' aftermath, with David Kane's *Dumbstruck*, a bleakly comic reversion to variety as a theatrical metaphor. Tron director Michael Boyd also shifted his 1990s' work in response to the new artistic experiences which international status brought to Glasgow's Tramway space in the shape of Peter Brook, Peter Stein, Robert Lepage and the Maly Theatre of St Petersburg. At the Tron, *Crow*, *The Bloody Chamber* (the work of Associate Director Caroline Hall) and *The Trick is to Keep Breathing* were all adaptations in which the director's visual and structural creativity had free rein.

In Edinburgh, the Traverse began the 1980s with a degree of creative burnout, though, before his departure in 1981, Chris Parr had played midwife to Tom McGrath's stylistically and technically innovative *1–2–3*. Peter Lichtenfels, Parr's successor, shifted the Traverse back towards an emphasis on the Edinburgh Festival and its role beyond Scotland. Among his successes were Liz Lochhead's *Blood and Ice* and Claire Luckham's *Trafford Tanzi*, with international input from the Market Theatre of Johannesburg's *Woza Albert!* and Teatr Stary's *Nastasia Filipovna*. None the less, audiences were at a low ebb and the SAC, resolved to extract better 'value for money' from the heavily subsidised operation, pruned its grants.

Between 1984 and 1987, under Lichtenfels's successor, Jenny Killick, the Traverse stimulated a rich new seam of writing talent, which included Chris Hannan, Simon Donald, Peter Arnott, John Clifford and, less directly, Sue Glover. During this period Clifford's *Losing Venice* provided the theatre with an international touring success, while his later *The Light in the Village* pointed the way forward, like *The Guid Sisters*, to an internationalism which was also rooted in Scotland. Unfortunately, Killick, whose main commitment was to her own direction, had very little sense of the Traverse's role in Scotland. Her Grassmarket regime flashed brilliantly but briefly and, faced with financial restrictions on the theatre's production schedule in 1988, she resigned. Had Killick stayed on to nurture her group of writers in the way that Chris Parr had

Figure 5.15 Chris Hannan's Elizabeth Gordon Quinn, *Traverse Theatre, 1985.*
(David Liddle: Scottish Theatre Archive)

done, Scottish playwriting in the 1990s would have been in a much stronger position. Killick's departure for film school was a portent of things to come.

Under Leslie Lawton, and then Ian Wooldridge, the Royal Lyceum, Edinburgh's principal producing theatre, failed to take fire. Compared to Clive Perry and Stephen MacDonald in the 1970s, the Lawton regime wavered between competent showmanship and the hackneyed. Ian Wooldridge's arrival from TAG began a new era but his physical and visual theatre style always seemed ill at ease in the Lyceum. However, his *Mother Courage*, in which the stage doors were flung open to reveal the stark profile of Edinburgh Castle, Tom McGrath's adaptation of Tankred Dorst's *Merlin*, and the Christmas productions of Stuart Paterson's plays were highpoints in a directorship which did go some way towards re-establishing the Lyceum as a base for Scottish acting and writing talent.

Another TAG Director, Ian Brown, followed Wooldridge to Edinburgh to succeed Jenny Killick at the Traverse in 1988. Under Brown, the Traverse moved, in 1992, to the new theatre under the Scottish Financial Centre which was built on the now culturally notorious Castle Terrace gap site, the 'Hole-in-the-Ground', which had been the intended site of the capital's new Opera House. Despite the best efforts of Edinburgh District Council's Labour administration, the Lyceum and the Traverse were unable to agree on joint operation of the new theatre space. The failure of two managements, both nursing straitened production resources, to collaborate in a multi-venue enterprise was regrettable. Despite some impressive successes, not least Sue Glover's *Bondagers*, the new Traverse quickly began to seem like a fashionable receiving theatre, while a reinvigorated Lyceum, under Kenny Ireland, clearly needed a variety of spaces to display its talents to best effect. Throw into the equation Gerry Mulgrew's Communicado company, which was based at the Lyceum during this period but provided a main strand of Traverse programming, and the scale of the missed opportunity in the early 1990s becomes apparent. At this time, Edinburgh's theatre community badly needed to anticipate the commercial challenge of the Festival Theatre, the Playhouse and the King's all competing to attract theatre audiences.

Even this brief survey of the 1980s reveals the extent to which Scottish theatre had come to depend for its development on the touring companies. It is, therefore, disturbing to record that in 1987, 7:84, the pathfinder company in touring, community outreach and festival development, lost the flair and theatrical intelligence of John McGrath as producer, director and playwright. The start of 7:84's troubles lay, ironically, in the success of the 1982 Clydebuilt Season of Scottish plays from the 1930s, 1940s and 1950s, which saw the company operating on a different scale and in a very different way from its previous touring incarnation. The season redefined possibilities for Scottish theatre as a whole by establishing a creative ancestry for popular and political theatre on which a new repertoire could be built. Not all of the plays, which included Joe Corrie's *In Time of Strife*, Ewan McColl's *Johnny Noble* and Ena Lamont Stewart's *Men Should Weep*, were equally successful, but a rich dramatic resource was demonstrated. *Men Should Weep* anticipated the 1980s in rewriting the genre of male, working-class drama, and gave context and heart to an emerging group of Scottish women playwrights. At this point, 7:84 desperately needed a new structure and a higher level of subsidy to enable it to move away from the small-scale touring treadmill, build on its 1982 achievements, and allow McGrath time to plan the next development. Instead the Scottish Theatre Company was already consuming the Scottish Arts Council's financial room for manoeuvre, while the changed political climate introduced a new wariness into the Council's attitude towards the company. 7:84 began to move into a position of conflict with its principal funder.

The problem was also political in a wider sense, as well as creative and organisational. During the 1970s, 7:84's message was iconoclastic, but predicated on hope that a radical analysis would lead to social and political progress. In the 1980s, the underlying hope had gone, pushing McGrath into an artistically difficult position of antagonism and alienation. This came to a head in the critically unpopular reworking of Aristophanes' *Women in Power* at the 1983 Edinburgh Festival, which divided 7:84 loyalists, led to a cancelled tour, and left McGrath in an exposed position. McGrath's isolation was compounded by the active hostility towards 7:84 England's 'Miners' Strike' tour of *Six Men of Dorset* in 1984, followed by the Arts Council's withdrawal of the English company's grant. The Scottish Arts Council was left between the rock of attracting the Conservative administration's notice, through its continued support for 7:84 Scotland, and the hard place of losing the already strained trust of the Scottish artistic community; so it prevaricated, awarded virtually standstill funding and pushed for management restructuring, while convincing itself that the company had run out of creative steam.

After 1982, McGrath concentrated on Highland touring with an adaptation of Fionn MacColla's *The Albannach*, *There is a Happy Land* and *Mairi Mhor, the Woman from Skye*. In these shows he fashioned a new relationship between

Figure 5.16 Sue Glover's Bondagers, *Traverse Theatre, 1991*. (Sean Hudson: Scottish Theatre Archive)

story-telling theatre and folk music, which later bore fruit, in 1989 and 1990, in his large-scale productions *Border Warfare* and *John Brown's Body*, and his adaptation, in 1994, of Neil Gunn's *The Silver Darlings*. However, all these later ventures were under the wing of Wildcat Stage Productions, since McGrath's resignation as artistic director of 7:84 in 1988 was effectively the SAC's price for the restoration of funding which it had withdrawn entirely earlier that year. In retrospect the withdrawal of funding is hard to justify on the basis of what 7:84 had achieved since 1980, nor was it vindicated by what the company achieved in the rest of the decade without John McGrath.

THE 1990s

If the 1980s was the decade of marketing, public relations became the 1990s' focus. Under the management of new director Seona Reid, the Scottish Arts Council, in association with other public bodies, launched its 'Charter' initiative, a large-scale consultative exercise on the future of the Scottish arts. Marginal adjustments in policy followed, such as a tiny percentage shift towards funding the traditional arts, which scored high in public-attitude surveys, and the setting up of a Working Party to examine the 'feasibility of a National Theatre Resource'. The main results were a worthwhile review of the 'state of the arts', ably summarised by Joyce McMillan,[15] and the promotion of the SAC itself as an agency for the arts offering information, expertise and advocacy, rather than just funding.

The 1990s continued the 1980s' trends towards a larger-scale, more physical style of theatre. Even subscription seasons could no longer guarantee audience loyalty unless there was a sense of event or occasion. Consequently, hard-pressed, building-based companies sought additional funding through special projects, tours and collaborations, while touring companies worked with festivals to ensure larger casts, media impact and high-tech production values. Peter Brooks's *Mahabharata*, at the Tramway in 1988, set a memorable standard of event marketing, though, as far back as 1980, Bill Bryden's National Theatre *The Mysteries* at the Edinburgh Festival had demonstrated the capacity of ensemble playing to break the mould of television naturalism and win back popular audiences for live theatre.

The existence of the Edinburgh International Festival and, later, Glasgow's Mayfest stimulated Scottish theatre throughout the post-war period by bringing international work to Scotland. In the mid 1990s the Edinburgh Festival celebrated its fiftieth anniversary and Mayfest (before it folded) its first decade, so proving the loyalty of the Scottish public to such keynote events. However, the prime importance of the festivals to the contemporary history of Scottish theatre has been their capacity to co-promote, and also co-produce, the work of Scottish companies. The marketing muscle and audience capacity of an

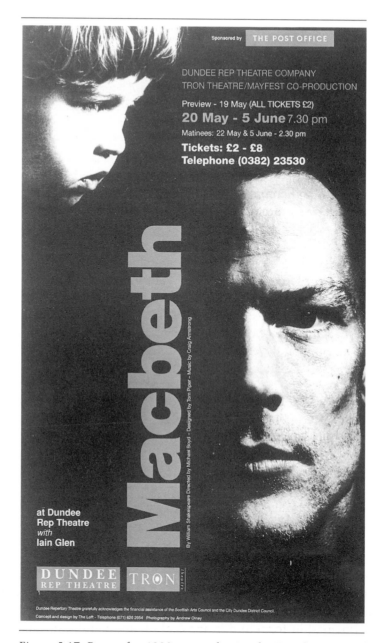

Figure 5.17 Poster for 1993 co-production by Dundee Rep and Glasgow's Tron Theatre of Macbeth *with Iain Glen.* (Tron Theatre)

Edinburgh Festival or a Mayfest run has effectively kept large-scale, large-cast professional theatre alive through lean times. The resultant sense of artistic ambition has benefited projects as culturally diverse as Glasgow Citizens' *Last Days of Mankind*, TAG's *A Scots Quair*, the Tron's version of C. P. Taylor's

Good and the Scottish Theatre Company's *Waiting for Godot*. It is unfortunate that Scottish theatre companies have not been resourced to transfer such successes abroad in the way that other nations subsidise their productions to come to Edinburgh and Glasgow.

One company which has developed a very Scottish form of ensemble process based on the strengths of the actors' imagination is Communicado. Communicado's work began at Theatre Workshop with the quest for new forms of political and community theatre. In director Gerry Mulgrew's hands text became just one aspect of the theatre process rather than its determinant, though some of the company's most successful performances, such as *Mary Queen of Scots Got Her Head Chopped Off* in 1987 and *Cyrano de Bergerac* in 1992, were based on a conjunction between the Communicado philosophy and the right kind of text, supplied in these cases by Liz Lochhead and Edwin Morgan respectively. In 1990 Communicado contributed to Glasgow's Year of Culture the epic experiment *Jock Tamson's Bairns*, a gigantic improvisation on Burns, which excited without fully satisfying, but overall the company has represented an original development in Scottish theatre art.

In 1987, Wildcat, originally a music theatre offshoot of 7:84, hit the jackpot with Tony Roper's *The Steamie*, which became the Scottish theatre's longest-running box-office success since Graham Moffat's mistitled rural satire *Bunty Pulls the Strings* in 1911. This warm-hearted celebration of Glasgow's lost community, seen from the wash-house perspective, confirmed that the old division between the play-going and the variety audience had been overtaken by the narrative music theatre of the 1980s and 1990s, though *The Steamie* also echoed an older genre of Scottish drama set at Hogmanay or some other key social ritual. As previously mentioned, Wildcat collaborated with John McGrath on three large-scale story-telling productions after *The Steamie* and, in 1994, toured a revival of Joan Littlewood's *Oh What a Lovely War*. During the same period, TAG also upped the scale of its work, achieving a major success with adaptations of Lewis Grassic Gibbon's *Sunset Song*, and then the whole *Scots Quair* trilogy. Once again this was narrative music theatre with an appeal to older communal rhythms. TAG's adaptation of Alasdair Gray's *Lanark* was more experimental in form and in musical idiom, and did not have the same box-office appeal.

7:84 Scotland entered a new phase in 1991 with the appointment of Iain Reekie as artistic director. The aim of the new team was to build on the work of John McGrath and his successor David Hayman, but to broaden the remit to include issues of personal politics and to find a way back into the changed communities of the 1990s. The result was a thoughtful commitment to new writing, extended rehearsal periods and a consistent outreach policy. The team's expressed reasoning behind the new policy is interesting, since it pinpoints

Figure 5.18 Tom Mannion in Cyrano de Bergerac, Communicado *Theatre
Company, 1992.* (Sean Hudson: Scottish Theatre Archive)

both the impact of the international theatre seasons in Glasgow and Edinburgh,
and the fundamental problems facing all Scottish companies who tried to rise
to the artistic challenge:

In recent years artists in this country have witnessed an influx of work
from abroad. Initially, this work left us in awe of the quality in the ideas

and the production. However, it was clear that some fairly fundamental differences existed between our work and theirs – minimum rehearsal times of two months, the development and continuation of work over years, ensemble companies and rigorous training, to name but a few. Present funding structures here obviously make it impossible for us to put all of these things into practice, but we felt that if our work was to develop properly we had not only to advocate change, but also to

Figure 5.19 Tony Roper's The Steamie, *Pitlochry Festival Theatre production, 1993.* (Sean Hudson: Scottish Theatre Archive)

institute it. Our first promise was that we would never rehearse anything for less than four weeks and we have stuck by this.[16]

To date this policy has borne fruit in productions such as Stephen Greenhorn's
Salt Wound and in the adaptation of Peter Sichrovsky's *Born Guilty*.

Another new direction was set by Clyde Unity Theatre, which looked for
its inspiration to the popular theatre traditions of Glasgow Unity and the
original 7:84 Scotland. Begun as a student company, Clyde Unity honed its art
by touring to community venues, often in large housing schemes. The result
was an impressive series of new plays by co-founders Aileen Ritchie and John
Binnie, which were unafraid of hard issues and sentiment, and able to engage
a demanding audience in small and large venues. Other new 1990s' companies
remained dependent on project funding from the SAC, and thus unable to plan
beyond the next production. Nevertheless, Wiseguise, Boilerhouse, Annexe
Theatre and Fifth Estate harnessed the energies and abilities of writers, directors
and actors to produce innovative, text-based and physical theatre work. The
emergence of Fifth Estate focused an unease about the neglect of playwrights
in favour of adaptation and spectacle and, from its base at the Netherbow

Figure 5.20 Clyde Unity Theatre's Accustomed to Her Face *by John Binnie, 1993.*
(Clyde Unity Theatre)

Theatre in Edinburgh, the company supported the work of George Rosie, Robert Forrest, Donald Campbell, Allan Sharpe and Stanley Eveling.

While touring and project companies pushed forward in a variety of directions, there was a revival in large-scale commercial touring theatre led by hit musicals such as *Les Miserables*, *Cats*, *Phantom of the Opera* and *Guys and Dolls*. In 1994 Edinburgh finally got its Lyric Theatre when the former Moss Empire (alias Mecca Bingo) was handsomely restored as the Festival Theatre. Since Apollo Leisure continued to operate the Playhouse and the city subsidised the King's as a touring house, this reintroduced the phenomenon of commercial competition to Edinburgh's theatres and placed the building-based producing companies in a situation of oversupply which has not yet been resolved. In Glasgow, in 1990, Bill Bryden created a large-scale visual spectacular *The Ship* in the former Harland and Wolff engine sheds; he followed this, in 1994, with *The Big Picnic*, a story-telling treatment of working-class Glasgow's share in the First World War. Attempts to transform the sheds into a permanent venue were frustrated, in 1995, by lack of SAC support, but the possibility of a new commercial venue south of the Clyde remained a live option.

The 1990s had left behind earlier polarities of popular versus art theatre, or Scottish versus Anglocentric culture, with which Scottish theatre had wrestled in the 1950s and 1960s. Audiences adapted flexibly to different styles and venues while moving comfortably along an axis of the Scottish and the international. The real issues now lay between the different elements in theatre-text, spectacle, music and idea, and the way the final theatre event revealed the values of its promoters and audience. The 1990s' tension was between those who grounded their creative process in real communities of experience and language, and those for whom the theatre event was part of a depersonalised consumer culture, in which marketing dictated content. This was the global situation around which a nexus of issues about the health of contemporary Scottish theatre clustered.

Translation has played a crucial role in theatre since the 1950s, because it is the link between the linguistic diversity of Scottish experience and the capacity of the indigenous theatre of a small northern European nation to absorb and reflect the international stage.[17] Translation also focused a characteristically Scottish concern for text and language which counterpointed the movement towards spectacle and visual theatre that had gathered pace through the 1980s and 1990s. Translation has increased in importance in Scottish theatre as part of the underlying linguistic confidence observable since the 1970s, because Scotland's trilingualism (Scots, Scots–English and Gaelic) thrives in the context of international cultural diversity in a way it was never entirely able to under the dominance of an artificially standardised southern English. Through translation, theatre production in Scotland could be seen as part of an international cultural ecology, or as the branch management of a global business.

Figure 5.21 Conversion of the 1928 Empire Theatre into the Edinburgh Festival Theatre, opened in 1994 to international acclaim as 'one of the best theatres in the world'. (Edinburgh Festival Theatre)

Another feature of the 1980s and 1990s was the increase in the number of women playwrights, balancing the predominantly male voices of the previous decade. These included Liz Lochhead, Sue Glover, Rona Munro, Marcella Evaristi, Sharman MacDonald and Anne-Marie di Mambro. Women writers brought new perspectives and experiences which enriched Scottish theatre and came to be reflected in the work of all playwrights, regardless of gender. In Jan McDonald's analysis:

> Despite the variety of backgrounds and settings . . . the women's plays consistently explore the relationship between national identity and culturally constituted codes of gender in which men and women are polarised into opposites and are arbitrarily allocated predetermined roles which inhibit fruitful relationships.[18]

The 1980s' playwrights widened the agenda just as, at the start of the 1970s, Stewart Conn had echoed and redefined the work of the 1950s. In *The Straw Chair* Sue Glover rewrote the genre of the Jacobite history play by foregrounding a personal tragedy of sexual politics against the 'romantic' background of a Hebridean island. Chris Hannan's *Elizabeth Gordon Quinn* remodelled the genre of heroic, male, working-class conflict, with an ambiguous female working-class heroine and a focus on the kind of women's rent strike which earns only a passing mention in Bill Bryden's *Willie Rough* in the early 1970s. In *Bold Girls* Rona Munro entered the same uncomfortable territory as Hector MacMillan's *The Sash* (1973), but from new perspectives. Twentieth-century Scottish theatre is alive with such echoes, refractions and revisions.

It is this irregular web of continuities and discontinuities, along with the re-emergence of a Scottish theatre profession since the Second World War, which can properly be described as a tradition, albeit a fragile one, which only the citizens of Scotland can reasonably be expected to sustain. The issue of responsibility was posed by the publication, in 1993, by the National Theatre for Scotland Campaign of a 'starter' list of 100 modern Scottish plays which might form the basis of a national theatre repertoire. Overall, the Campaign, the intensification of which coincided with the SAC's Working Party on a National Theatre Resource, failed to achieve momentum, but the repertoire list provoked a wide and lively debate because it tapped a common concern about the continuity of theatre writing as a litmus test for theatre health. The starter list was not a catalogue of twentieth-century masterpieces but its significance was perceptively summed up by Randall Stevenson:

> As well as suggesting a useful set of plays for revival or for the national repertoire, the list sketches a topography of the Scottish imagination in the 1990s whose markers for Scotland's present self-understanding, and what lies ahead, are at least as interesting as the past.[19]

As the Working Party proposed an, as yet, undefined 'Scottish National Theatre Initiative', the issue remained whether this imaginative landscape was to continue to depend on the individual preferences of artistic directors and managements, or whether there was a wider issue of responsibility, requiring some form of institutional definition.

In his stimulating introduction to *Scot-Free*, an anthology of plays from the 1980s, Alasdair Cameron, whose early death, in 1994, was an untimely loss to the nascent discipline of Scottish theatre history, presents an ebullient view of contemporary Scottish playwriting.[20] From his 1980s' perspective, however, Cameron tends to forget the experimental and political dimensions of the 1970s in favour of a general characterisation of earlier writing as male, working class and nostalgic. From the later viewpoint of a decade dominated by adaptations and narrative music theatre, it is incumbent to ask whether Scottish theatre in the last fifteen years has adequately responded to the changes in Scottish society. Has theatre writing in Scotland reflected the creation of an underclass, the loss of social cohesion, the disempowerment of employees and the increasing power of multinational business and the corporate state? Or has there been an inclination to become more safe and appealing, jettisoning a vital element of risk and danger? These unanswered mid-term questions were raised in an acute form by the theatrical hit of 1995, the adaptation of Irvine Welsh's best-selling novel *Trainspotting*. Moving swiftly from book to stage to screen, Welsh's portrayal of Edinburgh's narcotic sub-culture wavered uneasily between celebration, exposé and the exploitation of cult success marketing. The ultimate accolade of film adaptation required the sanitising of the novel and the stage adaptation's most authentic feature, its demotic Scots.

The year 1995 was not one of calm retrospect. The start of the National Lottery, and the allocation by statute of a proportion of its revenue to capital funding of the arts in Scotland, brought an unprecedented sudden influx of new money, doubling the Scottish Arts Council's disposable income overnight. At the same moment Hollywood discovered the appeal of Scottish myth and history with *Braveheart*, *Rob Roy* and *Loch Ness* achieving worldwide exposure in quick succession. Was this where the emphasis on adaptation and spectacle had been heading all along? Significantly, the one creative product, as opposed to bricks and cement, in which the SAC could invest its National Lottery winnings was film; productions of John Byrne's 1970s' play *The Slab Boys* and of Neil Gunn's novel *The Silver Darlings*, which 7:84 had dramatised, were scheduled to follow *Trainspotting* on to the big screen.

What will occupy Scotland's new and upgraded theatre spaces, and how will theatre react to the long-awaited birth of a Scottish film industry? These are the new questions. But the survival of live theatre and its vigorous contribution to Scotland's cultural development and self-questioning are not in doubt.

Notes

CHAPTER 1 BEGINNINGS TO 1700

1. The Plough Play is published as 'My Heartly Service' in *Music of Scotland*, ed. Kenneth Elliott and Helena Mennie Shire, *Musica Britannica XV* (London: Stainer and Bell, 1957), no. 30, pp. 141–7. See, too, Helena M. Shire and Kenneth Elliott, 'Pleugh Song and Plough Play', in *Saltire Review*, 2:6 (Winter 1955), pp. 39–44.
2. Sarah Carpenter, 'Early Scottish Drama', in *The History of Scottish Literature: Volume 1, Origins to 1660*, ed. R. D. S. Jack (Aberdeen: Aberdeen University Press, 1988), p. 201.
3. Walter Kennedy, *The Passioun of Crist*, in *Devotional Pieces in Verse and Prose*, ed. J. A. W. Bennett, Scottish Text Society (Edinburgh: William Blackwood, 1955), pp. 7–63. Dorothy W. Riach, 'Walter Kennedy's *The Passioun of Crist*: a reassessment', in *Scottish Literary Journal*, 9:1 (May 1982), pp. 5–20.
4. Simon Trussler, *Cambridge Illustrated History of British Theatre* (Cambridge: Cambridge University Press, 1994), p. 49.
5. I. D. McFarlane, *Buchanan* (London: Duckworth, 1981), p. 201.
6. *George Buchanan Tragedies*, ed. P. Sharratt and P. G. Walsh (Edinburgh: Scottish Academic Press, 1983), p. 1.
7. *The Cupar Proclamation* is included in Sir David Lindsay, *Ane Satyre of the Thrie Estaitis*, Canongate Classics 18, ed. Roderick Lyall (Edinburgh: Canongate, 1989).
8. Quoted in Trussler, *Cambridge Illustrated History of British Theatre*, p. 61.
9. Anna Jean Mill, *Mediaeval Plays in Scotland* (Edinburgh and London: William Blackwood, 1927), p. 84.
10. From an unpublished article by Jamie Reid-Baxter, 'John Burel's *Pamphilus speakand of Lufe*'. My thanks to him for generously letting me draw on that article and his acting-text of Burel's play translation.
11. L. E. Kastner and H. B. Charlton (eds), *The Poetical Works of Sir William Alexander, Earl of Stirling*, 2 vols (Manchester: Manchester University Press, 1921–9), p. xi.
12. David Masson, *Drummond of Hawthornden* (London: Macmillan, 1873), p. 198. There is an extensive description of this royal entry on pp. 196–9.
13. Terence Tobin, 'Popular Entertainment in Seventeenth Century Scotland', in *Theatre Notebook*, 23:1 (Autumn 1968), p. 48.
14. Quoted in Helen Bennett, 'The Perth Glovers' Sword-Dance Dress of 1633', in *Costume*, 19 (1985), p. 40.

15. Henry Grey Graham, *The Social Life of Scotland in the Eighteenth Century* (London: Adam & Charles Black, 1937), p. 440.
16. Alasdair Cameron, 'Theatre in Scotland 1660–1800', in *The History of Scottish Literature: Volume 2, 1660–1800*, ed. Andrew Hook (Aberdeen: Aberdeen University Press, 1987), p. 194.
17. Quoted in James C. Dibdin, *The Annals of the Edinburgh Stage* (Edinburgh: Richard Cameron, 1888), p. 28.

CHAPTER 2   THE EIGHTEENTH CENTURY

1. Terence Tobin, *Plays by Scots 1660–1800* (Iowa City: University of Iowa Press, 1974), pp. 9–10.
2. Robb Lawson, *The Story of the Scots Stage* (Paisley: Alexander Gardner, 1917), pp. 89–90.
3. Quoted in 'Anthony Aston', in Philip H. Highfill Jr., Kalman A. Burnim and Edward A. Langhans, *A Biographical Dictionary of Actors, Actresses, Musicians, Dancers, Managers and Other Stage Personnel in London, 1660–1800* (Carbondale and Edwardsville: Southern Illinois University Press, 1973–1993), vol. 1, p. 156.
4. *Caledonian Mercury*, 15 November 1736.
5. Quoted in David Masson, *Edinburgh Sketches and Memories* (London and Edinburgh: Adam and Charles Black, 1892), p. 105.
6. *Admonition and Exhortation by the Reverend Presbytery of Edinburgh to all within their Bounds* (Edinburgh: Presbytery of Edinburgh, 5 January 1757).
7. Mary Susan Carlson, *Political, Religious and Selected Social Influences on the Scottish Theatre in Edinburgh, 1750–1780* (unpublished MA thesis, Brigham Young University, 1981), pp. 109–10.
8. John Genest, *Some Account of the English Stage from the Restoration in 1660 to 1830* (Bath: H. E. Carrington, 1832), vol. 3, p. 257.
9. Tobin, *Plays by Scots 1660–1800*, p. 142.
10. James C. Dibdin, *The Annals of the Edinburgh Stage* (Edinburgh: Richard Cameron, 1888), p. 118.
11. Quoted in Dibdin, *The Annals of the Edinburgh Stage*, p. 493.
12. Ibid., p. 161.
13. Tobin, *Plays by Scots 1660–1800*, p. 51.
14. Dibdin, *The Annals of the Edinburgh Stage*, p. 227.
15. Ibid., p. 240.
16. J. Keith Angus, *A Scotch Play-House; being the Historical Records of the Old Theatre Royal, Marischal Street, Aberdeen* (Aberdeen: D. Wyllie & Son, 1878).
17. Peter Baxter, *The Drama in Perth: being a History of Perth's Early Plays, Playhouses, Pageants, Concerts, etc.* (Perth: Thos. Hunter & Sons, 1907), pp. 74, 75.
18. Alasdair Cameron, 'Theatre in Scotland, 1660–1800', in *The History of Scottish Literature: Volume 2, 1660–1800*, ed. Andrew Hook (Aberdeen: Aberdeen University Press, 1987), p. 203.

CHAPTER 3   THE NINETEENTH CENTURY

1. See also Barbara Bell, 'The National Drama', *Theatre Research International*, 17:2, pp. 96–108.

2. This document is amongst the Hannay papers held by the Archives and Manuscripts Department of the University Library, University of Dundee, to whom I am indebted for permission to quote from them.
3. I am indebted to Dundee City Archives for permission to quote from this document.
4. Quoted in 'No. 12: Theatre Royal, Dunlop St., 1782–1869', in *See Glasgow, See Theatre: A Guide to the Glasgow Theatres Trail*, text by Alasdair Cameron, illustrations by Graham Barlow (Glasgow: The Glasgow File, 1990), n.p.
5. John Coleman, *Fifty Years of an Actor's Life*, 2 vols (London: Hutchison, 1904).
6. Quoted in James C. Dibdin, *The Annals of the Edinburgh Stage* (Edinburgh: Richard Cameron, 1888), p. 439.
7. I am indebted to Professor Tracy C. Davis, Northwestern University, Illinois, for the account of the correspondence between the Examiner and the Glasgow managers.
8. James Houston, *Autobiography of Mr James Houston, Scotch Comedian* (Edinburgh and Glasgow: Menzies and Love, 1889), p. 10.
9. Alasdair Cameron, 'Popular entertainment in nineteenth-century Glasgow: background and context for the Waggle o' the Kilt exhibition', in Karen Marshalsay, *The Waggle o' the Kilt: Popular Entertainment and Theatre in Scotland* (Glasgow: Glasgow University Library, 1992), p. 11.
10. Albert Mackie, *The Scotch Comedians from the Music Hall to Television* (Edinburgh: Ramsay Head Press, 1973), p. 28.
11. As note 2 above.
12. This letter is part of the Hannay papers held by Glasgow University Archive. I quote from it by kind permission of the Clan Hannay Society.
13. E. Paget-Tomlinson, *The Railway Carriers* (Lavenham: Terence Dalton/Wordie Company, 1990), p. 91.
14. As note 2 above.
15. Terence Rees, *Theatre Lighting in the Age of Gas* (London: Society for Theatre Research, 1978), gives a fascinating account of the gas lighting in a number of Scottish theatres.
16. As note 2 above.
17. Alasdair Cameron, 'Scottish Drama in the Nineteenth Century', in *The History of Scottish Literature; Vol. 3, Nineteenth Century*, ed. Douglas Gifford (Aberdeen: Aberdeen University Press, 1988), p. 429.
18. See Martin Meisel, *Realizations: Narrative, Pictorial and Theatrical Arts in Nineteenth-Century England* (Princeton: Princeton University Press, 1983), pp. 164–5.
19. Quoted in L. Ormond, *J. M. Barrie* (Edinburgh: Scottish Academic Press, 1987).
20. Quoted in R. D. S. Jack, *The Road to the Never Land: A Reassessment of J. M. Barrie's Dramatic Art* (Aberdeen: Aberdeen University Press, 1991), p. 61.

CHAPTER 4   1900–1950

This chapter is largely a condensed, revised and, the author hopes, improved version of several chapters of his study *The Modern Scottish Theatre* (1977).

1. Figures obtained from a variety of sources: town clerks, librarians, archivists, chief constables and various editions of the *Stage Provincial Guide*. For fuller information about the number of theatres in Scotland in the twentieth century see David Hutchison, *The Modern Scottish Theatre* (Glasgow: Molendinar Press, 1977), pp. 152–4.

2. R. D. S. Jack, *The Road to the Never Land: A Reassessment of J. M. Barrie's Dramatic Art* (Aberdeen: Aberdeen University Press, 1991). Jack embarks on a detailed examination of several of Barrie's plays, contending that there is an underlying seriousness of purpose, of which full account has not been taken, and arguing that the ideas of Darwin and Nietzsche are central to a proper understanding of his work.

3. Figures obtained from several editions of the *Kinematograph Year Book*. See Hutchison, *The Modern Scottish Theatre*, pp. 152–4.

4. See W. H. McDowell, *The History of BBC Broadcasting in Scotland 1923–83* (Edinburgh: Edinburgh University Press, 1992).

5. See notes 1 and 3 above.

6. See Adrienne Scullion, 'Scottish Theatre and the Impact of Radio', *Theatre Research International*, 17:2, 1992, pp. 117–31; and Adrienne Scullion, 'BBC Radio in Scotland, 1923–39: Devolution, Regionalism and Centralisation', *Northern Scotland*, 15, 1995, pp. 63–93.

7. For information on the texts of the plays discussed here and elsewhere in the chapter, see Hutchison, *The Modern Scottish Theatre*. Several of the plays were published in the 1980s by 7:84 Theatre Company.

8. T. M. Watson, 'What I want to see on the Amateur Stage', *Scottish Stage*, September 1932.

9. James Bridie, *Dramaturgy in Scotland* (Glasgow: Proceedings of the Royal Philosophical Society of Glasgow, 1949).

10. Christopher Small, 'Bridie: the Unfinished Business', *Scottish Theatre*, January 1971.

11. See the interesting memoir by Bridie's son, Ronald Mavor, *Dr Mavor and Mr Bridie* (Edinburgh: Canongate, 1988), in which it is argued that if Bridie had been willing to cast off the rules of the morality to which he felt committed, 'he might have written the one great play of which he was capable'.

12. Quoted in Colin Milne, 'James Bridie and Drama in Scotland', *Scottish Field*, September 1945.

13. Joseph McLeod, 'Prospects of the Scottish Theatre', *Scots Theatre*, 2, 1946.

14. Robert Mitchell, 'Foundations of a Scots Theatre Tradition', *Scots Theatre*, 1, 1946.

CHAPTER 5   1950 TO 1995

Donald Smith would like to acknowledge help with research for this chapter from Kay Shanks, Anna Stapleton, Tony Paterson, Jamie Stuart, and Agnes Leitch (a 90-year-old veteran of Bertha Waddell's Children's Theatre). Thanks also to the staff of the Scottish Arts Council Library, and to Elizabeth Watson at the Scottish Theatre Archive at Glasgow University.

1. Figures based on David Hutchison, *The Modern Scottish Theatre* (Glasgow: Molendinar Press, 1977), pp. 152–5, supplemented by J. H. Littlejohn, *The Scottish Music Hall 1880–1990* (Wigtown: G. C. Book Publishers, 1990), *passim*.

2. Figure based on *Arts Council of Great Britain Annual Report 1959–60* (London, 1960).

3. Clifford Hanley, 'Civil War in the Civic Theatres', in *The London Illustrated News*, 20 January 1968.

4. For the response of the playwrights see Robert Kemp's preface to his *The Other Dear Charmer* (London: Duckworth, 1957).

5. Donald Campbell, *A Brighter Sunshine* (Edinburgh: Polygon, 1983), p. 206.

6. Joyce McMillan, *The Traverse Theatre Story* (London: Methuen, 1988), p. 80.
7. Elizabeth MacLennan, *The Moon Belongs to Everyone* (London: Methuen, 1990), p. 43.
8. Andrew Cruickshank, *Andrew Cruickshank* (London: Weidenfeld and Nicolson, 1988), pp. 105–6.
9. The National Theatre for Scotland Campaign is documented in Donald Smith (ed.), *The Scottish Stage* (Edinburgh: Candlemaker Press, 1993).
10. For this quotation and an excellent account of the SSP see Audrey Bain, 'Striking It Rich', in *Theatre Scotland*, 3:11 (Autumn 1994), pp. 16–24.
11. *Scottish Arts Council Annual Report 1972–73* (Edinburgh, 1973), p. 32.
12. *Scottish Arts Council Annual Report 1981* (Edinburgh, 1981), p. 4.
13. Figures drawn from the SAC Drama Committee's Policy Statement of 1987 prepared in response to the Review of the Scottish Theatre Company. Both documents are held by the SAC.
14. See *Local Authority Arts Expenditure 1992–93, Report of the SAC/COSLA Survey* (Edinburgh, 1994).
15. See Joyce McMillan, *Arts for a New Century* (Edinburgh, 1992). This consultative summary was succeeded by the more formal *Charter for the Arts in Scotland* (Edinburgh, 1993).
16. Quoted from an unpublished summary of the company's evolution, 7:84 Theatre Company Scotland, dated 10 January 1996.
17. See Bill Findlay, 'Scottish Translations 1970–1995', in Randall Stevenson and Gavin Wallace (eds), *Scottish Theatre Since the Seventies* (Edinburgh: Edinburgh University Press, 1996), pp. 186–97.
18. Jan McDonald, 'Scottish Women Dramatists Since 1945', in Douglas Gifford and Dorothy McMillan (eds), *A History of Scottish Women's Writing* (Edinburgh: Edinburgh University Press, 1997), pp. 494–513.
19. Quoted in 'The Hot One Hundred', in *Theatre Scotland*, 2:8 (Winter 1994), p. 18.
20. Alasdair Cameron (ed.), *Scot-Free: New Scottish Plays* (London: Nick Hern Books, 1990), pp. vii–xvii.

Select Bibliography

GENERAL

Angus, David, 'The Playfields of Scotland', in *The Scots Magazine*, New Series, 114:5 (February 1981), pp. 496–502.

Arnott, James and Randall Stevenson, 'Drama', in *The New Companion to Scottish Culture*, ed. David Daiches (Edinburgh: Edinburgh University Press, 1993), pp. 78–81.

Bain, Audrey, 'Striking it Rich', in *Theatre Scotland*, 3:11 (Autumn 1994), pp. 16–24. [Records the first twenty-one years of the Scottish Society of Playwrights.]

Bannister, Winifred, *James Bridie and His Theatre* (London: Rockliff, 1955). [Includes an account of his work for a Scottish national theatre.]

Barlow, Priscilla, *Wise Enough to Play the Fool: a biography of Duncan Macrae* (Edinburgh: John Donald, 1995).

Barrett, Wilson, *On Stage for Notes: The Story of the Wilson Barrett Company* (Edinburgh and London: William Blackwood, 1954).

Bell, Barbara, *Nineteenth-century Stage Adaptations of the Works of Sir Walter Scott on the Scottish Stage: 1810–1900* (unpublished Ph.D. thesis, University of Glasgow, 1991).

Bell, Barbara, 'The National Drama', in *Theatre Research International*, 17:2 (Summer 1992), pp. 96–108.

Bennett, Helen, 'The Perth Glovers' Sword-Dance Dress of 1633', in *Costume*, 19 (1985), pp. 40–57.

Bolton, H. Philip, *Scott Dramatized* (New York: Mansell, 1992; London: Mansell/Castle Imprint, 1993).

Cameron, Alasdair, 'Theatre in Scotland 1660–1800', in *The History of Scottish Literature, Vol. 2, 1660–1800*, ed. Andrew Hook (Aberdeen: Aberdeen University Press, 1987), pp. 191–205.

Cameron, Alasdair, 'Scottish Drama in the Nineteenth Century', in *The History of Scottish Literature, Vol. 3, Nineteenth Century*, ed. Douglas Gifford (Aberdeen: Aberdeen University Press, 1988), pp. 429–41.

Cameron, Alasdair, 'National Interests', in *Theatre Scotland*, 1:4 (Winter 1993), pp. 17–22. [Traces the history of efforts for a Scottish national theatre].

Cameron, Alasdair and Adrienne Scullion (eds), *Scottish Popular Theatre and Entertainment: Historical and Critical Approaches to Theatre and Film in Scotland* (Glasgow: Glasgow University Library, 1996).

Campbell, Donald, 'The Fraying Rope: Part 1, The Audience', in *Cencrastus*, 42 (Spring 1992), pp. 3–8.

Campbell, Donald, 'The Fraying Rope: Part 2, The Artists', in *Cencrastus*, 43 (Autumn 1992), pp. 32–6.

Campbell, Donald, 'The Fraying Rope: Part 3, The Authors', in *Cencrastus*, 44 (New Year 1993), pp. 6–10. [These three essays are published lectures on aspects of Scottish theatre history post-1700.]

Campbell, Donald, 'Introduction' to a reprint of John Jackson's *The History of the Scottish Stage* (Bristol: Thoemmes Press, 1996).

Campbell, Donald, *Playing for Scotland: A History of the Scottish Stage 1715–1965* (Edinburgh: Mercat Press, 1996).

Carlson, Mary Susan, *Political, Religious and Selected Social Influences on the Scottish Theatre in Edinburgh, 1750–1780* (unpublished MA thesis, Brigham Young University, 1981).

Carpenter, Sarah, 'Early Scottish Drama', in *The History of Scottish Literature, Vol. 1, Origins to 1660*, ed. R. D. S. Jack (Aberdeen: Aberdeen University Press, 1988), pp. 199–211.

Deans, Charlotte, *Charlotte Deans 1768–1839: A Travelling Actress in the North and Scotland* (Kendal: Titus Wilson, 1984).

Denholm, Reah Munro (ed.), *The Scottish National Theatre Venture (The Scottish National Players). Its Birth, History, Work and Influence 1921–1948* (Glasgow: Scottish National Players, 1953).

Dibdin, James C., *The Annals of the Edinburgh Stage: With an Account of the Rise and Progress of Dramatic Writing in Scotland* (Edinburgh: Richard Cameron, 1888). [As the sub-title indicates, Dibdin also discusses Scottish theatre history.]

Donaldson, W., *Fifty Years of Green Room Gossip: Recollections of an Actor* (London: Maxwell [1881]).

Genest, John, *Some Account of the English Stage from the Restoration in 1660 to 1830* (Bath: H. E. Carrington, 1832). [Has some Scottish coverage.]

Hayward, Brian, *Folk Drama in Scotland* (Ph.D. thesis, University of Glasgow, 1983). [A reduced version of the thesis, confined to c.1700 to the present, has been published: see next entry.]

Hayward, Brian, *Galoshins: The Scottish Folk Play* (Edinburgh: Edinburgh University Press, 1992).

Hill, John, 'Towards a Scottish People's Theatre: The Rise and Fall of Glasgow Unity', in *Theatre Quarterly*, 7:27 (Autumn 1977), pp. 61–70.

Houston, James, *Autobiography of Mr James Houston, Scotch Comedian* (Glasgow and Edinburgh: Menzies and Love, 1889).

Hutchison, David, *The Modern Scottish Theatre* (Glasgow: Molendinar Press, 1977).

Hutchison, David, 'Scottish Drama 1900–1950', in *The History of Scottish Literature, Vol.4, Twentieth Century*, ed. Cairns Craig (Aberdeen: Aberdeen University Press, 1987), pp. 163–77.

Inglis, Ralston, *The Dramatic Writers of Scotland* (Glasgow: G. D. MacKellar, 1868).

Jackson, John, *The History of the Scottish Stage* (Edinburgh: Peter Hill, 1793; repr. Bristol: Thoemmes Press, 1996).

Lawson, Robb, *The Story of the Scots Stage* (Paisley: Alexander Gardner, 1917).

[Logan, William H. and James Maidment (eds)], *Fragmenta Scoto-Dramatica: 1715–1758* (Edinburgh: [privately printed] 1835).

Lyall, R. J., 'The Lost Literature of Medieval Scotland', in *Bryght Lanternis: Essays on the*

Language and Literature of Medieval and Renaissance Scotland, ed. J. Derrick McClure and Michael R. G. Spiller (Aberdeen: Aberdeen University Press, 1989), pp. 33–47.

Mackenney, Linda, 'Scotland', in *The Cambridge Guide to World Theatre*, ed. Martin Banham (Cambridge: Cambridge University Press, 1988), pp. 873–6.

Mackenzie, Jack, *A Study of Eighteenth-Century Drama in Scotland (1660–1760)* (unpublished Ph.D. thesis, University of St Andrews, 1955).

Macleod, Joseph, 'Allan Ramsay – The Fight for his Theatre', *The Scotsman*, 22–4 April 1954.

Macleod, Joseph, 'The Earliest Amateur Playbill', in *Theatre Notebook*, 9 (October 1954–July 1955), pp. 11–15.

Maguire, Tom, 'Under New Management: The Changing Direction of 7:84 (Scotland)', in *Theatre Research International*, 17:2 (1992), pp. 132–7.

Marshalsay, Karen Anne, *'The Quest for a Truly Representative Scottish Native Drama': The Scottish National Players* (unpublished Ph.D. thesis, University of Glasgow, 1992).

Marshalsay, Karen Anne, '"The Quest for a Truly Representative Scottish Native Drama": The Scottish National Players', in *Theatre Research International*, 17:2 (1992), pp. 109–16.

Mill, Anna Jean, *Mediaeval Plays in Scotland* (Edinburgh: William Blackwood, 1927).

Mill, Anna Jean, 'The Records of Scots Medieval Plays: Interpretations and Misinterpretations', in *Bards and Makars*, ed. Adam J. Aitken, Matthew P. McDiarmid and Derick S. Thomson (Glasgow: University of Glasgow Press, 1977).

Murdoch, Helen, *Travelling Hopefully: the story of Molly Urquhart* (Edinburgh: Paul Harris, 1981).

Nicol, Allardyce, *History of the English Drama 1660–1900* (Cambridge: Cambridge University Press, 1955). [Has some Scottish coverage.]

Scullion, Adrienne, 'Scottish Theatre and the Impact of Radio', in *Theatre Research International*, 17:2 (1992), pp. 117–31.

Shire, Helena Mennie, *Song, Dance and Poetry of the Court of Scotland under King James VI* (Cambridge: Cambridge University Press, 1969).

[Smith, Donald (ed.)], *The Scottish Stage: A National Theatre Company for Scotland* (Edinburgh: Candlemaker Press, 1994).

Stevenson, Randall, 'Scottish Theatre Company: First Days, First Nights', in *Cencrastus*, 7 (1981–2), pp. 10–13.

Stevenson, Randall, 'Scottish Theatre 1950–1980', in *The History of Scottish Literature, Vol. 4, Twentieth Century*, ed. Cairns Craig (Aberdeen: Aberdeen University Press, 1987), pp. 349–67.

Stevenson, Randall, 'Looking for a Theatre, Looking for a Nation', in *Graph*, Winter 1988, pp. 21–4.

Stevenson, Randall, 'Recent Scottish Theatre: Dramatic Developments', in *Scotland: Literature, Culture, Politics*, ed. Peter Zenzinger (Heidelberg: Carl Winter/Universitätsverlag, 1989), pp. 187–213.

Stevenson, Randall and Gavin Wallace (eds), *Scottish Theatre Since the Seventies* (Edinburgh: Edinburgh University Press, 1996).

Tobin, Terence, 'Popular Entertainment in Seventeenth Century Scotland', in *Theatre Notebook*, 23:1 (Autumn 1968), pp. 46–54.

Tobin, Terence, 'The First Scottish Masters of Revels: Comptrollers of Popular Entertainment', in *Theatre Survey*, 9 (1968), pp. 65–71.

Tobin, Terence, 'School Plays in Scotland, 1656–93', in *Seventeenth Century News*, 23 (1969), p. 49.

Tobin, Terence, 'A List of Anonymous Pieces Presented at the Theatre Royal, Edinburgh,

1767–1800', in *Studies in Scottish Literature*, 7:1–2 (1969), pp. 29–34.

Tobin, Terence, 'A Checklist of Plays Presented in Scotland 1660–1705', in *Restoration and Eighteenth Century Theatre Research*, 12 (May 1973), pp. 51ff.

Tobin, Terence, *Plays by Scots 1660–1800* (Iowa City: University of Iowa Press, 1974).

Wells, Patricia, *Scottish Drama Comes of Age* (Ann Arbor: Michigan University Microfilms International, 1987).

White, Henry Adelbert, *Scott's Novels on the Stage* (New Haven: Yale University Press, 1927).

Worth, Christopher, '"A Very Nice Theatre at Edinr.": Sir Walter Scott and Control of the Theatre Royal', in *Theatre Research International*, 17:2 (Summer 1992), pp. 86–95.

SPECIFIC PLACES

There is an inevitable overlap between some items in the previous section and the categories below, so cross-checking is advised.

Aberdeen

Angus, J. Keith, *A Scotch Play-house; Being the Historical Records of the Old Theatre Royal, Marischal St., Aberdeen* (Aberdeen: D. Wyllie, 1878).

[Bulloch, John Malcolm], *The Playhouse of Bon Accord: Being a Short Survey of the Actor's Arts in the City of Aberdeen From Forgotten Times to the Erection of His Majesty's Theatre* (Aberdeen: [Robert Arthur Theatres] 1906).

Littlejohn, J. H., *Aberdeen Tivoli* (Aberdeen: Rainbow Books, 1986).

Arbroath

Carragher, P. Charles, *'Red Light' Recollections* (Arbroath: T. Buncle, 1906).

Ayr

Moore, John, *Ayr Gaiety: The Theatre Made Famous by the Popplewells* (Edinburgh: Albyn Press, 1976).

Morris, J., *Recollections of Ayr Theatricals from 1809* (Ayr: [privately circulated; printed at *Ayr Advertiser* office] 1872).

Dumfries

[Guild of Players], *Theatre Royal Dumfries* (Dumfries: Guild of Players, 1961).

Dundee

Boyd, Frank, *Records of the Dundee Stage from the Earliest Times to the Present Day* (Dundee: W. & D. C. Thomson, 1886).

MacKenzie, Alex, *On Stage, Dundee* (Dundee: [for the author] 1979).

Robertson, Alec, *History of the Dundee Theatre* (London: Precision Press, 1949).

Edinburgh

Armstrong, Norma, *The Edinburgh Stage 1715–1820: A Bibliography* (a Library Association Fellowship Thesis, 1968). [Held in the Edinburgh Room, Edinburgh Central Library.]

[Boswell, James], *A View of the Edinburgh Theatre During the Summer Season, 1759*

(London: A. Morley, 1760; repr. Los Angeles: The Augustan Reprint Society/UCLA, 1976).

Bruce, George, *Festival in the North: The Story of the Edinburgh Festival* (London: Robert Hale, 1975).

Campbell, Donald, *A Brighter Sunshine: A Hundred Years of the Edinburgh Royal Lyceum Theatre* (Edinburgh: Polygon, 1983).

Crawford, Iain, *Banquo on Thursdays: The Inside Story of 50 Years of the Edinburgh Festival* (Edinburgh: Goblinshead, 1997).

Dibdin, James C., *The Annals of the Edinburgh Stage* (Edinburgh: Richard Cameron, 1888).

[Edinburgh Gateway Company], *The Twelve Seasons of the Edinburgh Gateway Company 1953–1965* (Edinburgh: St Giles Press, 1965).

Edwards, Owen Dudley, *City of a Thousand Worlds: Edinburgh in Festival* (Edinburgh: Mainstream, 1991).

Mackenzie, Donald, *Scotland's First National Theatre* (Edinburgh: Stanley Press, 1963). [A history of Edinburgh's Theatre Royal.]

McMillan, Joyce, *The Traverse Theatre Story* (London: Methuen, 1988).

Miller, Eileen, *The Edinburgh International Festival, 1947–1996* (Aldershot: Scolar [sic] Press, 1996).

Moffat, Alistair, *The Edinburgh Fringe* (London: Johnston and Bacon, 1978).

Wishart, Ruth, *Edinburgh International Festival: Celebration! Fifty Years in Photographs* (Edinburgh: Edinburgh Festival Society, 1996).

Glasgow

Allen, Douglas, 'Glasgow Workers' Theatre Group and the Methodology of Theatre Studies', in *Theatre Quarterly*, 9:36 (Winter 1980), pp. 45–54.

Baynham, Walter, *The Glasgow Stage* (Glasgow: Robert Forrester, 1892).

Cameron, Alasdair, 'Popular theatre and entertainment in nineteenth-century Glasgow: background and context', in *The Waggle o' the Kilt*, ed. Karen Marshalsay (Glasgow: Glasgow University Press, 1992), pp. 5–12.

Cameron, Alasdair, 'Glasgow's Tramway: Little Diagilevs and Large Ambitions', in *Theatre Research International*, 17:2 (1992), pp. 146–55.

Coveney, Michael, *The Citz: 21 years of The Glasgow Citizens Theatre* (London: Nick Hern Books, 1991).

King, Elspeth, 'Popular Culture in Glasgow', *The Working Class in Glasgow, 1750–1914*, ed. R. A. Cage (London: Croom Helm, 1987).

McDonald, Jan, *What is a Citizens' Theatre?*, Proceedings of the Royal Philosophical Society of Glasgow, New Series, no. 1 (November 1984). [Traces the history of citizens' theatre in Glasgow through various twentieth-century companies.]

McNaughtan, Adam, 'Glasgow at Leisure, 1850', in *A Glasgow Collection: Essays in Honour of Joe Fisher*, ed. Kevin McCarra and Hamish Whyte (Glasgow: Glasgow City Libraries, 1990), pp. 107–15.

Inverness

Miller, J., *The Magic Curtain: The Story of Theatre in Inverness* (Inverness: Friends of Eden Court, 1986).

Isle of Mull

Hesketh, Barrie, *Taking Off: The Story of the Mull Little Theatre* (Inverness: New Iona Press, 1997).

Perth

Baxter, Peter, *The Drama in Perth: Being a History of Perth's Early Plays, Playhouses, Play Bills, Pageants, Concerts, etc.* (Perth: Thos. Hunter & Sons, 1907).

Boutcher, Roy and William G. Kemp, *The Theatre in Perth: Published to Mark the Fortieth Anniversary of Perth Theatre Company* (Perth: Perth Theatre Company, 1975).

Kordylewska, Agnes, 'David's Theatre', in *The Scots Magazine* (January 1992), pp. 369–78. [On the founding of Perth Theatre.]

[Perth Theatre], *Perth Theatre 1935–1985* (Perth: Perth Theatre Company, 1985).

Pitlochry

Bruce, George, *Pitlochry Festival Theatre: 21, A Record of Achievement 1951 to 1971* (Pitlochry: Pitlochry Festival Society, 1972).

Bruce, George, *Pitlochry Festival Theatre: Now we are Twenty-five; 1972–1975* (Pitlochry: Pitlochry Festival Society, 1976).

Rutherglen

Crichton, Mamie (ed.), *Rutherglen Repertory Theatre: The First Five Years, 1945–1950* (Rutherglen: [for the theatre] 1950).

St Andrews

Paterson, A. B., *History of the Byre Theatre* (St Andrews: [for the theatre] 1983).

MUSIC HALL, VARIETY, PANTOMIME

Bruce, Frank, Foley, Archie and George Gillespie (eds), *Those Variety Days: Memories of Scottish Variety Theatre* (Edinburgh: Scottish Music Hall Society, 1997).

Cameron, Alasdair, 'Pantomime', in *Keeping Glasgow in Stitches*, ed. Liz Arthur (Edinburgh: Mainstream, 1991), pp. 197–205.

Devlin, Vivien, *Kings, Queens and People's Palaces: An Oral History of the Scottish Variety Theatre* (Edinburgh: Polygon, 1991).

House, Jack, *Music Hall Memories* (Glasgow: Richard Drew Publishing, 1986).

Irving, Gordon, *The Good Auld Days: The Story of Scotland's Entertainers from Music Hall to Television* (London: Jupiter Books, 1977).

Kift, Dagmar, *The Victorian Music Hall: Culture, Class and Conflict* (Cambridge: Cambridge University Press, 1996). [This book's detailed analysis of regional halls includes Glasgow.]

Littlejohn, J. H., *The Scottish Music Hall 1880–1990* (Wigtown: G. C. Book Publishers, 1990).

Mackie, Albert D., *The Scotch Comedians from the Music Hall to Television* (Edinburgh: Ramsay Head Press, 1973).

Marchant, Josette Collins, *Journey Through Stageland: The Collins Family of Glasgow* (Wigtown: G. C. Book Publishers, 1995).

Mellor, G. J., *The Northern Music Hall* (Newcastle: Graham, 1970).

Index